LAND BIRDS

Continued ...

LAND BIRDS (continued)

THE COMPACT Australian BIRD GUIDE

Jeff Davies
Peter Menkhorst
Danny Rogers
Rohan Clarke
Peter Marsack
Kim Franklin

CSIRO PUBLISHING

First printed 2022. This reprint 2025.

A catalogue record for this book is available from the National Library of Australia.

ISBN: 9781486312245 (pbk)

Published exclusively in Australia and New Zealand by:

CSIRO Publishing
36 Gardiner Road, Clayton VIC 3168
Private Bag 10, Clayton South VIC 3169
Australia

Telephone: +61 3 9545 8400
Email: publishing.sales@csiro.au
Website: www.publish.csiro.au
Sign up to our email alerts: publish.csiro.au/earlyalert

Front cover: Magpie Goose (Kim Franklin); Spotted Pardalote (Peter Marsack)
Spine: Shy Albatross (Jeff Davies)
Back cover: Magnificent Riflebird (Peter Marsack); Red-backed Kingfisher (Kim Franklin); Sharp-tailed Sandpiper (Jeff Davies)
Title page: White-faced Heron (Kim Franklin)

Cover design by Cath Pirret
Typeset by Jeff Davies
Index by Indexicana
Printed in Singapore by Markono Print Media Pte Ltd

Oct25_R03

Contents

Alphabetical index to bird groups

Key to abbreviations and symbols

Ad	adult
Aus	Australia, Australian
br	breeding (plumage)
cf	compared with
c	central
cm	centimetre
e	east, eastern
ID	identification
Imm	immature
I	Island
Is	Islands
Juv	juvenile
min	minute
Mt	Mount, Mountain
n	north, northern
ne	north-east
NG	New Guinea
non-br	non-breeding (plumage)
NSW	New South Wales
NT	Northern Territory
nw	north-west
NZ	New Zealand

Qld	Queensland
s	south, southern
SA	South Australia
se	south-east
sec	second
ssp	subspecies
sw	south-west
Tas	Tasmania
Vic	Victoria
w	west, western
WA	Western Australia
~	approximately
♀	female(s)
♂	male(s)

○ likelihood of encounter score – very difficult

◔ likelihood of encounter score – may be difficult

◑ likelihood of encounter score – reasonable chance

◕ likelihood of encounter score – easy

● likelihood of encounter score – very easy

Acknowledgements

The many contributors to the mass of data distilled here have been acknowledged in *The Australian Bird Guide* (*ABG*) and we again express our heartfelt thanks and gratitude, but without reprinting the long list of names. We thank CSIRO Publishing for the opportunity to produce this compact version of the *ABG*, in particular, Briana Melideo and Tracey Kudis for guidance and forbearance. John Manger's advice, encouragement and support were also critical to completing the task.

Introduction

This book is a distillation of key identification information from *The Australian Bird Guide* (*ABG*) (Menkhorst *et al.* 2019 revised edition). Given that field identification is a constantly evolving process, new and improved field characters are also highlighted wherever relevant. Our express objective has been to produce a concise and portable version for field use on the Australian mainland and nearshore islands. We also hope that the compact and simplified presentation of information in this guide will enable readers (especially those who are quite new to birdwatching) to make rapid identifications of all species that one might reasonably expect to encounter. In this context, *The Compact Australian Bird Guide* is a companion to the more comprehensive *ABG* which specifically seeks to facilitate even the most complex of identification problems across all areas of Australian territory.

Area and species covered

The Compact Australian Bird Guide includes all bird species that are resident or regular visitors to the Australian mainland or Tasmania, and seas within a day's reach by boat. To maintain a focus on birds that most birdwatchers are likely to encounter, species that occur in Australia only as occasional visitors or vagrants are excluded, as are species found only in Australia's external territories. For details of those species refer to *ABG*.

Taxonomy and names

Species level taxonomy follows IOC version 11.1 (January 2021). Thus, some names may differ from those in *ABG*. English names follow those recommended by BirdLife Australia and its English Names Committee so that they most closely reflect common usage and tradition in Australia, including spelling (English), hyphenation and capitalisation. Spelling, hyphenation and capitalisation of other words throughout have also been simplified and may differ from *ABG*.

Sequence of species

As in *ABG*, we have adopted a pragmatic field guide sequence that groups bird families according to the broad habitats in which they are most likely to be encountered – marine, freshwater, aerial, terrestrial. Within these categories there is taxonomic structure to our sequence; birds in the same family are all presented in the same block of pages and birds in the same genus usually occur consecutively. This arrangement means that, as much as possible, species likely to be encountered together in the field are also placed close together in the book.

Structure of species accounts

Text has been deliberately kept to the minimum necessary to support the illustrations as the principal source of ID information. Information critical for ID is mostly summarised beneath the distribution map. This includes key points on plumage, habitat and voice, and sometimes behaviour. Other salient points are located close to the relevant illustrations.

Many Australian bird species vary geographically and have regional variants formally named as subspecies. In this compact edition we do not illustrate or list all subspecies. Rather, we only include illustrations of subspecies that are particularly distinctive and may pose identification questions. Accordingly, only a small number of distribution maps show subspecific distributions and then only for the most distinctive subspecies. For details of accepted subspecies and their distributions, see *ABG*.

Voice

We describe the most commonly heard calls, usually including phonetic renderings presented in italics. We use capitals to emphasise the loudest syllables and indicate speed of calls by use of spaces, hyphens or no breaks between syllables. However, bird calls are difficult to render in words. Published sound recordings and online bird sound databases, such as Xeno-canto, are very helpful tools in learning bird calls.

Size

In keeping with the concise format, the detailed measurements provided in *ABG* are not reproduced here. Instead, we present a single measure, total length (TL), which appears in cm next to the likelihood of encounter score. It is based on those presented at the beginning of each species account in the *Handbook of Australian, New Zealand and Antarctic Birds* (a seven-volume treatise published by Oxford University Press and the Royal Australasian Ornithologists Union/Birds Australia between 1990 and 2006). It is important to note that these measurements are taken by laying a dead bird on its back on a bench and measuring the distance from the tip of its bill to the tip of its tail or toes, whichever is longer. This means that the TL measurement is sometimes noticeably longer than a species appears when in a natural posture in the field – it is intended to provide an approximate guide only.

Likelihood of encounter score

To assist birders to assess the likelihood of their preliminary ID, we assigned a 'likelihood of encounter score' to every species and some distinctive subspecies. These scores assume that the observer is within the usual distribution for a given species, as shown in the distribution map, and in suitable habitat at the correct time of year for those species with clear seasonal patterns of movement. We used five likelihood classes varying from a closed circle (very easy to see) to an open circle (very difficult), using quarter circles as increments (see the key to symbols on page VI).

Artwork

The illustrations are sourced from *ABG*. Only a subset of illustrations is included for each species – those we judge to be most critical to allowing ID to species level. Where appropriate, new or revised illustrations have been prepared for this book.

Distribution maps

The maps are based on those presented within *ABG* with modifications to align with the objectives of this compact edition; most notably, subspecies distributions are generally not differentiated, nor are breeding islands for seabirds. Dark green shading shows regular occurrence; pale green shading shows irregular occurrence. Our understanding of species' distributions changes with time and these maps also incorporate updates where appropriate.

Describing bird morphology

A

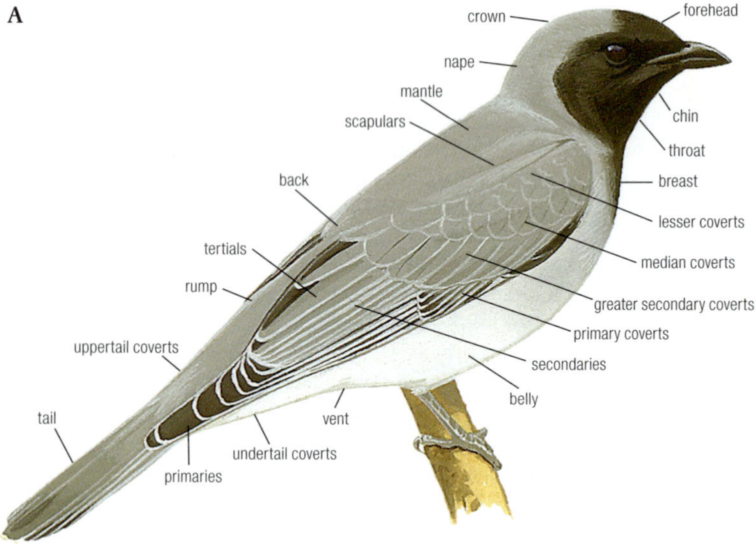

Figure 1: Terms used to describe the parts of a bird and major feather groups: A) general topography, Black-faced Cuckoo-shrike.

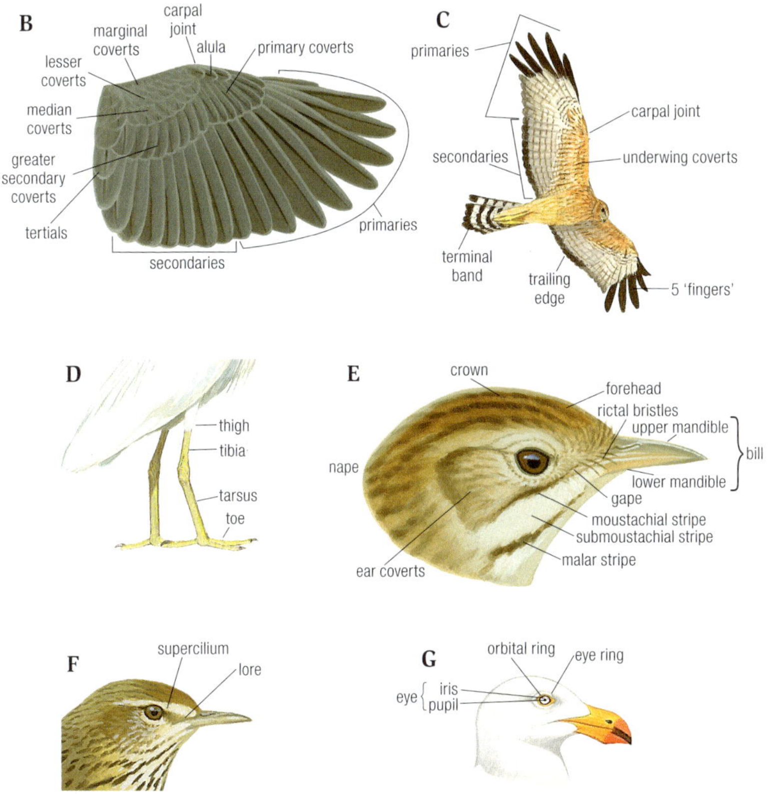

Figure 1 (continued): B) upperwing, Grey Shrike-thrush; C) underwing, Spotted Harrier; D) legs, Eastern Reef Egret; E) head markings, Australasian Pipit; F) head markings, Rufous Fieldwren; G) eye topography, Pacific Gull.

Ethical birding

Birding should not be an activity that harms the birds that fascinate us. Nevertheless, our presence in a bird's habitat can have negative effects on birds. We all share an obligation to keep disturbance of birds to a minimum. Usually this involves little more than common sense and some consideration of how our actions might affect the birds we want to see. Potential problems, and how to avoid these, include:

1. **Putting birds to flight.** The energy costs of alarm flight can be high. Whether observing or photographing, all birders should seek to avoid preventable disturbance. We have probably all seen observers and photographers approaching closer and closer until the bird or flock

flees. At times this causes little harm but there may be circumstances where it is harmful. An ethical objective for bird photographers is to attempt to obtain images without flushing the bird. Mostly, this simply requires patience, and some attention to the bird's behaviour. Signs that you are too close for comfort include: the bird stops foraging and pays attention to you; the bird stretches its wings; or it begins to move away. If any of these behaviours happen, it's best to freeze or to back off. If the bird resumes its former activities, you are more likely to get a better image of a more relaxed bird.

2. **Spending time close to an active nest.** Eggs and small chicks have little capacity to control their body temperature, in both hot and cold weather. They need help from their parents. For example, in beach-nesting Hooded Plovers, one cause of nest failure is disturbance of adults on hot days; if the parents cannot attend their nest to shade the eggs because humans are too close, the embryo inside the egg may die. Similarly, disturbance from nearby people can slow the provisioning of food to chicks, reducing their chances of survival. Often, if you are very close to an undiscovered nest or chicks, the parent birds will let you know – with distraction displays, alarm calls or allowing unusually close approach and appearing distressed.

3. **Using recorded bird calls (referred to as playback) to attract birds.** This is a vexed issue. Territorial birds may react strongly to broadcasts of their calls and approach the source, likely increasing their stress levels. Time that a bird spends on this kind of response is time that is lost from other activities; this is potentially a problem in the breeding season or in bad weather. On the other hand, it could be argued that judicious use of playback can be less harmful than other search methods, especially for cryptic species. For example, one can walk through Hummock Grass (genus *Triodia*) for hours, potentially causing lots of disturbance to Rufous-crowned Emu-wrens (and their habitat) without ever getting a decent view of them – yet, if done correctly, a 3-second snatch of playback may be sufficient to cause an emu-wren to hop briefly into view. Given the availability of sophisticated bird-call apps on smartphones, we simply ask that playback be used sparingly and efficiently to minimise impacts on birds.

Reference

Menkhorst P, Rogers D, Clarke R, Davies J, Marsack P, Franklin K (2019) *The Australian Bird Guide*. Revised edition. CSIRO Publishing, Melbourne.

Species accounts

Quick guide to tube-nosed seabirds: Albatross, petrels, shearwaters and storm-petrels all have raised tubular nostrils. They are adapted to an exclusively oceanic lifestyle, only coming ashore on islands to breed. A number of species can be seen from headlands, but most are to be found further out at the continental shelf. Organised seabird-watching boat trips are now held regularly and there are more than a dozen ports in Australia from which one-day 'pelagic trips' depart, providing the best opportunity to see this highly specialised group of birds.

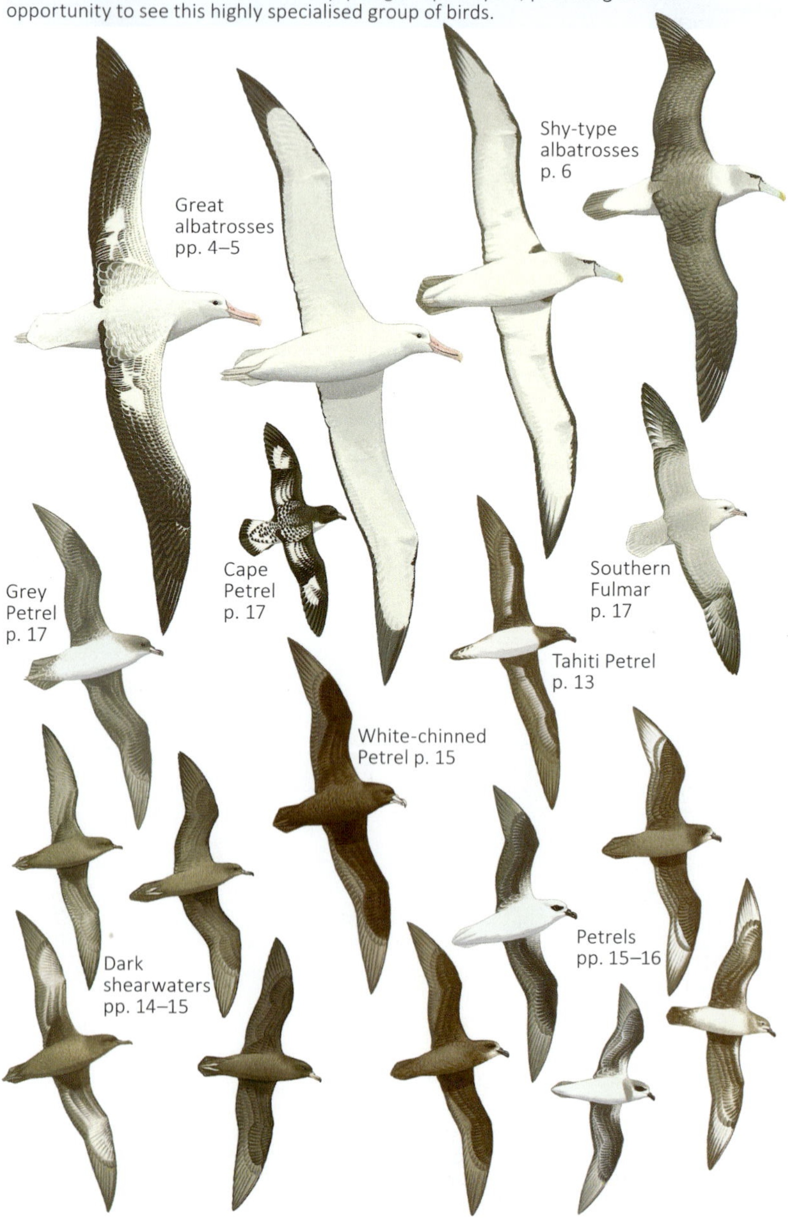

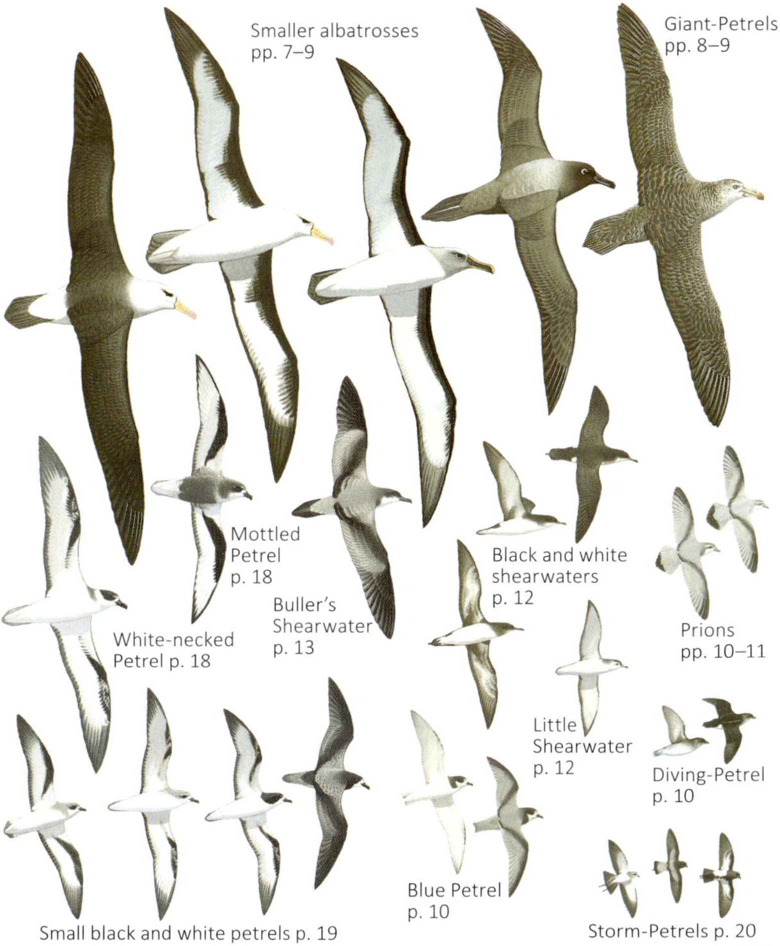

LITTLE PENGUIN ◑ 30 cm
Eudyptula minor

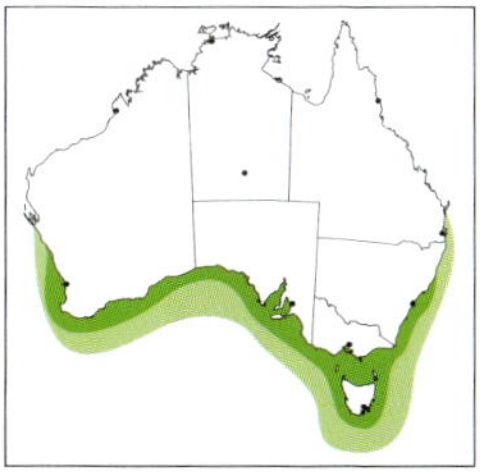

Sits low in water.

World's smallest penguin 20–30 cm tall. Slate-blue above, white below. Yapping at sea carries great distance in calm conditions. Loud braying at colonies. Often beach-washed. Nests in burrows and crevices.

SOUTHERN ROYAL ALBATROSS ◔ 118 cm
Diomedea epomophora

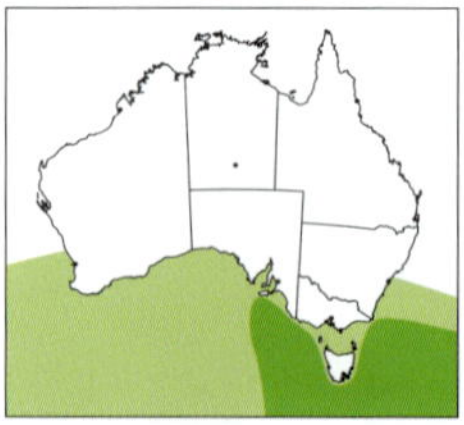

Largest albatross. Always white-backed. Extent of 'frosted' white in upperwings increases with age. Frequents deep marine waters, occurring most commonly off e Tas.

NORTHERN ROYAL ALBATROSS ◔ 112 cm
Diomedea sanfordi

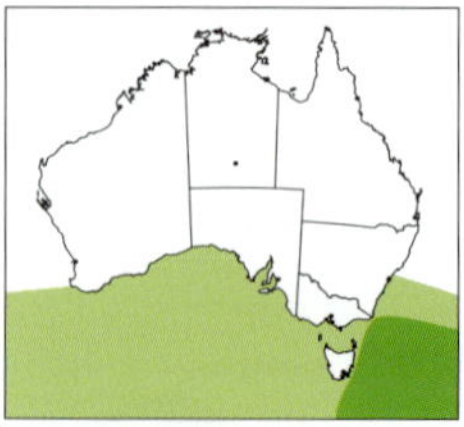

Very large albatross. Always white-backed with uniformly black upperwings. Over deep marine waters, rarely seen from land.

WANDERING ALBATROSS ◔ 116 cm
Diomedea exulans

Very large albatross, larger than NZ Albatross. Juvs mostly brown, Ads always white-backed. ♀ darker than ♂. Extent of 'blotchy' white in upperwings increases with age. Over deep marine waters.

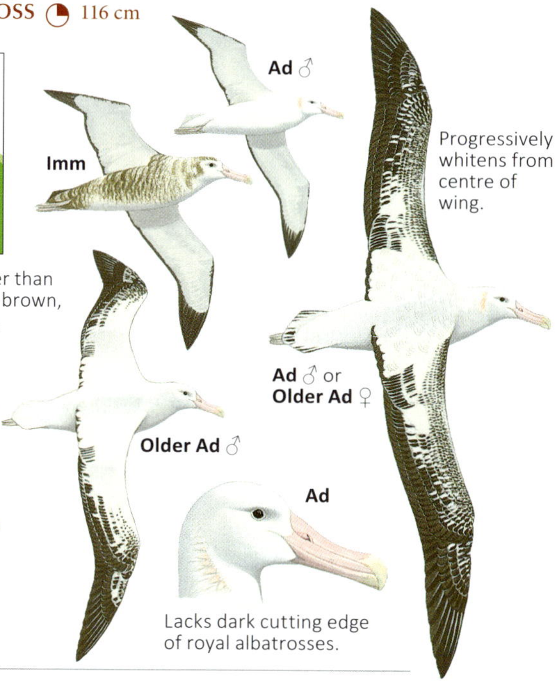

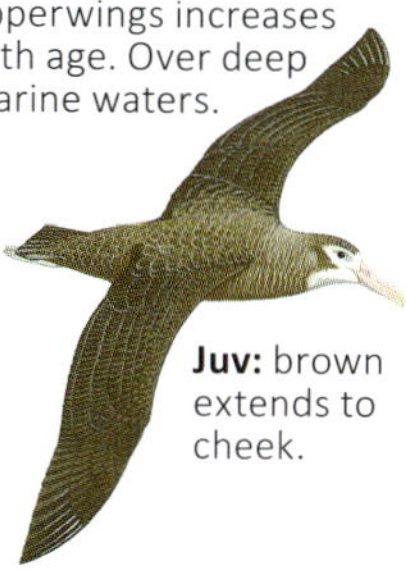

NEW ZEALAND ALBATROSS ◑ 112 cm
Diomedea antipodensis

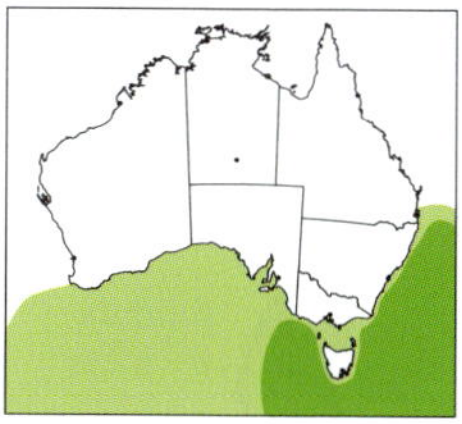

The most common great albatross off e and s Aus. Plumage progression like Wandering Albatross but never attains mostly white upperwings. Two subspecies: ssp *antipodensis* darker than ssp *gibsoni* in all Ad plumages.

SHY ALBATROSS ◕ 97 cm
Thalassarche cauta

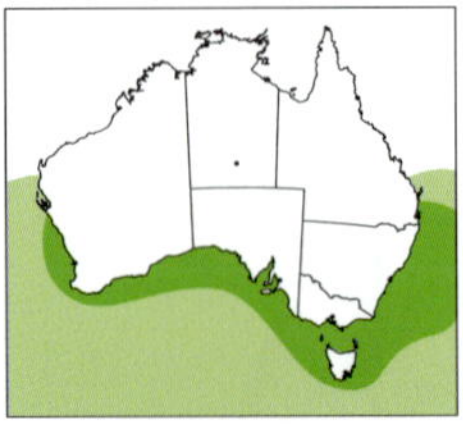

Medium–large albatross. Neat black margins to white underwing. Bill progressively paler with age. Coastal to deep marine waters. Most commonly seen albatross from land in e Aus.

SALVIN'S ALBATROSS ◔ 95 cm
Thalassarche salvini

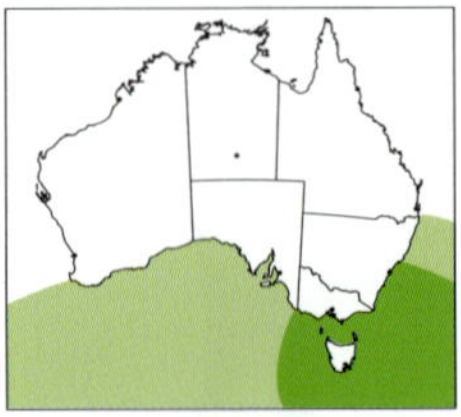

Always with grey hood like more common Juv Shy Albatross, but note all-dark tip to underwing without any white intrusion. Mostly at continental shelf where uncommon to rare.

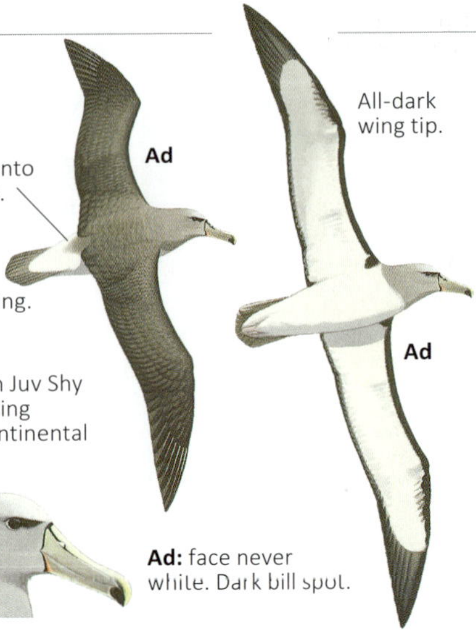

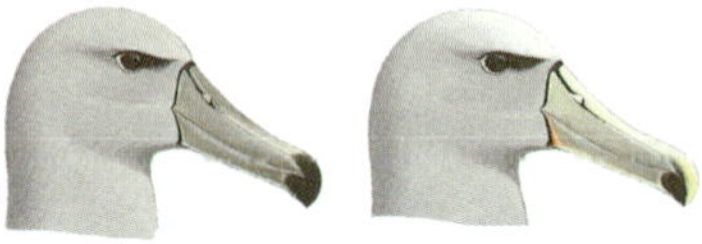

BLACK-BROWED ALBATROSS ◕ 87 cm
Thalassarche melanophris

Small–medium albatross. Dark underwing becomes paler with age. Black eye. Coastal to deep marine waters, often seen from land.

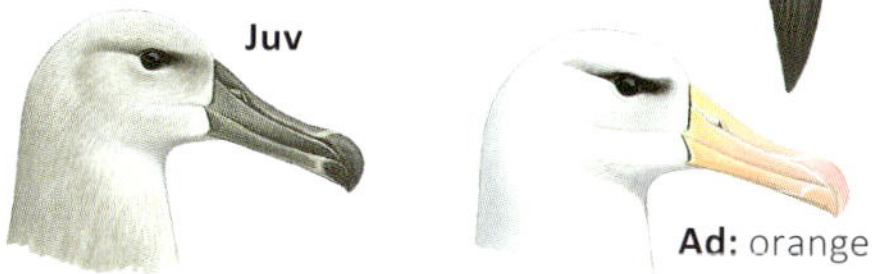

CAMPBELL ALBATROSS ◑ 87 cm
Thalassarche impavida

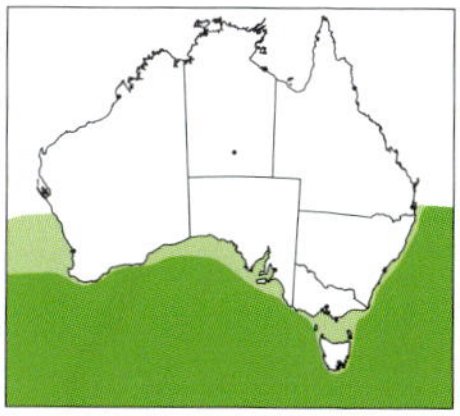

Very like Black-browed Albatross but note pale eye, darker underwing pattern.

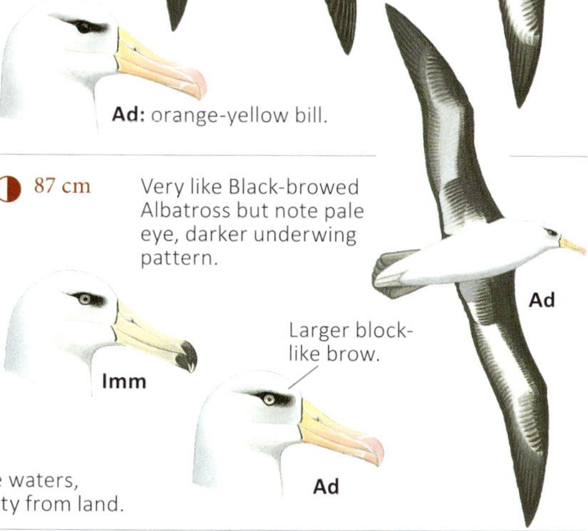

Typically over deeper marine waters, rarely identified with certainty from land.

GREY-HEADED ALBATROSS ○ 77 cm
Thalassarche chrysostoma

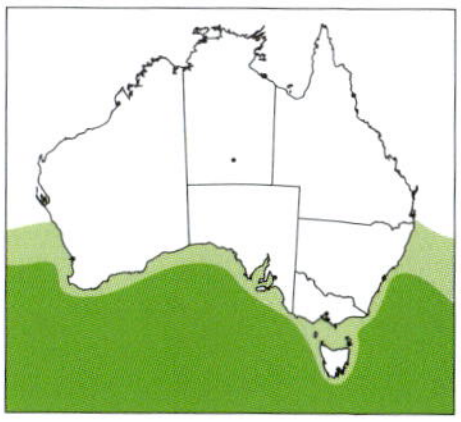

Small–medium albatross with grey hood. Dark underwing becomes paler with age. A rare winter–spring visitor to deep marine waters off s Aus.

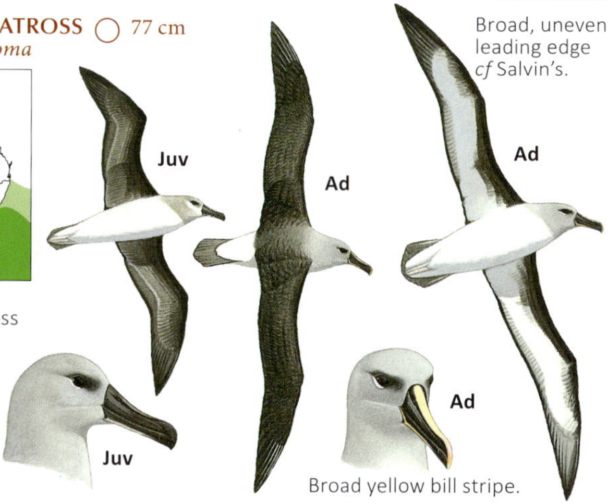

INDIAN YELLOW-NOSED ALBATROSS ◑ 75 cm
Thalassarche carteri

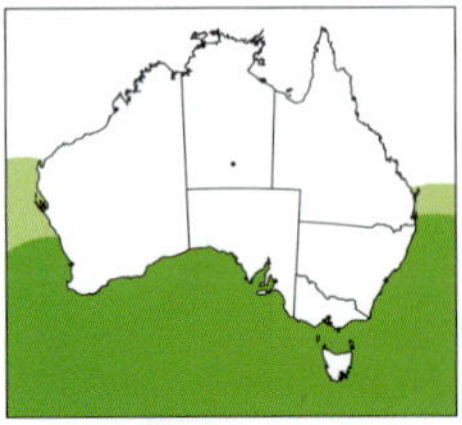

Smallest albatross in s oceans. In all ages, white head contrasts with black bill, neat black margins to underwing. Coastal to deep marine waters. Most common off sw Aus.

BULLER'S ALBATROSS ◑ 78 cm
Thalassarche bulleri

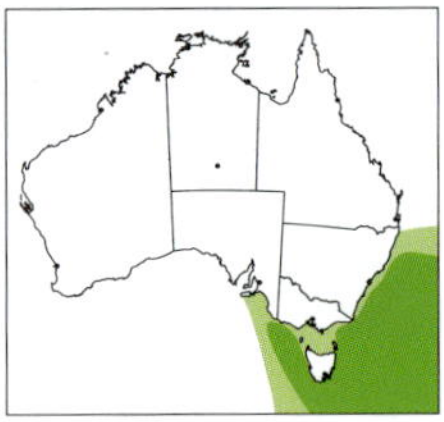

Small–medium albatross. In all ages, grey hood and broad black leading edge to underwings. Coastal to deep marine waters. Common e Tas, uncommon elsewhere.

SOUTHERN GIANT-PETREL ◔ 92 cm
Macronectes giganteus

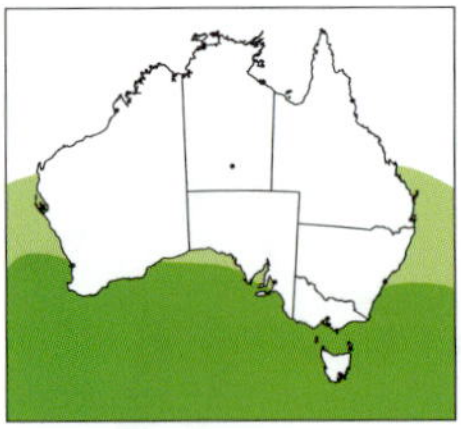

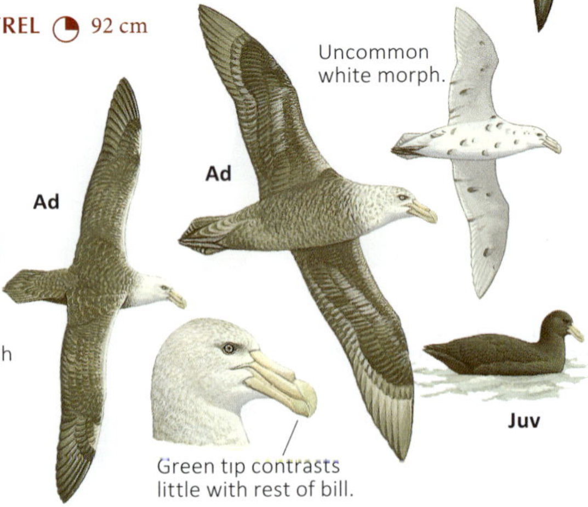

Thickset albatross-sized petrel, always with greenish tip to bill. Voracious scavenger and predator. Uncommon off s Aus in winter.

SOOTY ALBATROSS ◔ 86 cm
Phoebetria fusca

Small–medium albatross with slender, elongated structure and warm brown tones. Effortless wheeling flight in strong winds. Mostly beyond continental shelf, rarely seen from land.

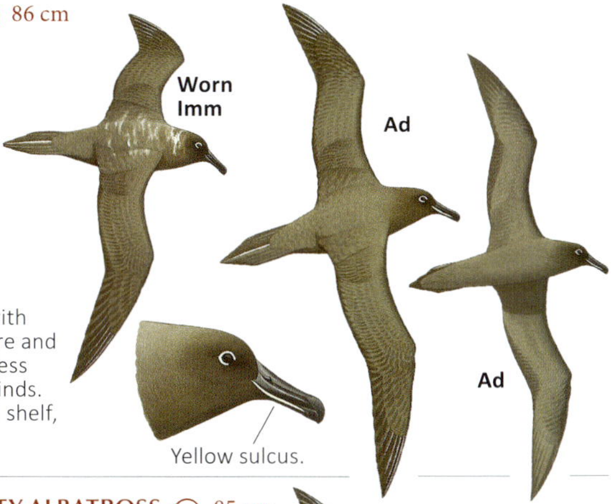

LIGHT-MANTLED SOOTY ALBATROSS ○ 85 cm
Phoebetria palpebrata

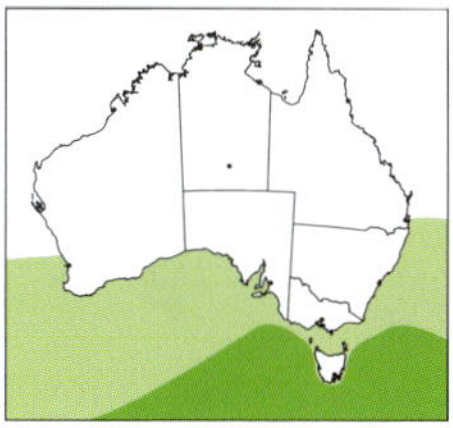

As for Sooty Albatross but mostly cold-grey tones with blackish face. Usually beyond continental shelf over cold marine waters, very rarely seen from land.

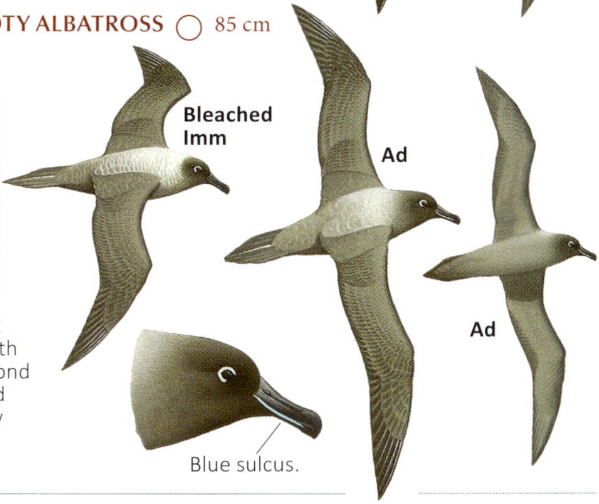

NORTHERN GIANT-PETREL ◑ 87 cm
Macronectes halli

Thickset albatross-sized petrel, always with reddish tip to bill. Voracious scavenger and predator. Attends fishing boats. Common off s Aus in winter.

COMMON DIVING-PETREL ◑ 22 cm
Pelecanoides urinatrix

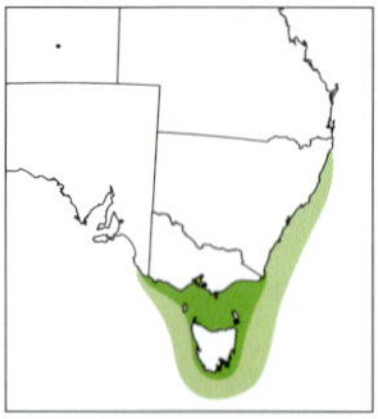

Small, dumpy petrel with stubby wings. Flight low to sea with continuous, frantic wing beats. Mostly over depths of 50–180 m. Infrequently seen from land.

BLUE PETREL ◔ 29 cm
Halobaena caerulea

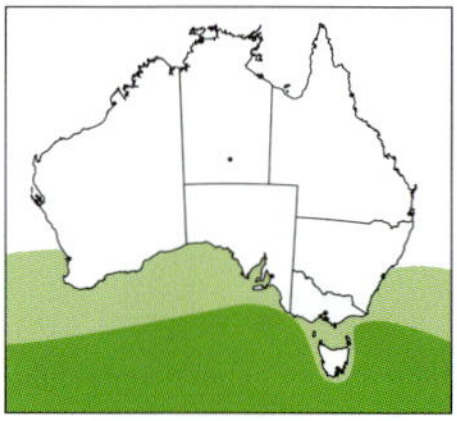

Small prion-like petrel with blackish helmet, white-tipped tail. Wheels above sea surface, more dynamic flight than prions. Scarce winter–spring visitor to deep marine waters.

FAIRY PRION ◕ 25 cm
Pachyptila turtur

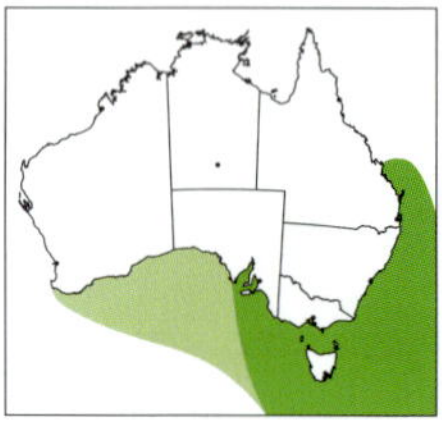

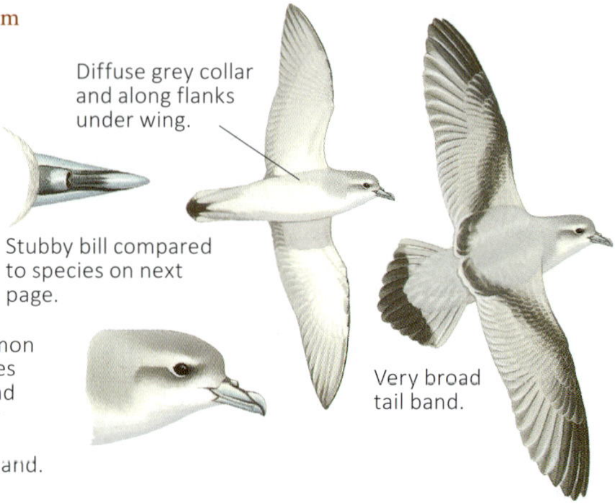

Pale silvery grey, the common prion off se Aus. Sometimes abundant over offshore and pelagic waters. Commonly beach-washed, but only occasionally sighted from land.

SLENDER-BILLED PRION ◔ 26 cm
Pachyptila belcheri

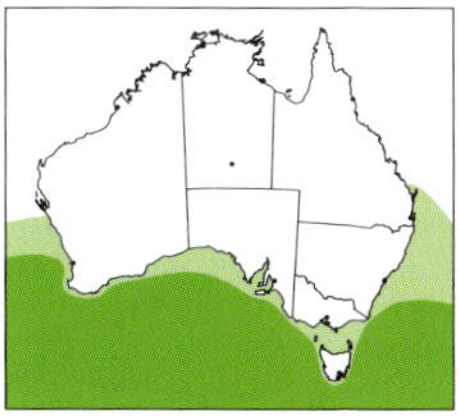

Pale-faced prion with weakly contrasting M-mark across spread wings and lower back. Occasionally beach-washed, otherwise mostly over cold marine waters far from land.

Look for individuals of all three species on this page hidden within flocks of Fairy Prion.

ANTARCTIC PRION ◔ 27 cm
Pachyptila desolata

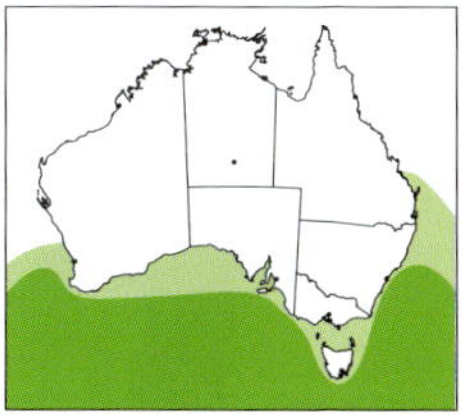

Darker grey than Fairy Prion with bolder facial pattern and collar. Bill size varies. Occasionally beach-washed, otherwise mostly over cold marine waters far from land.

SALVIN'S PRION ○ 28 cm
Pachyptila salvini

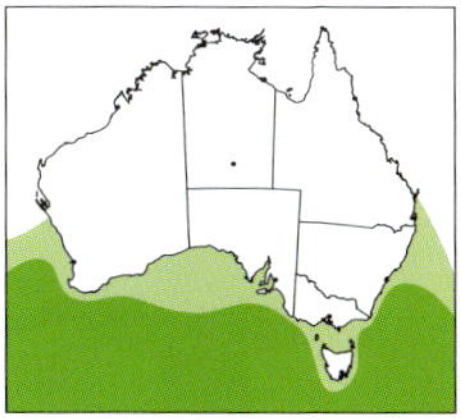

Very similar to largest-billed Antarctic Prions, but with steeper square forehead and small nail at tip of duller bill. Scarce winter visitor only identifiable in good photographs or when beach-washed.

LITTLE SHEARWATER 27 cm
Puffinus assimilis

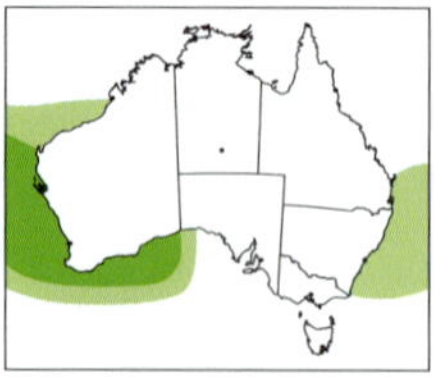

Small, white-faced shearwater. Flies low to water with rapid series of shallow wing beats, interspersed by short glides. Breeds on islands off sw Aus, very rare off e Aus.

FLUTTERING SHEARWATER 34 cm
Puffinus gavia

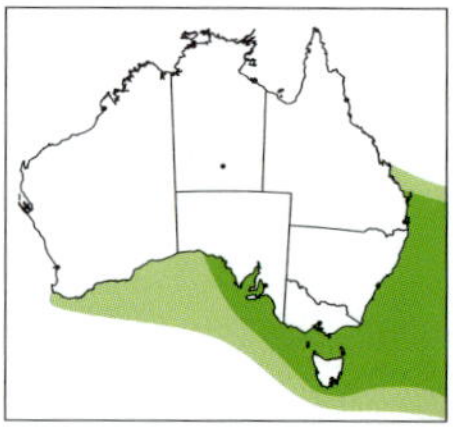

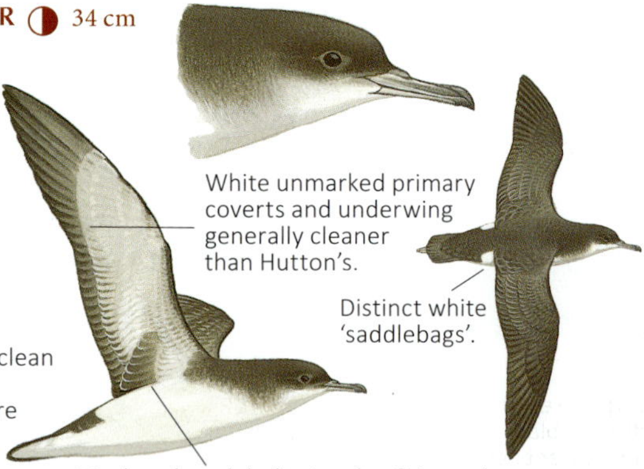

Small shearwater with rather clean white underwings. Common migrant to coastal and offshore waters. Flocks of pale-bellied shearwaters in se Aus mostly comprise this species.

HUTTON'S SHEARWATER 37 cm
Puffinus huttoni

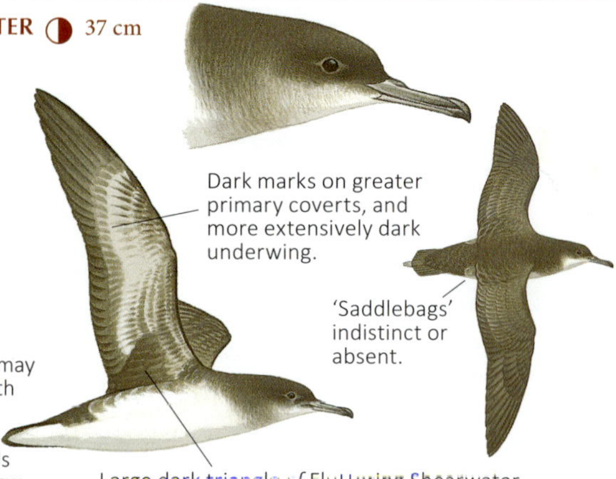

Very similar to Fluttering Shearwater, with which it may flock, but subtly darker with more well-defined collar. Frequents coastal and offshore waters. Most birds migrate to nw Aus via the sw, large numbers occur on passage.

STREAKED SHEARWATER 48 cm
Calonectris leucomelas

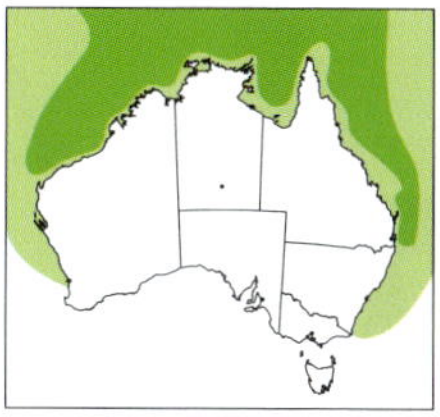

Large, pale-faced tropical shearwater. Long, straight wings and relaxed flight recalls small albatross. Long, wedge-shaped tail and prominently streaked wing coverts. Non-breeding migrant from Japan. Regular in small numbers to tropical seas but rarely seen from land.

BULLER'S SHEARWATER 46 cm
Ardenna bulleri

Large, grey and white shearwater with distinct black 'M' across spread wings and lower back. Clean white below. Long, tapered tail and black cap. Subtropical and temperate seas of e Aus, Oct to Apr but rarely seen from land.

TAHITI PETREL 45 cm
Pseudobulweria rostrata

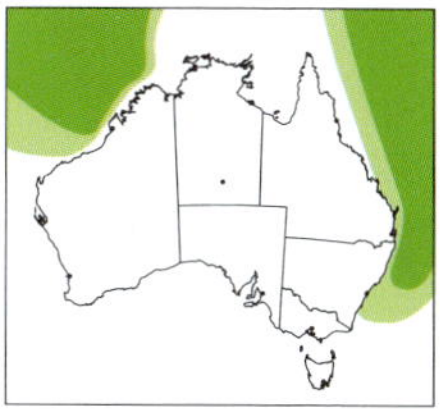

Very heavy bill.

Large, chocolate-brown petrel with sharply demarcated white lower breast and belly. Effortless, powerful, gliding flight, wings typically held straight, appear especially long and narrow. Long, tapered tail. Tropical seas, at and beyond continental shelf.

SHORT-TAILED SHEARWATER 42 cm
Ardenna tenuirostris

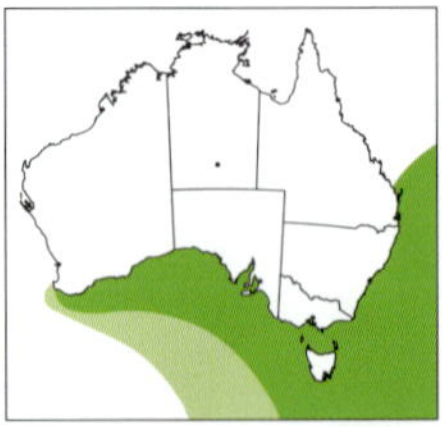

Abundant dark shearwater. Millions breed in se Aus from Sep to May. Often frequents coastal waters, huge flocks can be seen from land in fast gliding, undulating flight on stiff wings. Common beach-wreck.

SOOTY SHEARWATER 43 cm
Ardenna grisea

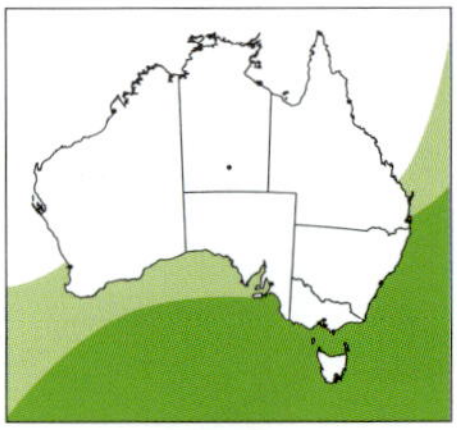

Like Short-tailed Shearwater but larger with longer, heavier bill, pale bar in underwing. Small numbers frequent offshore and pelagic waters, rarely identified from land.

WEDGE-TAILED SHEARWATER 42 cm
Ardenna pacifica

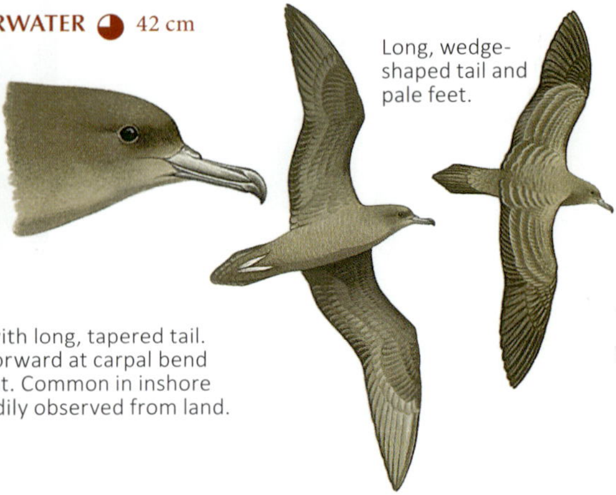

Lightly built shearwater with long, tapered tail. Angular wings held well forward at carpal bend in relaxed, unhurried flight. Common in inshore and offshore waters. Readily observed from land.

FLESH-FOOTED SHEARWATER 42 cm
Ardenna carneipes

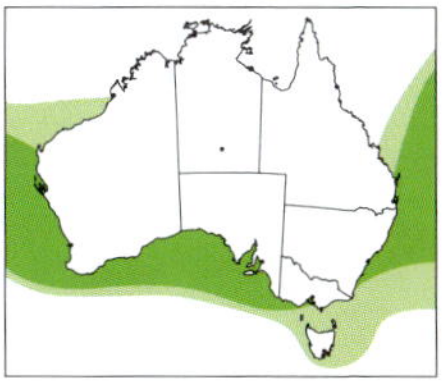

Large, robust, all-dark shearwater with broad wings. Flight more casual and unhurried than other shearwaters. Tropical to temperate waters. Occasionally seen from land. Summer migrant present Sep to May.

GREAT-WINGED PETREL 40 cm
Pterodroma macroptera

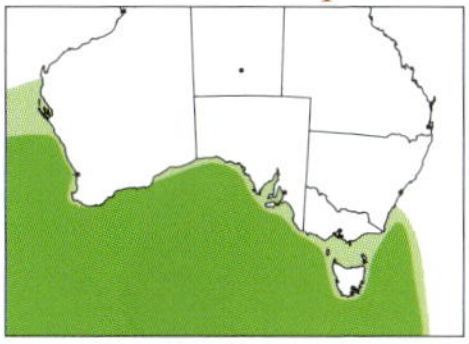

Large, all-dark petrel. Can show indistinct grey wash to face. Rhythmic flight, with regular high arcs. More common in w Aus. Rarely seen from land except in winter storms.

GREY-FACED PETREL 40 cm
Pterodroma gouldi

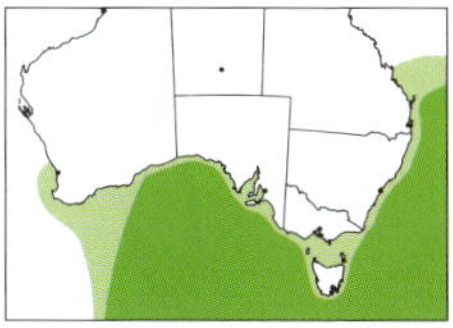

Very similar to Great-winged Petrel; most show much paler face and are structurally more thickset. Common over deep marine waters in e Aus, scarce off sw WA.

WHITE-CHINNED PETREL 54 cm
Procellaria aequinoctialis

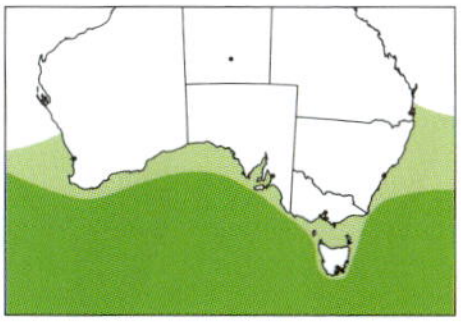

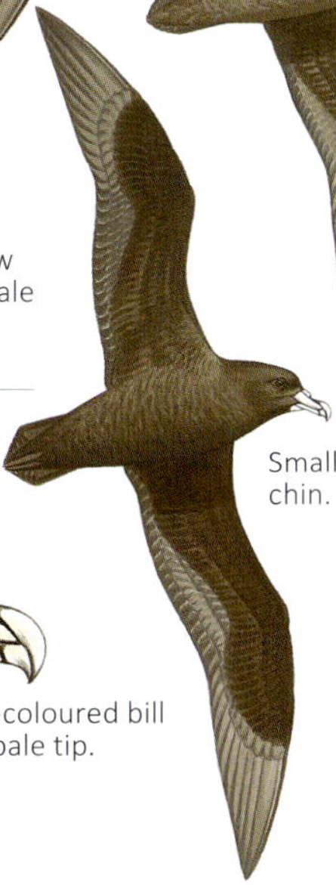

Large, almost uniformly black-brown petrel with pale bill. Not all show white chin, but diagnostic when present. Deep marine waters off s Aus. Common in summer, scarce in winter.

KERMADEC PETREL ◔ 38 cm
Pterodroma neglecta

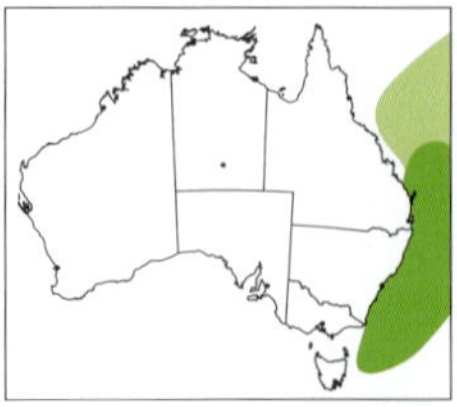

Enormously variable plumage, but always shows skua-like pale flash in upperwing. Frequents deep pelagic waters in subtropical seas. Occurs year-round but most common in summer.

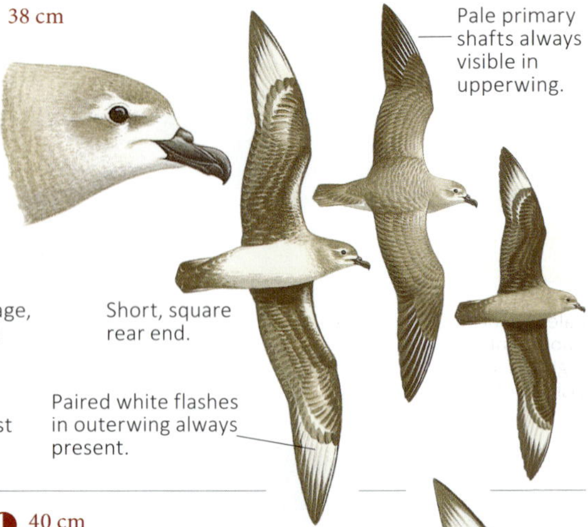

PROVIDENCE PETREL ◑ 40 cm
Pterodroma solandri

Large, robust petrel with pale flashes in underwing. Chunky bill *cf* Kermadec Petrel. Restricted to deep pelagic waters off e Aus where regular in small numbers, mostly Mar–Nov. Very rarely seen from land.

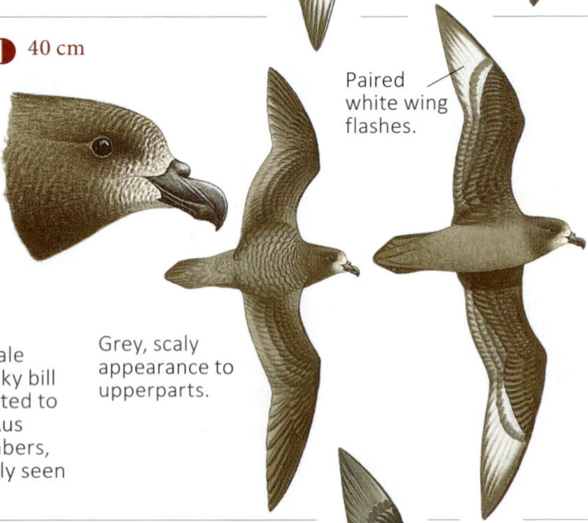

WHITE-HEADED PETREL ◑ 43 cm
Pterodroma lessonii

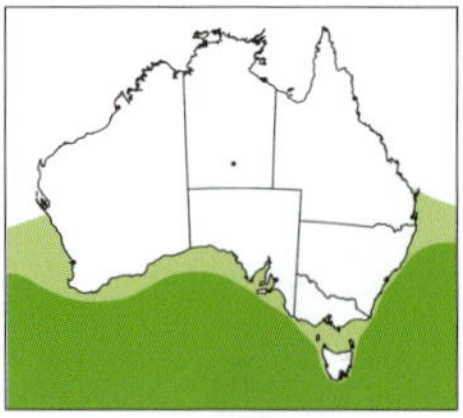

Powerful flight with regular deep arcs. Over deep marine waters, very rarely seen from land. Occurs year-round but most common in spring.

SOUTHERN FULMAR ◯ 47 cm

Fulmarus glacialoides

Pale southern petrel with gull-like upperwing pattern. Effortless flight on stiff wings. Rare winter visitor from Southern Ocean.

CAPE PETREL ◐ 38 cm

Daption capense

Unmistakable black and white petrel with chequered upperparts and largely white underparts.

Common in cold marine waters but generally absent in summer. Readily attracted to boats and occasionally seen from land.

GREY PETREL ◯ 50 cm

Procellaria cinerea

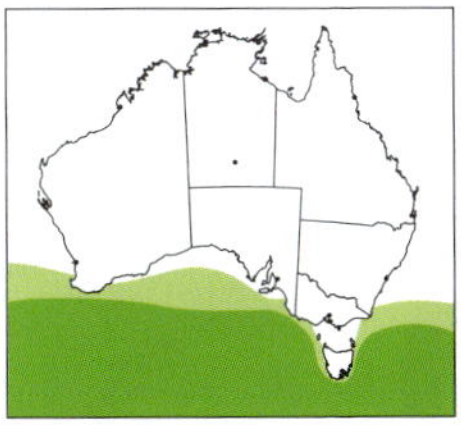

Large southern petrel, slate-grey above. Stiff-winged, gliding flight. Occurs in pelagic waters beyond the continental shelf in winter and spring.

WHITE-NECKED PETREL ◔ 43 cm
Pterodroma cervicalis

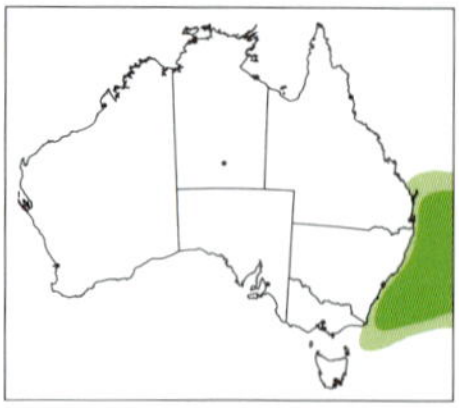

Large petrel with clean white collar, neat black cap and mask, distinct black carpal bar on underwing.

Effortless gliding, occasional relaxed series of wing beats. Mostly summer visitor to deep, warm waters off e coast. Very rarely seen from land.

SOFT-PLUMAGED PETREL ◔ 34 cm
Pterodroma mollis

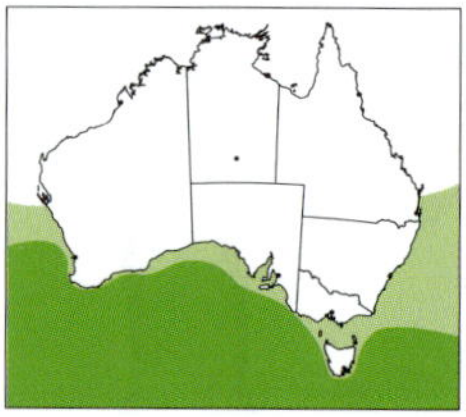

Medium-sized petrel with dusky underwing and grey breast band.

Rare dark morph.

Zig-zagging flight on angled wings. Deep marine waters. Common winter–spring off sw WA, scarce year-round se Aus.

MOTTLED PETREL ◔ 35 cm
Pterodroma inexpectata

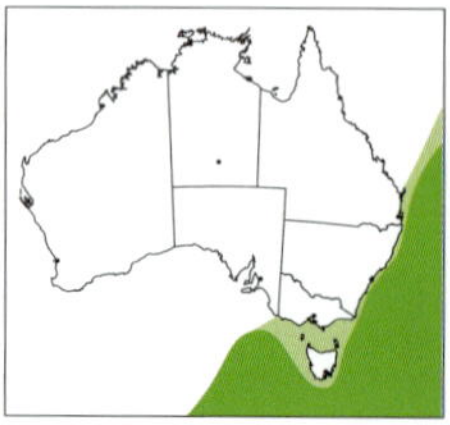

Very broad black carpal bar on underwing.

Medium-sized, grey and white petrel with sooty belly, thickset body and neck. Powerful flight, towering into sky, dashing past vessels. Over deep marine waters. Scarce spring migrant off e Aus, summer visitor off Tas.

BLACK-WINGED PETREL ◔ 29 cm
Pterodroma nigripennis

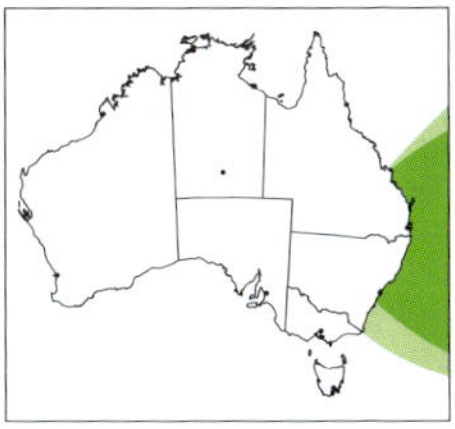

Small, grey and white petrel with very broad black underwing bar, distinct blackish eye smudge and soft-grey semi-collar. Active flight with rapid twists and turns. Deep pelagic waters off e Aus in summer. Breeds on offshore islands in Pacific.

GOULD'S PETREL ◔ 30 cm
Pterodroma leucoptera

Small petrel with distinctive neat, black hood, darkish upperparts and moderately broad black carpal bar on underwing. Rapid gliding flight with regular twists and turns. Breeds on islands off n NSW but otherwise frequents deep waters beyond the continental shelf.

COOK'S PETREL ○ 27 cm
Pterodroma cookii

All grey above with small, crescent-shaped, black eye patch. White below with weak, narrow, black carpal bar on underwing. Scarce summer visitor to deep pelagic waters off se Aus. Unlikely to be seen from land.

WHITE-FACED STORM-PETREL 19 cm
Pelagodroma marina

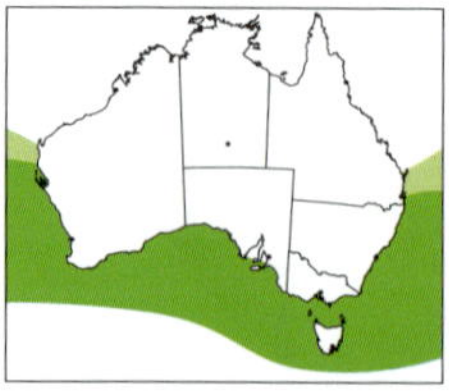

Medium-sized with unique dark mask in white face. Broad wings. Common, can be abundant in offshore and pelagic waters Sep–May.

Characteristically bounds with paired feet when feeding, kicks off water surface, changes direction abruptly.

GREY-BACKED STORM-PETREL 17 cm
Garrodia nereis

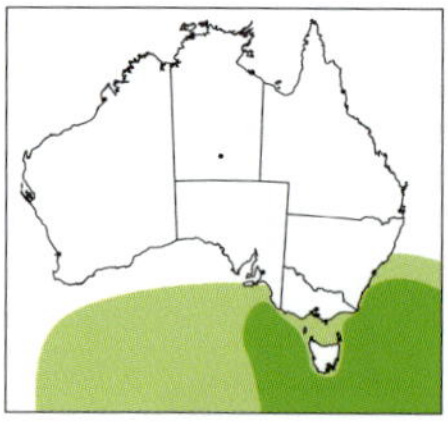

Tiny compact storm-petrel with black hood. Rapid, fluttery flight on direct path low to water. Frequents deep marine waters off se Aus where most common Apr–Oct.

Silvery grey wing panels and rump.

Runs across water surface when feeding.

WILSON'S STORM-PETREL 17 cm
Oceanites oceanicus

Small, black storm-petrel with white rump and distinct white flanks. One of world's most abundant seabirds. Flies low to water with weaving path. Mostly on deep marine waters. Common Oct–Jun off s Aus, mostly Apr–Nov off n Aus.

Patters feet on surface when feeding.

BLACK-BELLIED STORM-PETREL 20 cm
Fregetta tropica

White-rumped with pale underparts. In flight swings from side to side whilst skipping off sea, doesn't patter. Deep marine waters well beyond shelf, Nov–Apr off s Aus, May–Oct off n Aus.

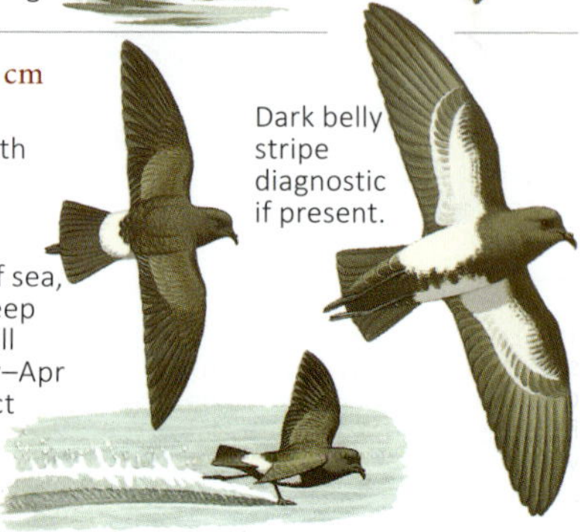

Dark belly stripe diagnostic if present.

Skims surface with one foot.

AUSTRALIAN PELICAN 170 cm
Pelecanus conspicillatus

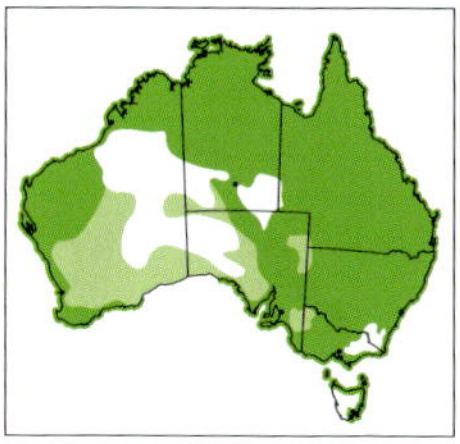

Unmistakable, our only pelican. Gregarious in small to large flocks at inland and coastal wetlands, estuaries and bays. Powerful and majestic gliding flight interspersed with methodical wing beats. Small flocks usually fly in a line formation.

WHITE-TAILED TROPICBIRD 40 cm
Phaethon lepturus

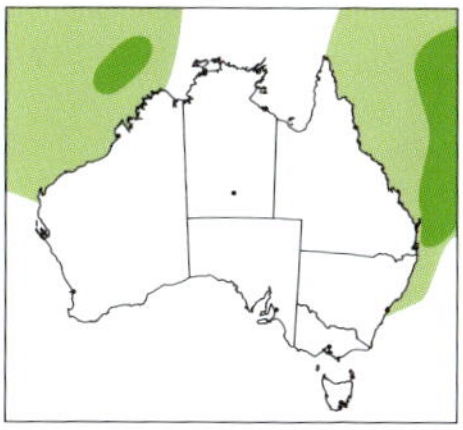

Tropical pelagic waters, rarely seen from land. Solitary, plunge dives from height for fish and squid. Purposeful and direct flight, more graceful than Red-tailed with rapid tern-like wing beats, often high above sea surface.

RED-TAILED TROPICBIRD 49 cm
Phaethon rubricauda

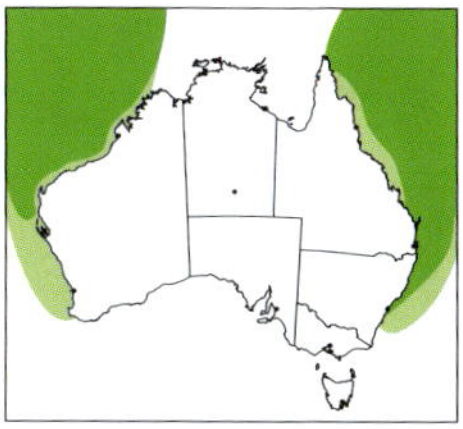

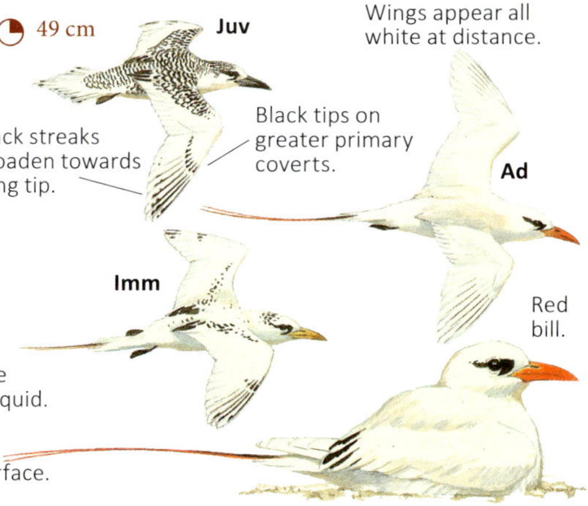

Tropical pelagic waters, rarely seen from land. Solitary, plunge dives from height for fish and squid. Purposeful and direct flight with steady, rhythmic wing beats, often high above sea surface.

AUSTRALASIAN GANNET ● 87 cm
Morus serrator

Common black and white gannet of s Aus. Long glides interspersed with methodical wing beats. Can be very common in coastal waters, routinely seen from land.

MASKED BOOBY ◔ 80 cm
Sula dactylatra

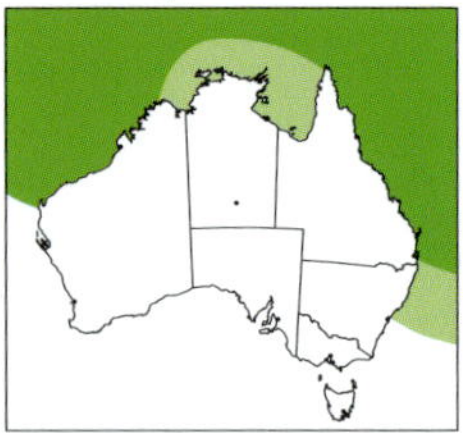

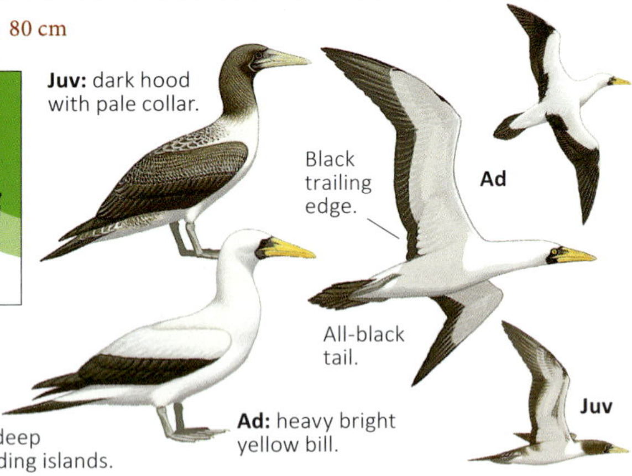

Large, black and white booby of tropics and subtropics. Very scarce around Aus mainland, mostly singletons over deep water except near breeding islands.

BROWN BOOBY ◕ 70 cm
Sula leucogaster

Common booby of tropics and subtropics. Chocolate brown with sharply demarcated white underparts.
Frequents coastal waters, rests on pylons and markers. Abundant at breeding islands.

RED-FOOTED BOOBY 75 cm
Sula sula

Small, slightly built, polymorphic booby of tropical seas. Striking red feet. Breeds on tropical islands, approaches vessels at sea, but rare on mainland where mostly storm-driven.

LESSER FRIGATEBIRD 75 cm
Fregata ariel

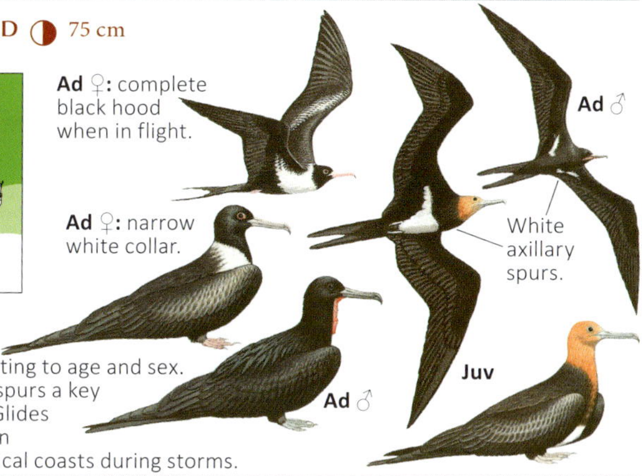

Large, mostly black seabird with much plumage variation relating to age and sex. Narrow white axillary spurs a key ID feature in all ages. Glides effortlessly. Often seen soaring high over tropical coasts during storms.

GREAT FRIGATEBIRD 95 cm
Fregata minor

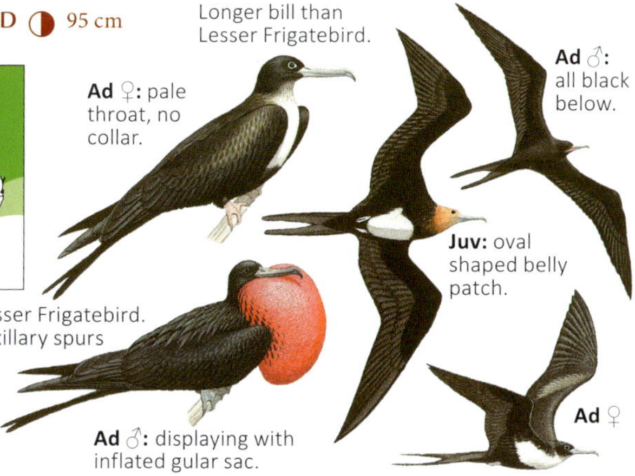

Slightly larger than Lesser Frigatebird. Lacks distinct white axillary spurs in all plumages. ♂ all black, ♀ and Juvs with white breast or belly. Tropical seas, rare in w Aus.

AUSTRALASIAN DARTER ◕ 90 cm
Anhinga novaehollandiae

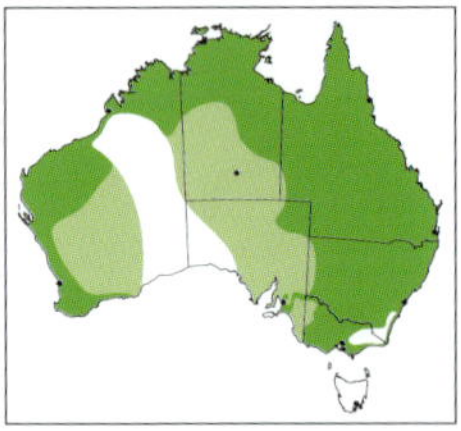

Large with long, kinked neck and dagger-shaped bill. Hunts underwater for fish in most freshwater habitats, can stay underwater for long periods. Mostly solitary or in small groups. **Voice:** a series of ratchet-like, croaking clicks.

GREAT CORMORANT ◕ 82 cm
Phalacrocorax carbo

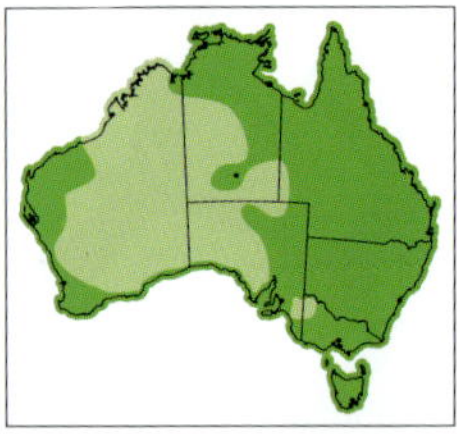

All black with white and yellow face, largest cormorant in Aus. Occurs on both inland and coastal waters, preferring larger bodies of water. Singly or in small flocks.

Comparative sizes of cormorant species.

LITTLE BLACK CORMORANT ● 60 cm
Phalacrocorax sulcirostris

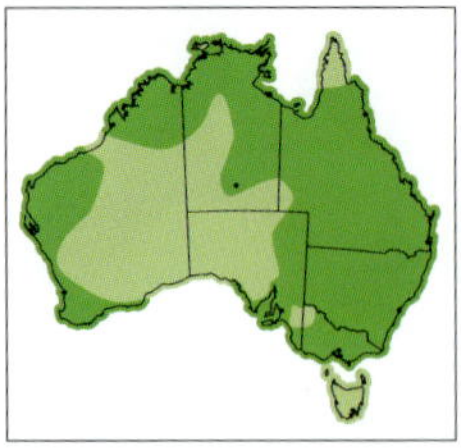

Small and all black. Occupies a wide range of inshore marine and freshwater wetlands. Often in large, tight flocks that feed cooperatively over dense schools of fish, birds surfacing at rear fly to front of flock and dive.

LITTLE PIED CORMORANT ● 60 cm
Microcarbo melanoleucos

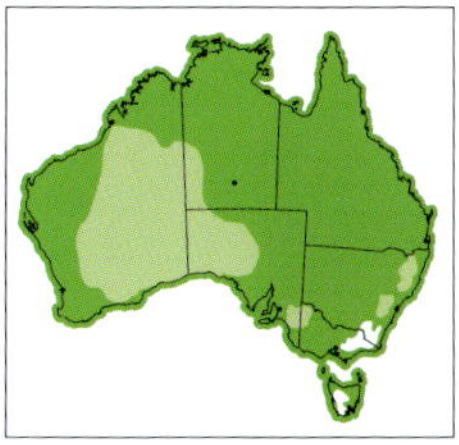

Tail as long as head and neck.

Smallest Aus cormorant. Black and white with short orange bill and long tail. Common in most wetland types, including inshore marine waters. Usually alone but can form groups.

Feeds on aquatic invertebrates, especially yabbies, so often on smaller wetlands where other cormorant species are not often present.

AUSTRALIAN PIED CORMORANT ◕ 75 cm
Phalacrocorax varius

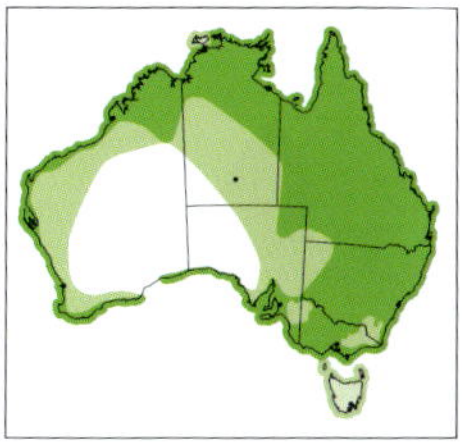

In flight kinked neck and head held above axis of body.

Large, black and white cormorant with long, pale bill. Inhabits coastal marine waters and larger, deep freshwater lakes and reservoirs. Alone or in groups, often well offshore in coastal bays.

Single Australian Pied with three Black-faced.

BLACK-FACED CORMORANT ◕ 65 cm
Phalacrocorax fuscescens

In flight head held below axis of body with straight neck.

Large, black and white cormorant with black cap reaching eye, and slate-grey facial skin. Entirely marine, prefers high-energy coastal waters near rocky islands, stacks and reefs used for roosting. Seldom ventures far into bays.

BROWN SKUA ◑ 64 cm
Stercorarius antarcticus

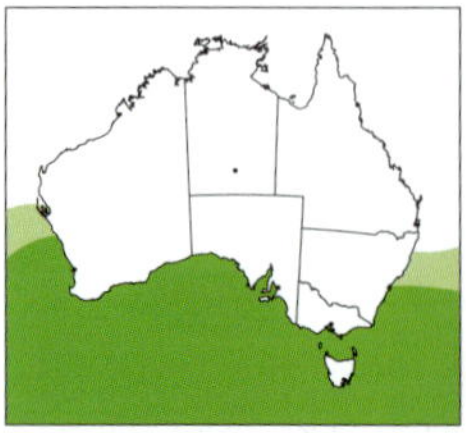

Large, gull-like predator with distinctive pale flashes in wings. Strictly marine, occasionally seen from land, but rarely ashore in Aus. A winter–spring visitor from sub-Antarctic waters.

SOUTH POLAR SKUA ○ 53 cm
Stercorarius maccormicki

Like Brown Skua, but most individuals with paler body. A rare autumn and spring migrant that mostly passes through Aus seas far from land.

Non-breeding jaeger heads: see also next page.

POMARINE JAEGER 46 cm
Stercorarius pomarinus

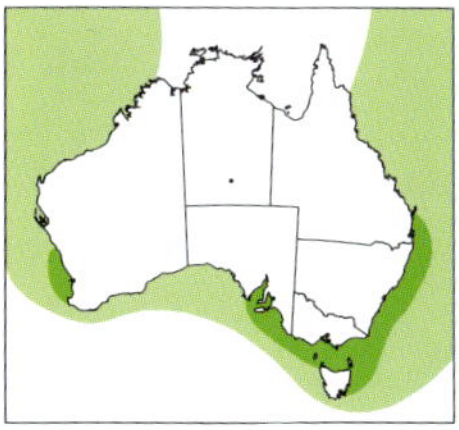

Largest jaeger, heavily built with broad, spatulate tail streamers. Dark and pale morphs occur. Summer migrant present Oct–Apr. Occasionally seen from land off e Aus. More predatory than piratical.

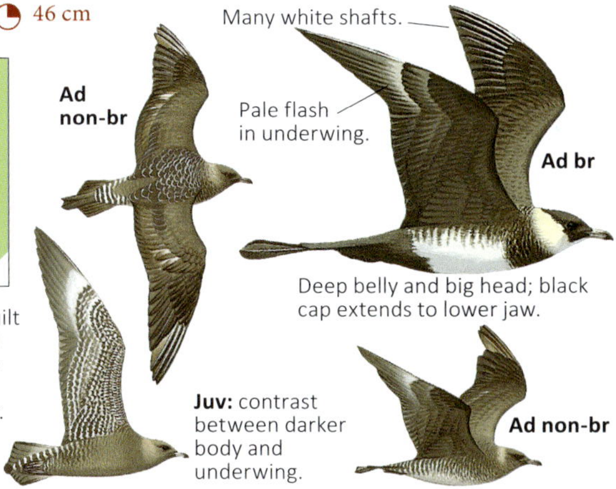

ARCTIC JAEGER 41 cm
Stercorarius parasiticus

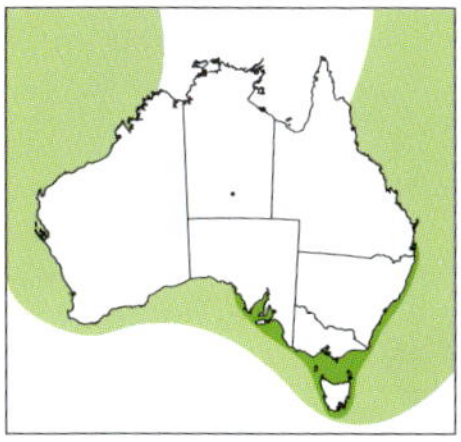

Mid-sized jaeger with both dark and pale morphs. Common summer migrant to coastal waters, routinely enters bays, often seen from land. Chases terns and gulls to steal their food.

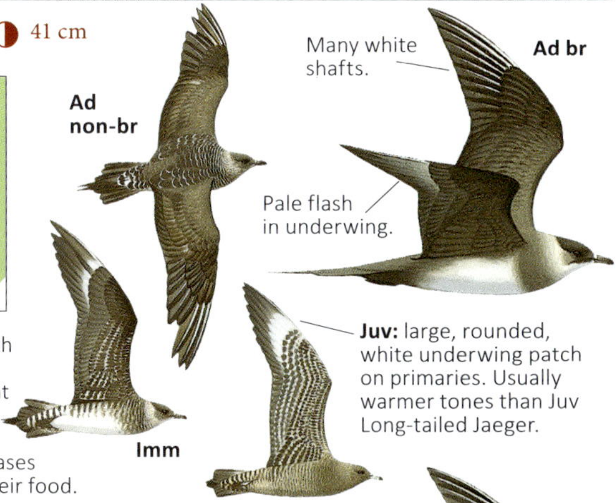

LONG-TAILED JAEGER 38 cm
Stercorarius longicaudus

Smallest jaeger with paler grey tones. Scarce summer migrant mostly to deep pelagic waters. Only seen from land during storms or when migrating.

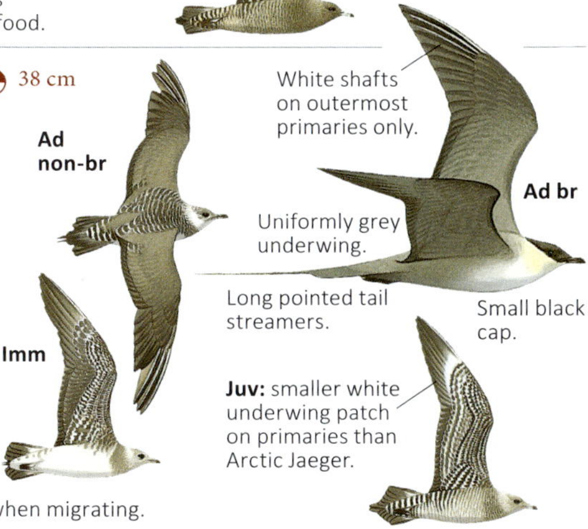

SILVER GULL
Chroicocephalus novaehollandiae

40 cm

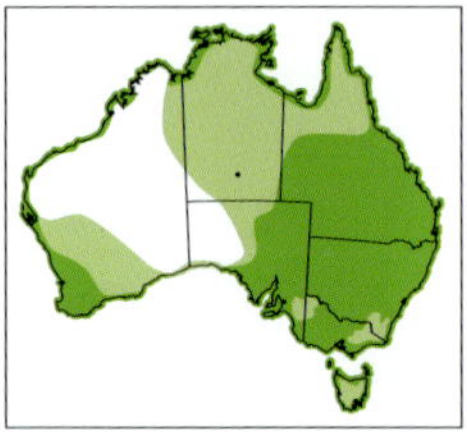

Our only regularly occurring small 'seagull', with light grey upperparts. Familiar and abundant on coasts, many waterways and urban areas; often in flocks. **Voice:** loud harsh squeal *we* or *kwee-aar.*

PACIFIC GULL
Larus pacificus

58 cm

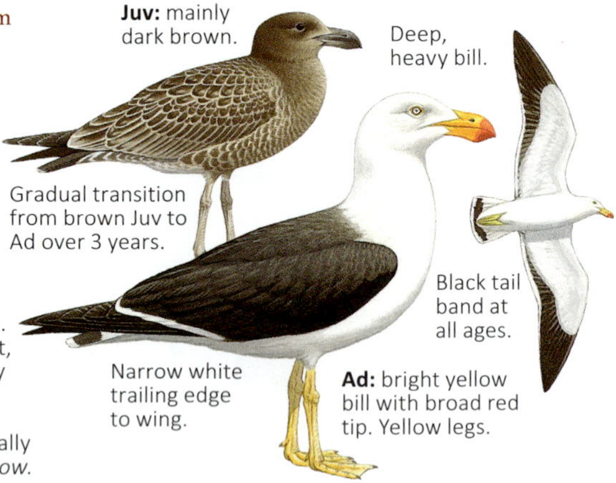

Huge gull with massive bill. Thinly spread along s coast, mainly on sheltered, sandy shores, but also on ocean beaches and rocky coasts. **Voice:** not vocal, occasionally gives gruff, nasal bark *ow-ow.*

KELP GULL
Larus dominicanus

55 cm

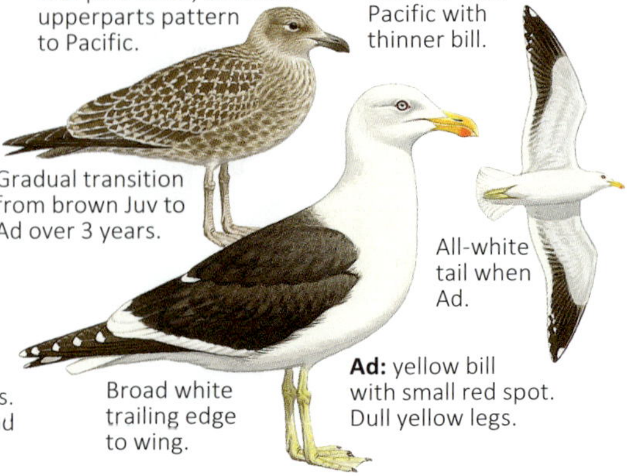

Large gull with medium bill, patchy along s coast, most common in NSW and se Tas. Sandy shores and rocky coasts. **Voice:** noisy, raucous yelps and cackling wail *ee-ah-ha-ha-ha.*

Quick guide to terns: Slim seabirds with pointed bills, long pointed wings. Most species occur in flocks, roost with other terns, gulls or shorebirds, nest colonially and feed on the wing.

CASPIAN TERN ◑ 50 cm
Hydroprogne caspia

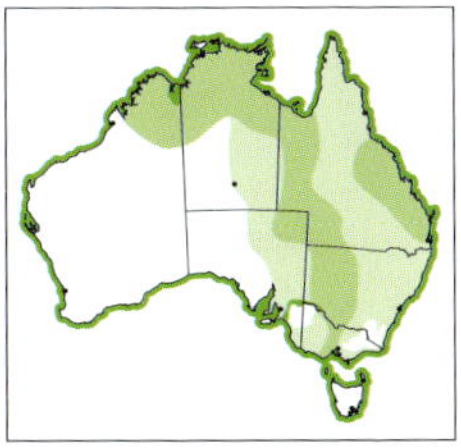

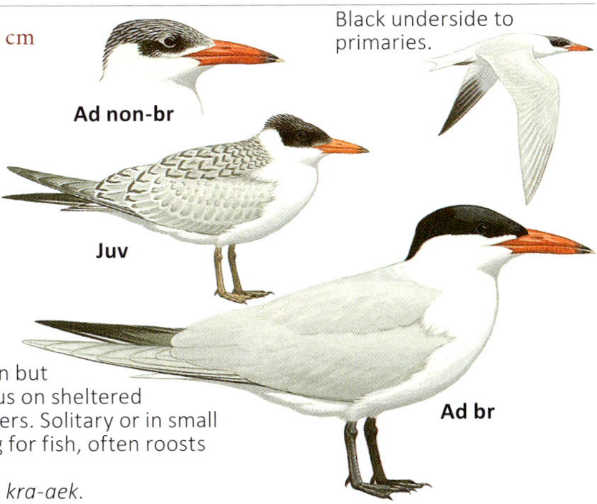

Largest tern: pale, with massive red bill. Uncommon but widespread and conspicuous on sheltered coasts and large inland waters. Solitary or in small flocks; hovers before diving for fish, often roosts with gulls and shorebirds.
Voice: deep, very loud rasp *kra-aek*.

AUSTRALIAN GULL-BILLED TERN ◕ 36 cm
Gelochelidon macrotarsa

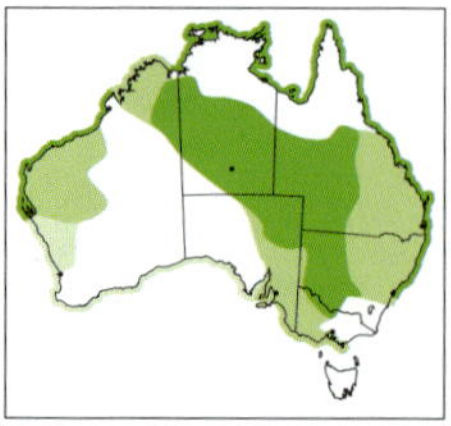

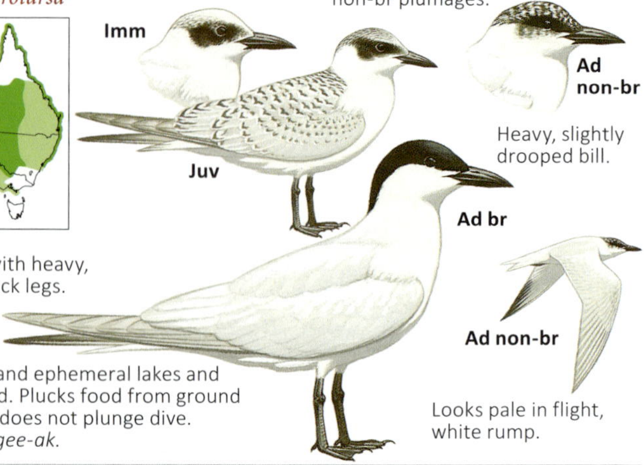

Large, pale tern with heavy, black bill, long black legs. More common in n Aus, on coasts with tidal flats, and inland ephemeral lakes and adjacent grassland. Plucks food from ground or water surface, does not plunge dive.
Voice: gruff yelp *gee-ak*.

COMMON GULL-BILLED TERN ◔ 35 cm
Gelochelidon nilotica

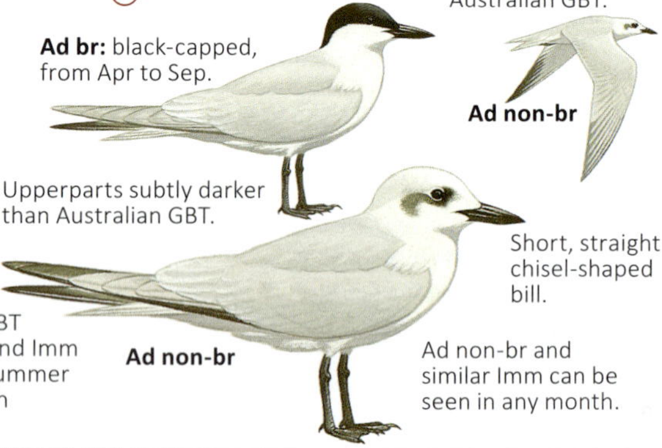

Smaller than Australian GBT with shorter bill; non-br and Imm have smaller eye patch. Summer visitor to n Aus coasts with tidal flats; breeds in Asia.

SOOTY TERN ◕ 34 cm
Onychoprion fuscatus

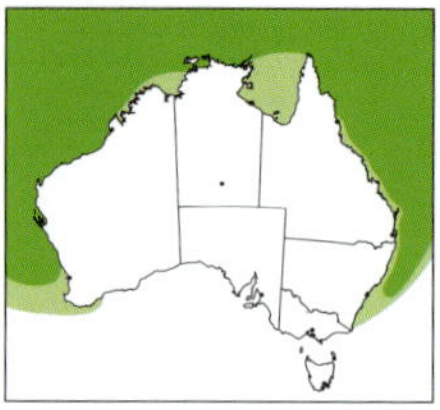

Long-winged, oceanic tern with black upperparts. Mostly in flocks at sea, plucks prey from surface, shallow plunge dives. Only near mainland shores in bad weather; nests colonially on offshore islands.
Voice: noisy at colonies, main call harsh *ker-wacky-wak*.

GREATER CRESTED TERN ● 45 cm
Thalasseus bergii

Large coastal tern with shaggy crest. Common, mainly feeds near shore, plunge dives for fish.
Voice: noisy, main call a loud, harsh *kerack*.

LESSER CRESTED TERN ◕ 40 cm
Thalasseus bengalensis

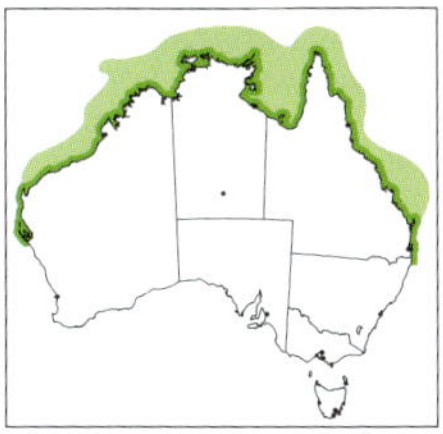

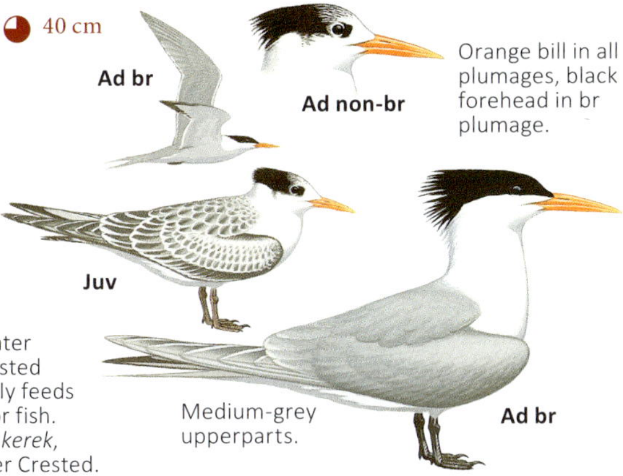

Coastal, looks slimmer, neater and paler than Greater Crested Tern with orange bill. Mainly feeds near shore; plunge dives for fish.
Voice: loud, rasping *kek* or *kerek*, higher-pitched than Greater Crested.

BRIDLED TERN ◕ 31 cm
Onychoprion anaethetus

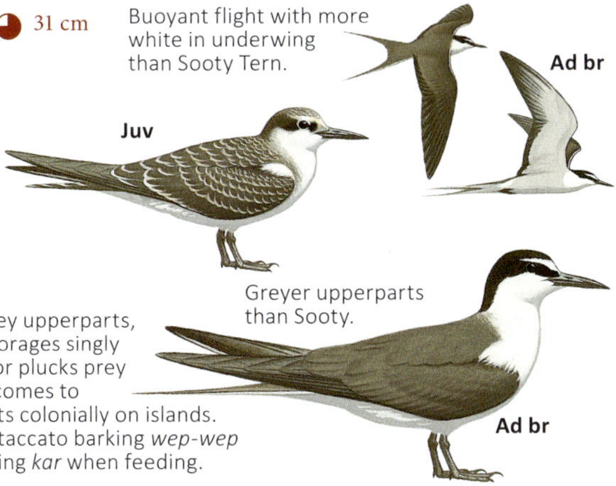

Oceanic tern with dark-grey upperparts, long, white supercilium. Forages singly or in flocks, plunge dives or plucks prey from water surface, only comes to coast in bad weather; nests colonially on islands.
Voice: noisy at colonies, staccato barking *wep-wep* when alarmed, harsh grating *kar* when feeding.

WHISKERED TERN ◕ 24 cm
Chlidonias hybrida

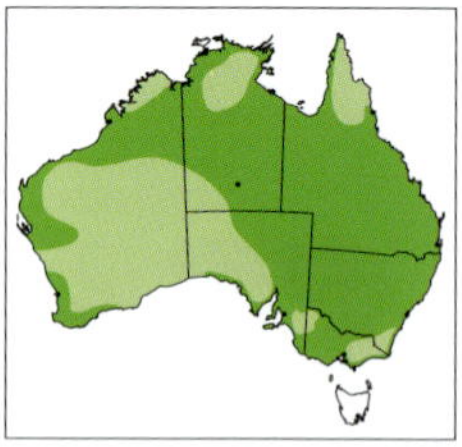

Smallish, stocky tern with broad wings, plain upperwing, short, forked tail. Flocks roam over vegetated inland wetlands and nearby plains; also on sheltered coasts. Summer visitor to s, present year-round in n Aus.
Voice: harsh, snipe-like *keirch*.

WHITE-WINGED BLACK TERN ◑ 21 cm
Chlidonias leucopterus

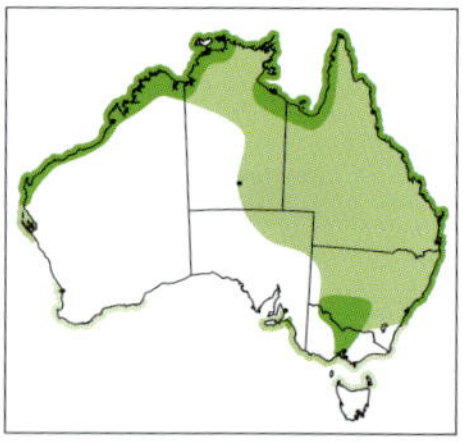

Small, slim tern, with short, forked tail. Often flocks with Whiskered Tern. Summer visitor to freshwater wetlands and grasslands, sometimes on sheltered coasts. More common in n Aus.
Voice: dry *krip* or *keek-keek*, less harsh than Whiskered.

ROSEATE TERN ◑ 34 cm
Sterna dougallii

Medium–small tern of tropical and subtropical seas, near coral reefs or sparsely vegetated islands. Seldom dives.
Voice: high-pitched, rising *cher-VICK*.

WHITE-FRONTED TERN ◑ 39 cm
Sterna striata

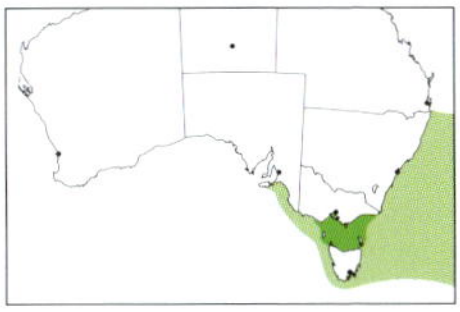

Medium sea-tern with large head. Like Roseate but unlike Common, has white inner edge to primaries forming white line along top of folded wing. Most seen in Aus are Imm with black carpal bars. Forages offshore, plunge dives; mostly roosts on rocky coasts, rarely with Common Terns on beaches. **Voice:** variety of harsh cries.

COMMON TERN ◑ 34 cm
Sterna hirundo

The standard medium-sized tern on Aus coasts. Migrant from Asia, mainly seen in non-br plumages. Slimmer and smaller-headed than White-fronted. Forages near shore, plunge dives; roosts in flocks on beaches, rocks and jetties. **Voice:** sharp hoarse *kip* in flight, *kyee-hah* when agitated.

ARCTIC TERN ○ 31 cm
Sterna paradisaea

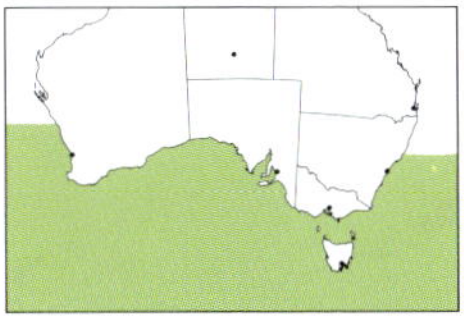

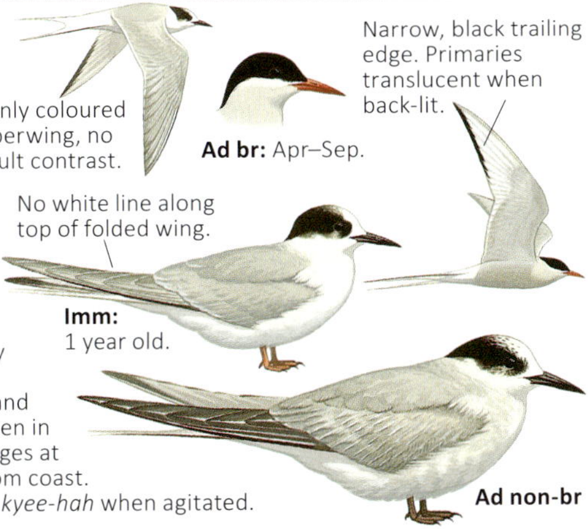

Rare sea-tern, migrant from the Arctic. Shorter neck, bill and legs than Common, but relatively long wings. Best distinguished from Common on wing pattern and lack of moult contrast. Mainly seen in non-br plumages, Jun–Dec. Forages at sea, plunge dives; rarely seen from coast. **Voice:** sharp hoarse *kip* in flight, *kyee-hah* when agitated.

BLACK-NAPED TERN ◑ 31 cm
Sterna sumatrana

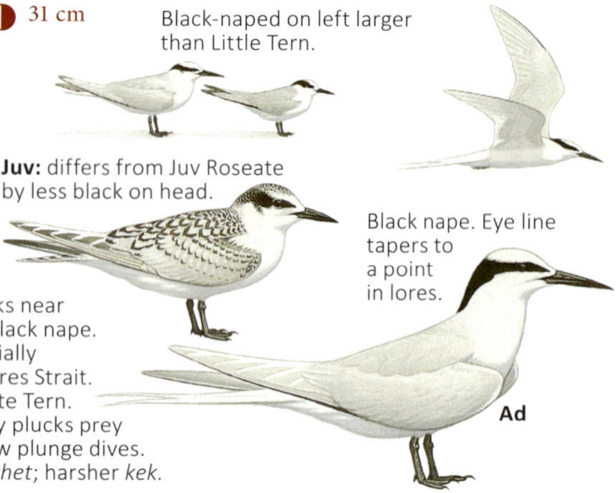

Pale tropical sea-tern; looks near white in flight except for black nape. Mainly near islands, especially Great Barrier Reef and Torres Strait. Often in flocks with Roseate Tern. Forages near shore, mostly plucks prey from surface, some shallow plunge dives.
Voice: yapping *chet-chet-chet*; harsher *kek*.

FAIRY TERN ◑ 24 cm
Sternula nereis

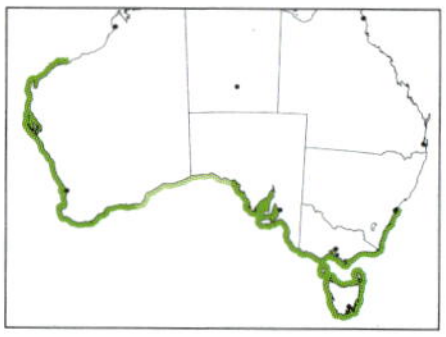

Small, uncommon coastal tern. Stockier than similar Little Tern. Ad br differs in bill colour and loral pattern. In non-br, Fairy has paler outer primaries and usually yellow tinge in bill. Hovers and plunge dives for fish in sheltered coastal waters; roosts on shore; nests mainly on beaches where threatened by human disturbance.
Voice: vocal; hard *ker-vik* or *ker-ker-vik*, rarely monosyllabic.

LITTLE TERN ◑ 24 cm
Sternula albifrons

Small coastal tern: population includes uncommon Aus residents and numerous Asian migrants. Similar to Fairy Tern, note darker outer primaries. Ad br differs in bill colour and loral pattern. In non-br develops all-black bill.
Voice: vocal; loud sharp *kip* or *zweek*, sometimes given as double note or chatter; higher-pitched than Fairy.

BROWN NODDY ◕ 42 cm
Anous stolidus

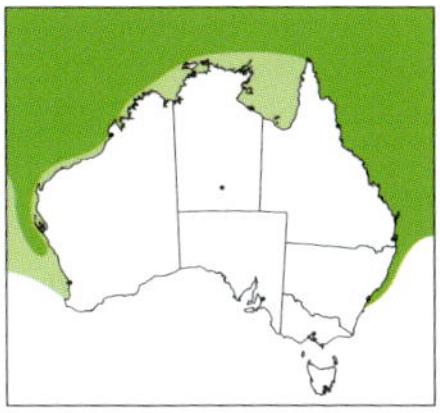

Found in tropical seas, all noddies have dark plumage, white cap and wedge-shaped tail.

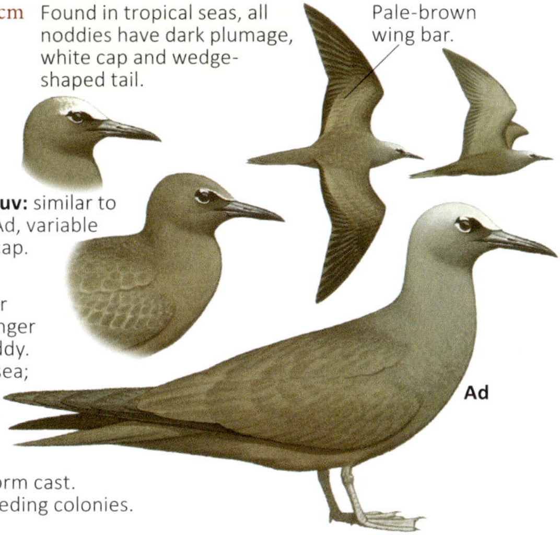

Largest noddy, with browner plumage, shorter bill and longer tail than Black or Lesser Noddy. Forages in flocks far out to sea; mainly plucks prey from surface, occasionally settles on water in large rafts. Nests colonially on islands, mainland records mainly storm cast.
Voice: cawing chorus at breeding colonies.

BLACK NODDY ◑ 37 cm
Anous minutus

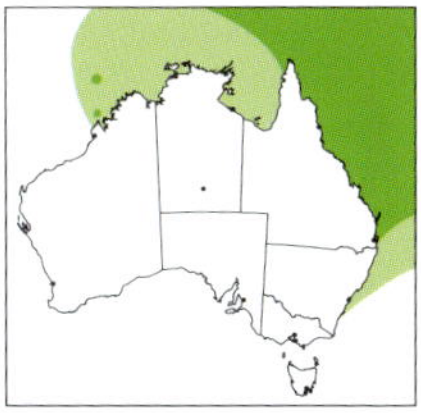

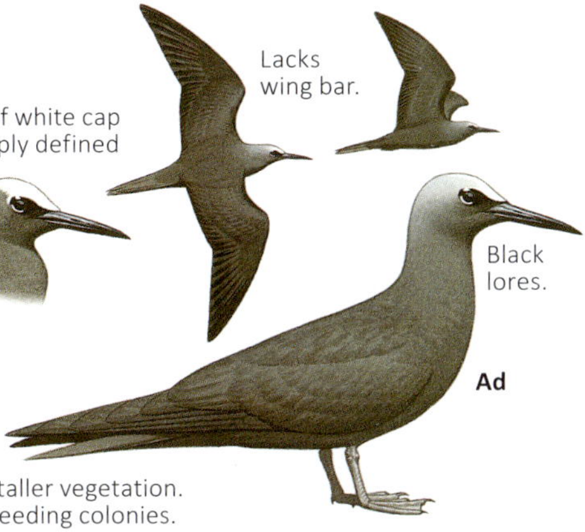

Small noddy with blacker plumage and whiter cap than other noddies. Bill longer and more slender than Brown Noddy. Similar behaviour to Brown Noddy but nests often set in taller vegetation.
Voice: incessant varied chatter at breeding colonies.

LESSER NODDY ○ 31 cm
Anous tenuirostris

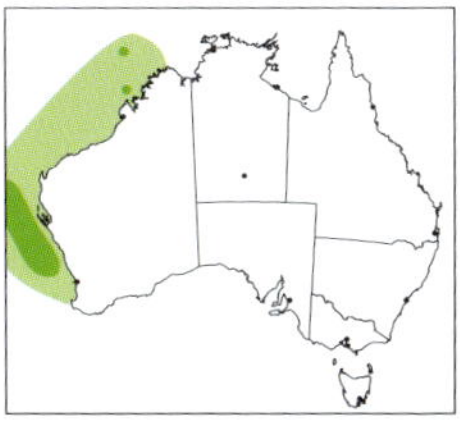

Indian Ocean counterpart of Black Noddy: grey-tinged cap merges into pale lores.
Voice: just as vocal as other noddies, calls a bit softer.

Quick guide to shorebirds: Shorebirds (also known as waders, especially in Europe) are the main focus of many birdwatchers. Watching shorebirds usually involves visiting wetlands and shores to see elegant birds that often gather in large, mixed flocks in open settings (e.g. wide beaches, sandspits). Views are often at long range, and a tripod-mounted telescope hugely enhances the viewing experience. Some shorebird species nest in Australia, but more of our species are long-distance migrants from Siberia, northern Asia and Alaska. Adults arrive in Australia ~Sep–Oct and depart ~Feb–Apr. In many species, immature birds remain in Australia through the austral winter. Confident ID of shorebirds requires an understanding of their seasonal changes in appearance. In many species, breeding and non-breeding plumages look very different. Migratory species are in non-breeding plumage through most of the Australian summer. In late summer they begin moult to breeding plumage, and some are very brightly coloured before they depart north. In our spring (~Sep–Oct) many adults still have remnant breeding plumage. At the same time, birds in their first year are moulting out of their juvenile plumage, which in some species looks quite different to the non-breeding plumage of adults.

BUSH STONE-CURLEW ◕ 56 cm

Burhinus grallarius

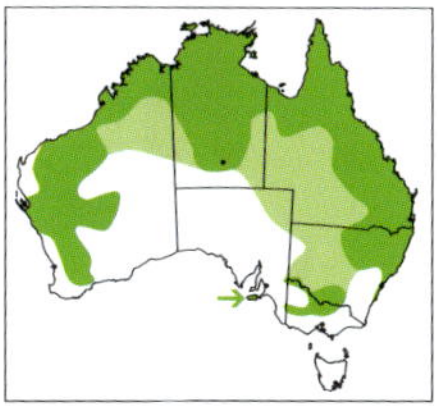

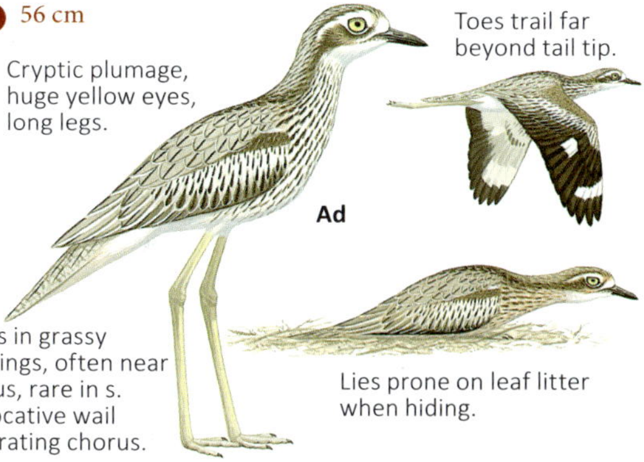

Nocturnal, shy; singles or pairs in grassy woodlands and adjacent clearings, often near fallen timber. Common in n Aus, rare in s. **Voice:** vocal at night; loud evocative wail *wee-loo*, often given in accelerating chorus.

BEACH STONE-CURLEW ◑ 55 cm

Esacus magnirostris

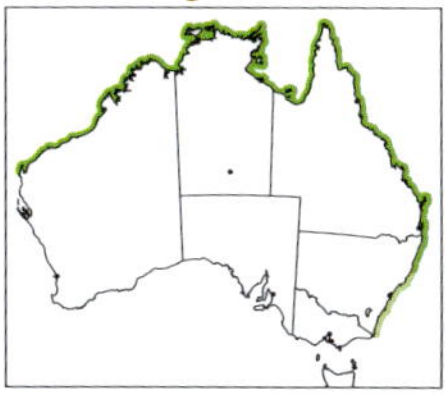

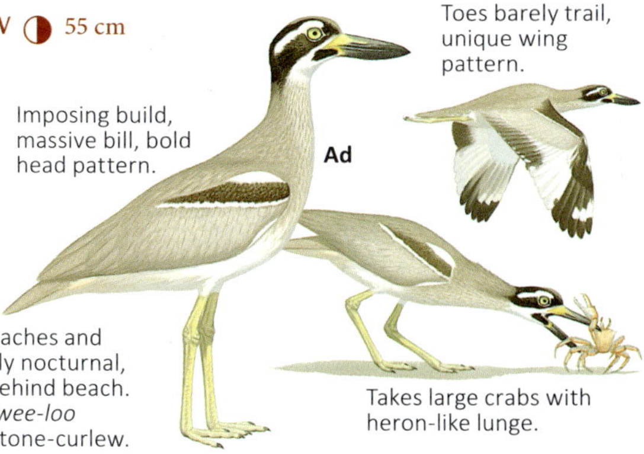

Singles or pairs on quiet beaches and nearby tidal flats. Shy, partly nocturnal, often hides in vegetation behind beach. **Voice:** fairly quiet; wailing *wee-loo* higher-pitched than Bush Stone-curlew.

SOOTY OYSTERCATCHER ◑ 46 cm
Haematopus fuliginosus

All-black oystercatcher of rocky coasts. Singly or in pairs; some join flocks in winter.
Voice: piping *plic* and flight calls *pit-chew* more shrill than Pied Oystercatcher.

PIED OYSTERCATCHER ◕ 46 cm
Haematopus longirostris

Mostly on tidal flats and nearby beaches; sometimes on rocky shores. Territorial pairs when breeding, flocks at other times.
Voice: vocal; piercing repeated *pic*, also *petey-pete* in flight.

PIED STILT ◕ 35 cm
Himantopus leucocephalus

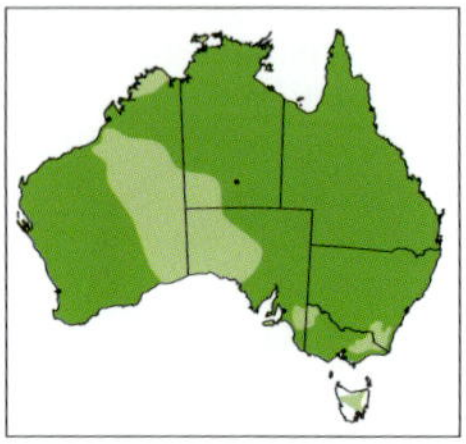

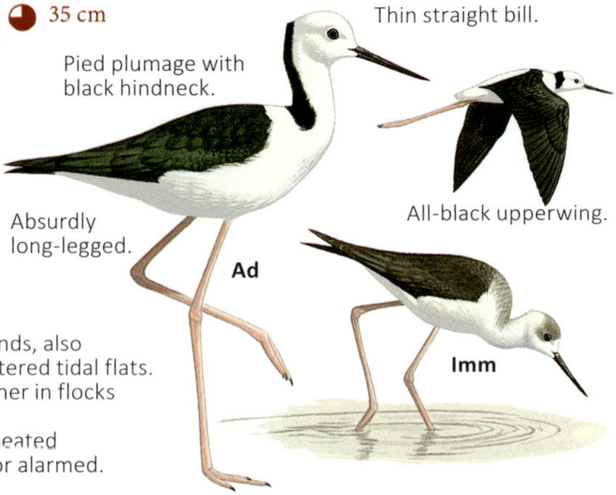

Mostly in freshwater wetlands, also brackish wetlands and sheltered tidal flats. Wades in shallows, can gather in flocks when roosting.
Voice: strident yap *kek*, repeated persistently when excited or alarmed.

BANDED STILT

Cladorhynchus leucocephalus

◐ 39 cm

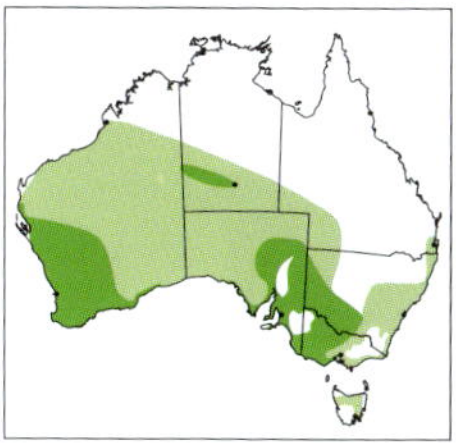

Highly gregarious stilt, mainly seen on salt lakes or saltworks. Gathers in dense flocks when roosting, nests in huge colonies in remote inland salt lakes soon after they flood.

Voice: nasal bark *chowp*.

Stockier and shorter-winged than Pied Stilt, always has white head.

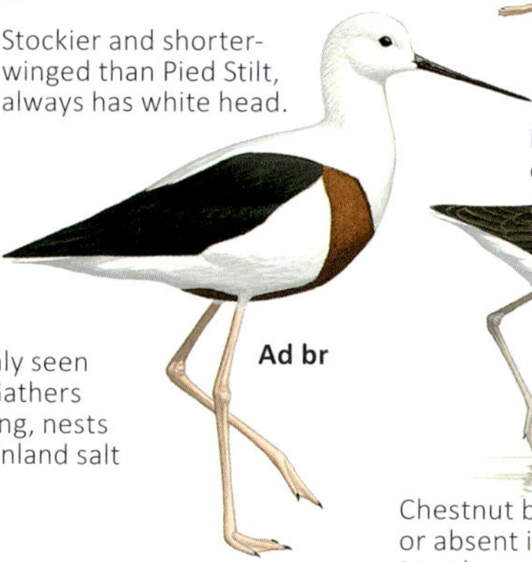

Broad white trailing edge to wing.

Chestnut breast band is faint or absent in Ad non-br and Juv plumages.

Usually swims when foraging, taking brine shrimp from surface.

Often flocks with Red-necked Avocet.

RED-NECKED AVOCET

Recurvirostra novaehollandiae

◐ 44 cm

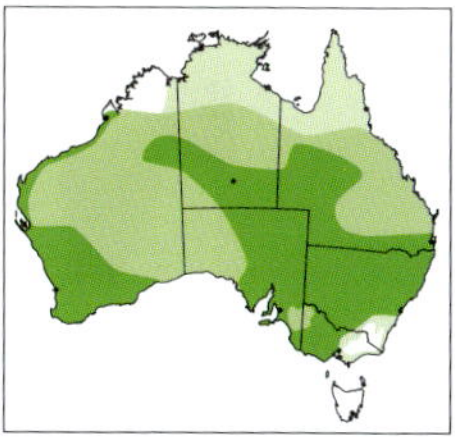

Elegant, social shorebird found in shallow wetlands, ranging from saline to fresh, sometimes in sheltered marine inlets. Swims or wades to feed, with sideways bill sweeps to locate tiny prey.

Voice: in flight, repeated reedy yelp *toot*.

White upperwing with big black panels.

Fine, upcurved bill, chestnut head and neck.

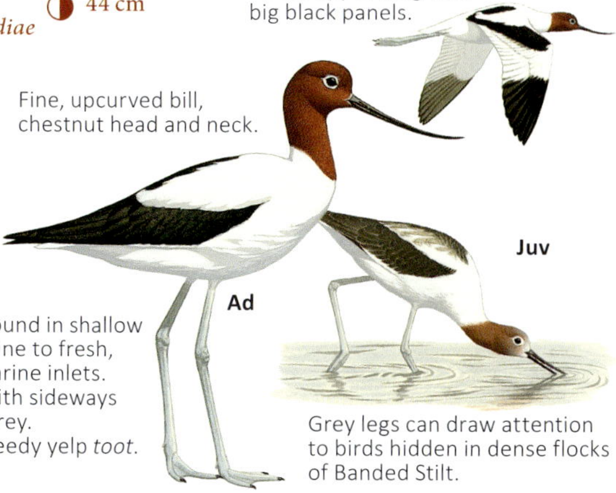

Grey legs can draw attention to birds hidden in dense flocks of Banded Stilt.

COMB-CRESTED JACANA ◔ 25 cm
Irediparra gallinacea

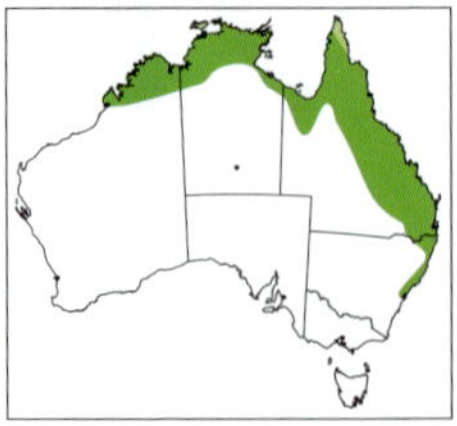

Greatly elongated toes used to walk on floating vegetation (especially lily pads) on freshwater wetlands.
Voice: wide repertoire of short quiet calls.

MASKED LAPWING ● 33 cm
Vanellus miles

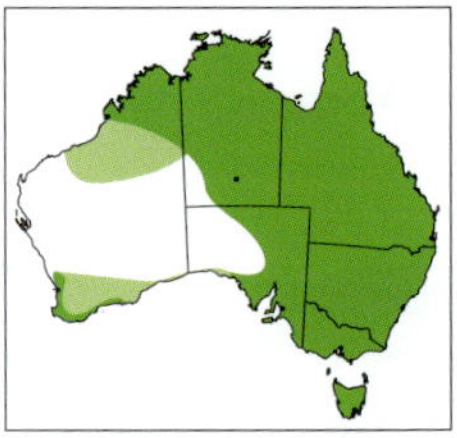

Large, familiar lapwing with yellow facial wattles.
Open habitats including farmland and urban parks; usually near water but rarely wades. In pairs or small flocks; aggressive in defence of nest and young.
Voice: vocal; noisy grating *keer-ki-ki-ki-ki* ... and single-note calls.

BANDED LAPWING ◑ 27 cm
Vanellus tricolor

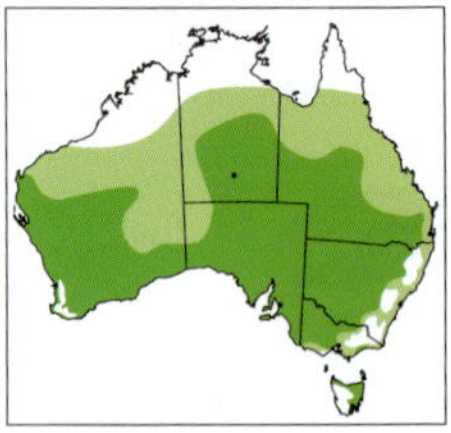

Unobtrusive, on plains and farmlands with bare ground or very short grass; often far from water. Usually in small flocks.
Voice: rattling alarm calls in staccato burst of 3–4 notes *e-chi-chi-chi*.

INLAND DOTTEREL 21 cm
Peltohyas australis

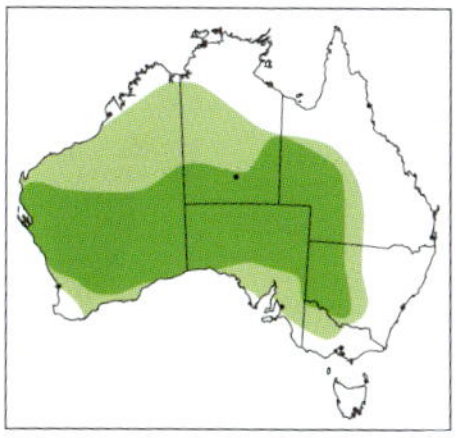

Singles, pairs and small flocks on arid inland plains: gibber and claypans with very sparse vegetation, occasionally on bare fields of wheatbelt. Well-camouflaged, mostly nocturnal, hard to see.
Voice: not vocal. Quiet trill *kroot* in flight.

RED-CAPPED PLOVER 15 cm
Charadrius ruficapillus

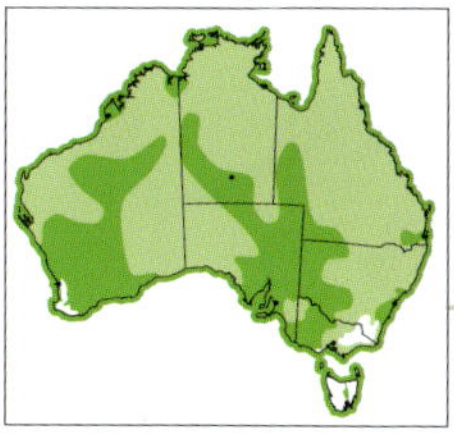

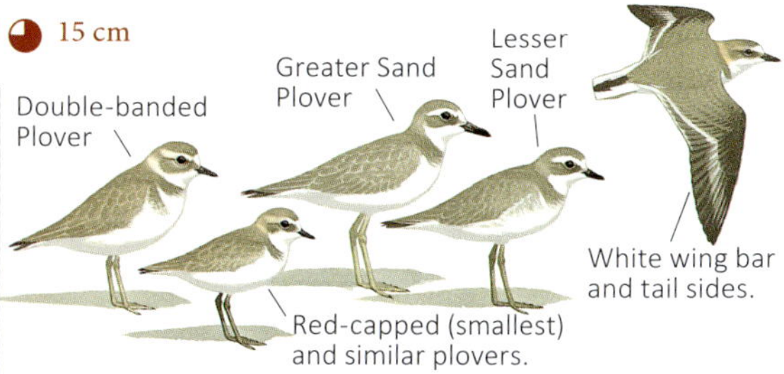

Our smallest plover. Found singly, in pairs or small flocks on inland wetlands and coast. Rarely wades; usually on moist or dry ground near water.
Voice: sharp quiet *wit*.

LITTLE RINGED PLOVER 15 cm
Charadrius dubius

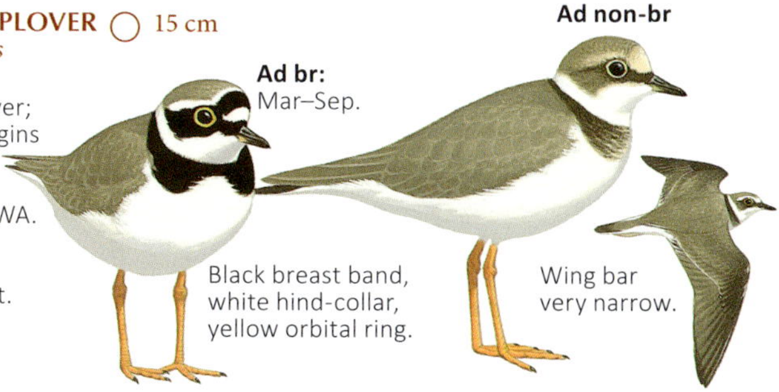

Small migrant plover; rare visitor to margins of freshwater wetlands in tropical NT and n WA.
Voice: soft, downslurred whistle *piu* in flight.

BLACK-FRONTED DOTTEREL ◔ 17 cm
Elseyornis melanops

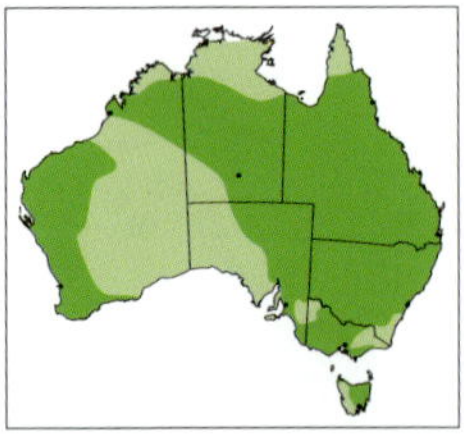

Small, dainty plover found on bare ground or mud beside freshwater wetlands, including small water bodies like farm dams. Singly or in pairs, occasionally in small flocks. **Voice:** sharp, high-pitched *pit* repeated rapidly.

RED-KNEED DOTTEREL ◔ 19 cm
Erythrogonys cinctus

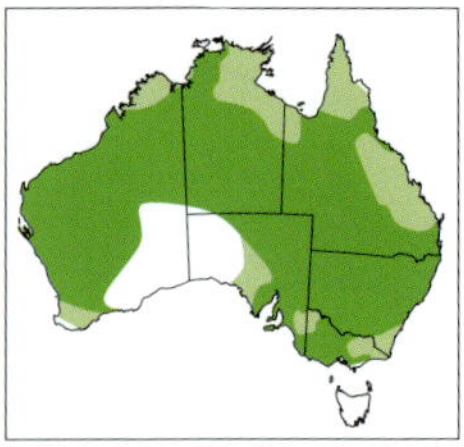

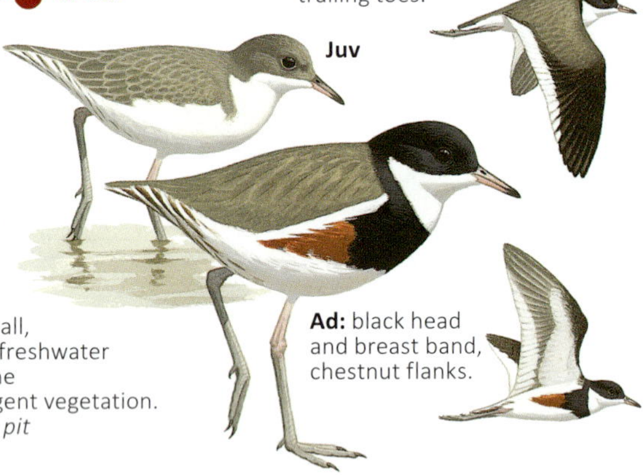

Elegant plover found in small, loose flocks in shallows of freshwater wetlands, usually with some bare mud and some emergent vegetation. **Voice:** sharp, high-pitched *pit* repeated rapidly.

HOODED PLOVER ◑ 21 cm
Thinornis cucullatus

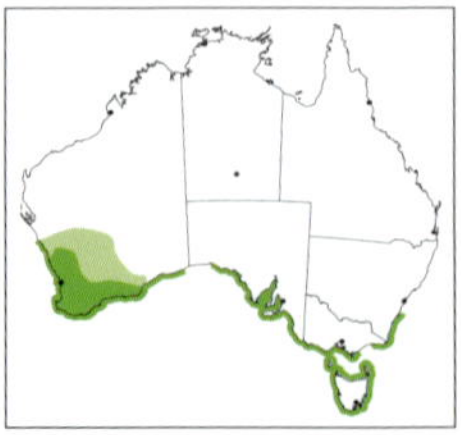

Pale, stocky plover with black head. In se Aus on broad ocean beaches; usually in pairs, some small flocks in winter. WA ssp mainly on inland salt lakes and found in larger flocks. **Voice:** soft, low-pitched *chook* in flight.

DOUBLE-BANDED PLOVER ◐ 19 cm
Charadrius bicinctus

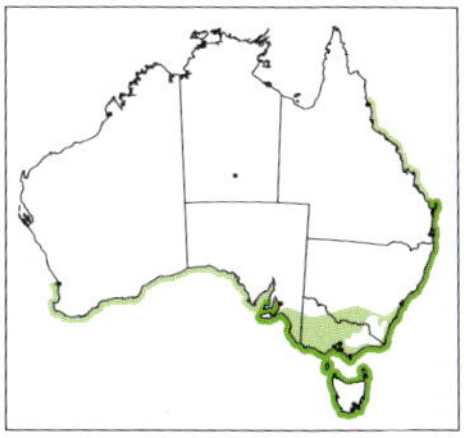

Medium-sized plover with upright stance, short bill and unique breast pattern. Migrant from NZ, present in Aus Feb–Aug. In flocks on coasts with tidal flats, also uses inland wetlands and adjacent close-cropped pasture.
Voice: clear sharp *chip* in flight.

LESSER SAND PLOVER ◐ 19 cm
Charadrius mongolus

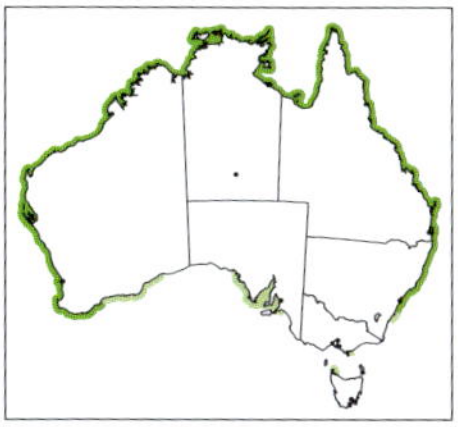

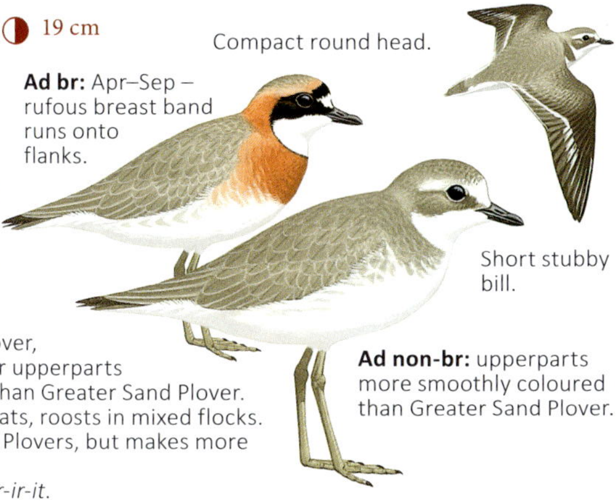

Medium-sized migrant plover, with shorter bill, smoother upperparts and more upright stance than Greater Sand Plover. Coastal; forages on tidal flats, roosts in mixed flocks. Usually with Greater Sand Plovers, but makes more use of rocky roosts.
Voice: brisk rippling trill *tir-ir-it*.

GREATER SAND PLOVER ◐ 23 cm
Charadrius leschenaultii

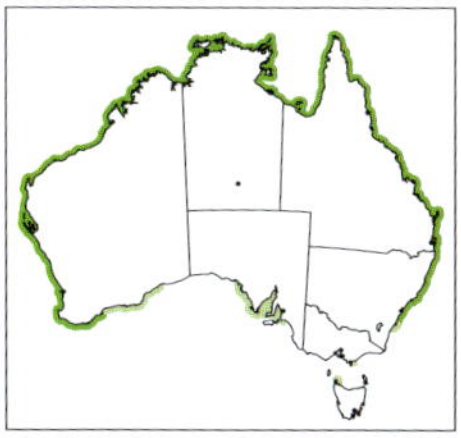

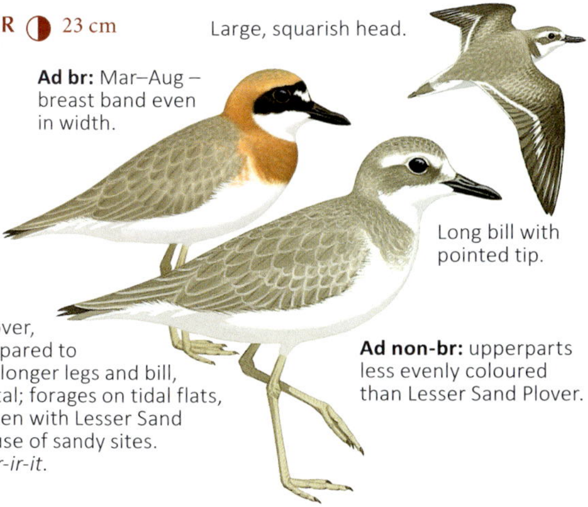

Medium-sized migrant plover, looks a little ungainly compared to Lesser Sand Plover due to longer legs and bill, larger squarer head. Coastal; forages on tidal flats, roosts in mixed flocks. Often with Lesser Sand Plovers, but makes more use of sandy sites.
Voice: brisk rippling trill *tir-ir-it*.

GREY PLOVER ◑ 29 cm
Pluvialis squatarola

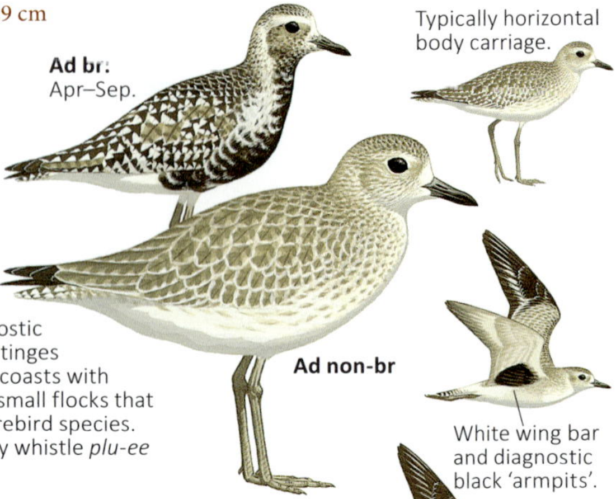

Largest plover, with diagnostic black 'armpits', no golden tinges in upperparts. Migrant to coasts with large tidal flats. Roosts in small flocks that sometimes join other shorebird species. **Voice:** far-carrying breathy whistle *plu-ee* or *plee-oo-ee*.

PACIFIC GOLDEN PLOVER ◑ 24 cm
Pluvialis fulva

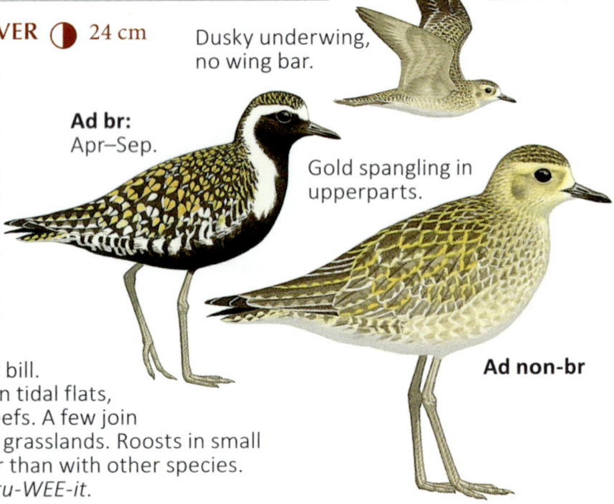

Smaller than Grey Plover; has rounder head, smaller bill. Migrant, mainly coastal, on tidal flats, saltmarsh, beaches and reefs. A few join Oriental Plovers on inland grasslands. Roosts in small flocks, often beside rather than with other species. **Voice:** clear shrill whistle *tu-WEE-it*.

ORIENTAL PLOVER ◑ 23 cm
Charadrius veredus

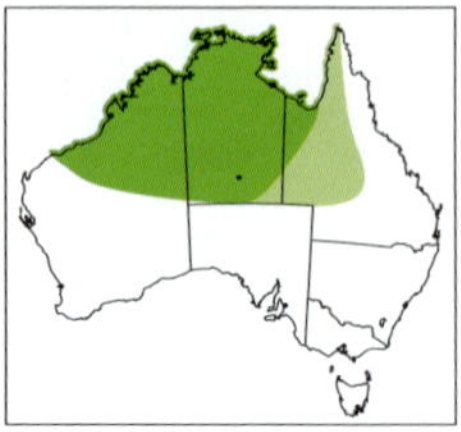

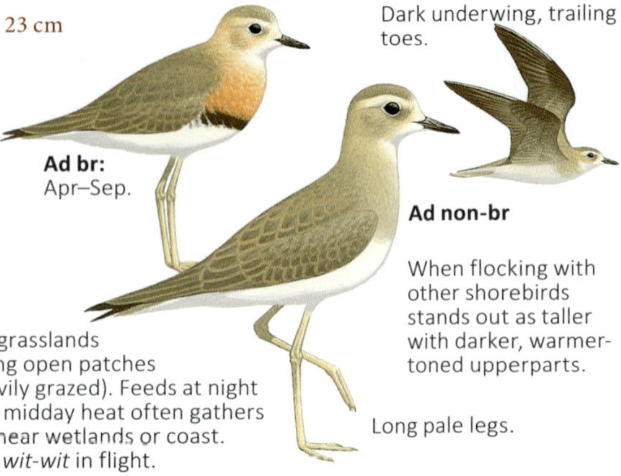

Slender migrant plover of grasslands and inland plains, preferring open patches (e.g. recently burnt or heavily grazed). Feeds at night and cooler parts of day; in midday heat often gathers in flocks on moist ground near wetlands or coast. **Voice:** soft whistle *twik* or *wit-wit* in flight.

AUSTRALIAN PRATINCOLE ◑ 21 cm
Stiltia isabella

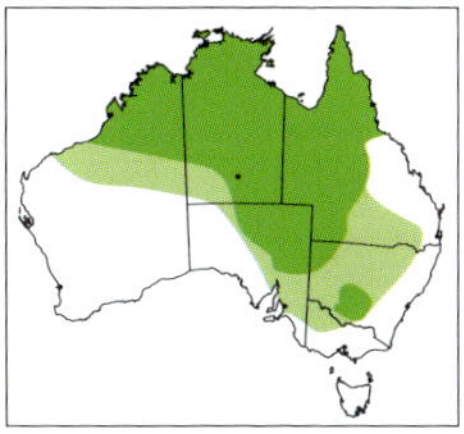

Elegant, tern-like flight, trailing toes, short square tail.

Slender, stands tall; sandy upperparts contrast with long, black primaries. Small flocks on arid or semi-arid plains, not far from drinking water. Catches insects on the wing or by running.
Voice: shrill upslurred whistle *weeteet*.

ORIENTAL PRATINCOLE ◔ 23 cm
Glareola maldivarum

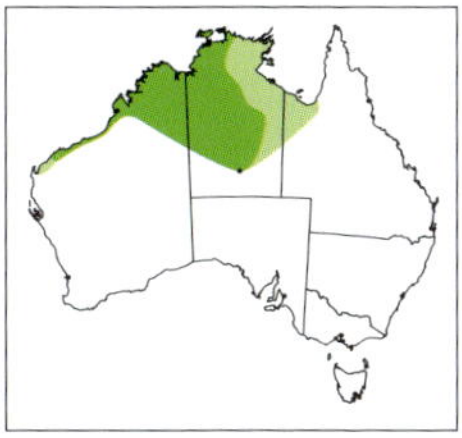

Tern-like flight with forked tail and chestnut underwing, toes don't trail.

Greyer than Australian Pratincole with shorter legs, horizontal posture. Migrant to n Aus; present ~Oct–Apr. Occurs in large (sometimes huge) flocks over open country, usually foraging on the wing; walks and runs well. Gathers near water or coast to loaf in midday heat. **Voice:** sharp grating *kyik*.

AUSTRALIAN PAINTED-SNIPE ○ 27 cm
Rostratula australis

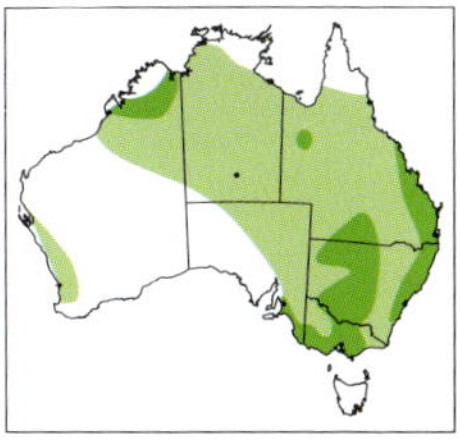

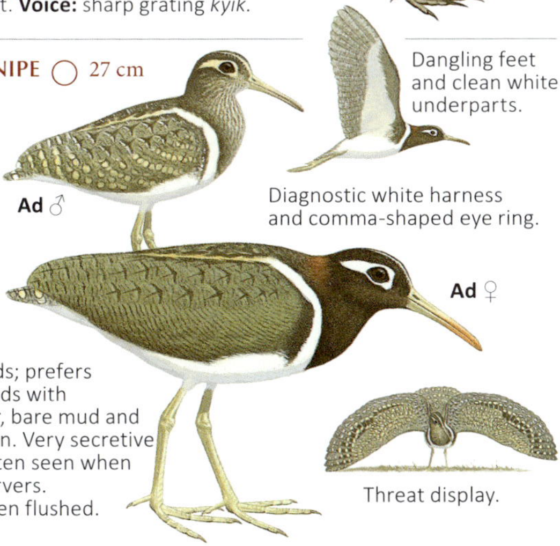

Dangling feet and clean white underparts.

Diagnostic white harness and comma-shaped eye ring.

Threat display.

Rare nomad of inland wetlands; prefers temporary freshwater wetlands with combination of shallow water, bare mud and dense, low, fringing vegetation. Very secretive and often nocturnal; most often seen when flushed, or by quiet still observers.
Voice: not vocal, loud *kek* when flushed.

LATHAM'S SNIPE ◐ 31 cm
Gallinago hardwickii

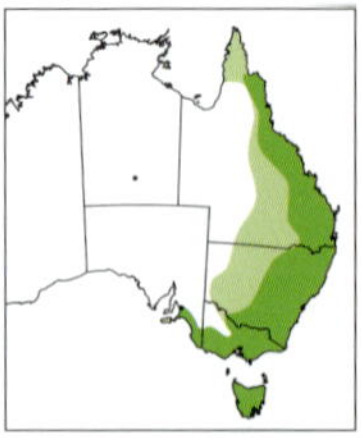

Our largest, longest-winged snipe. The only true snipe in s and e Aus.

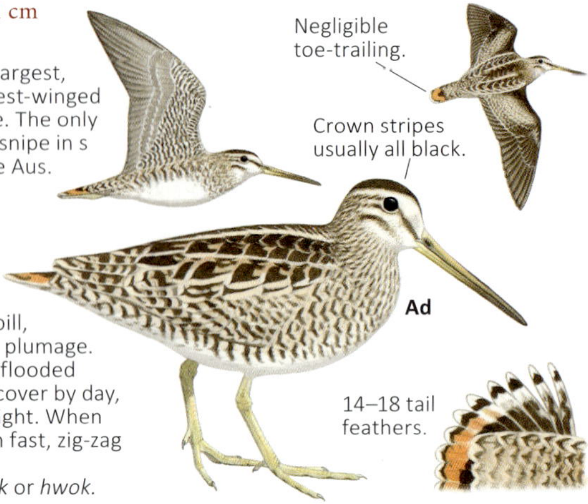

Migrant with long, straight bill, densely barred and mottled plumage. Small flocks in marshes and flooded grasslands; roosts in dense cover by day, forages in muddy areas at night. When flushed erupts from cover in fast, zig-zag flight.
Voice: explosive rasping *kerk* or *hwok*.

SWINHOE'S SNIPE ◔ 28 cm
Gallinago megala

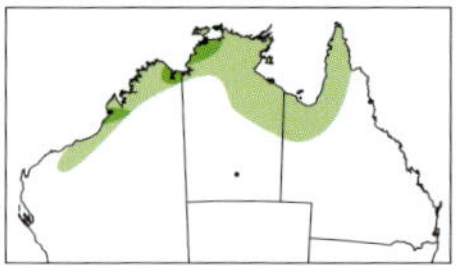

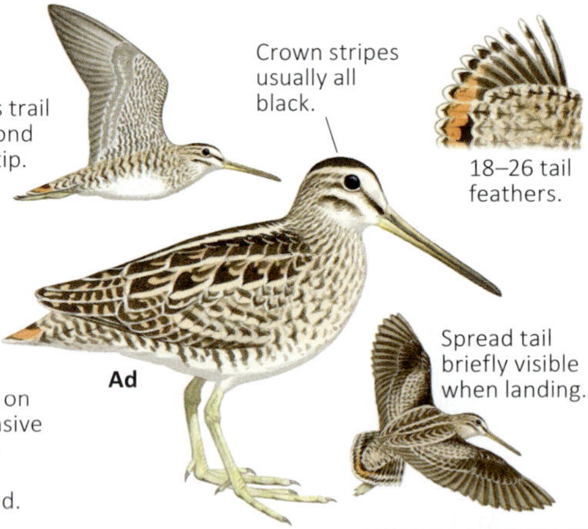

Migrant to freshwater wetlands of n Aus; very similar to other snipe in appearance and behaviour. Confident ID requires views of hard-to-see tail structure. From Latham's on shorter rear-end structure, extensive toe-trailing; even more similar to Pin-tailed Snipe.
Voice: rasping *skaak* when flushed.

PIN-TAILED SNIPE ○ 26 cm
Gallinago stenura

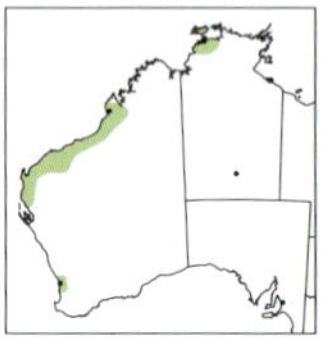

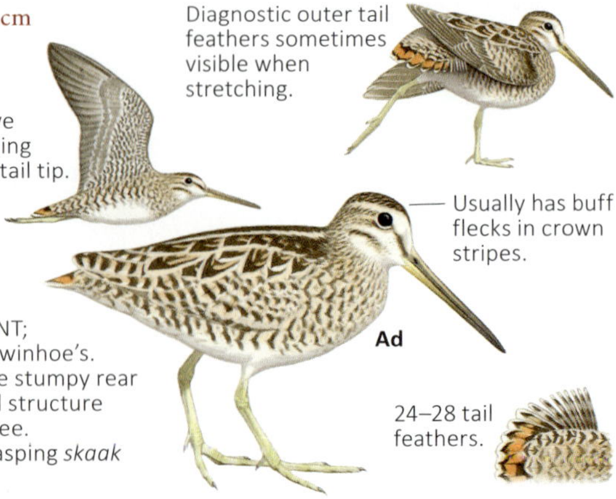

Migrant to freshwater wetlands of coastal WA and NT; co-occurs with very similar Swinhoe's. Pin-tailed tends to have more stumpy rear end, buff flecks in crown; tail structure distinctive but very hard to see.
Voice: higher-pitched, less rasping *skaak* than Swinhoe's.

ASIAN DOWITCHER 34 cm
Limnodromus semipalmatus

Rare, coastal migrant, usually hidden in Bar-tailed Godwit flocks when roosting. Regular in Roebuck Bay, n WA, occasional singles elsewhere in n Aus.
Voice: quiet; soft yelp *chowp* in alarm.

BAR-TAILED GODWIT 38 cm
Limosa lapponica

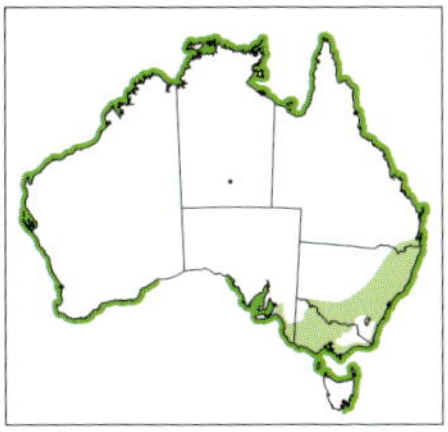

Coastal migrant mainly at sites with large tidal flats. Sociable; often roosts on seaward side of large shorebird flocks.
Voice: nasal bark *kwik* or *kwikwick*.

BLACK-TAILED GODWIT 42 cm
Limosa limosa

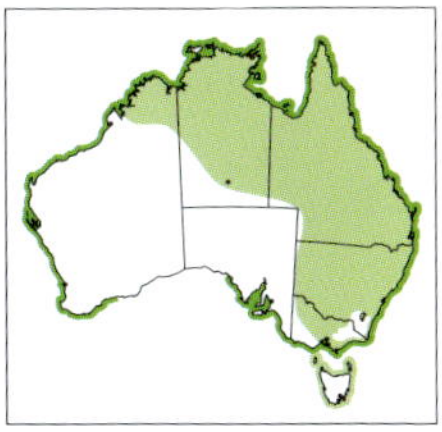

Coastal migrant preferring soft tidal flats; also uses shallow, fresh inland wetlands. Roosts in mixed flocks.
Voice: fairly quiet; short, firm *tuk* in flight.

LITTLE CURLEW ◑ 29 cm
Numenius minutus

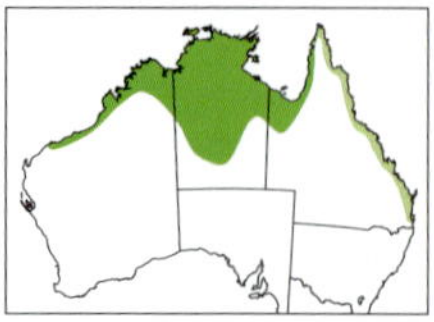

Small curlew with plain face, small bill. Migrant to tropical grasslands and plains.

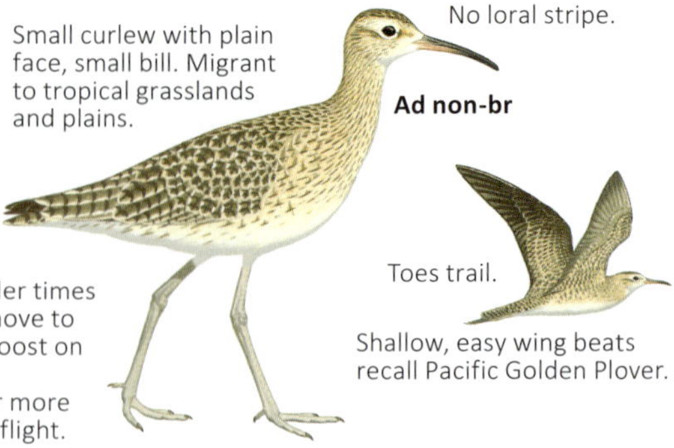

Flocks forage at night and cooler times of day; in midday heat often move to wetlands or coast to drink or roost on moist ground.
Voice: soft whistled *te-te-te* or more rasping *tchew-tchew-tchew* in flight.

WHIMBREL ◕ 42 cm
Numenius phaeopus

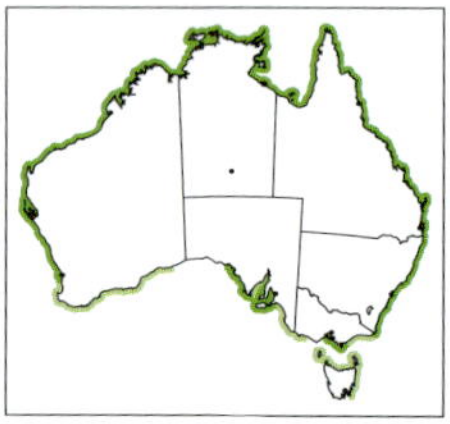

Coastal migrant. Most common in n Aus, at sites with tidal flats and mangroves.

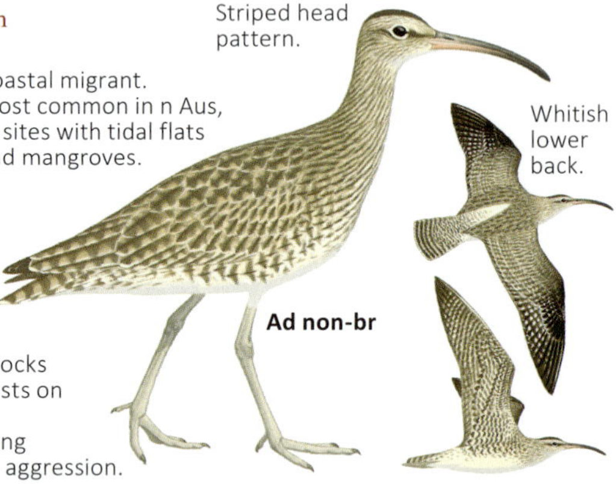

Hunts crabs. Roosts in mixed flocks on beaches and rocks; also roosts on mangrove branches.
Voice: noisy. Main call a bubbling *ti-ti-ti-ti* ...; also harsher calls in aggression.

FAR EASTERN CURLEW ◕ 63 cm
Numenius madagascariensis

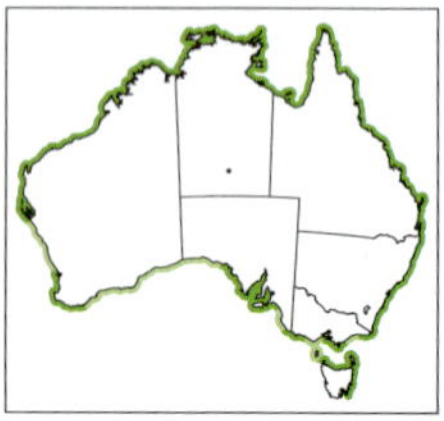

World's largest shorebird.

Ad ♀ non-br: improbably long bill, ♂ bill shorter. Lacks obvious face markings.

Migrant to coasts with large tidal flats. Roosts in single-species flocks; if congregating with other species is always the wariest of shorebirds. Sometimes prefers quieter sites in saltmarsh or large mangrove clearings. Uncommon, declining.
Voice: loud hoarse wail *corr-ee, corr-ee* ...

COMMON GREENSHANK ◕ 32 cm

Tringa nebularia

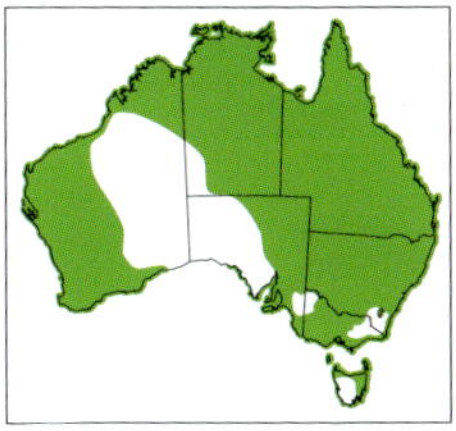

Tall migrant with long, yellowish-green legs; wades in shallow water from tidal flats to inland wetlands. Solitary when feeding, small flocks when roosting, wary and excitable at all times.
Voice: loud ringing *tchu-tchu-tchu*.

MARSH SANDPIPER ◑ 24 cm

Tringa stagnatilis

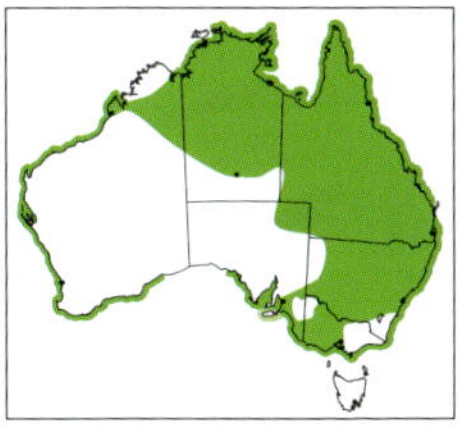

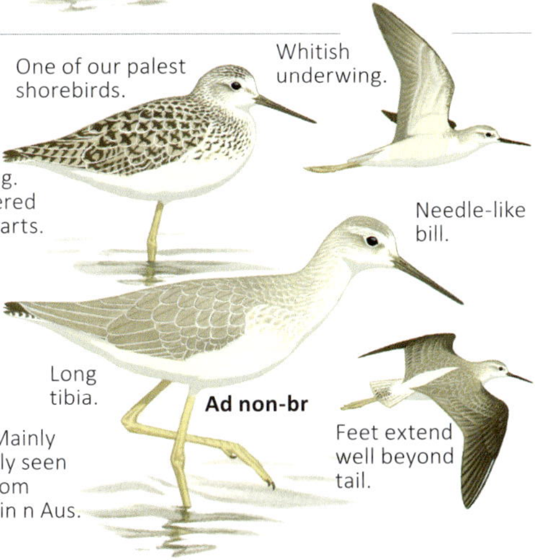

Slim, elegant migrant; paler than Common Greenshank with finer, needle-like bill, longer tibia. Mainly in fresh to brackish wetlands, usually seen wading, daintily picking tiny prey from water surface. Some use tidal flats in n Aus.
Voice: clear *tew* in flight.

COMMON REDSHANK ○ 28 cm

Tringa totanus

Tall migrant with orange-red legs, straight bill. Uncommon and mainly coastal in Aus, on sheltered tidal flats, especially mudflats surrounded by mangroves. **Voice:** noisy; loud *TEU-hu-hu*; recalls Common Greenshank but more emphasis on first note.

GREY-TAILED TATTLER ◑ 25 cm
Tringa brevipes

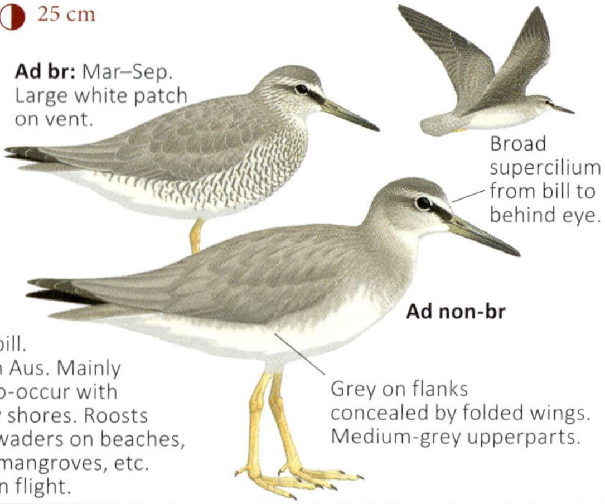

Sturdy, grey migrant with yellow legs, thick, straight bill. Coastal, more common in n Aus. Mainly near tidal flats, but some co-occur with Wandering Tattler on rocky shores. Roosts in flocks, often with other waders on beaches, but also perches on rocks, mangroves, etc. **Voice:** clear whistle *chu-it* in flight.

WANDERING TATTLER ◔ 27 cm
Tringa incana

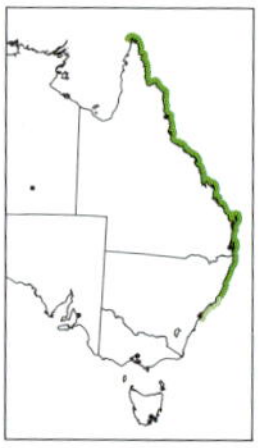

Uncommon migrant, restricted to rocky shores. Slightly larger and darker than Grey-tailed with smaller supercilium, darker flanks. Solitary or in small flocks. **Voice:** diagnostic: ringing whistling trill *wee-wi-wi-wi* ...

TEREK SANDPIPER ◑ 23 cm
Xenus cinereus

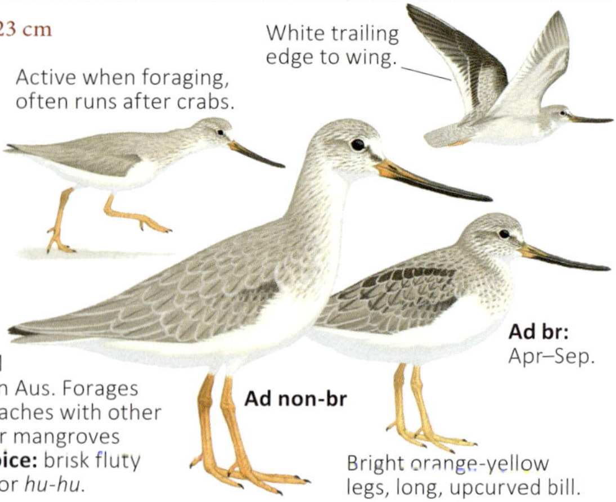

Only small shorebird with long, upcurved bill. Coastal migrant, most common in n Aus. Forages on tidal flats. Roosts on beaches with other shorebirds; also on rocks or mangroves with Grey-tailed Tattler. **Voice:** brisk fluty upslurred whistles *pi-pi-pi* or *hu-hu*.

COMMON SANDPIPER ◑ 20 cm
Actitis hypoleucos

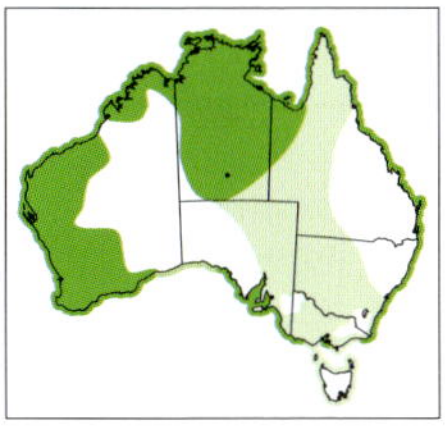

Smallish migrant.
Solitary or in small groups;
uses both coastal and inland wetlands,
(especially mangrove-lined creeks)
with narrow and often steep shorelines.
Voice: vocal; thin, penetrating whistle *tsee-wee-wee*.

WOOD SANDPIPER ◔ 21 cm
Tringa glareola

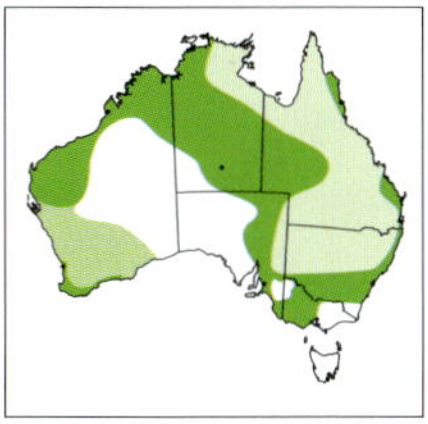

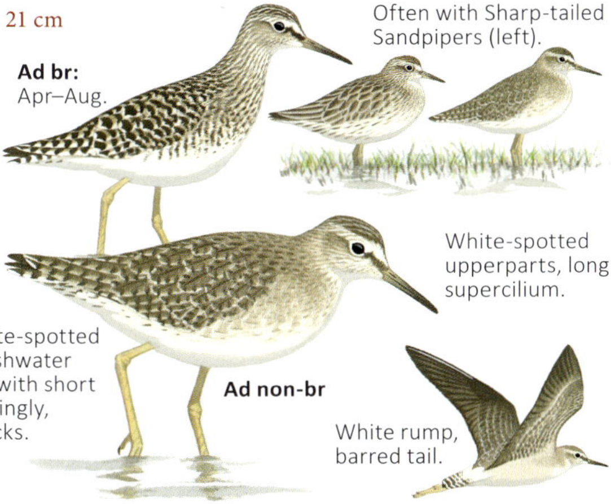

A small sandpiper with white-spotted upperparts. Migrant to freshwater wetlands, especially those with short emergent plants. Forages singly, occasionally joins small flocks.
Voice: excitable; 1–4 note, shrill whistled *chif-iff-iff*.

RED-NECKED PHALAROPE ○ 18 cm
Phalaropus lobatus

Small migrant, usually seen swimming. Mainly pelagic but most Aus records on shallow, fresh to saline, near-coastal wetlands with muddy margins.
Voice: short loud *pit* or *twik*.

SANDERLING ◑ 20 cm
Calidris alba

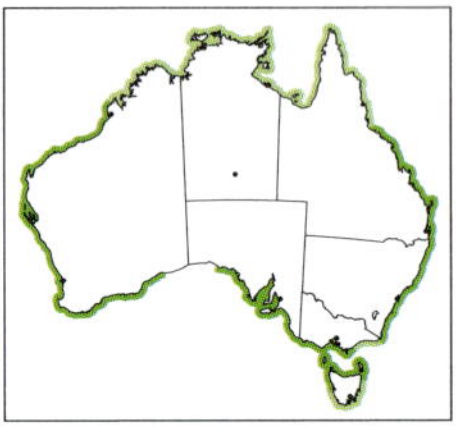

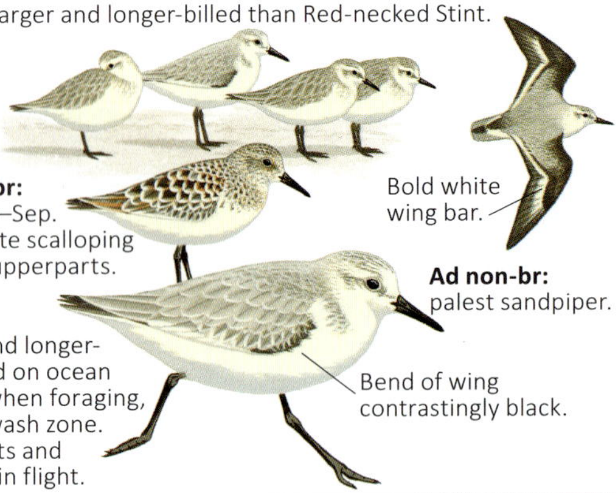

Small, chunky migrant, larger and longer-billed than stints. Coastal, found on ocean beaches and sandflats. Active when foraging, often runs in and out of wave-wash zone. Roosts in flocks, often with stints and small plovers. **Voice:** soft *twick* in flight.

BROAD-BILLED SANDPIPER ◔ 17 cm
Calidris falcinellus

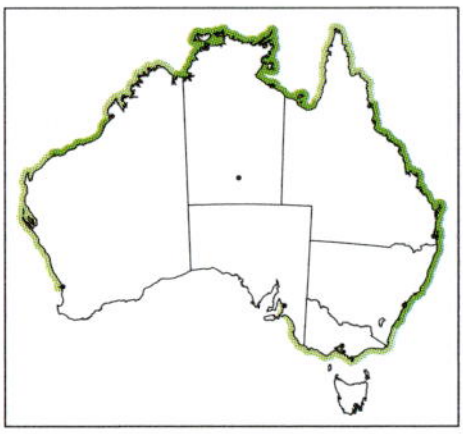

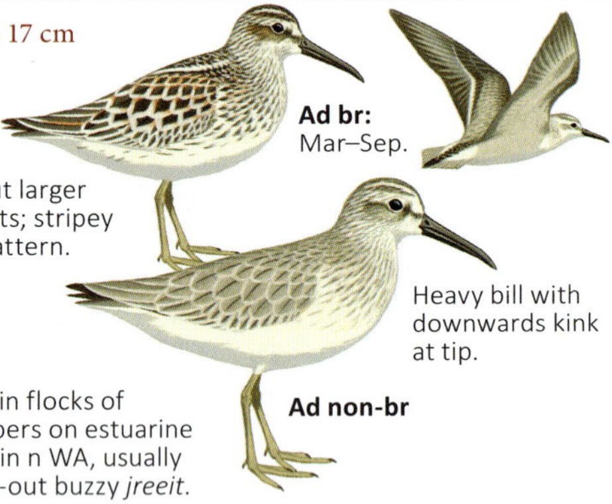

Uncommon migrant, usually hidden in flocks of Red-necked Stints or Curlew Sandpipers on estuarine mudflats. Sometimes in small flocks in n WA, usually seen singly elsewhere. **Voice:** drawn-out buzzy *jreeit*.

RUFF ○ 29 cm
Calidris pugnax

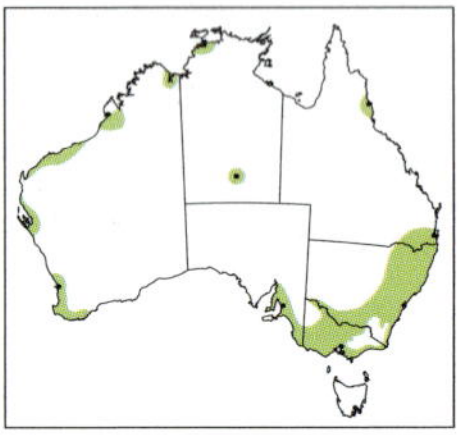

Large sandpiper, ♂ much larger than ♀. Variable plumage but distinctive shape: deep-bodied and long-legged with small head and bill; white feathers run onto base of bill causing 'snouted' appearance. Uncommon migrant, mainly to freshwater wetlands. Seen singly, often with Sharp-tailed Sandpipers. **Voice:** usually silent.

RUDDY TURNSTONE ◕ 23 cm
Arenaria interpres

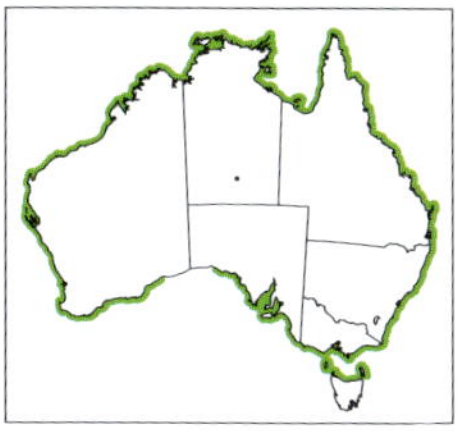

Ad br: Mar–Sep.

In flight, strong pattern includes white 'diamond' in back.

Ad non-br: black bib, short, orange legs.

Distinctive coastal migrant: rocky shores, tidal flats and beaches. Found in flocks. Vigorous feeding behaviour, often overturns wrack and pebbles in search of prey.
Voice: variations on rattling chuckle *tuk-a-ti-ti*.

GREAT KNOT ◑ 27 cm
Calidris tenuirostris

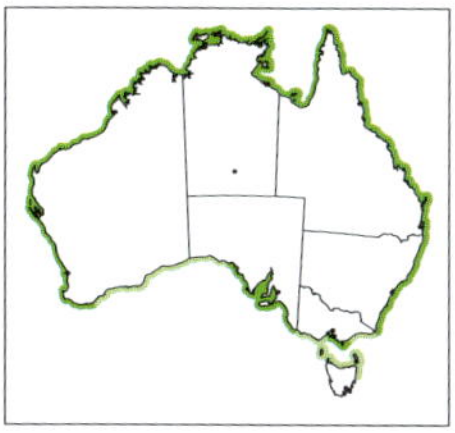

Ad br: Mar–Aug. Black-spotted breast, rufous blaze in scapulars.

U-shaped white rump.

Bill slightly downcurved, longer than head. Striped crown.

Ad non-br: streaked flanks.

Rump looks pale grey.

Large, sturdy sandpiper, migrant to extensive tidal flats. Most common in n Aus, where often the most numerous large shorebird. Hunts buried bivalves, roosts in dense, mixed flocks.
Voice: flight call *nyut* or *nyut-nyut* higher-pitched and more rasping than Red Knot.

RED KNOT ◑ 24 cm
Calidris canutus

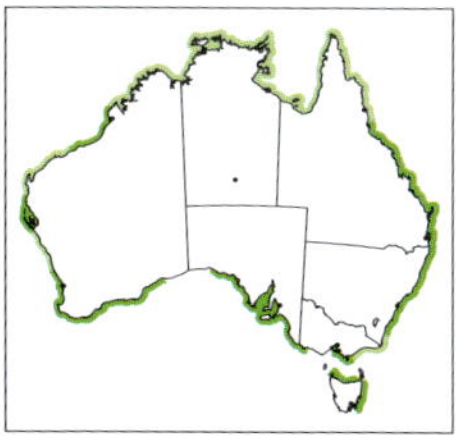

Imm br: Red Knot on left with two Great Knots.

Ad br: Mar–Sep.

Plain grey crown.

Bill straight, no longer than head.

Ad non-br: grey chevrons in flanks.

Sturdy sandpiper, migrant to extensive tidal flats. In n Aus usually outnumbered by Great Knot. Highly specialised to locate and extract buried bivalves. Roosts in dense flocks, often mingling with Great Knot.
Voice: not noisy, flight call a short mellow bark *puk* or *puk-puk*.

RED-NECKED STINT ● 14 cm
Calidris ruficollis

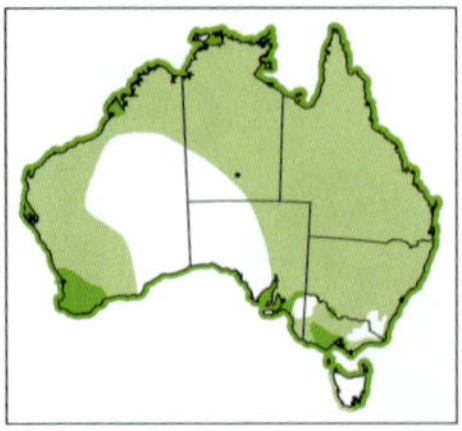

Tiny migrant with black legs and bill; one of our smallest and most numerous shorebirds. In flocks on coasts with tidal flats and unvegetated fringes of fresh to brackish wetlands. **Voice:** short *prrp* in flight and alarm.

Ad br: fresh plumage Mar–Apr. Grey-white fringes to tertials and coverts. Rufous throat above black streaking of upper breast.

Ad br: Apr–Aug. Full colour.

Ad non-br

Juv: Sep–Oct. Weak mantle V. Small black centres to scapulars.

LITTLE STINT ○ 13 cm
Calidris minuta

Rare in Aus and difficult to ID. Possible anywhere Red-necked Stint occurs, hidden within flocks. **Voice:** short *chit* in flight, shorter and less trilled than Red-necked Stint.

Ad br: Apr–Aug. Broad rufous fringes to tertials and coverts, looks 'rufous-sided'. White V on mantle. Black streaking over rufous.

White throat.

Double supercilium.

Bold V on mantle.

Dark centres to scapulars and coverts.

Juv: Sep–Oct.

Non-br very similar to Red-necked Stint, has shorter body, longer legs, smaller head with finer bill.

Ad non-br

LONG-TOED STINT ◔ 14 cm
Calidris subminuta

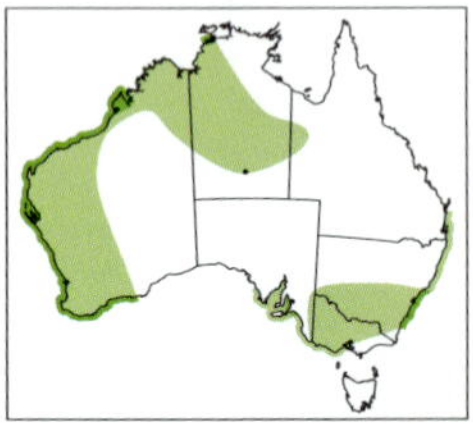

From Sharp-tailed Sandpiper (right) by tiny size, finer bill, no streaks on flanks or undertail.

Trailing toes.

Ad br: Apr–Aug.

Ad non-br

Yellow legs, toes longer than tarsus.

Our smallest migratory shorebird; note yellow legs, streaky upperparts, short fine bill. Uncommon in n and w Aus, rare in se Aus. Solitary on fringes of freshwater wetlands, often in short, emergent vegetation. **Voice:** short *prrp* in flight, deeper than Red-necked Stint.

CURLEW SANDPIPER ◕ 20 cm
Calidris ferruginea

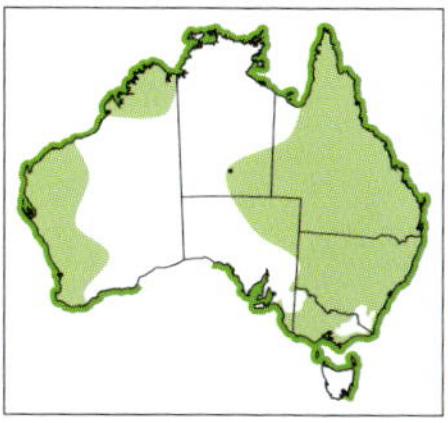

Slender migrant with long, decurved, black bill. Forages in shallows of coastal and inland wetlands; roosts nearby in dense flocks. Fairly common, though declining.
Voice: pleasing short trill *chirrup*.

PECTORAL SANDPIPER ◔ 21 cm
Calidris melanotos

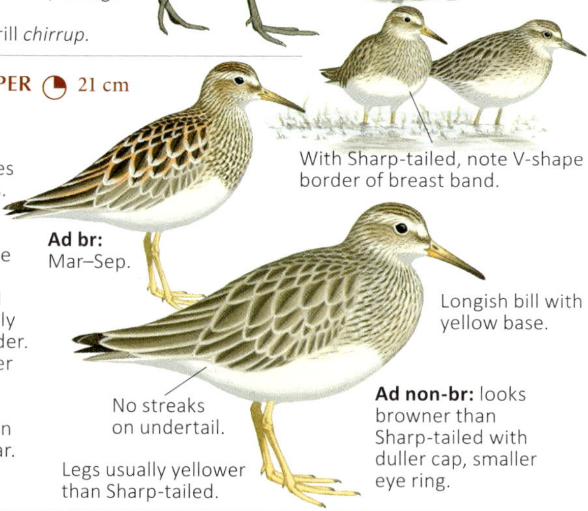

Uncommon migrant to shallows or grassy edges of freshwater wetlands. Easily overlooked among Sharp-tailed Sandpipers and possible anywhere that species occurs. Heavily marked breast band with sharply demarcated lower border. Longer bill with yellower base than Sharp-tailed Sandpiper.
Voice: low trill *chirrup* in flight, recalls Budgerigar.

SHARP-TAILED SANDPIPER ◕ 20 cm
Calidris acuminata

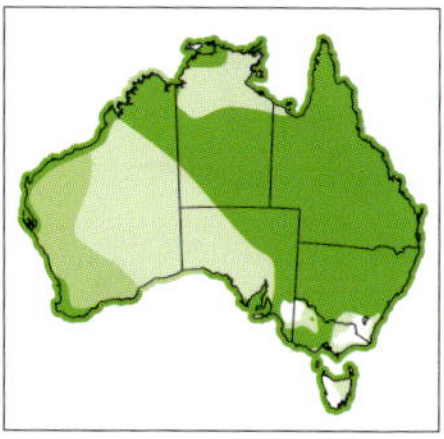

Medium-sized migrant with short bill, streaky upperparts, ginger cap. Flocks in fresh to saline wetlands, including flooded vegetation and saltmarsh. Most common in se Aus, on both coast and inland wetlands; on inland wetlands it is often the most common shorebird.
Voice: soft *pleep* in flight, short trills.

BLACK SWAN ● 125 cm
Cygnus atratus

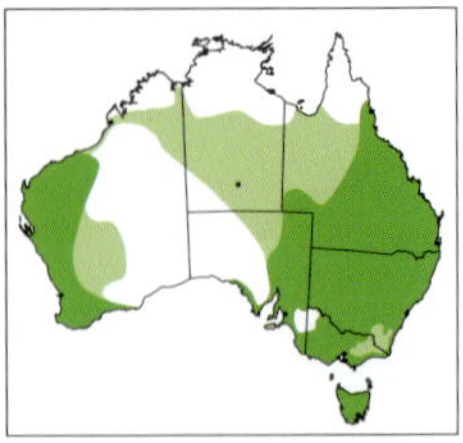

Unmistakable, black plumage except for white outerwing feathers. Pairs, family groups or flocks of up to several thousand on a variety of shallow wetlands, freshwater or brackish, and sheltered coastal waters.
Voice: pleasant musical bugle.

CAPE BARREN GOOSE ◑ 90 cm
Cereopsis novaehollandiae

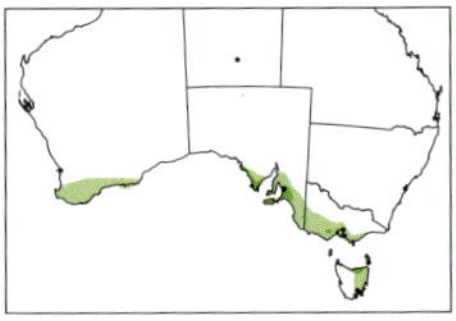

Pale grey with striking green-yellow skin on bill. Sturdy pink-purple legs. Mostly breeds on islands, moves to adjacent mainland in non-breeding period where grazes in pasture. Powerful flight with slow wing beats.
Voice: honk is a loud *arrk,* also low grunts.

MAGPIE GOOSE ◕ 82 cm
Anseranas semipalmata

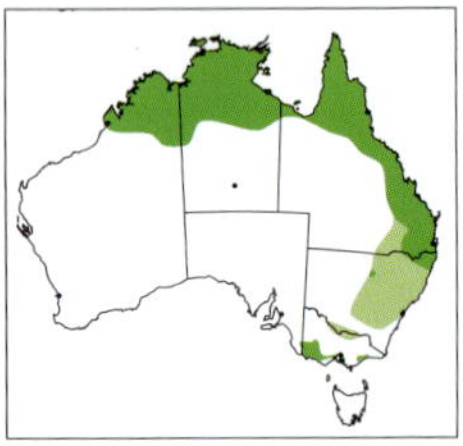

Primitive waterfowl. Black and white with orange-yellow legs and feet. Most common in tropics where flocks of many thousands feed in shallow freshwater and grassland. Roosts communally in waterside trees.
Voice: loud honking.

PLUMED WHISTLING-DUCK ◕ 50 cm
Dendrocygna eytoni

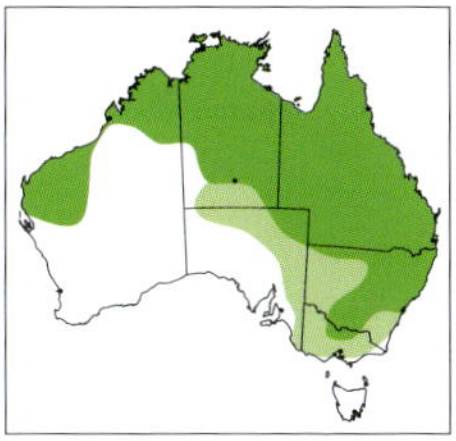

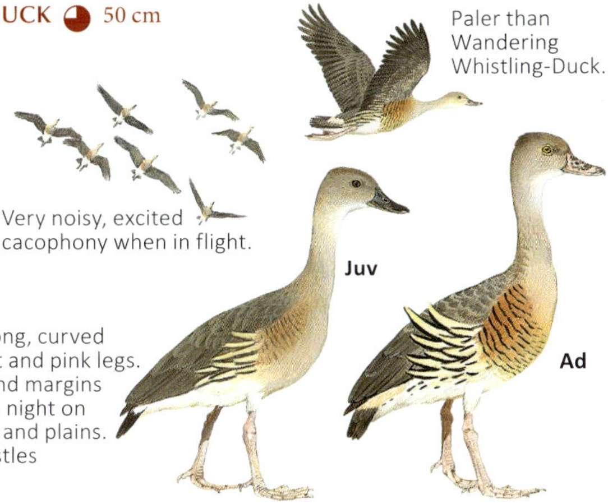

Upright stance. Pale with long, curved flank plumes, barred breast and pink legs. Large flocks stand at wetland margins during day. Feeds mostly at night on margins of grassy wetlands and plains. **Voice:** garrulous, shrill whistles and twittering.

WANDERING WHISTLING-DUCK ◑ 50 cm
Dendrocygna arcuata

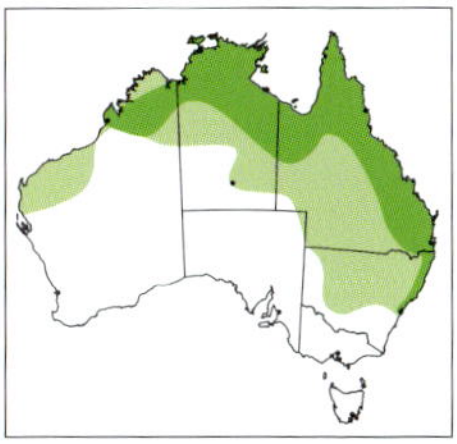

Darker than Plumed Whistling-Duck, chestnut underparts, blackish bill and legs, short, straight flank plumes. Freshwater and estuarine wetlands often in large numbers. Feeds in wetland, often dives unlike Plumed Whistling-Duck. **Voice:** garrulous, shrill descending whistle and twittering.

SPOTTED WHISTLING-DUCK ○ 46 cm
Dendrocygna guttata

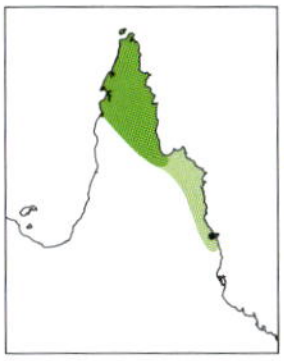

Dark brown above with large white spots on flanks. Colonised n Qld from PNG in recent decades. Small flocks and family groups in freshwater or estuarine swamps. Spends most of day loafing, mostly feeds at night. **Voice:** nasal *wheeow*, piping *pi-pi-pi*.

AUSTRALIAN WOOD DUCK ● 47 cm
Chenonetta jubata

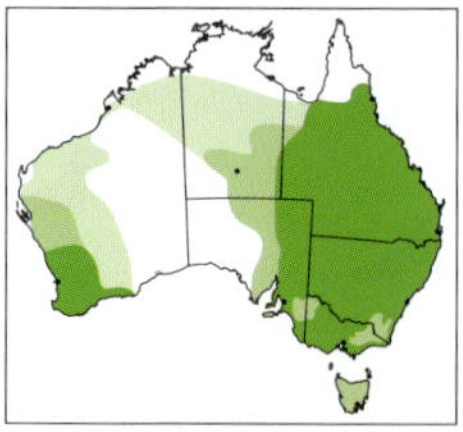

Small flocks graze short herbage near margins of wetlands, including farm dams and along inland rivers. Often grazes on sports fields. **Voice:** nasal rising *gnaarrk*.

RADJAH SHELDUCK ◑ 55 cm
Radjah radjah

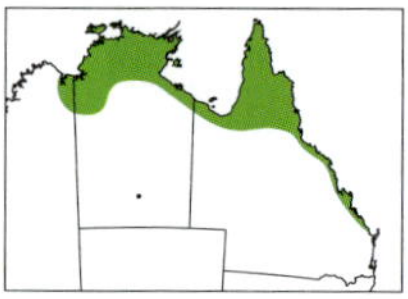

White and chestnut with narrow breast band, bill and legs pale pink. Coastal brackish wetlands, mangroves and estuaries. Dabbles in shallow water and grazes adjacent grassland. Walks strongly and perches readily. **Voice:** highly vocal, ♂ hoarse whistles, ♀ harsh rattle.

AUSTRALIAN SHELDUCK ◕ 65 cm
Tadorna tadornoides

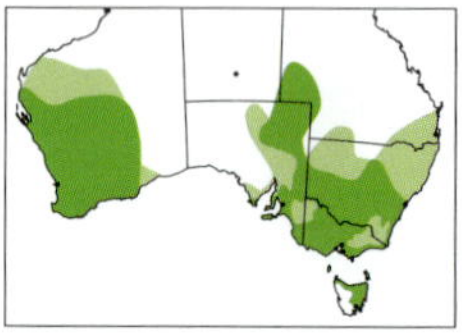

Large blackish duck with rich orange-brown breast. Grazes, often in large flocks on pasture or crop stubble sometimes far from water. Congregates at large wetlands, fresh or saline. **Voice:** ♂ low honk, ♀ higher-pitched, nasal *ang gankrr*.

COTTON PYGMY-GOOSE ◔ 36 cm

Nettapus coromandelianus

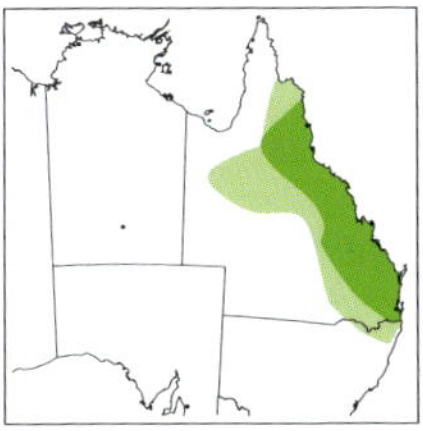

Ad ♂ non-br: smudgy collar.

Ad ♂: bold white band along flight feathers (not present in ♀).

Ad ♀: grey-brown mottling, eye stripe does not extend to nape.

Ad ♂: white face, narrow black necklace.

Very small duck with short, goose-like bill. Almost wholly aquatic in deep coastal lagoons with abundant aquatic vegetation, particularly waterlilies. Shy, rarely close to shore. **Voice:** ♂ loud, staccato chatter, ♀ soft quacks.

GREEN PYGMY-GOOSE ◑ 33 cm

Nettapus pulchellus

Ad ♂ non-br

Ad ♂: primaries all dark.

Ad ♀: eye stripe reaches nape.

Ad ♂: dark green neck, white cheek.

Dark head and neck, glossy green upperparts, boldly patterned underparts. Similar jizz and behaviour to Cotton but more widespread in greater range of habitats with waterlilies. **Voice:** ♂ whistled *phee-wit*, ♀ down-slurred whistle *pee-yew*.

PINK-EARED DUCK ◑ 41 cm

Malacorhynchus membranaceus

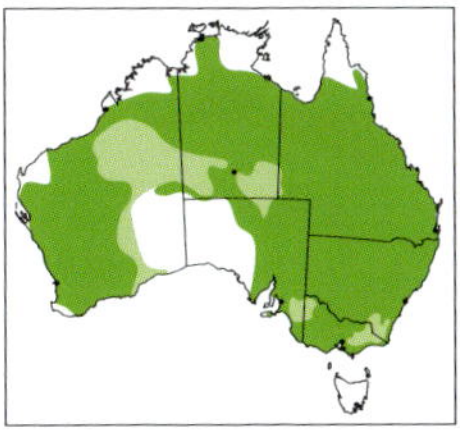

Size comparison with Grey Teal (upper right), two at front filter feeding.

Plain dark upperwing.

Ad: tiny pink ear spot behind black face mask.

Small, boldly striped. Long, specialised bill with noticeable side flaps to aid filter feeding. Nomadic, often in great numbers on shallow wetlands.
Voice: garrulous, distinctive, high-pitched chirruping whistles, very obvious when flock takes to the air.

CHESTNUT TEAL 45 cm
Anas castanea

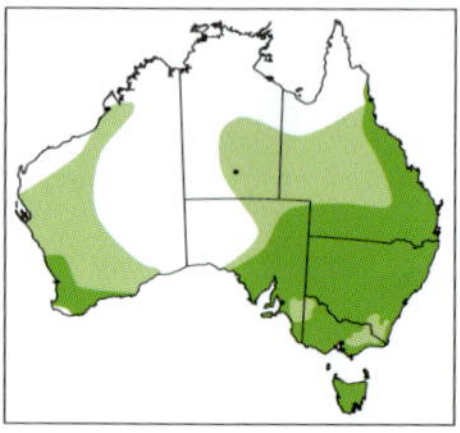

Small, sexually dimorphic, commonly in sheltered marine waters and coastal wetlands, less common on inland lakes.
Voice: ♀ loud repeated *wree-ark* run together with a series of quick descending laughing quacks, ♂ an excited *peep*.

GREY TEAL 43 cm
Anas gracilis

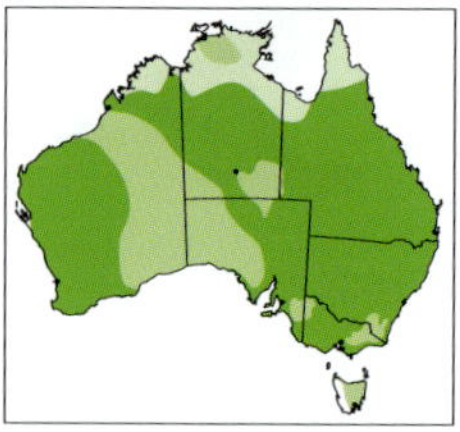

Comparison with ♀ Chestnut Teal (right).

Small, sexes alike, paler grey-brown than ♀ Chestnut and more extensive white throat sharply demarcated from grey breast. Nomadic, can occur on almost any wetland type including ephemeral inland flood waters.
Voice: as for Chestnut Teal.

AUSTRALASIAN SHOVELER 50 cm
Spatula rhynchotis

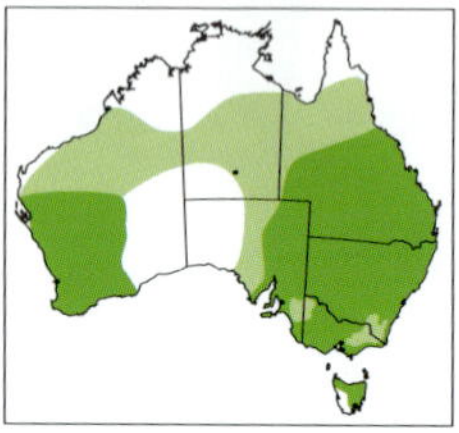

Long broad bill, sloping forehead, short neck and flattened back profile. Prefers well-vegetated wetlands but will use most wetland types. Wary, often first to fly when disturbed. Filter feeds with bill or whole head in water, but also up-ends. **Voice:** quiet, pleasant chattering *tuk tuk*.

FRECKLED DUCK ◔ 53 cm
Stictonetta naevosa

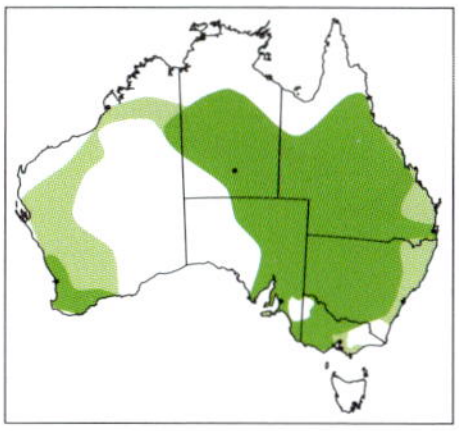

Uniformly dark with pale speckles, distinctive peaked crown and scooped bill profile. Scarce, mostly on larger inland wetlands including flooded lignum. Also coastal wetlands, especially in drier years. Rests during day, feeds mostly at night.
Voice: mostly silent.

PACIFIC BLACK DUCK ● 53 cm
Anas superciliosa

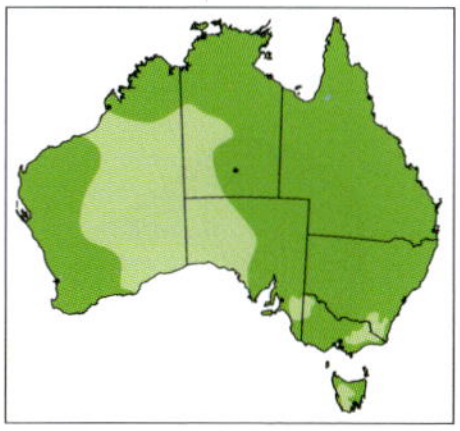

Large, brown with pale-yellow and black striped face. Bright green speculum in wing. Prefers wetlands with plenty of green vegetation but found on most wetland types, tame at urban wetlands.
Voice: ♂ soft *rab-raabraah*, ♀ loud, raucous, descending *quack-quark quarrk*.

MALLARD ◔ 60 cm
Anas platyrhynchos

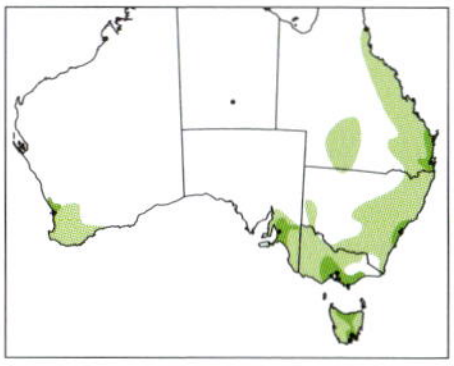

Domesticated forms common on urban wetlands, whereas true, wild Mallard rare in Aus. Mostly larger than Pacific Black Duck with which it can hybridise. Wing speculum blue (green on Pacific Black Duck), bright orange legs, ♀ facial pattern not as bold as Pacific Black Duck.
Voice: like Pacific Black Duck.

HARDHEAD ◔ 52 cm
Aythya australis

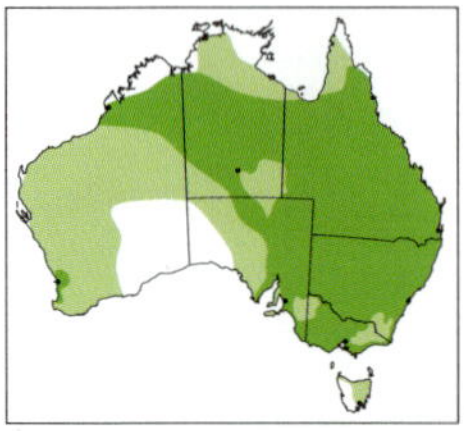

In flight note flashing white wing panels and very rapid wing beats.

Rich brown with white undertail, bicoloured bill. ♂ mahogany head with white eye. ♀ paler face and dark eye. Wary, often first species to fly when approached. A diving duck that feeds in open water on deeper freshwater wetlands. **Voice:** mostly silent.

MUSK DUCK ◑ 60 cm
Biziura lobata

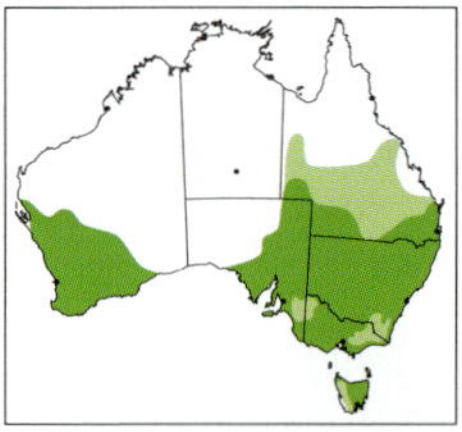

Voice: ♂ courtship display includes loud whistle and *whump* sounds while splashing water. ♀ mostly silent.

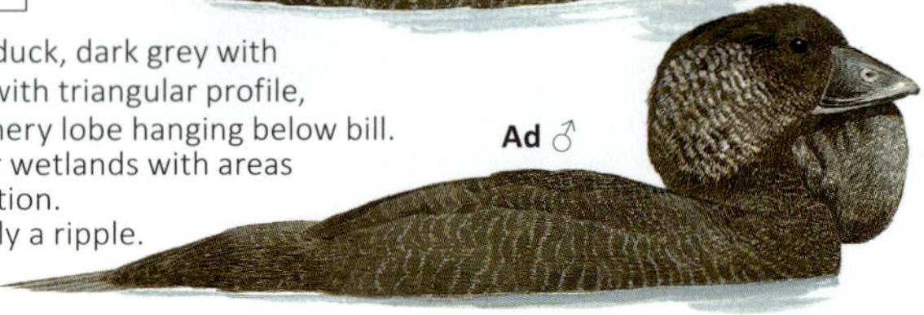

Large, powerful, diving duck, dark grey with flat spiky tail. Stout bill with triangular profile, ♂ has conspicuous leathery lobe hanging below bill. Prefers deep freshwater wetlands with areas of dense aquatic vegetation. Submerges leaving barely a ripple. Rarely seen ashore or in flight.

BLUE-BILLED DUCK ◑ 40 cm
Oxyura australis

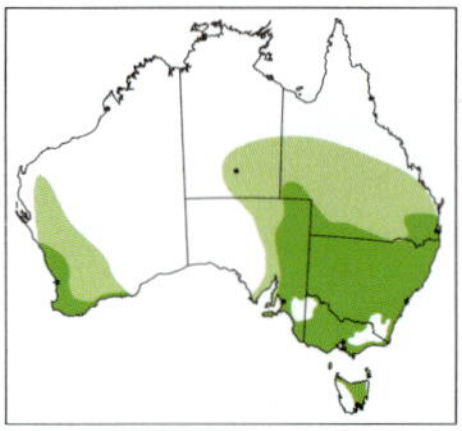

In mixed groups note erect tail on loafing birds.

Small, compact, wholly aquatic diving duck. Large rounded head and flat, spiky tail. Bill profile scooped *cf* Musk Duck. Distinguish ♀ from Musk Duck by smaller compact body and bill shape. Prefers deep freshwater wetlands, usually away from shore. **Voice:** usually silent.

GREAT CRESTED GREBE ◑ 54 cm
Podiceps cristatus

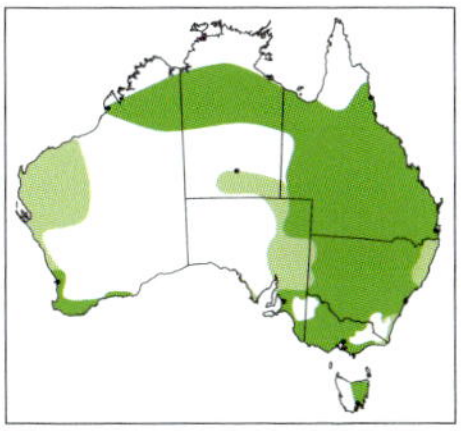

In flight note rapid wing beats, narrow wings with white panels. Long slender neck and bill.

Imm: lacks head adornment of Ad.

Our largest grebe, slender neck most obvious feature at distance with long straight bill and very distinctive head plumage. Dives for food on deep freshwater or saline wetlands and sheltered coastal waters.
Voice: mostly silent.

HOARY-HEADED GREBE ◕ 29 cm
Poliocephalus poliocephalus

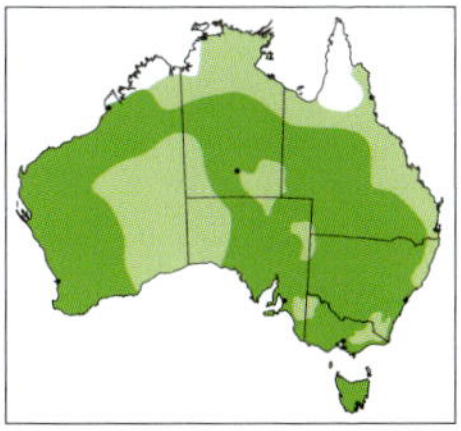

Ad non-br: dark cap encloses eye and extends to gape.

Readily takes flight low across water, note very rapid wing beats, narrow wings with white panels, slender neck.

Ad br: unmistakable hoary head.

Small, dives for food. Typically in large flocks on open lakes both freshwater and brackish, sheltered coastal waters and, less frequently, smaller wetlands.
Voice: mostly silent *cf* Australasian Grebe.

AUSTRALASIAN GREBE ◕ 24 cm
Tachybaptus novaehollandiae

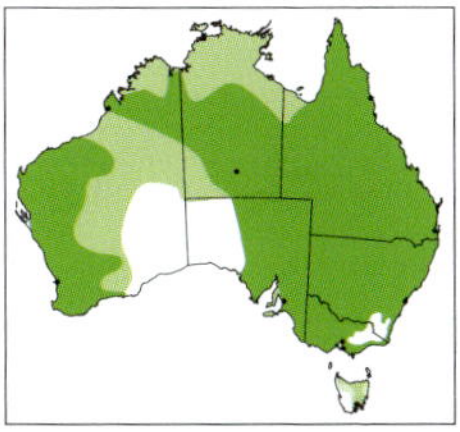

Ad non-br: dark cap does not fully enclose eye. Obvious yellow eye and gape flange.

In flight note rapid wing beats, narrow wings with white panels, slender neck.

Ad br: chestnut blaze on nape of dark-grey head.

Small, dives for food. Only in freshwater including small dams, often just a pair or family group. Reluctant to fly, prefers to dive when disturbed.
Voice: calls often, characteristic loud rattling trills.

Great Egret, gape extends behind eye.

Intermediate Egret, shorter gape and stouter bill than Great Egret.

Cattle Egret, short sturdy bill looks slightly downcurved.

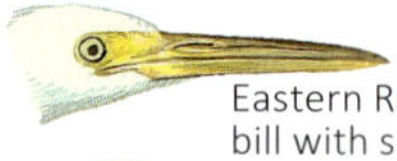
Eastern Reef Egret, stout bill with slit-like nostril.

Little Egret, slim bill with slit-like nostril.

GREAT EGRET ◕ 93 cm
Ardea alba

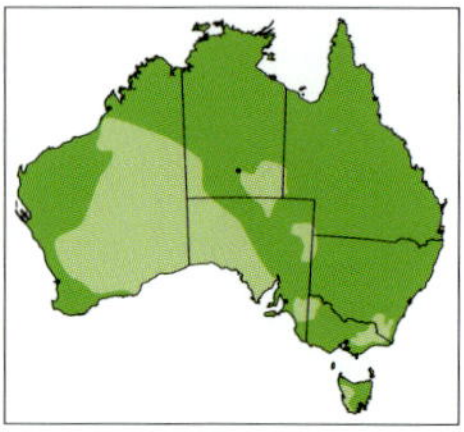

Largest, longest-necked egret; gape diagnostic, extending behind eye.

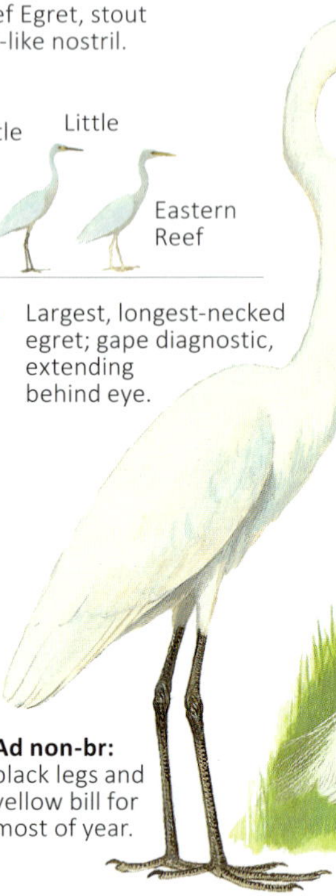

Ad non-br: black legs and yellow bill for most of year.

Legs trail far beyond tail tip.

Ad br: briefly has black bill, colourful lores and legs.

Widespread in fresh to tidal wetlands; wades quietly and slowly when foraging. Nests colonially in trees near or in wetlands.
Voice: deep staccato *ar-ar-ar* when flushed.

INTERMEDIATE EGRET ◑ 63 cm
Ardea intermedia

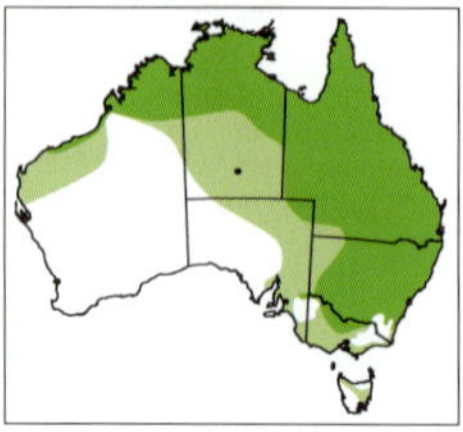

Smaller than Great Egret with rounder head, shorter gape; shorter neck looks 'smoother', less angular.

Ad non-br

Black legs and yellow bill for most of year.

Longer toes than other egrets.

Legs trail less than Great Egret.

Long plumes on breast and scapulars when breeding.

Ad br: briefly has red bill, colourful lores and legs.

Most common in n Aus. Prefers shallow, vegetated, freshwater wetlands, also wet pasture; wades slowly and deliberately.
Voice: quiet, usually silent except at nesting colonies.

EASTERN CATTLE EGRET ◔ 55 cm
Bubulcus coromandus

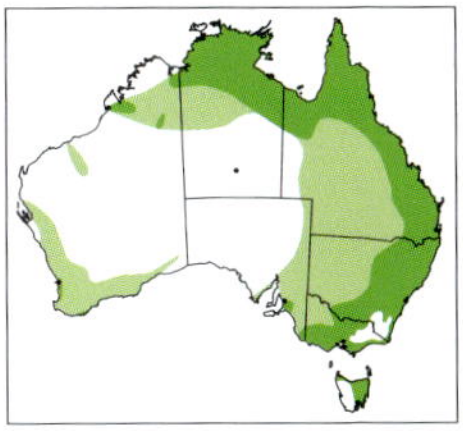

Ad br: orange-buff neck.

Follows stock, sometimes perches on cattle.

Ad non-br

Shorter neck, toes and bill than Intermediate Egret; often has traces of diagnostic orange-buff plumage, especially in crown.

Stocky yellow-billed egret of moist pasture where mostly seen in flocks with livestock; also shallow freshwater wetlands with emergent veg. **Voice:** mostly silent apart from croaking or husky calls at nesting colonies and roosts.

EASTERN REEF EGRET ◑ 62 cm
Egretta sacra

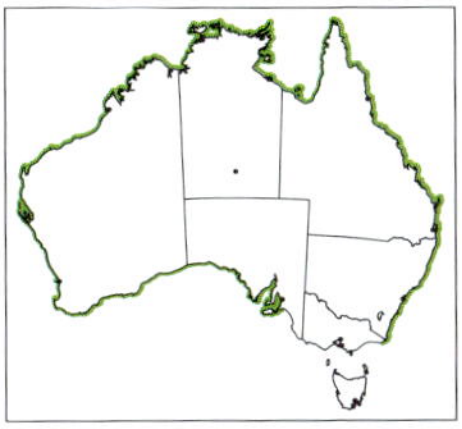

Ad br grey morph: darker than White-faced Heron, lacks white on face.

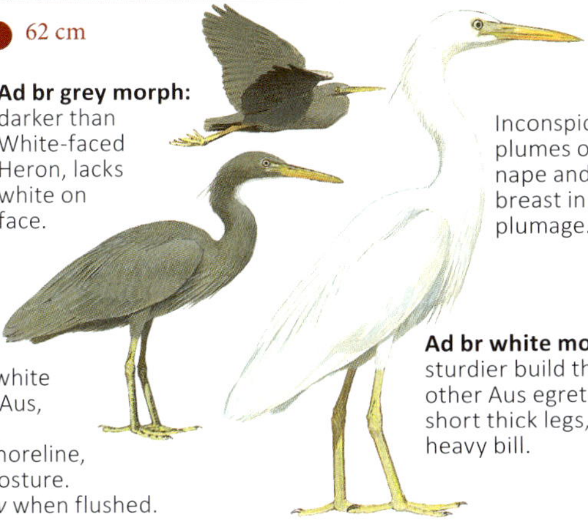

Inconspicuous plumes on nape and breast in br plumage.

Ad br white morph: sturdier build than other Aus egrets; short thick legs, deep heavy bill.

Exclusively coastal, mainly on rocky shores. Grey and white morphs both common in n Aus, grey predominates in s. Forages in shallows or on shoreline, stalking prey in crouched posture. **Voice:** harsh guttural *kraaw* when flushed.

LITTLE EGRET ◑ 60 cm
Egretta garzetta

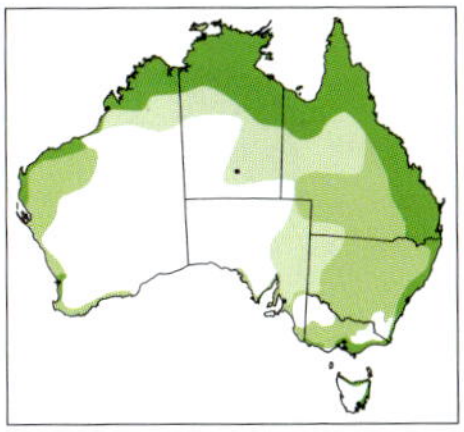

Active when feeding.

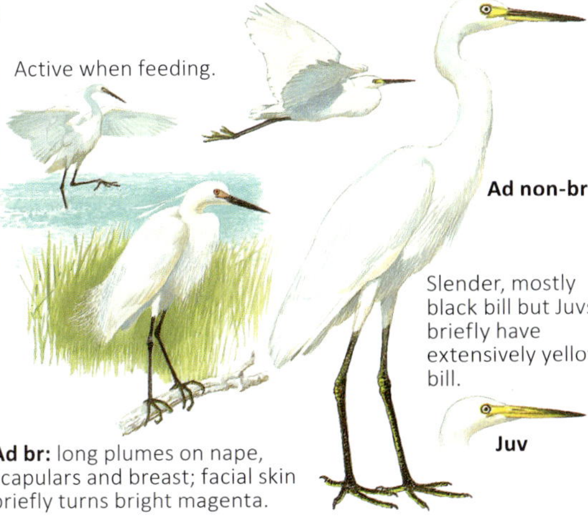

Ad non-br

Slender, mostly black bill but Juvs briefly have extensively yellow bill.

Juv

Ad br: long plumes on nape, scapulars and breast; facial skin briefly turns bright magenta.

Small dainty egret with long, slender, usually black bill. Typically active when feeding, chasing prey with high-stepping gait and raised wings. **Voice:** long grating alarm call *aaah* when flushed.

WHITE-FACED HERON ● 67 cm
Egretta novaehollandiae

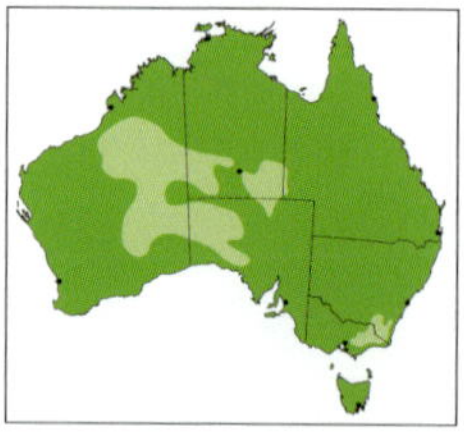

Our most common heron, widespread in freshwater and brackish wetlands, including damp pasture, sports fields and sheltered coastlines.
Voice: when disturbed a harsh *oork*.

WHITE-NECKED HERON ◑ 91 cm
Ardea pacifica

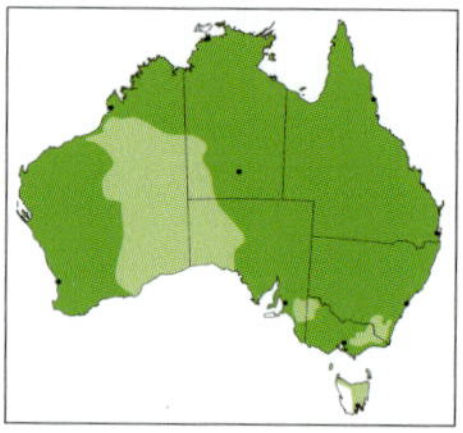

Uses a variety of shallow freshwater wetlands and flooded grasslands. Avoids saline and coastal areas, more common inland. Mostly singles or pairs but can congregate in loose flocks, numbers fluctuate with rainfall.
Voice: guttural croak when disturbed.

PIED HERON ◔ 49 cm
Egretta picata

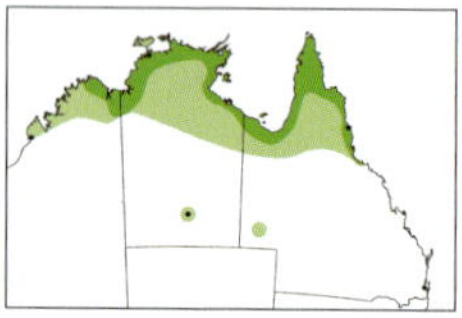

Small tropical heron, found on freshwater wetlands and floodplains, also coastal saline wetlands and estuaries. Often in low emergent vegetation. Typically small, loose flocks but also larger gatherings. **Voice:** gruff croak when disturbed.

NANKEEN NIGHT-HERON ◑ 60 cm
Nycticorax caledonicus

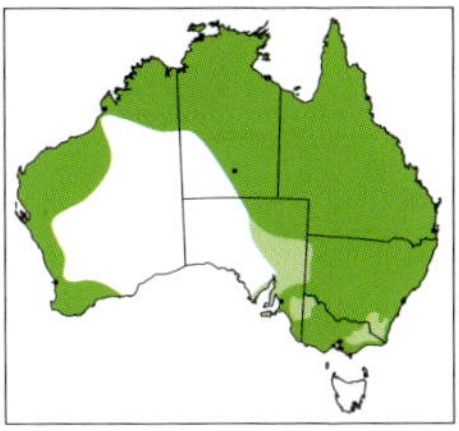

Juv: coarsely streaked brown, buff spots on wings.

Ad br: black cap and bill. Two white plumes extend from nape.

During day roosts communally in trees near water, including in suburban parks. Disperses at dusk to feed in freshwater wetlands, less commonly in saline environments. **Voice:** gruff croak in flight when disturbed.

STRIATED HERON ◑ 43 cm
Butorides striata

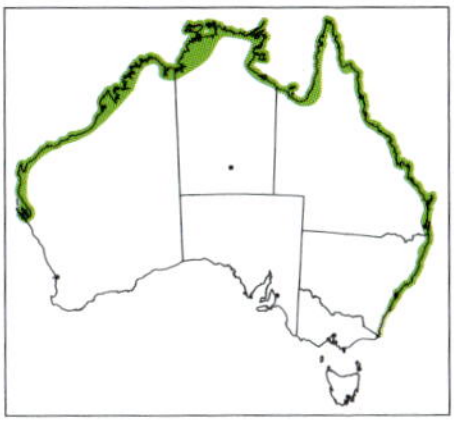

Flight low and fast.

Juv: darker with smaller spots on wing than Juv Nankeen Night-Heron.

Ad: Pilbara WA form.

Ad

Small compact heron of mangroves and riverine vegetation. Secretive, feeds along shorelines at low tide, never far from cover. Feeds by stealth, often motionless in crouched posture. **Voice:** alarm call, loud repeated, scratchy *kek* or *kyow*.

GREAT-BILLED HERON ◔ 105 cm
Ardea sumatrana

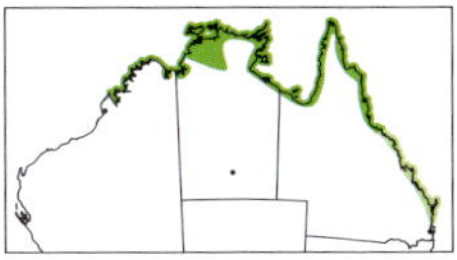

Ad non-br: all grey with massive bill.

Heavy ponderous flight, uniformly grey wings.

Juv: rich brown.

Large secretive heron of tropical coasts. Forest-lined rivers, mangrove estuaries and near-coastal permanent wetlands. Shy and solitary, best seen from boat. **Voice:** when breeding, a loud resonant roar, day and night.

BLACK BITTERN ◔ 60 cm
Ixobrychus flavicollis

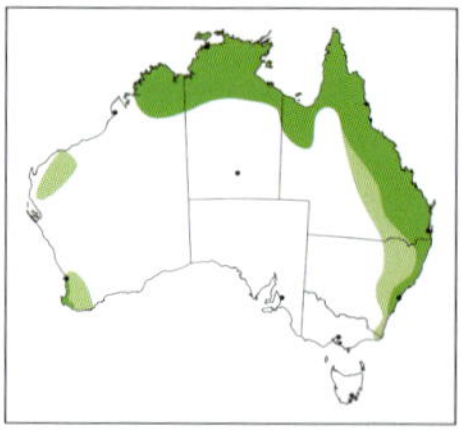

Dark plumage and secretive behaviour. Along forested waterways with dense, overhanging vegetation. Usually seen when flushed, or perching quietly in tree beside water.
Voice: when breeding, loud *whoo-oo-oo.*

AUSTRALIAN LITTLE BITTERN ○ 30 cm
Ixobrychus dubius

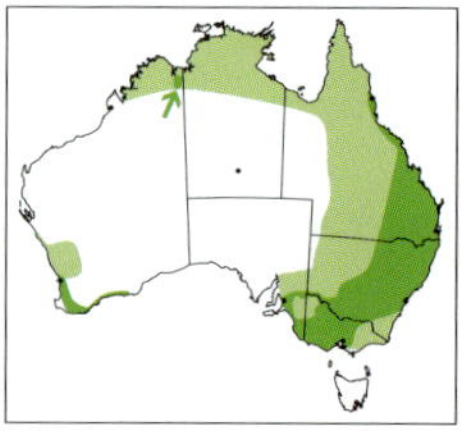

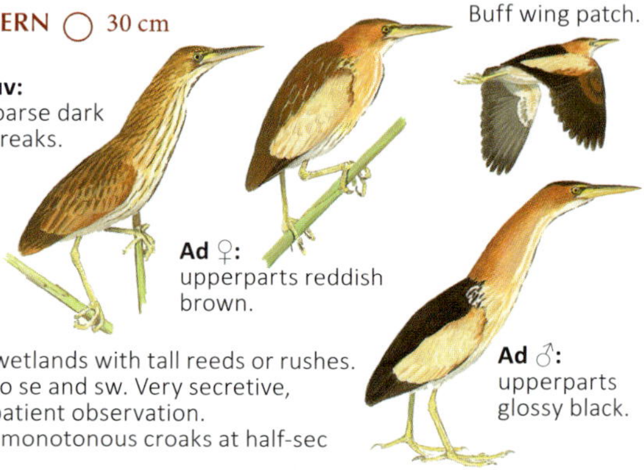

Small, cryptic. In freshwater wetlands with tall reeds or rushes. Spring and summer migrant to se and sw. Very secretive, detected by call, flushing or patient observation.
Voice: when breeding, deep, monotonous croaks at half-sec intervals.

AUSTRALASIAN BITTERN ◕ 71 cm
Botaurus poiciloptilus

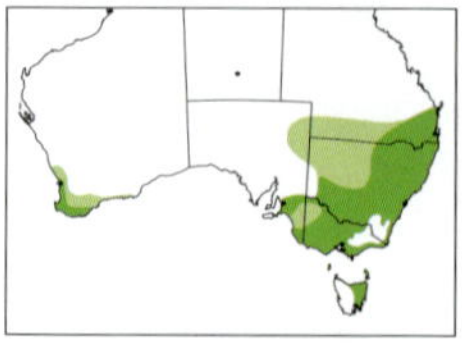

Large, heavy-set with thick neck. Secretive. Inhabits freshwater and brackish swamps with reeds, rushes or sedges, rice crops and occasionally saltmarsh. Usually solitary, freezes when found in open.
Voice: when breeding, deep, loud booms at 1–2 sec intervals.

BROLGA ◑ 115 cm
Antigone rubicunda

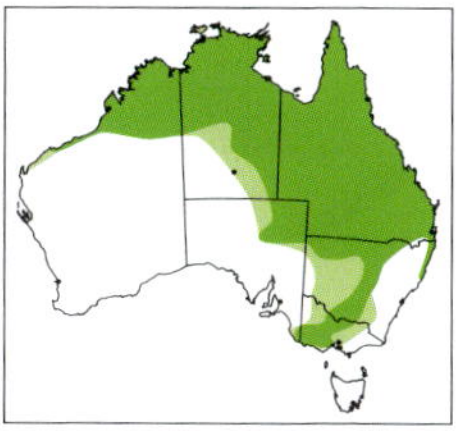

Tall, stately crane with red face and band across hindneck, pale-grey crown and dark-grey legs. In shallow wetlands, pasture, fallow and ploughed paddocks.
Voice: loud bugling duets between members of a pair or dance group.

SARUS CRANE ◑ 125 cm
Antigone antigone

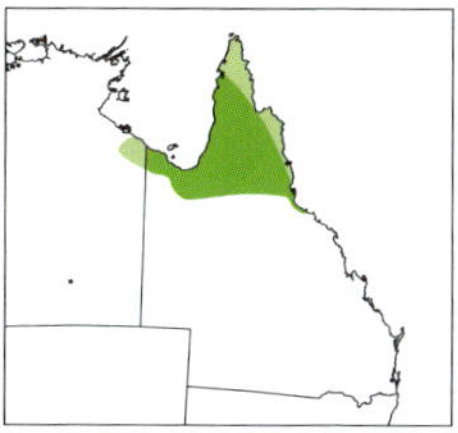

Easily confused with Brolga. Red extends partway down neck, pinkish legs. Some birds regularly move between breeding areas near Gulf of Carpentaria and cropland in e Qld.
Voice: similar to Brolga, perhaps somewhat higher-pitched.

BLACK-NECKED STORK ◑ 123 cm
Ephippiorhynchus asiaticus

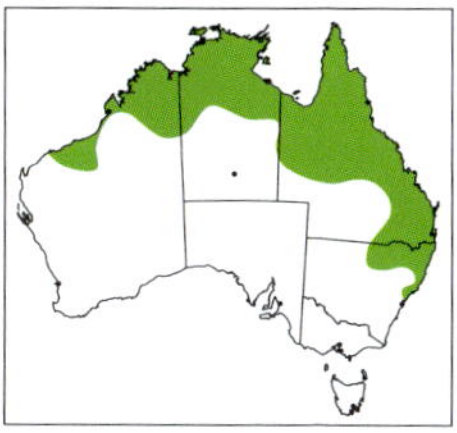

Tall, iridescent black and white waterbird with massive black bill and bright pink legs. Freshwater wetlands and coastal tidal flats. Walks slowly with bill held low and slightly open to catch fish or other prey. Usually singly or in pairs.
Voice: mostly silent, loud rattling sound produced by clattering mandibles together.

AUSTRALIAN WHITE IBIS 70 cm
Threskiornis molucca

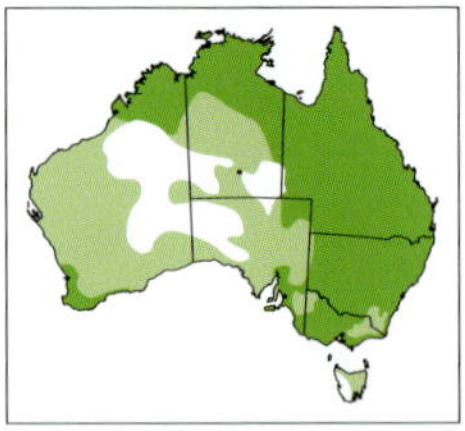

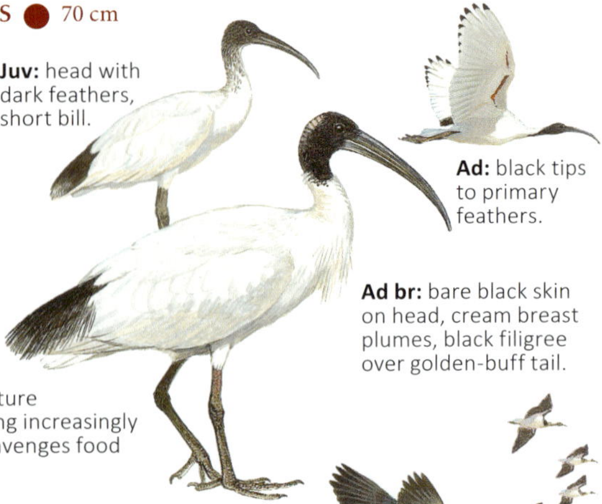

Juv: head with dark feathers, short bill.

Ad: black tips to primary feathers.

Ad br: bare black skin on head, cream breast plumes, black filigree over golden-buff tail.

Large, familiar, dirty white with long, black, curved bill. Found in most shallow wetland types, flooded pasture and tidal mudflats. Becoming increasingly common in cities where scavenges food waste in parks.
Voice: hoarse bark.

STRAW-NECKED IBIS 65 cm
Threskiornis spinicollis

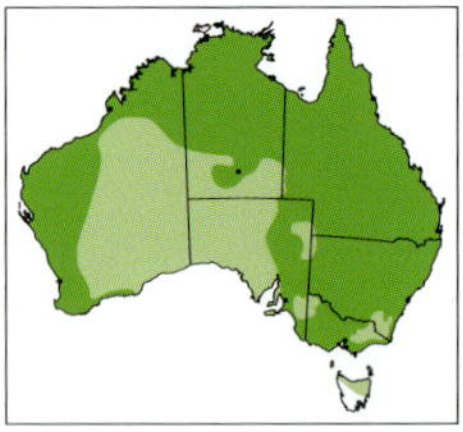

Juv: dark feathers on head, no neck plumes, dull body with reduced gloss.

Ad: iridescent black back and wings, straw-coloured neck plumes, bare black skin on head.

Forages in flocks, mainly in wet and dry grassland, pasture, crops, ploughed paddocks and sports grounds, less frequently in shallow wetland margins. Flocks fly high on thermals to feeding sites, often in a V formation.
Voice: mostly silent.

GLOSSY IBIS 60 cm
Plegadis falcinellus

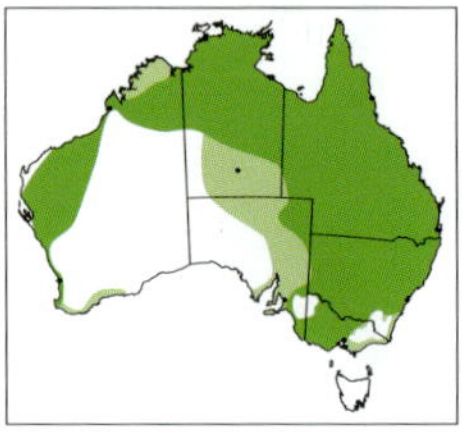

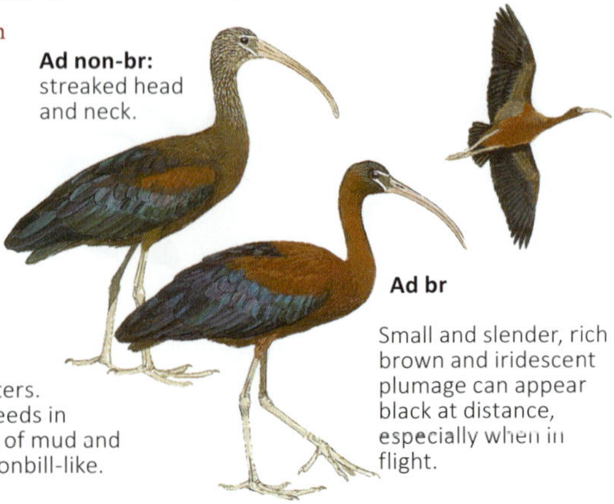

Ad non-br: streaked head and neck.

Ad br

Small and slender, rich brown and iridescent plumage can appear black at distance, especially when in flight.

Mostly in shallow freshwater wetlands and inland floodwaters. Less common in s of range. Feeds in flocks with energetic probing of mud and sweeping water with bill, spoonbill-like.
Voice: mostly silent.

ROYAL SPOONBILL ◕ 77 cm
Platalea regia

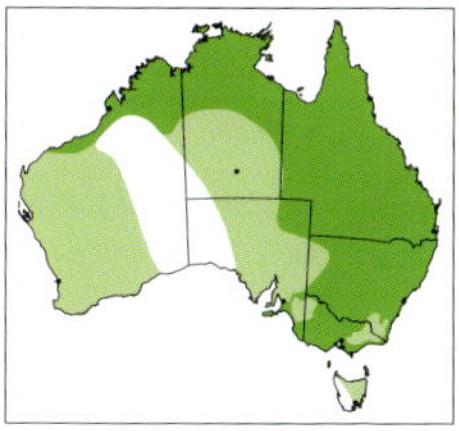

Juv: dusky wing tips.

Juv: lacks plumes and face pattern.

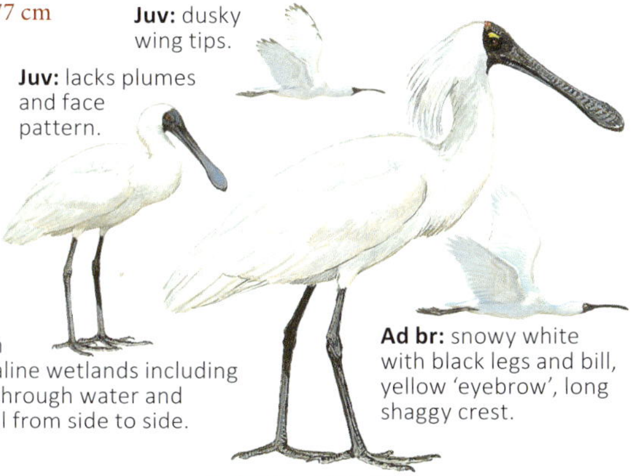

Gregarious in small flocks on extensive shallow fresh or saline wetlands including mudflats. Feeds by striding through water and sweeping the partly open bill from side to side. **Voice:** mostly silent.

Ad br: snowy white with black legs and bill, yellow 'eyebrow', long shaggy crest.

Mixed flock of both Royal and Yellow-billed Spoonbills plus Australian White Ibis. Note each has a different tone of white.

YELLOW-BILLED SPOONBILL ◕ 84 cm
Platalea flavipes

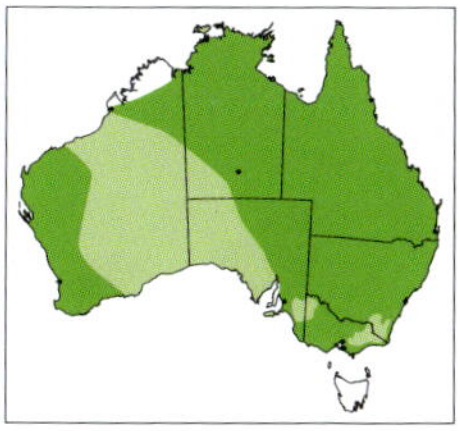

Juv: plain face.

Inhabits a wide range of wetlands, freshwater or saline, including ephemeral pools and farm dams. In small groups but single birds are common. Feeds in similar way to Royal Spoonbill. **Voice:** mostly silent.

Ad br: creamy white, pale bill, bright facial skin, dark narrow border around face, sparse black filigree over rump.

CHESTNUT RAIL ◔ 48 cm
Eulabeornis castaneoventris

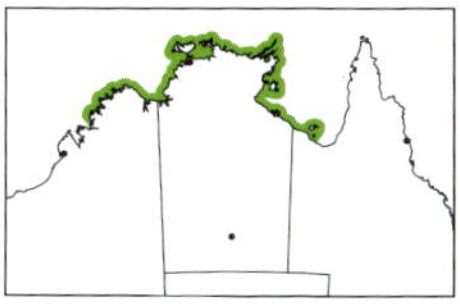

Forages on exposed tidal mudflats but never far from cover.

Very large rail of tropical mangroves and adjacent mudflats. Best seen from boat in tidal creeks and channels. Chestnut body with grey head, but Kimberley birds have olive upperparts. **Voice:** deep drumming followed by loud, repeated *whack-whack-whack*.

LEWIN'S RAIL 23 cm
Lewinia pectoralis

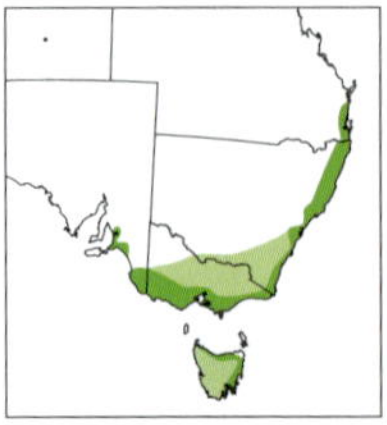

Long-billed rail with rufous crown and hindneck. Heavily vegetated wetland fringes, wet heath and saltmarsh. Mostly near coast. More often heard than seen. **Voice:** repeated *kek-kek-kek,* also low growling and drumming calls.

BUFF-BANDED RAIL 31 cm
Hypotaenidia philippensis

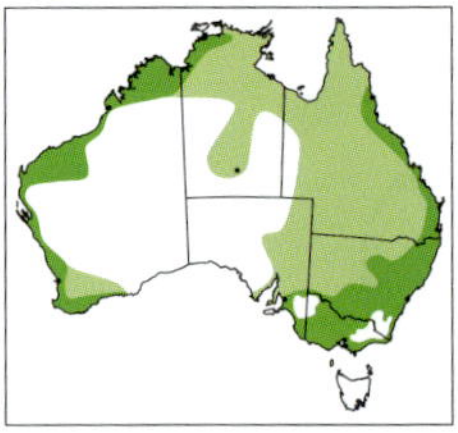

Medium-sized rail, finely barred with ginger breast band. Found in diverse wetland settings, also undergrowth on islands. Can be tame. **Voice:** most common call a high-pitched, forced *seeip.*

RED-NECKED CRAKE 26 cm
Rallina tricolor

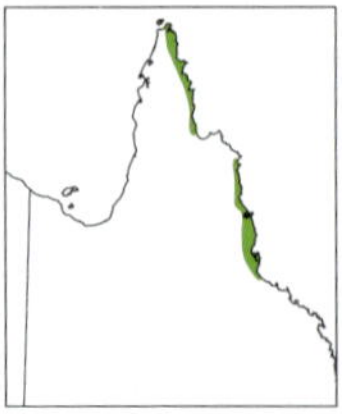

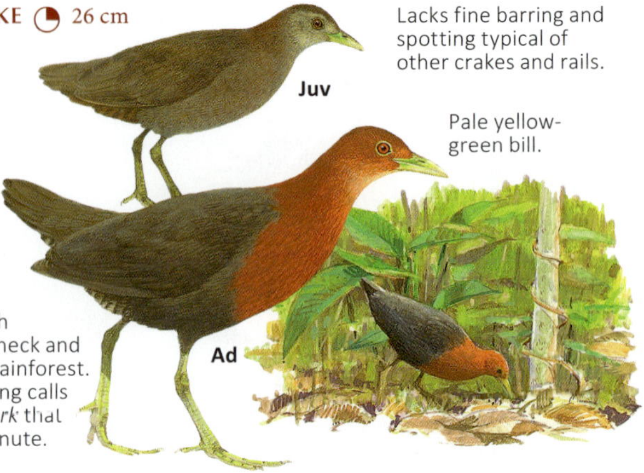

Medium-sized rail with reddish-brown head, neck and breast. Restricted to rainforest. **Voice:** loud, far-carrying calls *guuurk-guurk-gurk-gurk* that may continue for a minute.

BAILLON'S CRAKE ◔ 16 cm
Zapornia pusilla

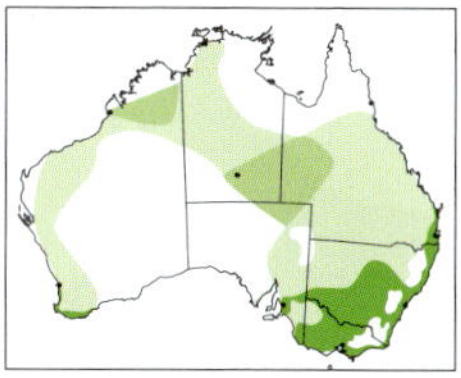

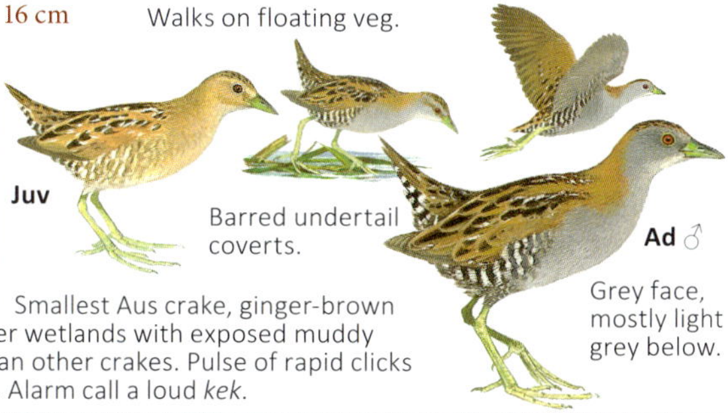

Smallest Aus crake, ginger-brown above. Mostly in freshwater wetlands with exposed muddy edges. **Voice:** less vocal than other crakes. Pulse of rapid clicks *pd.pd.pd.pd* lasting ~1 sec. Alarm call a loud *kek*.

AUSTRALIAN SPOTTED CRAKE ◑ 21 cm
Porzana fluminea

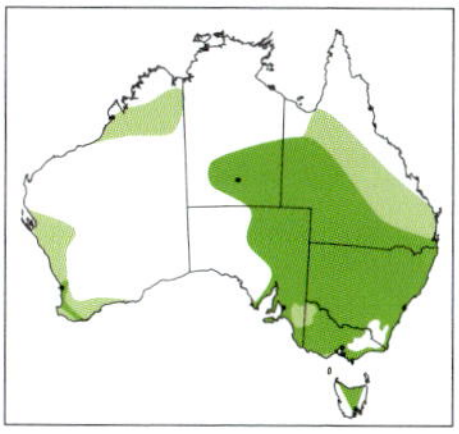

White sides to black-centred undertail. Black and white barring on flanks.

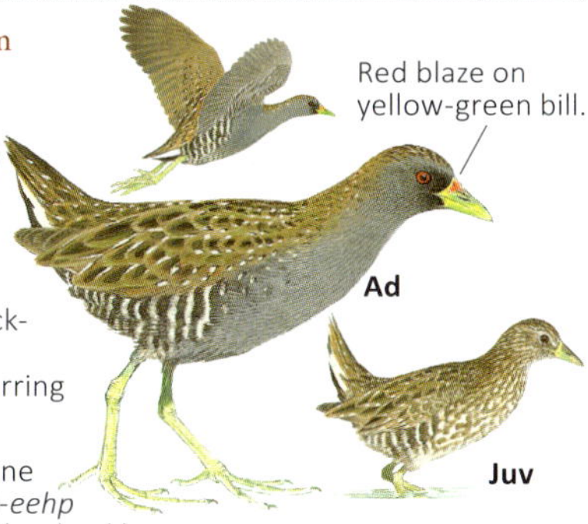

Marshy edges of well-vegetated fresh and saline wetlands. **Voice:** sharp, double-note call *eehp-eehp* from cover. Territorial calls a series of hyena-like chuckles.

SPOTLESS CRAKE ◔ 18 cm
Zapornia tabuensis

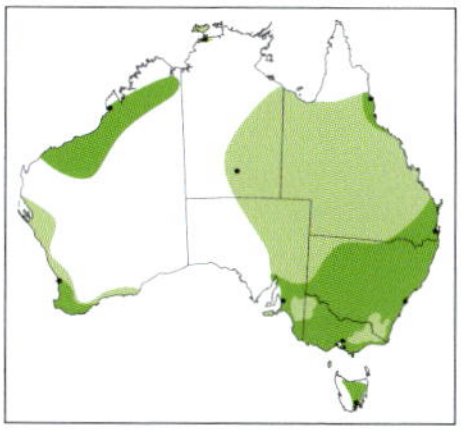

Barred undertail coverts.

In vegetated wetlands, including urban ponds, especially those with inundated lignum, reeds or sedges.

Voice: a series of soft *woop-woop-woop* notes followed by loud, sewing machine-like rattle.

WHITE-BROWED CRAKE ◑ 19 cm
Poliolimnas cinereus

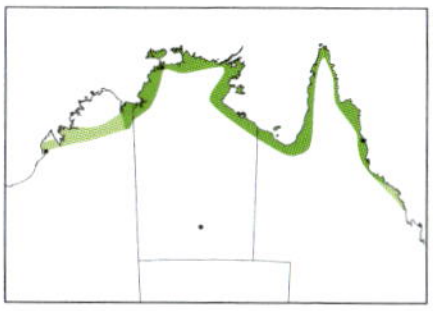

Small crake of near-coastal freshwater wetlands where routinely walks on floating vegetation, especially lily pads. **Voice:** loud, far-carrying *eeehk-eeehk-eeehk* repeated up to a dozen times.

AUSTRALASIAN SWAMPHEN ● 46 cm
Porphyrio melanotus

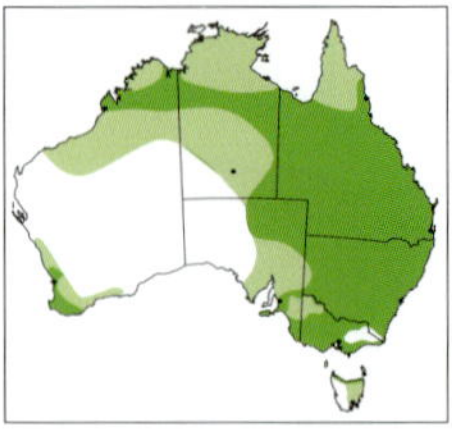

Large, gangly legged, blue and black waterhen. In reedbeds of lakes, rivers, swamps, estuaries and urban wetlands.
Voice: series of 5–10 loud shrieks increasing in duration, initially *kreek,* finishing *quinquinkrrkrrquinquinquinkrrkrr.*

DUSKY MOORHEN ◕ 37 cm
Gallinula tenebrosa

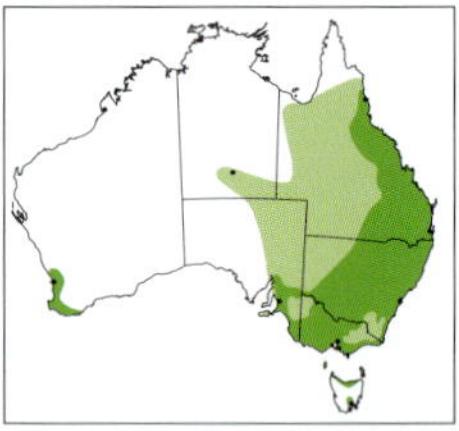

Dark slate-grey waterhen. In reedbeds of lakes, rivers, swamps and urban wetlands.
Voice: explosive wavering *kuuurk* or *krrruk-uk*, short *kook-kook-kook*. Also short, sharp notes when alarmed.

EURASIAN COOT ● 37 cm
Fulica atra

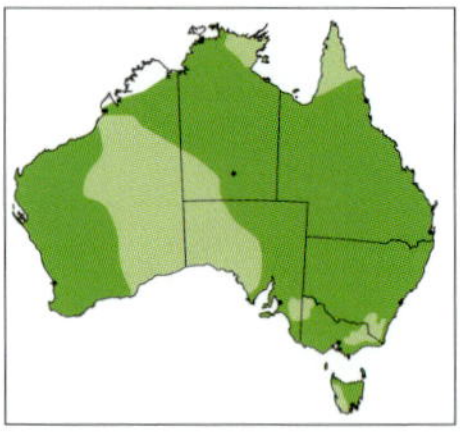

Sooty waterbird with white bill and frontal shield. Dives readily for aquatic veg. On large lakes, rivers, estuaries and urban wetlands, often in large numbers.
Voice: loud scratchy *krarrk* or *kriak,* also *kratack-krat-krat-krat*. Also clipped repeated squeak *pip-pip-pip* and soft *pit-pit-pit*.

PALE-VENTED BUSH-HEN ◔ 27 cm
Amaurornis moluccana

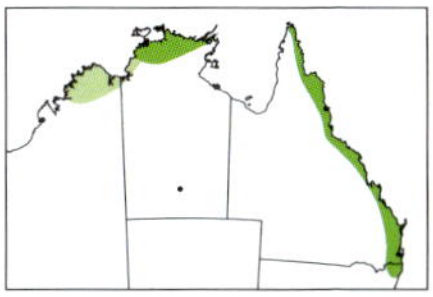

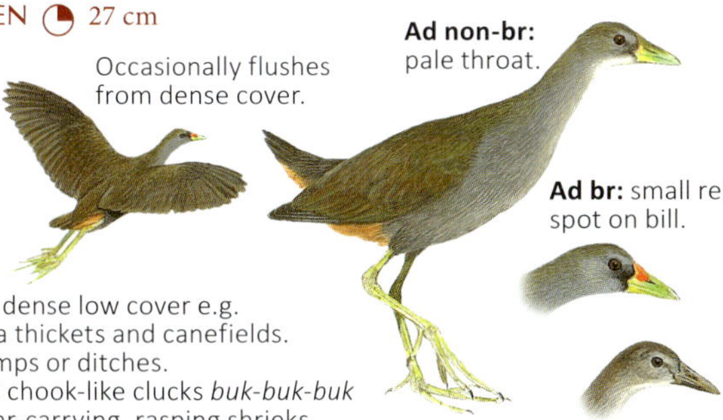

Furtive, plain waterhen. In dense low cover e.g. tall grass or rushes, lantana thickets and canefields. Usually near streams, swamps or ditches.
Voice: call a series of rapid chook-like clucks *buk-buk-buk* followed by 8–12 paired, far-carrying, rasping shrieks or wails each pair rising then falling, becoming more urgent *whiiie-chhuu—whiiie-chhuu*. Also a rapid, monotonous *woup-woup-woup* ...

BLACK-TAILED NATIVE-HEN ◑ 34 cm
Tribonyx ventralis

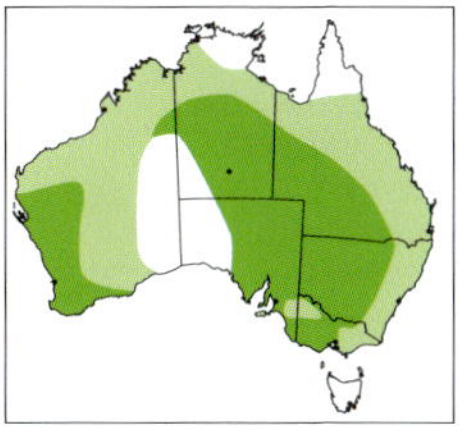

Fleet-footed, terrestrial waterhen. Dispersive and eruptive on shallow, inland habitats, especially with flooded lignum.
Voice: less vocal than other waterhens, usually flush in silence. A clean, high-pitched whistle, series of loud, sharp, urgent notes *eeip-eeip-eeip*, also explosive *tiip* or *tiup* and *ehk* or *ehk-ek*.

TASMANIAN NATIVE-HEN ◕ 47 cm
Tribonyx mortierii

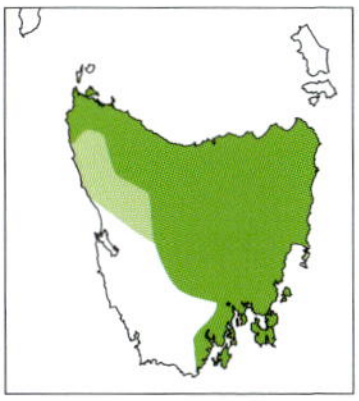

Large, flightless, olive-brown, terrestrial waterhen. In tussock grassland and rough pasture, usually close to wetlands.
Voice: a series of loud see-sawing notes or rapid, breathless donkey-like braying. Multiple birds calling leads to a cacophony of unpleasant noise. An abrupt high-pitched alarm.

EMU
Dromaius novaehollandiae

170 cm

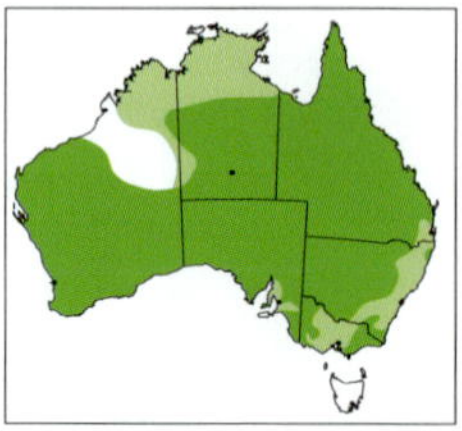

Unmistakable tall, flightless bird of most habitats but not closed forest and true deserts.
Voice: usually silent, ♀ gives low, far-carrying boom.

SOUTHERN CASSOWARY
Casuarius casuarius

160 cm

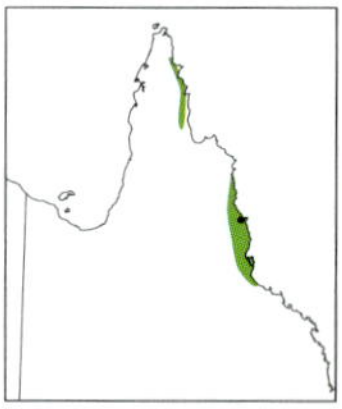

Large, stocky, flightless bird with powerful legs, can be aggressive if approached too closely. Tropical rainforest and adjacent vegetation, orchards and quiet gardens. Solitary or small family groups.
Voice: generally silent. Loud booming and rumbling territorial calls, often at night.

AUSTRALIAN BUSTARD
Ardeotis australis

100 cm

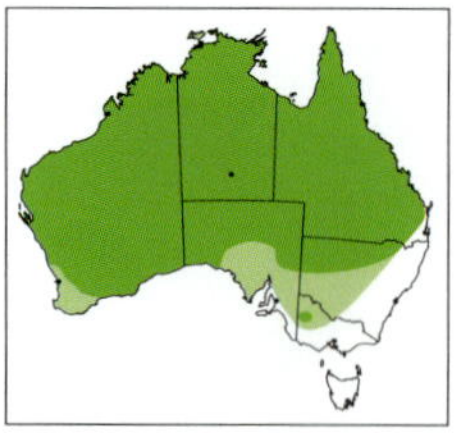

Tall, stately manner with head held high. Inhabits dry, open grassland and savanna, in pairs or family parties. Mostly restricted to inland and n Aus.
Voice: displaying ♂ gives loud roars and grunts.

MALLEEFOWL ◔ 60 cm
Leipoa ocellata

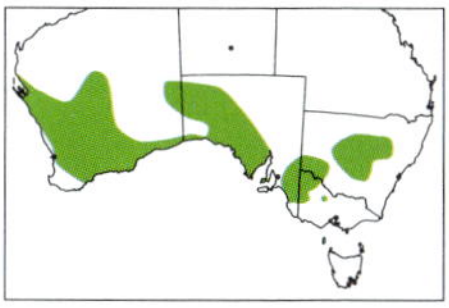

Large ground bird of dry forest, especially mallee. Incubates eggs within a large mound of sand covering composting leaves and twigs. Shy, walks slowly, freezes when disturbed, reluctant to fly. Difficult to observe except from distance when birds working mound. Solitary, or pair at mound. **Voice:** soft *oom* contact calls.

AUSTRALIAN BRUSH-TURKEY ◕ 65 cm
Alectura lathami

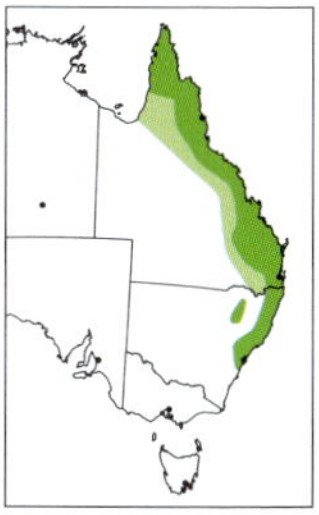

Ad br: purple neck wattle on Cape York.

Large ground bird of mostly closed forest, increasingly in gardens of towns and cities. Incubates eggs in large nest mound of leaf litter. Mostly solitary, often shy, quiet and unobtrusive but becomes tame around people. Roosts high in tree. **Voice:** low grunts and clucks, loud nasal *gok*.

ORANGE-FOOTED SCRUBFOWL ◕ 44 cm
Megapodius reinwardt

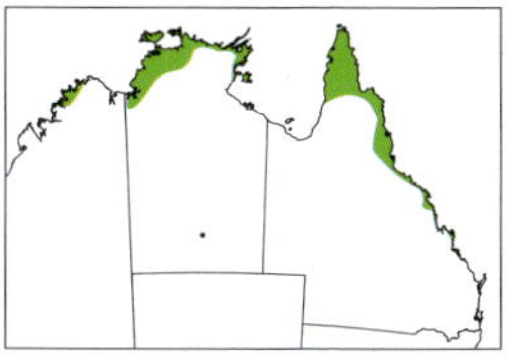

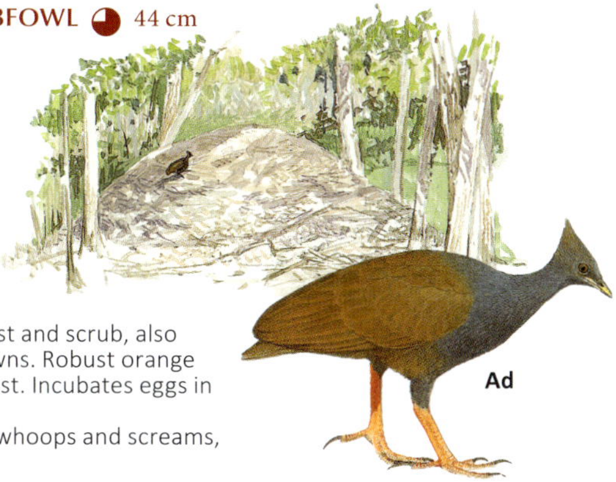

Medium-sized ground bird of tropics, inhabits moist forest and scrub, also parks in tropical cities and towns. Robust orange legs and feet, pointed hindcrest. Incubates eggs in massive mound of leaf litter. **Voice:** loud chuckles, rattles, whoops and screams, day and night.

INDIAN PEAFOWL ♀ 90 cm ♂ 215 cm
Pavo cristatus

Introduced species. Feral on French I, King I and some other Bass Strait Is; occasional escapes elsewhere.

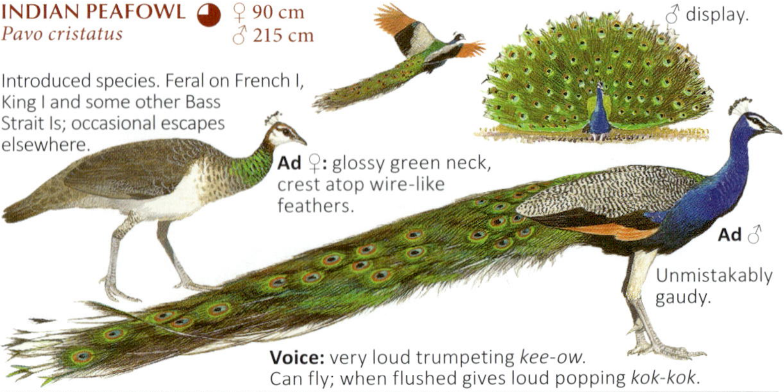

Voice: very loud trumpeting *kee-ow*. Can fly; when flushed gives loud popping *kok-kok*.

WILD TURKEY 122 cm
Meleagris gallopavo

Introduced species. Large body, tiny bare head. Feral on King, Flinders and Kangaroo Is, where flocks include white birds indicative of captive origins.

Voice: loud throaty gobble; also sharp *tuk* given by ♀.

COMMON PHEASANT 70 cm
Phasianus colchicus

Long-tailed ground bird, about the size of lyrebird.

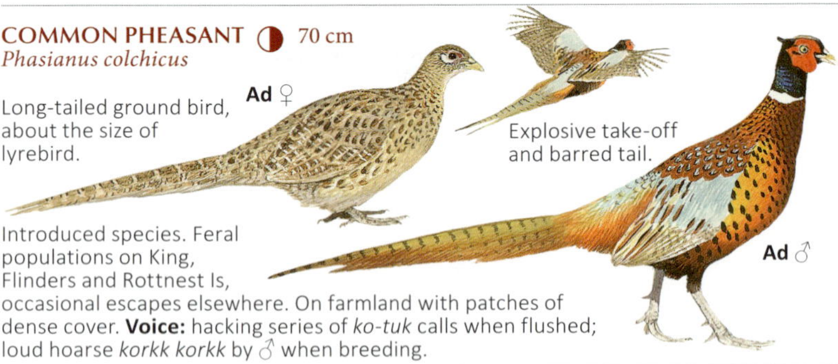

Introduced species. Feral populations on King, Flinders and Rottnest Is, occasional escapes elsewhere. On farmland with patches of dense cover. **Voice:** hacking series of *ko-tuk* calls when flushed; loud hoarse *korkk korkk* by ♂ when breeding.

HELMETED GUINEAFOWL 60 cm
Numida meleagris

Hen-sized ground bird with rotund body, tiny bare head.

Introduced species. Feral populations in dry grassy woodlands in a few sites in e Qld, including Mt Molloy, Chillagoe and Charters Towers. Occurs in noisy alert flocks. **Voice:** far-carrying, grating cackles.

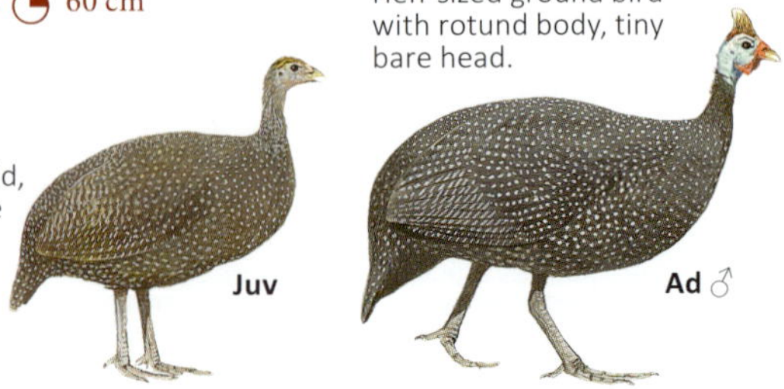

STUBBLE QUAIL ◐ 19 cm
Coturnix pectoralis

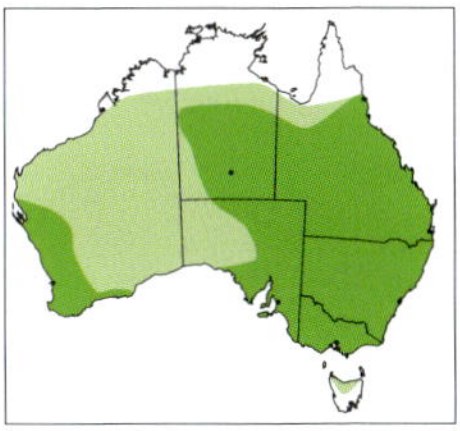

Flies low and fast with whirring wing beats.

Cryptic, usually seen when flushed. In small coveys in grassland and cereal crops.

Ad ♂: rufous face, black breast.

White supercilium, black-streaked underparts.

Ad ♀

Voice: most often found by call, a clear, brisk whistle *tutchewup* in breeding season. Usually silent when flushed.

BROWN QUAIL ◐ 19 cm
Coturnix ypsilophora

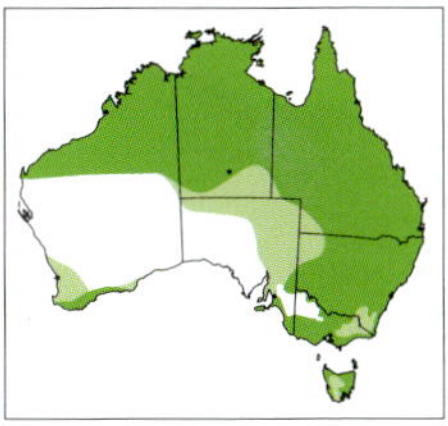

Flushes explosively with steep take-off, clattering wing beats. Rounder wing tips than Stubble.

Prefers denser, wetter areas than Stubble Quail, often near wetlands. Cryptic, small coveys venture into open near dense cover, especially at dawn and dusk.

Ad ♀

Ad ♂

Plain face, barred flanks.

Voice: penetrating 2-note whistle *pit-FWEER*; sharp chirp when flushed.

KING QUAIL ○ 13 cm
Excalfactoria chinensis

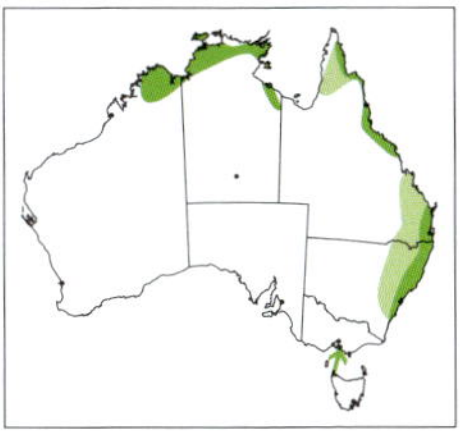

Looks tail heavy when flushed; dark upperwings lack pale wing panels of similarly small button-quails.

Tiny quail found in dense cover in swampy grassland, fernland and heath. Very cryptic, usually seen when small covey flushed.

Ad ♂

Ad ♀

Voice: high-pitched nasal descending crow or whistle *pyew or ke-er*. Cheeps and rapid peeping when flushed.

CALIFORNIA QUAIL ◐ 25 cm
Callipepla californica

Feral population on King I. Pairs and family parties in rough pasture with nearby cover; sometimes feeds in open, perches on posts. Flies on whirring, short, stiff wings. **Voice:** displaying ♂ gives loud crowing *cu-CA-cow*.

Ad ♂

Large introduced quail with diagnostic plume on forecrown.

Ad ♀

PAINTED BUTTON-QUAIL 18 cm
Turnix varius

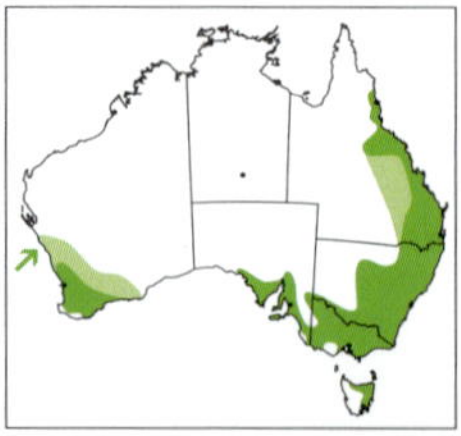

Large button-quail with rufous blaze on 'shoulders'. Pairs or small coveys in dry eucalypt forest and woodland with sparse to moderate understorey.

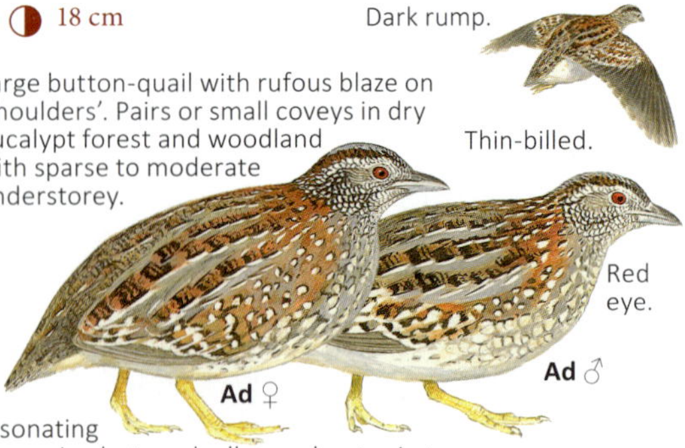

Often makes saucer-shaped depressions in leaf litter when foraging. **Voice:** deep resonating *oom* notes – like Common Bronzewing but gradually accelerates in tempo.

BUFF-BREASTED BUTTON-QUAIL 20 cm
Turnix olivii

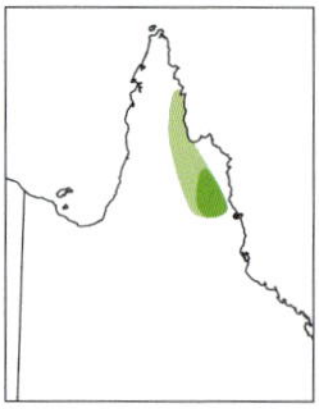

Large, elusive button-quail of tropical woodland with sparse, grassy understorey. Critically endangered; any sightings noteworthy.

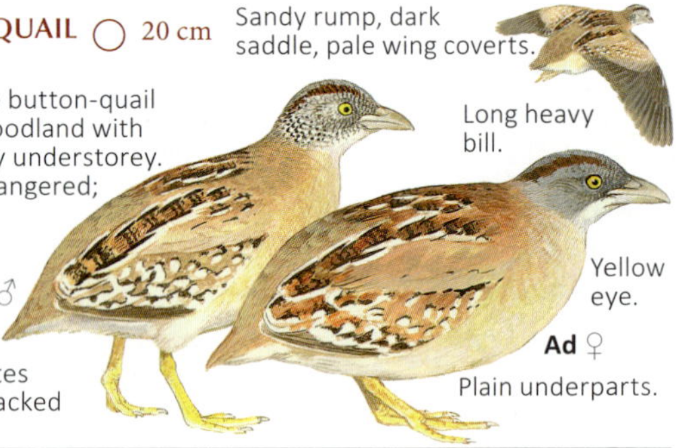

Voice: deep resonating *oom* notes – possibly similar to Chestnut-backed Button-quail.

CHESTNUT-BACKED BUTTON-QUAIL 15 cm
Turnix castanotus

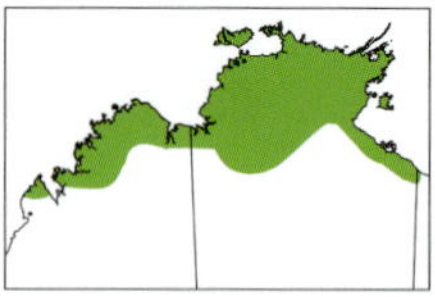

Heavily built button-quail of monsoonal eucalypt woodland and open forest with short, sparse understorey.

Voice: series of deep tremulous *oom* notes, each with vibrating, multisyllabic, rising quality.

BLACK-BREASTED BUTTON-QUAIL 18 cm
Turnix melanogaster

Large, secretive button-quail of thick forest with deep leaf litter, especially dry rainforest. Pairs or small coveys. Foraging birds make saucer-shaped depressions in leaf litter, often first clue to their presence.

Voice: low, tremulous drumming comprises repeated quavering *oom* notes, each *oom* with 5–7 syllables.

RED-BACKED BUTTON-QUAIL ◔ 13 cm
Turnix maculosus

Dense grasslands, especially tussock grasses on blacksoil plains; often near wetlands. Cryptic; pairs or small coveys most often seen when flushed.

Strongly contrasting pale wing panels; buff flanks.

Tiny button-quail with yellow bill and legs. **Voice:** subdued series of upslurred *oom* notes, increasing in volume and tempo.

LITTLE BUTTON-QUAIL ◑ 13 cm
Turnix velox

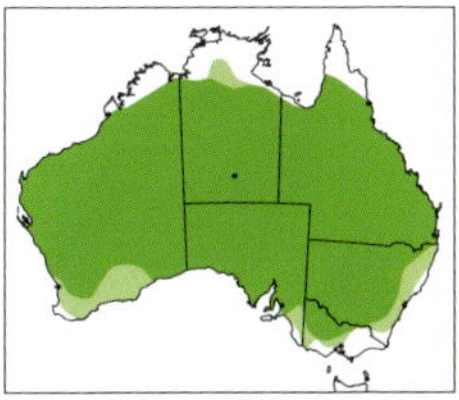

Small, thick-billed button-quail of dryish grasslands and grassy woodlands. Partly migratory; most common in inland in winter, in temperate regions in spring and early summer.

White rear-flanks. Strong contrast between black flight feathers and rufous wing panels.

Pink legs.

Voice: repeated disyllabic *hoo-oo*; also 2–3 squeaking chip notes when flushed.

RED-CHESTED BUTTON-QUAIL ◔ 13 cm
Turnix pyrrhothorax

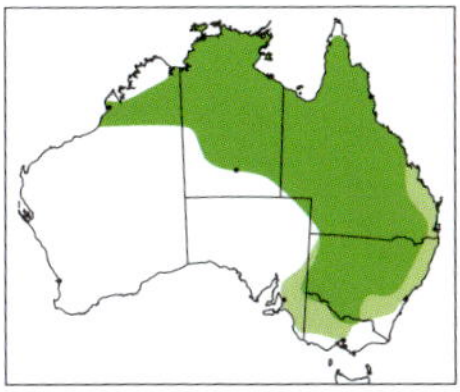

Small, thick-billed button-quail of grassland and grassy woodland. Often with Little Button-quail but prefers denser cover. Partly nomadic or migratory.

Rufous rear-flanks. Weak contrast between flight feathers and dark grey-brown upperparts.

Pink legs.

Voice: rapidly repeated *oom* notes, each slightly upslurred, rising in pitch and intensity. Can give sharp chatter when flushed.

PLAINS-WANDERER ○ 17 cm
Pedionomus torquatus

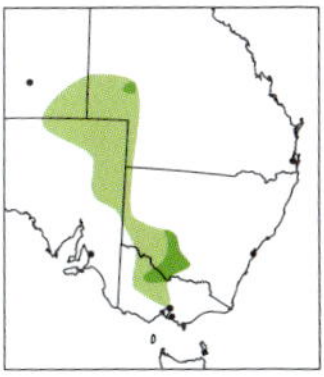

Very secretive ground bird of sparsely vegetated inland plains. Most often seen by spotlight at night.

Slow flight with trailing feet, buff wing bar.

Long legs, often stands tall.

Ad ♀: rufous bib, pied collar.

Densely vermiculated upperparts without white streaking. **Voice:** repeated low resonant *oo* at dawn and dusk.

Quick guide to raptors: A diverse group of predators, but usually showing a hook-tipped bill, powerful feet with long sharp claws and nostrils that open within a cere. Most often seen flying overhead where ID is based on flying style, plumage pattern and structure. Most species can soar exploiting thermals, often to great heights.

Swamp Harrier p. 87
Spotted Harrier p. 87
Osprey p. 84
Pacific Baza p. 89
Goshawks p. 88
Elanus kites p. 89
Falcons pp. 90–91
Nankeen Kestrel p. 90

EASTERN OSPREY 57 cm
Pandion cristatus

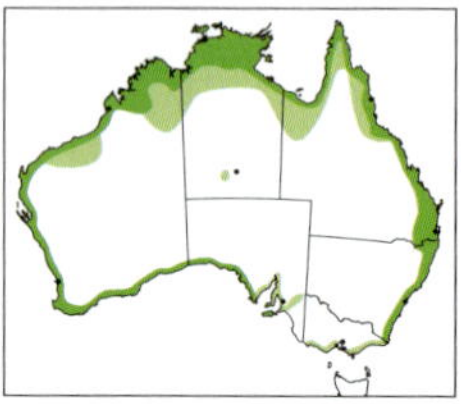

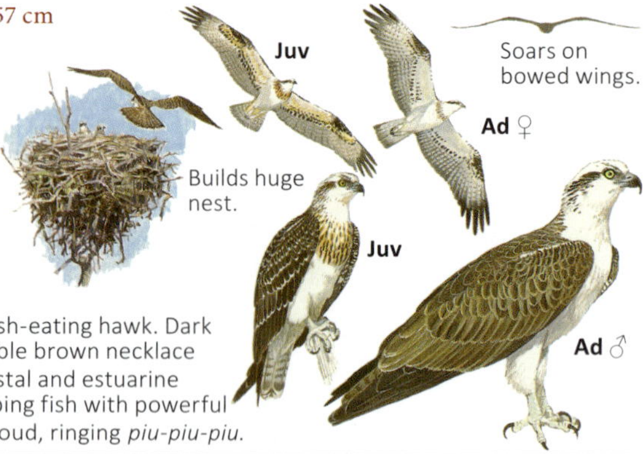

Large, brown and white, fish-eating hawk. Dark line behind pale eye, variable brown necklace most developed in ♀. Coastal and estuarine waters. Plunge dives grabbing fish with powerful talons. **Voice:** distinctive, loud, ringing *piu-piu-piu*.

WHITE-BELLIED SEA-EAGLE 80 cm
Haliaeetus leucogaster

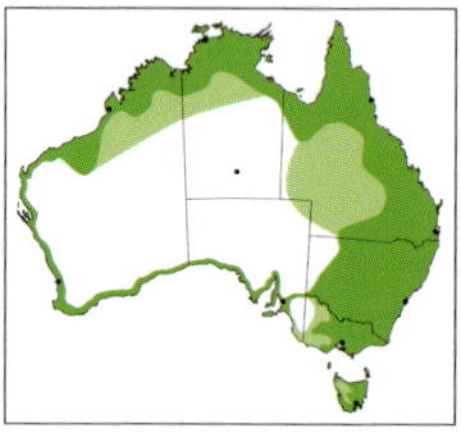

Imposing grey and white eagle of coast and large inland waters. Soars on stiffly upswept, broad-based wings. Huge talons and deep bill. **Voice:** when breeding, loud, goose-like honks and yelps.

WEDGE-TAILED EAGLE 95 cm
Aquila audax

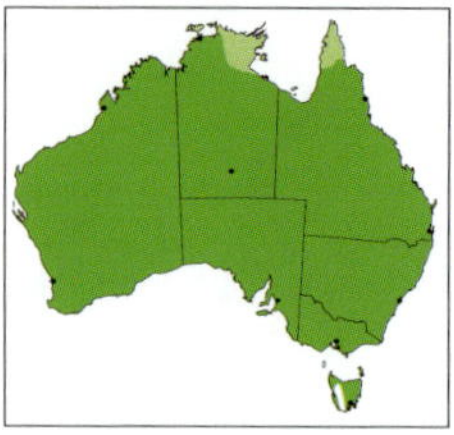

Our largest bird of prey, dark with heavy, deep bill. Perches atop dead tree or telegraph pole in early morning sun. Hunts small vertebrates, especially rabbits, but carrion, including roadkill, can be an important part of the diet. Juv paler, golden-brown head and wing coverts. **Voice:** mostly silent, meek trills and whistles.

LITTLE EAGLE ◑ 50 cm
Hieraaetus morphnoides

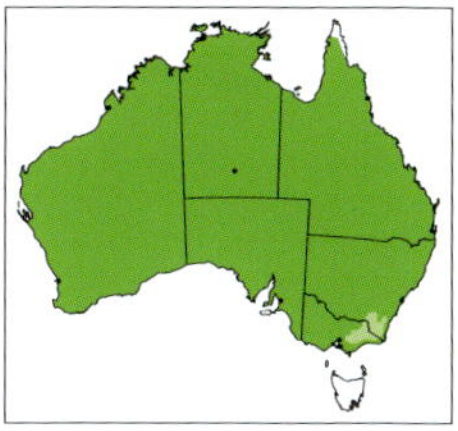

Soars on flat wings, shortish, barred, tail. Red-brown underwing coverts, black limited to outer half of primaries (*cf* Whistling Kite).

Small, compact eagle of open wooded habitats. Mostly solitary, often soars high in tight circles with rectangular wings and squarish tail. Pale and dark morphs. When perched note 'trousers', short crest on nape, folded wings do not reach tail tip.
Voice: vocal; loud 2–3-syllable whistle *fee-few or fee-fee-few.*

WHISTLING KITE ● 55 cm
Haliastur sphenurus

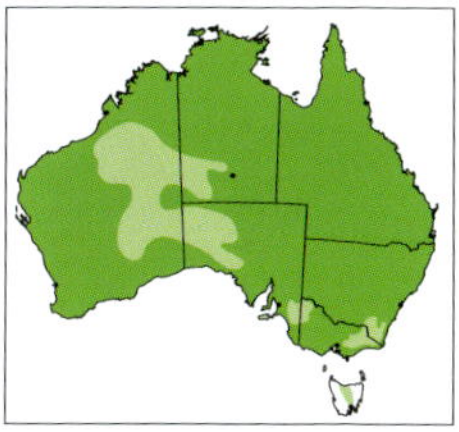

Lazy, buoyant flight, gliding and soaring. Pale underwing coverts (*cf* Little Eagle) outer primaries all dark.

Soars on slightly bowed wings.

Juv: white spots on back and wing coverts.

Untidy, loose-winged scavenger of open country usually close to water. Also flood plains, farmland and tidal flats. Longish, rounded, pale tail. When perched tail clearly extends beyond wing tips.
Voice: very vocal; 2-note descending *see-ooo* immediately followed by ascending staccato whistle *si-si-si-si*.

BRAHMINY KITE ◔ 47 cm
Haliastur indus

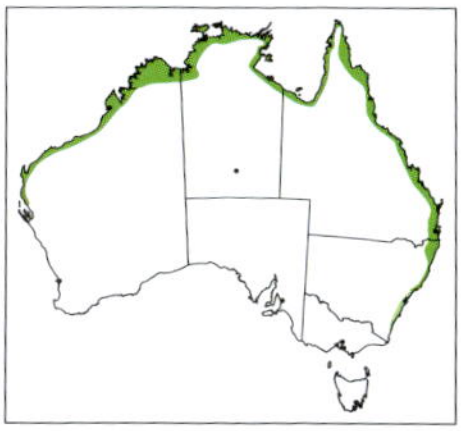

Soars on slightly raised wings.

Juv: recalls Whistling Kite and Little Eagle. Dark patch behind eye, undertail with terminal dark band.

Mid-sized, compact kite of tropical and subtropical coasts. Patrols beaches and estuaries snatching prey and carrion from shoreline. When perched, tail tip just short of wing tip.
Voice: alarm call a loud, drawn out quavering *beee-yah.*

BLACK KITE ● 50 cm
Milvus migrans

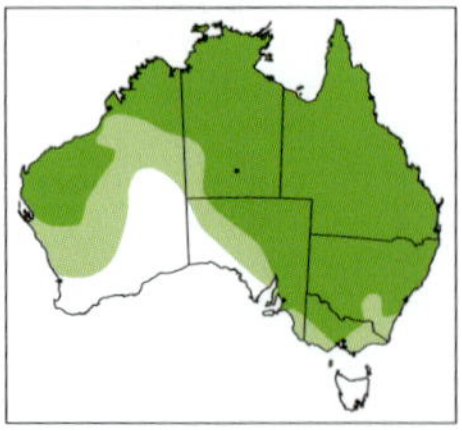

Familiar dark kite with pale face and yellow cere. Forked tail extends well beyond wing tip when perched. Inland plains, pastoral land and towns, abundant in n Aus. Gathers in loose flocks, sometimes totalling 100s, around food sources such as carcasses and around bushfires. A bold and opportunistic predator and scavenger.
Voice: recalls Whistling Kite with less descending start and staccato finish does not ascend.

SQUARE-TAILED KITE ◔ 52 cm
Lophoictinia isura

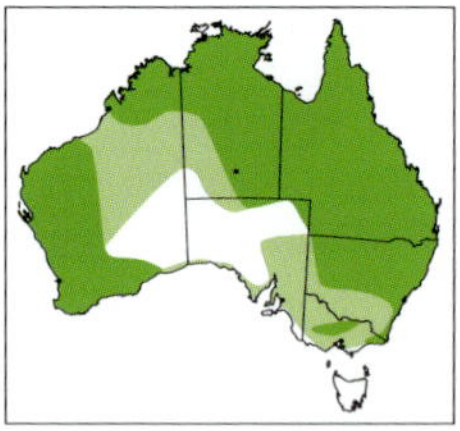

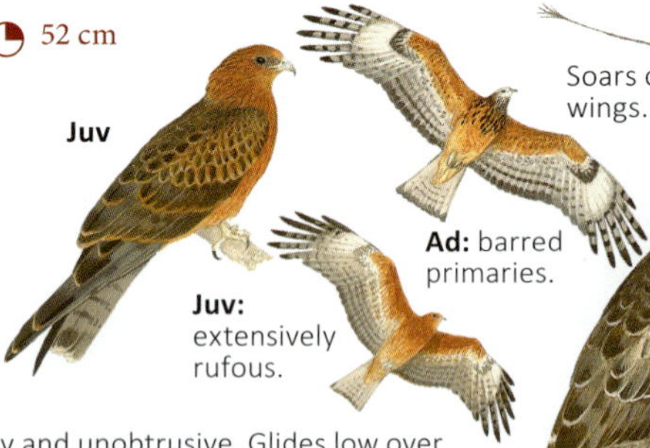

Uncommon, usually solitary and unobtrusive. Glides low over canopy of open forest and woodland with much jinking and side slipping. Very long 'fingered' wings in flight, extend well beyond tail tip when perched. Mostly absent from tropics during the wet season and a spring–summer visitor in s of range.
Voice: mostly silent, a short, hoarse yelp and incessant chattering when nesting.

BLACK-BREASTED BUZZARD ◔ 55 cm
Hamirostra melanosternon

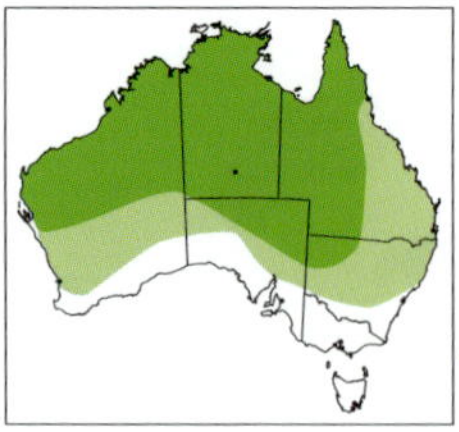

Large, black and rufous soaring hawk of inland plains and savanna. Long, broad wings deeply fingered, with conspicuous white patch at base of black outer primaries. Folded wings extend well beyond short grey tail.
Voice: mostly silent, a short hoarse yelp and whinnying sounds.

RED GOSHAWK ○ 52 cm
Erythrotriorchis radiatus

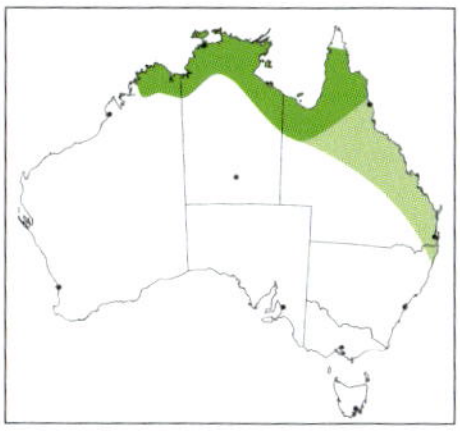

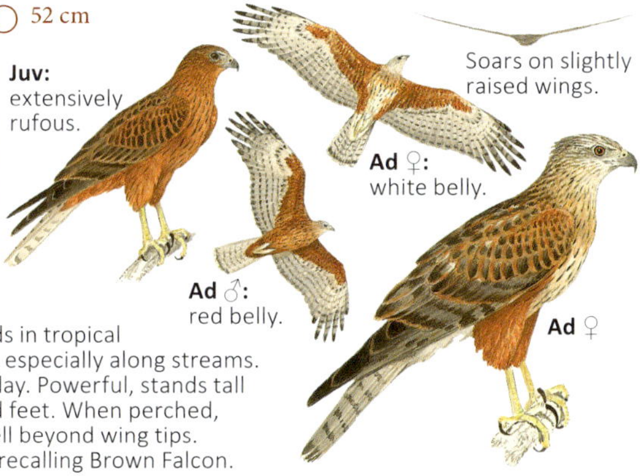

Rare ambush hunter of birds in tropical woodland and open forest, especially along streams. Sits quietly during heat of day. Powerful, stands tall on massive, yellow legs and feet. When perched, barred grey tail extends well beyond wing tips. **Voice:** vocal; loud cackling recalling Brown Falcon.

SWAMP HARRIER ◔ 55 cm
Circus approximans

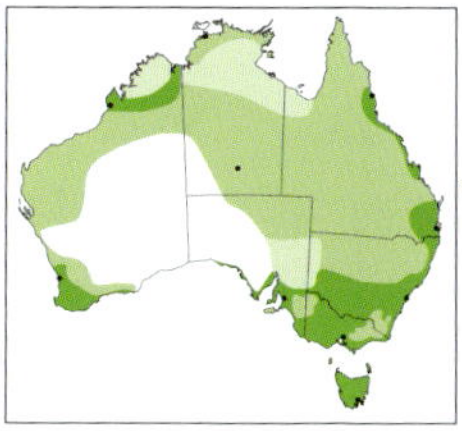

Menacing, wary, long-legged hawk. Flies low and slow over wetlands and adjacent country. In most plumages white rump usually sufficient for ID, but dark Juv has tawny rump. **Voice:** mostly silent, breeding birds give short, far-carrying whistle *see-u*.

SPOTTED HARRIER ◑ 56 cm
Circus assimilis

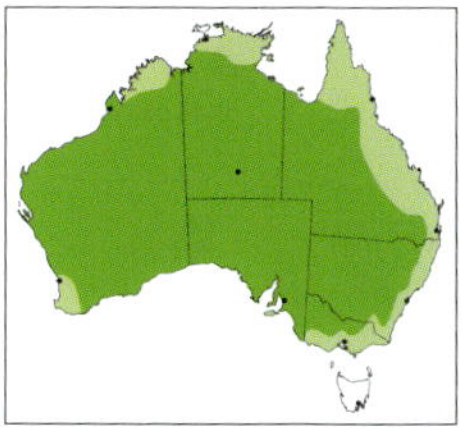

Striking rufous and grey, broad rectangular wings, long black primaries. Flight slow, buoyant, long glides with subtle jinking. Over crops, grassland and sparsely timbered country, mostly inland. **Voice:** mostly silent, chattering threat call *kik-kik-kik*.

BROWN GOSHAWK ◕ 47 cm
Accipiter fasciatus

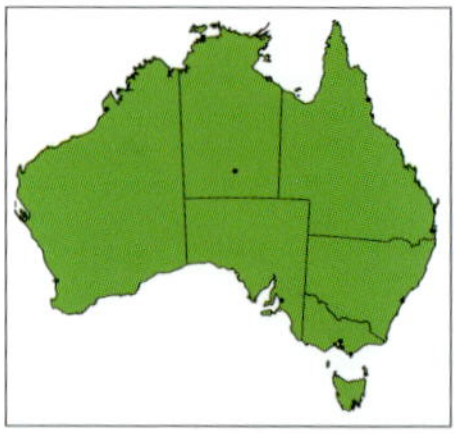

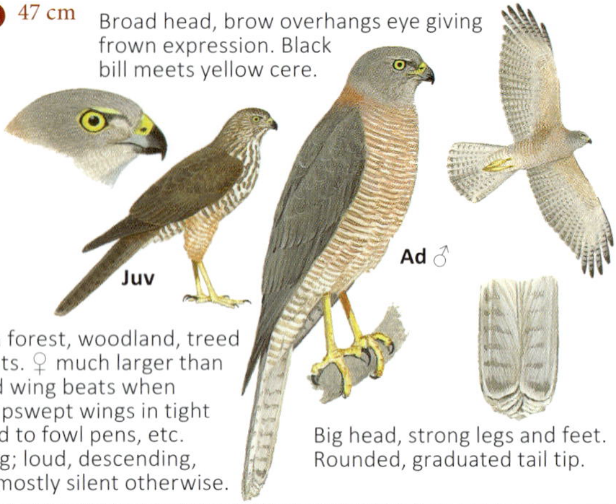

Broad head, brow overhangs eye giving frown expression. Black bill meets yellow cere.

Big head, strong legs and feet. Rounded, graduated tail tip.

Powerful hunter of birds in forest, woodland, treed farmland and urban habitats. ♀ much larger than ♂. Powerful bursts of rapid wing beats when hunting, soars on slightly upswept wings in tight circles. Juvs often attracted to fowl pens, etc. **Voice:** vocal when breeding; loud, descending, strident chatter *ee-ee-ee*, mostly silent otherwise.

COLLARED SPARROWHAWK ◑ 35 cm
Accipiter cirrocephalus

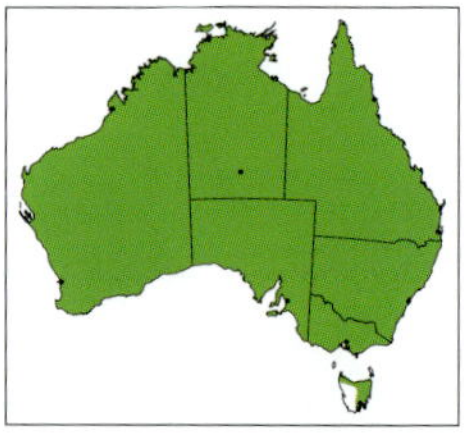

Small head with less brow overhang giving staring expression.

Ad has narrow blue between yellow cere and black bill.

Slender legs and toes. Tail square-tipped, often notched.

Small but fierce bird hunter, easily confused with Brown Goshawk and lives in similar habitats. ♀ much larger than ♂. Dashing flight, will chase prey through dense bushes. More flickering wing beats and buoyant gliding than Brown Goshawk. Soars in tight circles. **Voice:** recalls Brown Goshawk but sharper, higher-pitched *ki-ki-ki*.

GREY GOSHAWK ◑ 47 cm
Accipiter novaehollandiae

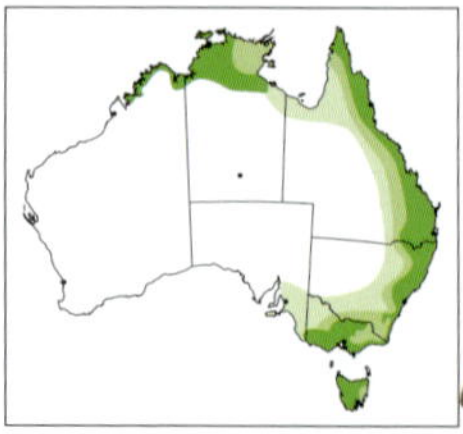

Red eye.

Compact flight profile with broad wings and tail.

Robust, polymorphic hawk, inhabits wetter forest, occasionally in more open country. Secretive and uncommon, often seen perched quietly watching for prey. White morph predominates in Vic, only morph in Tas. **Voice:** rather vocal, a series of ringing whistles *klooee klooee klooee*.

BLACK-SHOULDERED KITE ◕ 35 cm
Elanus axillaris

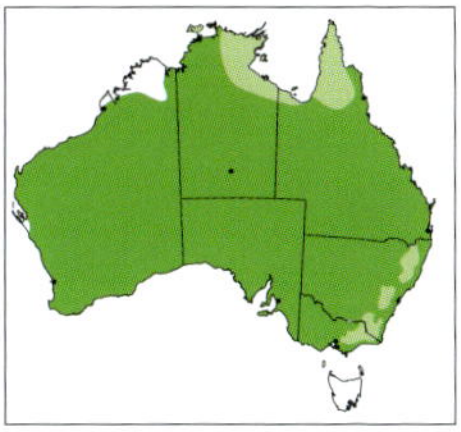

Juv: orange-brown on head and chest, broad buff scaling on back.

Hovering.

Glides with wings upswept.

Ad: black eye patch extends behind eye, white head.

Small pale hawk of grasslands and agricultural areas, less common in the arid inland. Often seen perched conspicuously or hovering over grassland searching for prey, mostly rodents.
Voice: raspy contact call *scree scree scree.*

LETTER-WINGED KITE ○ 35 cm
Elanus scriptus

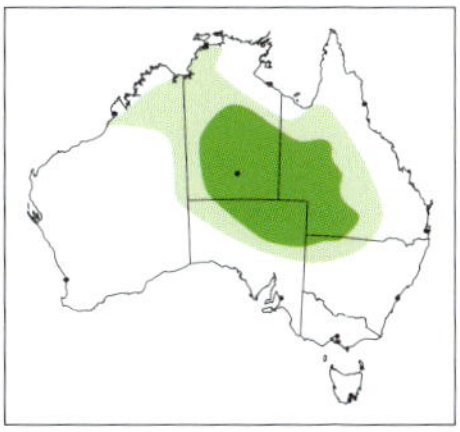

Juv: orange-brown on chest and grey on head, rusty plain back.

Glides with wings upswept.

Distinctive underwing.

Ad ♂: white head

Black eye patch does not extend behind eye.

Ad ♀: grey on crown and hindneck.

Gregarious, mostly nocturnal kite on arid plains of eastern central Aus. Roosts communally by day in leafy trees, becomes active towards dusk. Resembles Black-shouldered Kite, underwing diagnostic.
Voice: a short clear whistle.

PACIFIC BAZA ◑ 40 cm
Aviceda subcristata

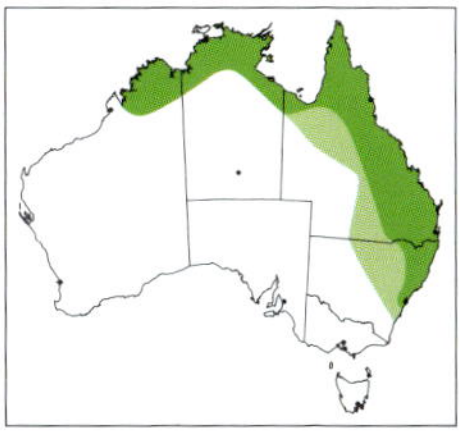

Juv: rufous scalloping on back and wing, white areas on face.

Soars on slightly bowed wings.

Ad: grey head, short crest, yellow eye, barred chest.

Long, broad, paddle-shaped wings pinched-in close to body. Barred primaries, broad black terminal band on tail.

Small crested hawk, bold bars on chest. Forest edges in tropics and subtropics, including parks and urban areas. Feeds in tree canopy taking large insects, tree frogs, etc. Unobtrusive, sits quietly on shaded perch when not active.
Voice: main call a reedy, 2-note whistle *wee-choo wee-choo.*

NANKEEN KESTREL ● 32 cm
Falco cenchroides

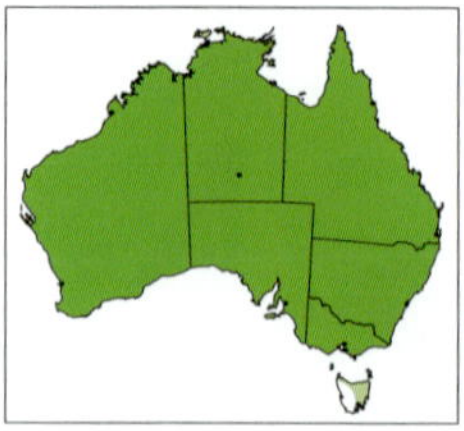

Common and widespread in open country – plains, farmland and coasts. Small and slender with long, rounded tail and narrow wings.
Voice: territorial call an excited, shrill chatter *keekeekee*.

BROWN FALCON ● 45 cm
Falco berigora

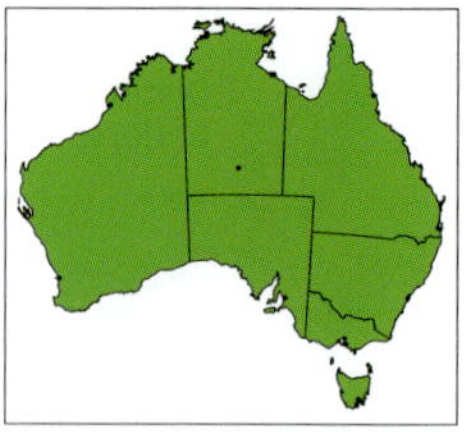

Common in open country. Medium-sized with large head, two black stripes on face, sluggish flight. Many plumages, rufous to dark brown. Bare skin around eye blue-grey becoming yellow with age.
Voice: loud cackling often given in flight.

BLACK FALCON ◔ 50 cm
Falco subniger

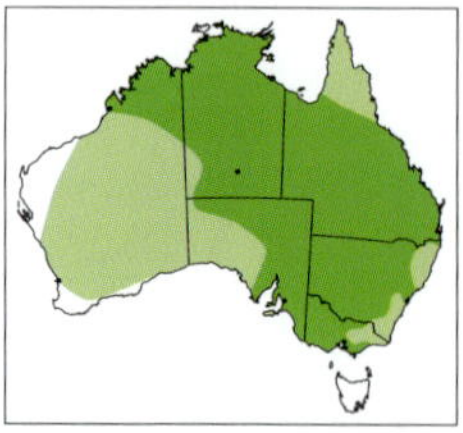

Powerful and agile hunter of birds in lightly timbered country. Sooty-brown, long wings and long, rounded tail, small head, broad shoulders.
Voice: when breeding, a deep, guttural cackle, whinnying sounds.

AUSTRALIAN HOBBY ◑ 33 cm
Falco longipennis

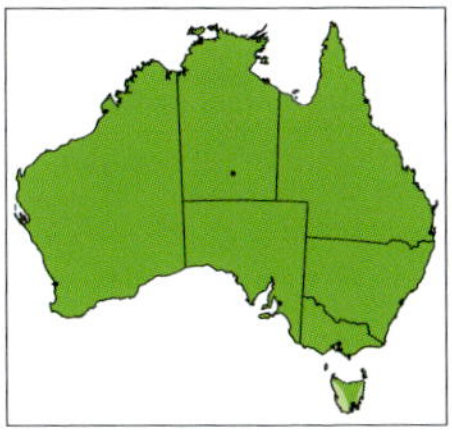

Juv: broad rufous fringes.

Ad

Small, dark bird hunter with narrow, angular wings. Dashing, agile flight rising in arcs and low through terrain. In open country with scattered trees, tree-lined watercourses and urban areas. Perches on high emergent branch. Rufous, black-streaked underparts. Slimmer and longer tailed than Peregrine, lacks full black helmet. **Voice:** excited high-pitched *ke-ke-ke*.

PEREGRINE FALCON ◑ 42 cm
Falco peregrinus

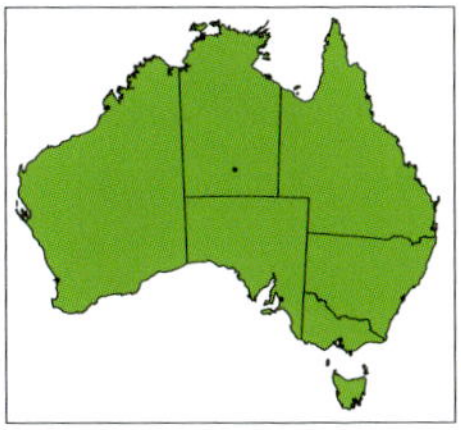

Juv

Juv: streaked underparts.

Ad: black helmet, bright yellow cere, legs and feet.

Ad: barred underparts.

Fast aerial bird hunter found in most habitats. Solid build with rather short, broad wings and tail. Powerful flight with shallow wing beats, makes spectacular high speed stoops onto prey. Often soars for short periods.
Voice: harsh screaming chatter *kik kik kik*.

GREY FALCON ○ 37 cm
Falco hypoleucos

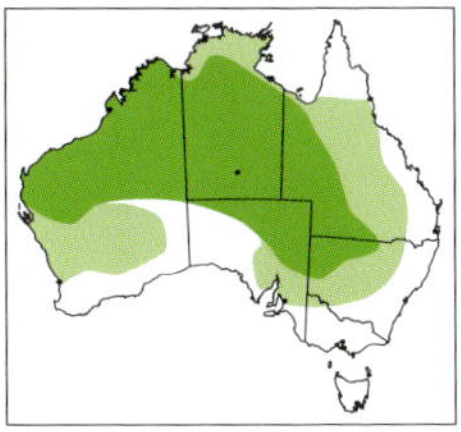

Juv: darker with duller facial bare parts.

Juv: more heavily marked underwing than Ad.

Ad: pale blue-grey, bright-yellow bare parts.

Ad: very pale underwing with dark wing tips.

Rarely encountered falcon of arid inland plains and treed watercourses. Powerful flight with shallow wing beats. Often soars for extended periods high in the sky. When not hunting, sits quietly within tall, shady tree.
Voice: harsh screaming chatter *kik kik kik*.

EASTERN BARN OWL ◑ 33 cm
Tyto javanica

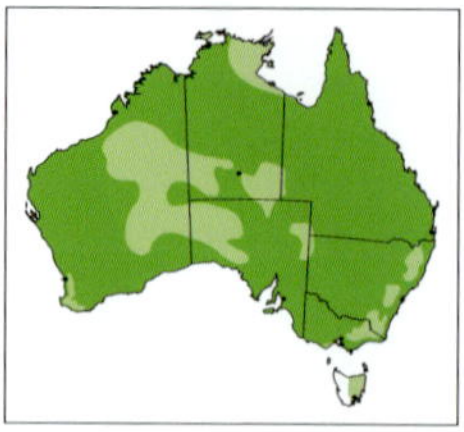

Small, pale owl, widespread in open country, farmland and urban areas. Often seen perched on fence post. **Voice:** territorial call a falsetto, rasping screech *skee-aaar*, reedy screams and squeals.

Ad ♂

Ad ♀: warmer toned than ♂, bolder marks on chest.

Buoyant flight with very pale underwing. No foot projection beyond tail.

Facial disc white with narrow black rim to lower half. Skinny legs sparsely covered with hair-like feathers.

AUSTRALIAN MASKED OWL ○ 41 cm
Tyto novaehollandiae

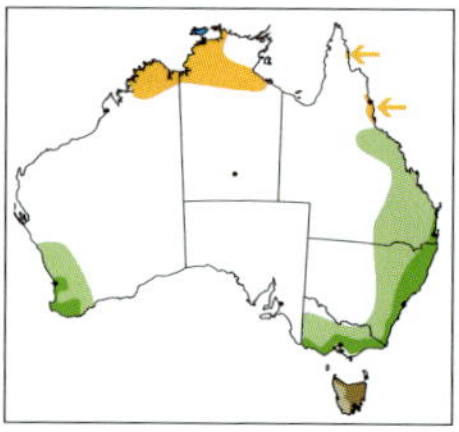

Highly variable in size and plumage. Largest birds in Tas, smallest in n Aus.
Voice: loud, hissing screech *h-a-a-a*, louder, deeper and harsher than Eastern Barn Owl.

Ad ♀

Elusive, occurring at low densities in forest and woodland, sightings often at forest edge.

Ad ♀

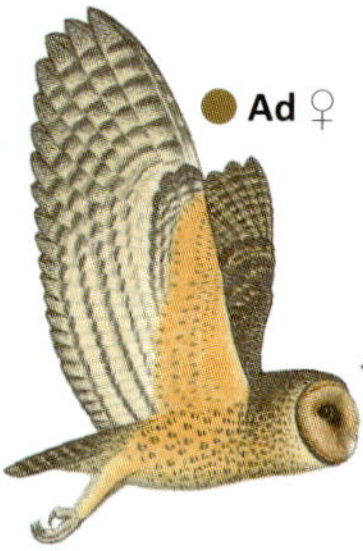

Ad ♀

No foot projection beyond tail in flight.

Ad ♂

Ad ♀

Ad ♂

Ad ♂

Ad ♀

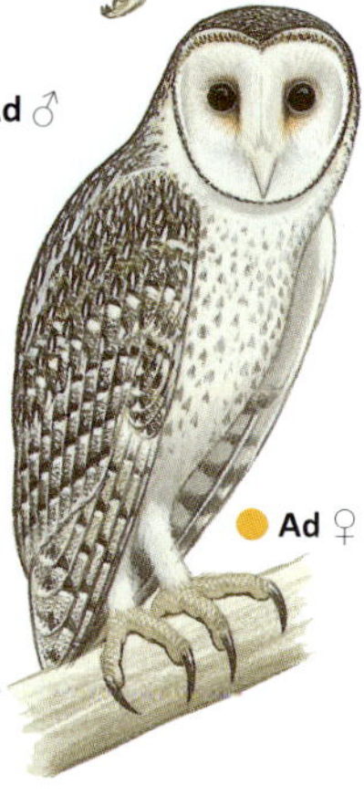

Smallest, palest birds from e and n Aus easily confused with Eastern Barn Owl. In all plumages more coarsely patterned, facial disc rounder with continuous narrow black rim. Powerful, densely feathered legs with large feet.

EASTERN GRASS OWL 34 cm
Tyto longimembris

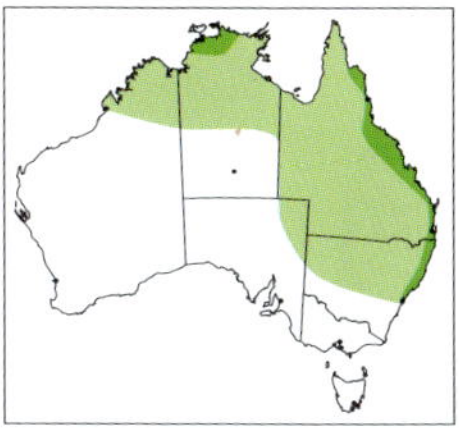

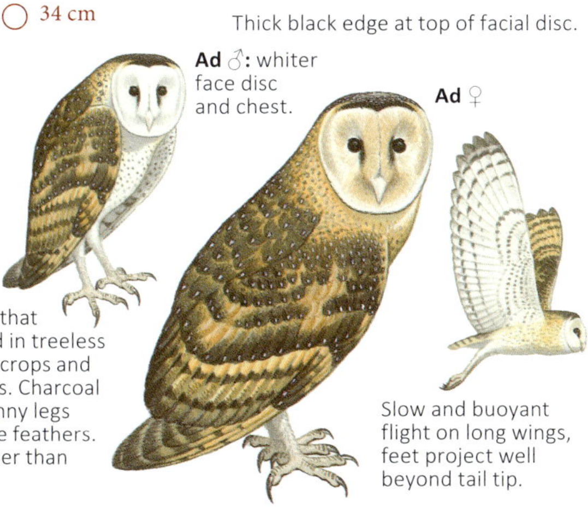

Localised, long-legged owl that roosts and nests on ground in treeless habitats; grassland, heath, crops and canefields, sedge and reeds. Charcoal and rich buff markings, skinny legs sparsely covered in hair-like feathers. **Voice:** harsh screech, deeper than Eastern Barn Owl.

GREATER SOOTY OWL 34 cm
Tyto tenebricosa

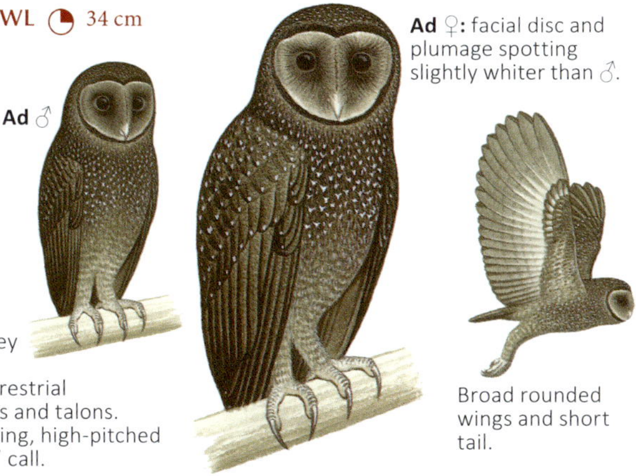

Large, heavy, sooty-grey owl of tall wet forest, hunts arboreal and terrestrial mammals. Massive legs and talons. **Voice:** a long, descending, high-pitched wail, the 'falling bomb' call.

LESSER SOOTY OWL 33 cm
Tyto multipunctata

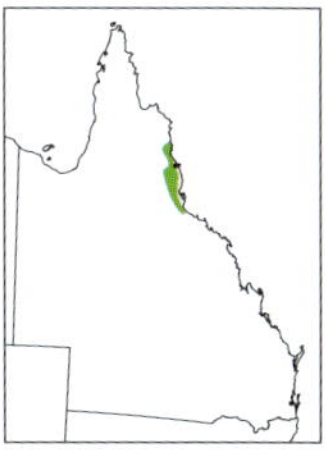

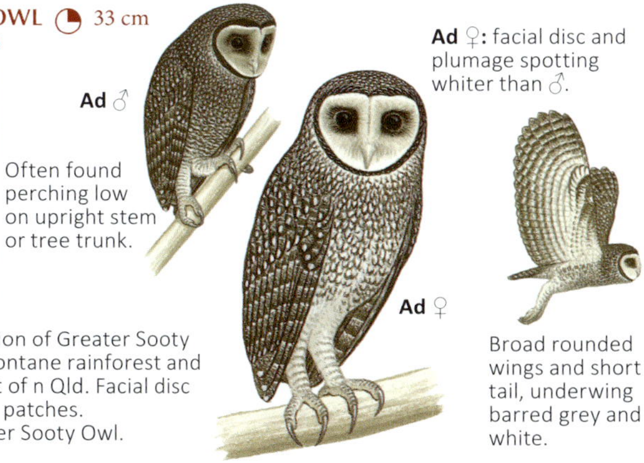

Smaller, paler, version of Greater Sooty Owl confined to montane rainforest and wet eucalypt forest of n Qld. Facial disc clear with dark eye patches. **Voice:** as for Greater Sooty Owl.

POWERFUL OWL ◔ 55 cm
Ninox strenua

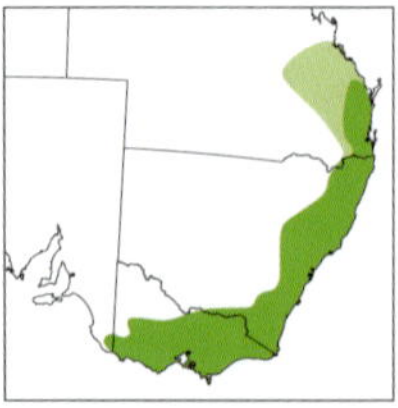

Our largest owl, hunts arboreal mammals and large birds. Roosts by day on substantial horizontal branch of tall, shady tree, often clasping remains of previous night's prey. Inhabits wet and some drier eucalypt forests, also urban areas with good populations of possums. **Voice:** loud, far carrying double hoot *whoo-hoo*.

Ad: piercing yellow eyes, underparts with diagnostic grey-brown chevrons.

RUFOUS OWL ◔ 51 cm
Ninox rufa

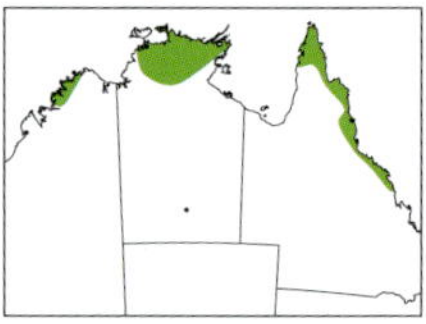

Large rufous and brown owl of tropical n, in rainforest and also some city parks. More squat than Powerful Owl with shorter tail. **Voice:** slow, low-pitched, double hoot similar to Powerful Owl.

Ad: Qld.

Ad: NT and Kimberley, richer colour than darker ssp in Qld.

BARKING OWL ◑ 41 cm
Ninox connivens

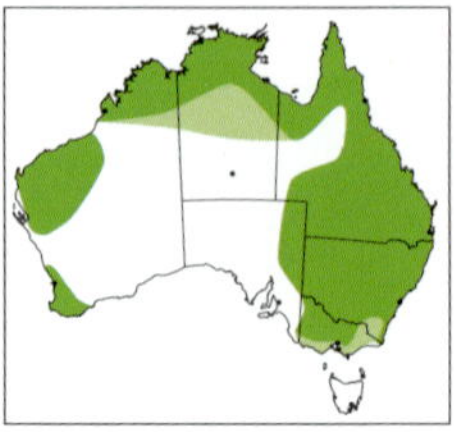

Ad: n and nw Aus, smaller, paler with warmer-toned streaking. Compare with Australian Boobook.

Ad: e and s Aus.

Fast and agile flight on long wings.

Medium-sized, cool-grey owl of open forest, woodland, treed watercourses, farmland and city parks in the n. **Voice:** regular, dog-like bark *woof-woof* and a rarely heard long, wavering scream.

AUSTRALIAN BOOBOOK ◔ 32 cm
Ninox boobook

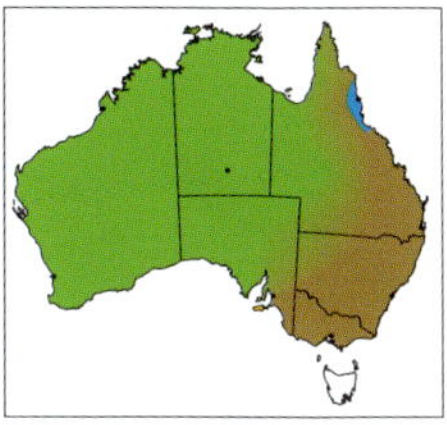

● **Ad**

● **Ad:** sw and c Aus, rich rufous.

● **Ad:** n Aus, reduced, paler patterning.

Small brown owl with large head, blackish patch around each eye, regional variation in plumage. Occupies all treed habitats of mainland Aus, often found roosting within dense foliage.
Voice: familiar double hoot *boo-book,* commonly heard shortly after dusk.

● **Ad:** dark reddish brown with densely spotted belly, but reduced spots on back. Rainforest specialist.

MOREPORK ◔ 32 cm
Ninox novaeseelandiae

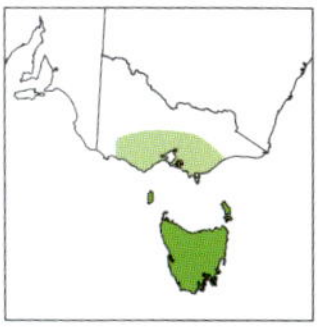

More densely spotted than Australian Boobook. Bright yellow eyes.

Ad

Some migrate to s Vic in winter.
Voice: as for Australian Boobook.

AUSTRALIAN OWLET-NIGHTJAR ◔ 22 cm
Aegotheles cristatus

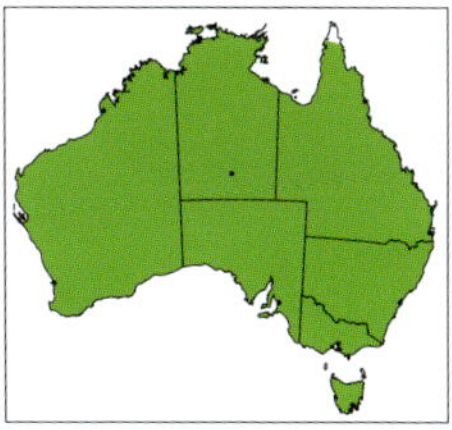

Small, dainty, nocturnal insectivore, roosts in hollow by day. Widespread in most treed environments, common in drier woodlands, avoids rainforest. Many plumage morphs.
Voice: loud *chirr* repeated 2–3 times, often at dusk, occasionally during day from hollow.

Large eye, short, broad-based bill.

WHITE-THROATED NIGHTJAR ◔ 32 cm
Eurostopodus mystacalis

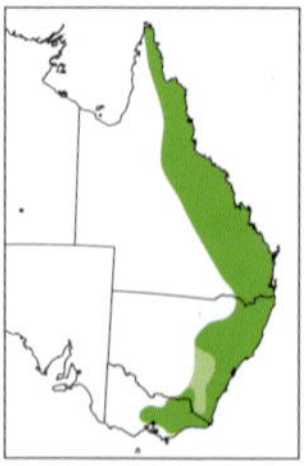

In flight most often seen hawking over forest road or clearing. No white panels in wing or tail.

Juv: darker throat and chest than Spotted.

Our largest and darkest nightjar, crepuscular and nocturnal forest dweller. By day roosts on ground in leaf litter. Folded wings reach almost to tail tip.
Voice: weird laugh, accelerating and ascending staccato gobble.

SPOTTED NIGHTJAR ◑ 31 cm
Eurostopodus argus

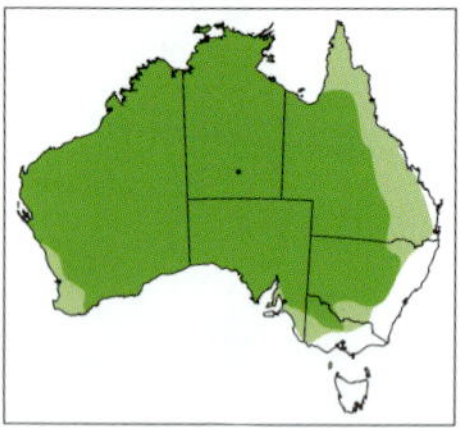

In flight found hawking over track or clearing, note prominent white patch in outerwing.

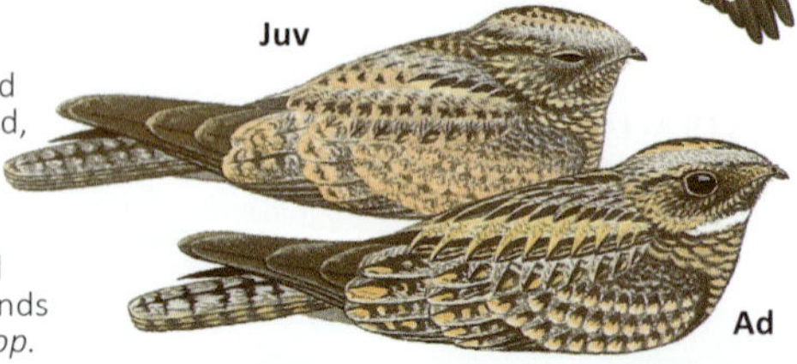

Dry country nightjar, crepuscular and nocturnal often found sitting on road, bright eye shine in car headlights. Roosts on ground, tail reaches well past folded wing tip.
Voice: weird laugh, accelerating and ascending, ending with gurgling sounds *coor caw caw … dipdop dipdop dipdop.*

LARGE-TAILED NIGHTJAR ◑ 26 cm
Caprimulgus macrurus

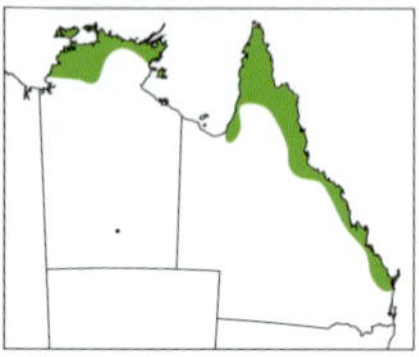

Wet tropical environments. Crepuscular and nocturnal,roosts on ground in leaf litter. Feeds over clearings and forest edges.

Ad ♀: cream patches.

Ad ♂: prominent white patches in outerwing and tail.

Voice: loud, repeated *chop chop chop* at ~1 sec intervals, often given from exposed perch.

TAWNY FROGMOUTH ◕ 42 cm
Podargus strigoides

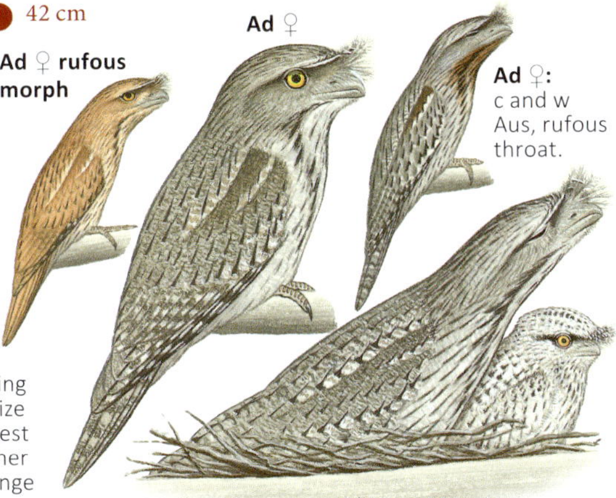

Ad ♀ rufous morph

Ad ♀

Ad ♀: c and w Aus, rufous throat.

Ad ♂: with nestling. ♂ typically has coarser patterning and less brown on shoulder and back than ♀.

Familiar, much loved nightbird. By day perches in rather open position, relying on camouflage. Variable in size and colour across Aus, smallest in n. Shorter tail than the other two frogmouths. Yellow-orange eye, black-streaked breast. **Voice:** soft continuous *oom oom oom* repeated over long period.

PAPUAN FROGMOUTH ◑ 55 cm
Podargus papuensis

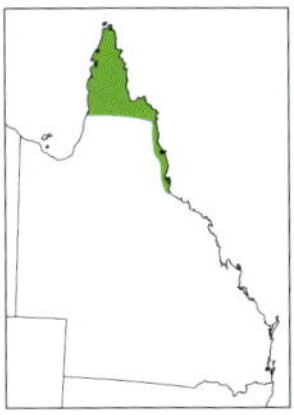

Ad ♀: less coarsely patterned and warmer toned.

Ad ♂: darker morph.

Ad ♂: large white spots on wing coverts.

Very large with big head and bill, red eye, and relatively long tail (half total length). Rainforest and tropical scrub, also mangroves. Usually roosts behind dense vegetation. **Voice:** as for Tawny Frogmouth but slower and deeper.

MARBLED FROGMOUTH ○ 37 cm
Podargus ocellatus

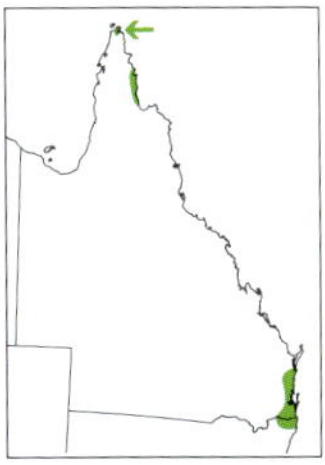

Two ssp well separated geographically.

Ad ♂: n Cape York.

Orange eye and long forehead plumes.

Ad ♀: n Cape York, rufous morph.

Ad ♂: se Qld.

Small to medium-sized rainforest frogmouth, long graduated tail. **Voice:** monotonous *whoor-loo* recalling cuckoo, nightjar-like rapid bubbling and falling gobble, ending with loud popping sounds (bill clapping).

PALM COCKATOO ◔ 56 cm
Probosciger aterrimus

Huge, all black. Active and conspicuous in pairs or small groups. Rainforest and tropical woodland.
Voice: loud, disyllable whistle, the second note drawn out with an upward inflection.

RED-TAILED BLACK-COCKATOO ◑ 57 cm
Calyptorhynchus banksii

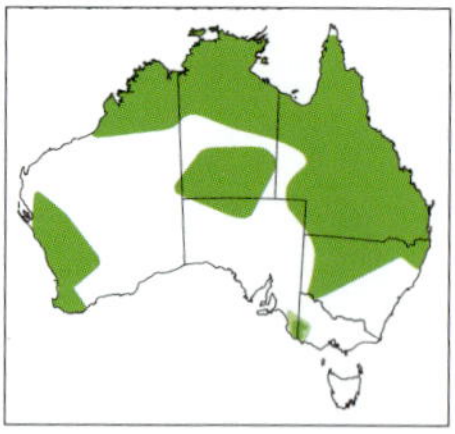

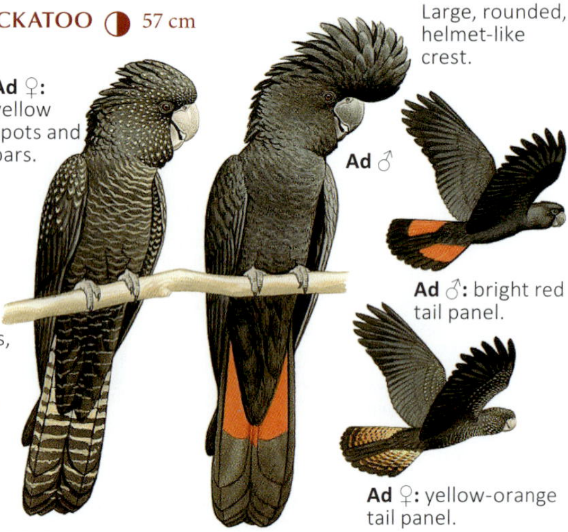

Large, noisy flocks in a wide range of treed habitats, including monsoon woodland, tall eucalypt forest, semi-arid woodland and savanna.
Voice: a rolling, grating *krurr-rurr-kee*, often given in flight, also squeaky whistling sounds.

GLOSSY BLACK-COCKATOO ◔ 48 cm
Calyptorhynchus lathami

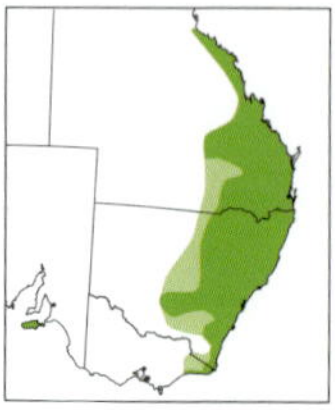

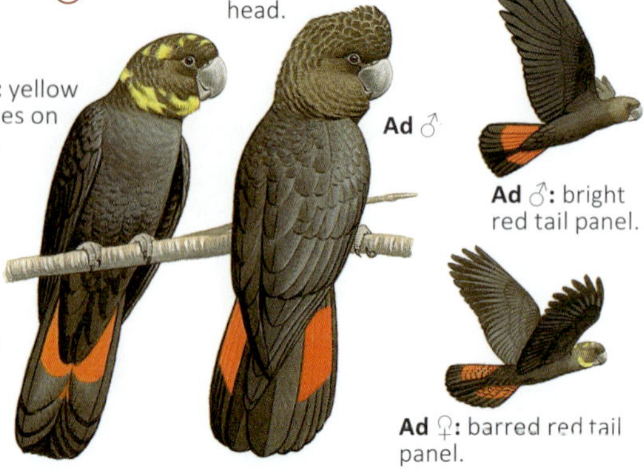

Small black-cockatoo. Diet confined to seeds of she-oaks in forest, heath and on coast.
Voice: metallic *tarr-red* often given in flight, softly while feeding.

YELLOW-TAILED BLACK-COCKATOO ◕ 60 cm
Zanda funereus

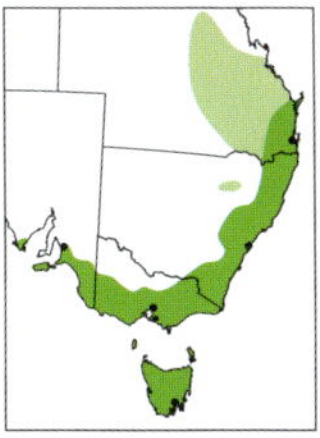

Long-tailed, black cockatoo of eucalypt forest, coastal *Banksia* woodland, heath and pine plantations. Feeds in trees and shrubs. Mostly eats seeds but supplements with insect larvae. Majestic, buoyant flight, deep, slow wing beats. **Voice:** sad, wailing cry *weer-lew* usually given in flight.

♂ has clearer yellow tail panel than ♀.

Gouges trees to extract borers.

CARNABY'S BLACK-COCKATOO ◑ 55 cm
Zanda latirostris

Similar to Yellow-tailed. Found mostly in wheatbelt eucalypt woodland, mallee, heath and pine plantations. Feeds in trees and shrubs, also spilt grain on ground. **Voice:** sad, wailing cry *whee-la,* more drawn out and more clearly disyllabic than Baudin's.

BAUDIN'S BLACK-COCKATOO ◑ 54 cm
Zanda baudinii

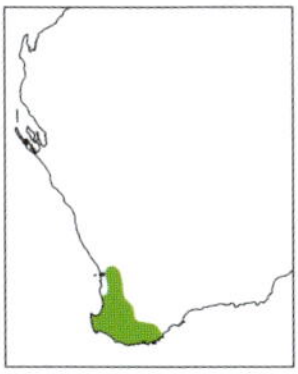

Difficult to separate from Carnaby's. Inhabits wetter, taller forests. Uses elongated bill to extract seeds from eucalypt fruit.

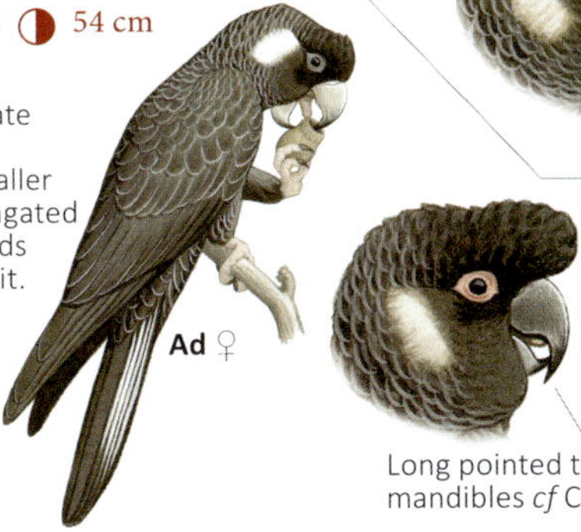

Voice: slightly shorter wailing cry, more clipped than Carnaby's.

Long pointed tips to both mandibles *cf* Carnaby's.

MAJOR MITCHELL'S COCKATOO 39 cm
Lophochroa leadbeateri

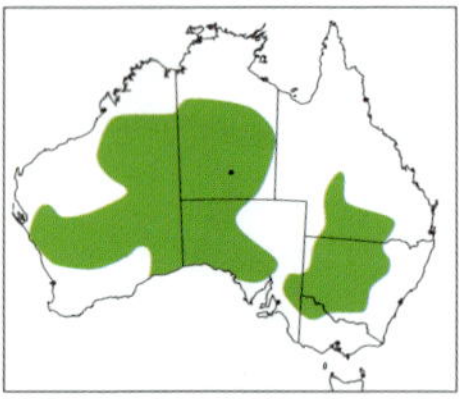

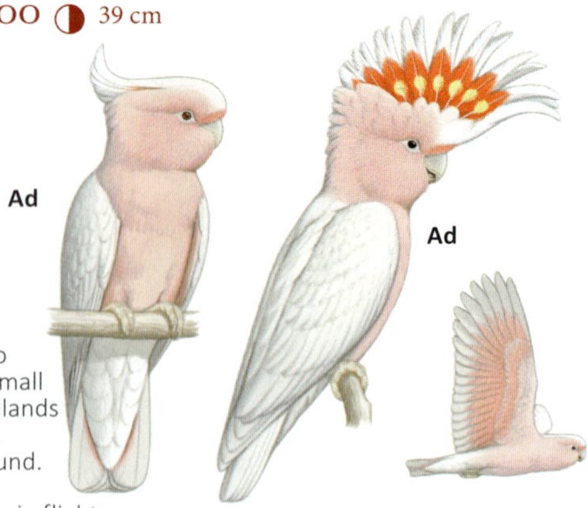

Gorgeous pink and white cockatoo with flamboyant crest. Pairs and small groups in arid and semi-arid woodlands of mallee, mulga and callitris pine. Feeds in trees, bushes and on ground. **Voice:** a 3-note, slightly subdued falsetto *creek-ery-cree,* often given in flight.

GALAH 35 cm
Eolophus roseicapilla

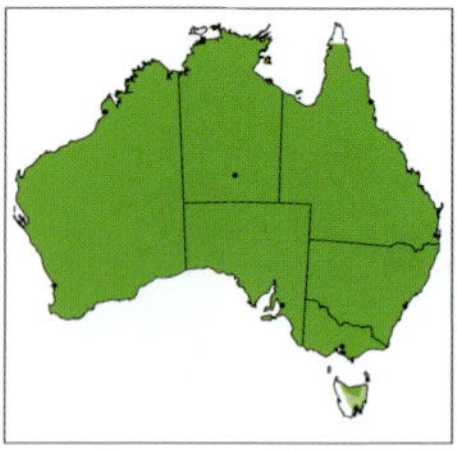

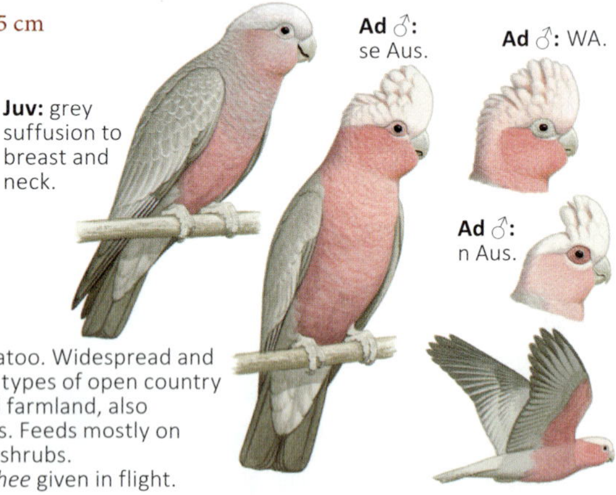

Familiar pink and grey cockatoo. Widespread and common in noisy flocks. All types of open country from arid interior to coastal farmland, also suburban parks and gardens. Feeds mostly on ground but occasionally on shrubs.
Voice: loud, strident *chee chee* given in flight.

GANG-GANG COCKATOO 34 cm
Callocephalon fimbriatum

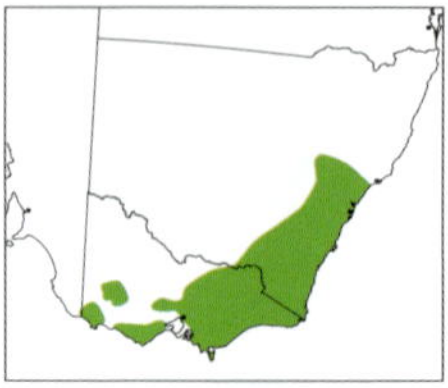

Small, stocky, forest cockatoo with wispy crest. In small, mobile groups in temperate eucalypt forest. Partial altitudinal migrant moving to foothills and cities in winter. Very approachable when feeding in trees or bushes.
Voice: slow, creaking, scratchy 'rusty hinge'.

LONG-BILLED CORELLA ● 40 cm
Cacatua tenuirostris

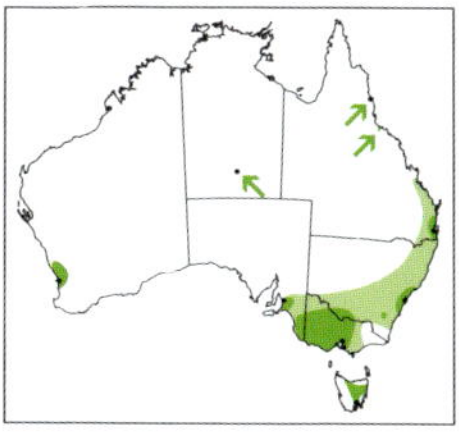

Short-tailed cockatoo with short, blunt crest. Gathers in large flocks in grassy open eucalyptus woodland, agricultural areas, parks and semi-urban habitats. **Voice:** wavering *curr-ur-up* given in flight.

Ad: red face and crescent across throat, long bill.

Narrower wings than other corellas, quicker, more agile flight.

Feeds on ground digging for tubers with elongated upper mandible.

LITTLE CORELLA ● 37 cm
Cacatua sanguinea

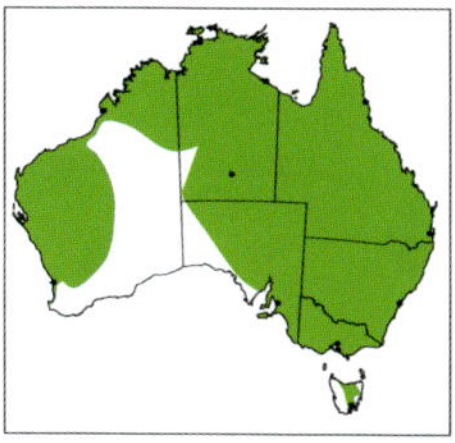

Smallest corella. Large noisy flocks in a wide variety of habitats from monsoonal forest, swamps and mangroves, to semi-arid grassland, farmland, parks and urban areas. Feeds on ground but also in trees and bushes. **Voice:** as for Long-billed Corella.

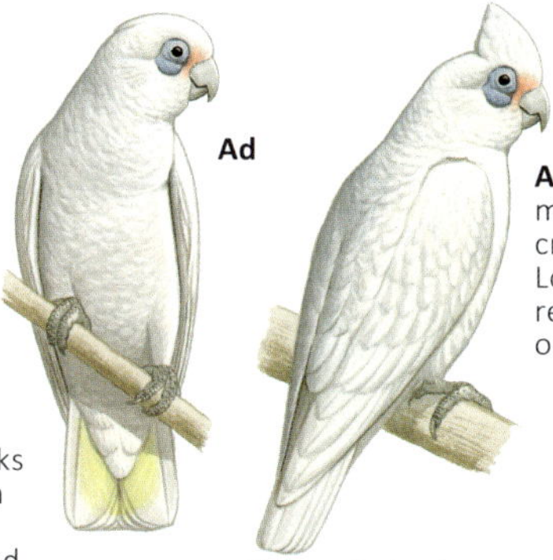

Ad

Ad: taller, more-pointed crest than Long-billed, red-pink only on face.

Slower flight than Long-billed Corella on broader wings.

WESTERN CORELLA ◑ 42 cm
Cacatua pastinator

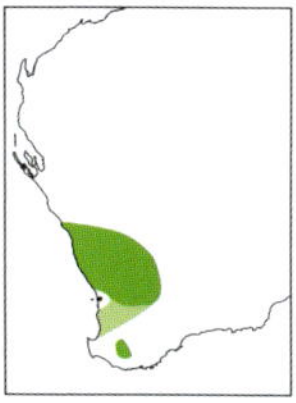

Compared to Little Corella note tall, pointed crest, bulkier body with rather big head and elongated upper mandible.

Largest corella. Ssp *pastinator* mostly in part-cleared farmland with tall trees, ssp *derbyi* in semi-arid wheatbelt, sometimes in mixed flock with Little Corella. Feeds on ground, digging for tubers with elongated upper mandible. **Voice:** as for other Corellas.

Ad: smallest in n.

Ad: larger in s.

Note rather upright posture when perched.

SULPHUR-CRESTED COCKATOO ● 51 cm

Cacatua galerita

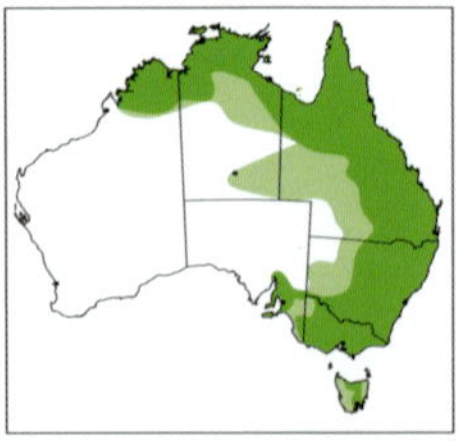

Ad

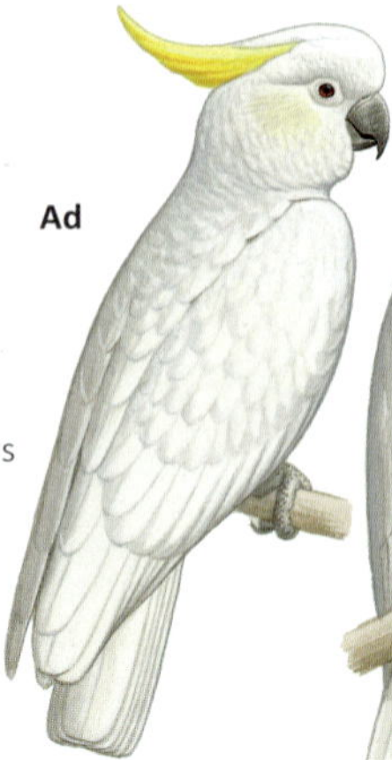

Ad

Conspicuous, large, noisy, white cockatoo. Gregarious in small to large flocks, in most forest types, also treed farmland and urban parks and gardens. Feeds in canopy, on bushes and on ground.
Voice: very loud, harsh screeches ending with an upward inflection.

In flight, rapid rather stiff wing beats, often a brief pause after every three beats.

DOUBLE-EYED FIG-PARROT ◐ 14 cm

Cyclopsitta diophthalma

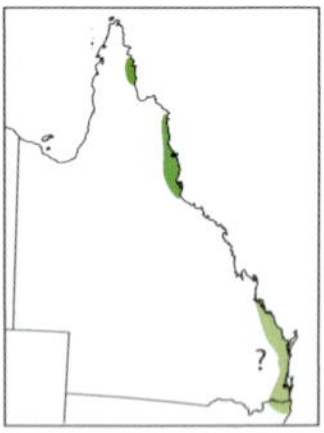

Ad ♂: n Cape York.

Ad ♀: n Cape York.

Pale underwings.

Ad ♂: Wet Tropics s Cape York.

Ad ♀: Wet Tropics s Cape York.

Tiny, dumpy-bodied parrot of rainforest, gallery forest, mangroves, gardens and isolated fruiting figs. Unobtrusive when feeding, sometimes allowing a close approach. Southern ssp Coxen's Fig-Parrot likely extinct.
Voice: a sharp, piercing, metallic *tzing tzing*.

VARIED LORIKEET ◐ 19 cm

Psitteuteles versicolor

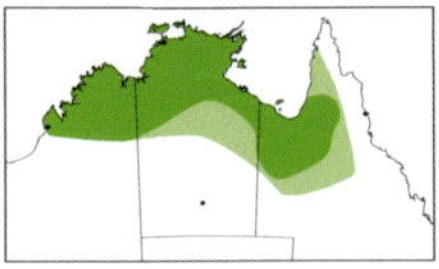

Small, pastel-coloured, blossom nomad with fine yellow streaking and white skin around eye.

Juv

Ad ♂

In small flocks on flowering eucalypts and paperbarks.
Voice: incessant, shrill, high-pitched screeching.

RAINBOW LORIKEET ● 30 cm

Trichoglossus moluccanus

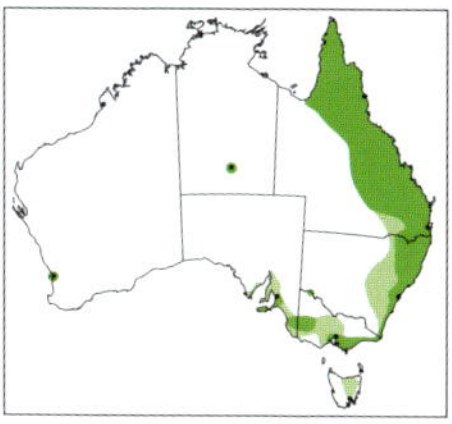

Large and colourful, our most familiar lorikeet in many towns and cities. Noisy flocks locally abundant where flowering trees and shrubs provide nectar flows.

Voice: loud metallic screeches, also clear melodious whistles.

RED-COLLARED LORIKEET ◕ 30 cm

Trichoglossus rubritorquis

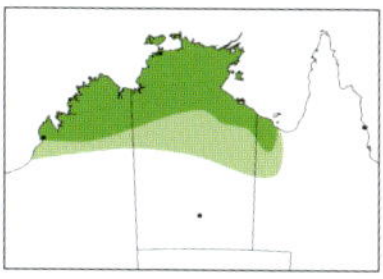

Ecological equivalent of Rainbow Lorikeet in the Top End and Kimberley. Differs by orange hindneck, blue mantle and blackish belly.

Voice: as for Rainbow Lorikeet.

SCALY-BREASTED LORIKEET ◕ 24 cm

Trichoglossus chlorolepidotus

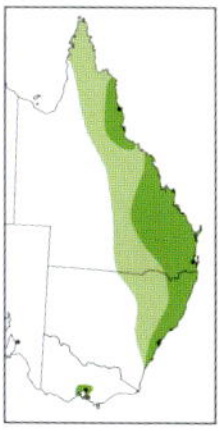

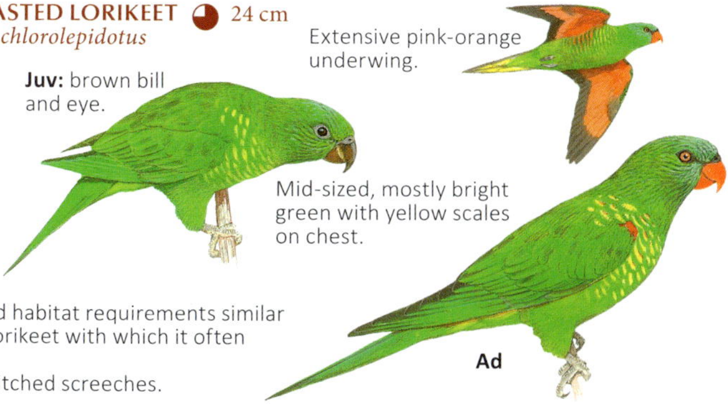

Behaviour and habitat requirements similar to Rainbow Lorikeet with which it often associates.

Voice: high-pitched screeches.

LITTLE LORIKEET ◔ 17 cm
Parvipsitta pusilla

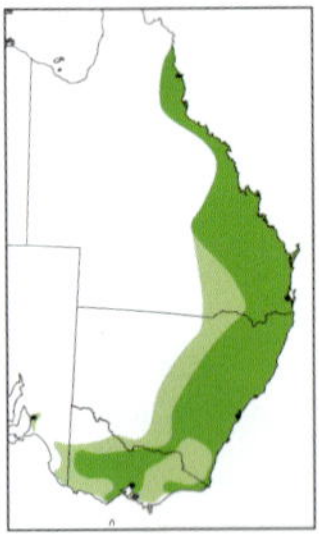

Smallest Aus lorikeet. Bright green with red face, green underwing coverts. Feeds in canopy of flowering eucalypts where can be difficult to see within foliage due to small size.

Juv: face dull, bill pale, lacks bronze mantle of Ad.

Voice: thin, sharp, shrill *zit-zit-zit* given incessantly in flight. Constant high-pitched feeding chatter.

PURPLE-CROWNED LORIKEET ◑ 18 cm
Parvipsitta porphyrocephala

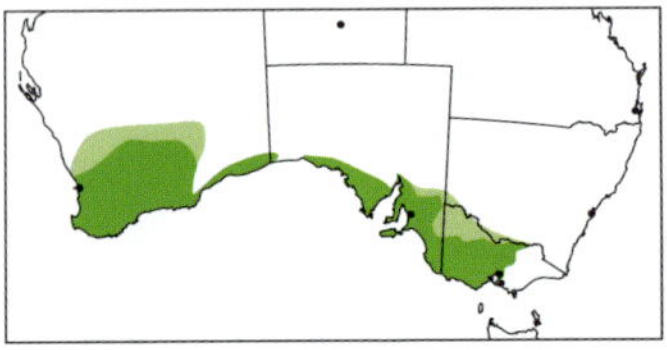

Juv: face dull, lacks bronze mantle of Ad.

Small lorikeet with leaden purple crown, red underwing coverts seen in good views in flight. Similar in form and behaviour to Little Lorikeet but has proportionately longer tail. Inhabits dry open forest, woodland and mallee, where eucalypts are in flower. Commonly in town parks and gardens, can be rather tame when feeding.

Voice: harsh *tsit-tsit-tsit* not as shrill or metallic as Little Lorikeet. Constant high-pitched feeding chatter softer than Little Lorikeet.

MUSK LORIKEET ◕ 21 cm
Glossopsitta concinna

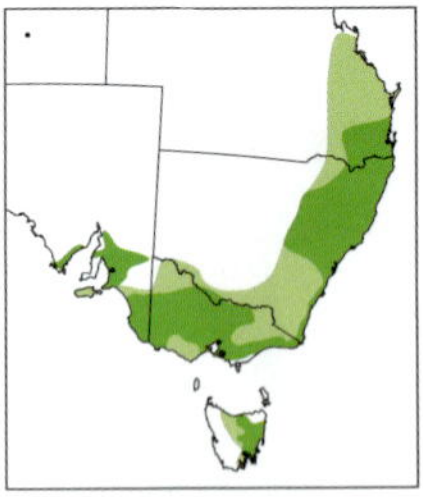

Juv: reduced blue on head, brown bill, lacks bronze mantle.

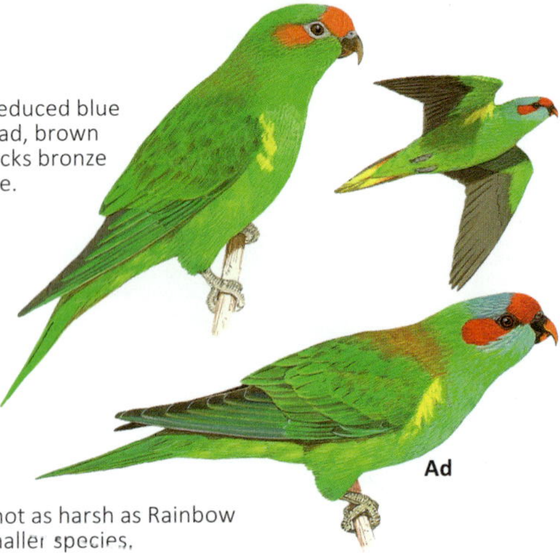

Mid-sized, stocky build. Noisy flocks in forest, woodland, treed farmland and urban areas where eucalypts are in flower. Occasionally seen in backyard apple trees eating fruit.

Voice: constant shrill screeching not as harsh as Rainbow Lorikeet or as sharp as the two smaller species.

ECLECTUS PARROT ◔ 45 cm
Eclectus roratus

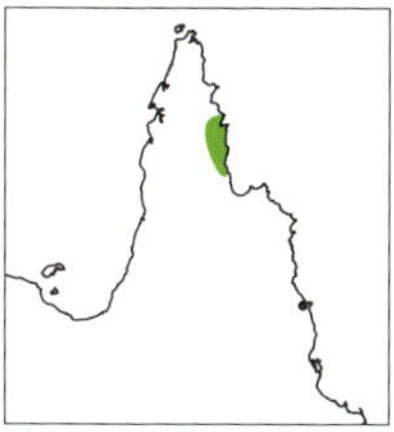

Large and robust, brilliant plumage and reverse sexual dimorphism with ♀ brighter than ♂. Only found in rainforest.
Voice: ear-splitting, 2-note screech, also mellow flute-like whistle.

Ad ♀

Ad ♂

Ad ♀

RED-CHEEKED PARROT ◔ 23 cm
Geoffroyus geoffroyi

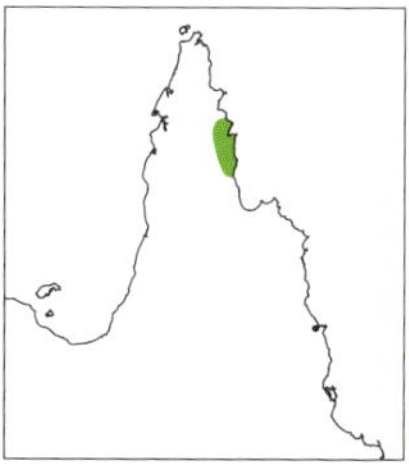

Only found in rainforest. Feeds high in canopy where difficult to see.
Voice: loud metallic *aark-aark-aark*.

Ad ♀**:** brown head.

Ad ♂**:** pastel blue and red head.

Blue underwing coverts.

SWIFT PARROT ◔ 25 cm
Lathamus discolor

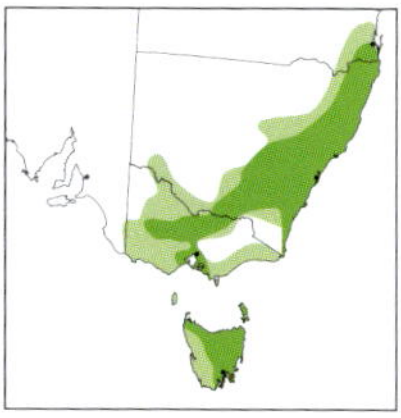

Nectivorous. Breeds only in Tas, migrates to mainland in winter where wanders widely searching for flowering eucalypts. Also gleans lerps and honeydew from leaves.
Voice: mellow, disyllabic, tinkling *chit chit*.

Juv: subdued plumage.

In flight, long, narrow tail, red underwing coverts.

Ad ♂

CRIMSON ROSELLA ● 36 cm
Platycercus elegans

All rosellas have an undulating flight style with rapid shallow wing beats interspersed with brief glides.

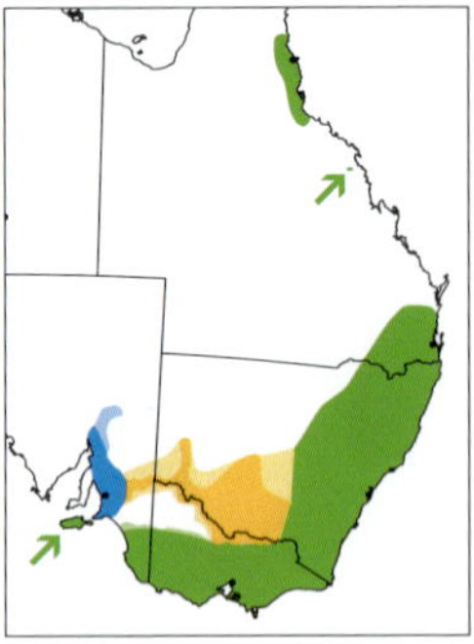

The three morphological groups hybridise readily along their interface zones.

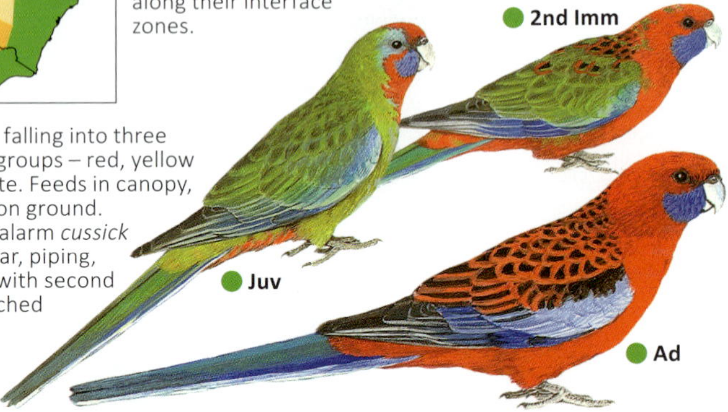

Highly variable, falling into three morphological groups – red, yellow and intermediate. Feeds in canopy, on bushes and on ground. **Voice:** strident alarm *cussick cussick*, also clear, piping, 3-note whistle with second note higher-pitched *kink-kwee-kink*.

Crimson Rosella (ssp *elegans, nigrescens, melanoptera*): widespread in moist forest, woodland, treed farmland, orchards, town parks and gardens. In Qld and ne NSW mainly in wet forest at higher altitude. In s occurs at all altitudes and in greater variety of habitats.

Ssp *nigrescens*: of far n rainforests, smaller and darker. Juv plumage resembles that of Ad.

Yellow Rosella (ssp *flaveolus*): closely associated with River Red Gum forest on floodplains of the Murray river system and associated Riverina Plains. Visits adjacent box and mallee eucalypt habitats and town parks and gardens.

Adelaide Rosella (ssp *fleurieuensis, subadelaidae*): inhabits open eucalypt forest, treed farmland, town parks and gardens. Common in Adelaide. Intermediate in appearance between crimson and yellow types. Yellower ssp *subadelaidae* in n merges with redder ssp *fleurieuensis* of the s, intermediate types found around Adelaide.

Ad: tip of Fleurieu Peninsula.

Ad: Flinders Ranges.

Ad: Adelaide and Mt Lofty Ranges.

GREEN ROSELLA
Platycercus caledonicus

36 cm

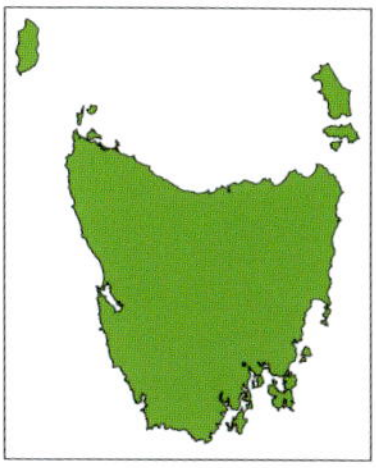

Large, solidly built, dark-backed rosella. Present in most wooded habitats in Tas, at all altitudes, also visits heathland, grassland, orchards and gardens. Feeds at all levels – canopy, shrub, ground.

Voice: alarm similar to Crimson but slightly less raucous *cussick cussick,* also clear, piping, 3-note whistle with second note higher-pitched *kink-kwee-kink.*

Ad ♀: orange-red on throat.

Ad ♂

EASTERN ROSELLA 30 cm
Platycercus eximius

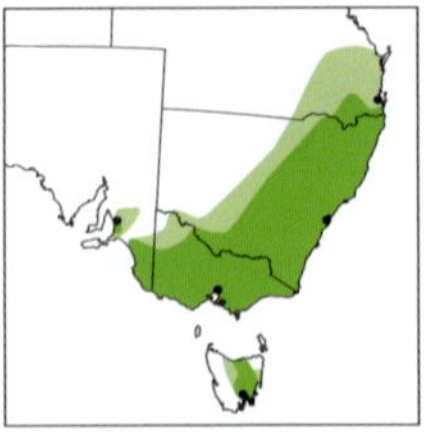

Common in lightly treed country: woodland, forest edge, treed farmland, parks and gardens. In pairs and small family groups. Feeds at all levels – canopy, shrub, ground. **Voice:** loud repeated clinking *chit chit* or *chit chit chut*. Also a piping *pwink pwink*, a 3-note whistle with emphasis on the 1st note and fast chatter.

PALE-HEADED ROSELLA 31 cm
Platycercus adscitus

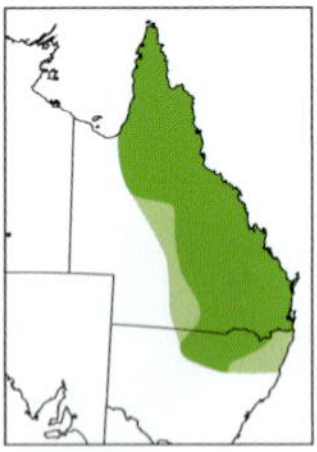

Mostly in lowland open country: woodland, treed farmland, edges of coastal swamp forest, parks and gardens. Pairs and small family groups. Feeds at all levels – canopy, shrub, ground. **Voice:** as for Eastern Rosella.

NORTHERN ROSELLA 30 cm
Platycercus venustus

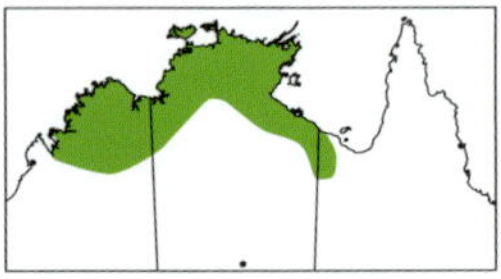

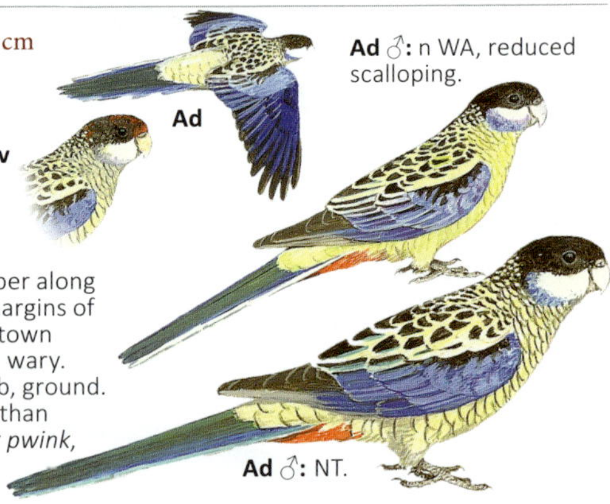

Tropical woodland, savanna, timber along streams, often in hilly country, margins of monsoon forest. Occasionally in town parks and gardens, but quiet and wary. Feeds at all levels – canopy, shrub, ground. **Voice:** loud *chit chit* less clinking than Eastern. Also a fast ringing *pwink pwink*, 3-note whistle with emphasis on the 1st note and fast chatter.

WESTERN ROSELLA ◕ 27 cm

Platycercus icterotis

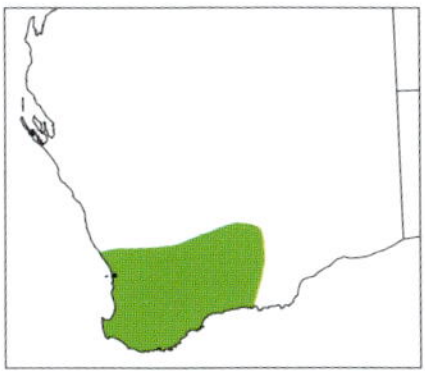

Smallest rosella and only one in s WA. Quiet and easily overlooked in a variety of forest, treed farmland and parks. Two ssp differ in both plumage and habitat preference. Ssp *icterotis* of wetter forest of the sw; less red, rump green. Ssp *xanthogenys* in remnant woodland and dry forest of the WA Wheatbelt; extensively red with blue tail and rump. A broad hybrid zone occurs from Perth to Albany. Feeds at all levels – canopy, shrub, ground.
Voice: soft bell-like *quink-quink*; however, often rather quiet.

RED-CAPPED PARROT ◑ 36 cm

Purpureicephalus spurius

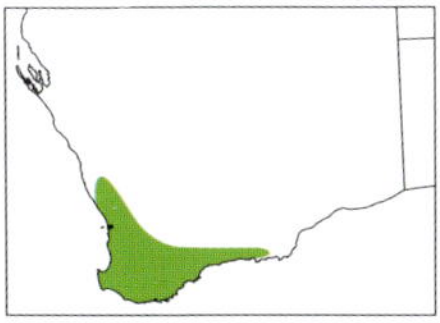

Unique, long-tailed parrot of tall eucalypt forest and woodland, roadside remnants and city parks. Elongated upper mandible specialised to extract seeds from large-fruited eucalypts, especially Marri. Also feeds quietly on ground where can be surprisingly difficult to see.
Voice: metallic *checkacheck* or *krakk-rak*.

PRINCESS PARROT ○ 42 cm
Polytelis alexandrae

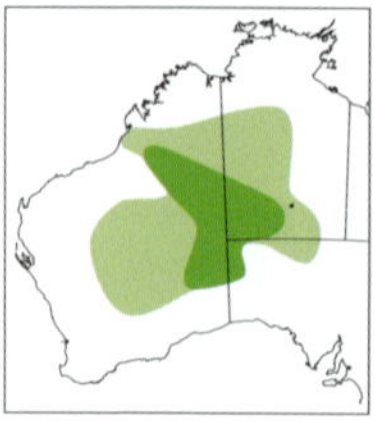

Elegant and elusive desert nomad with very long tail. Follows rainfall in w and c deserts, core distribution Great Sandy Desert.

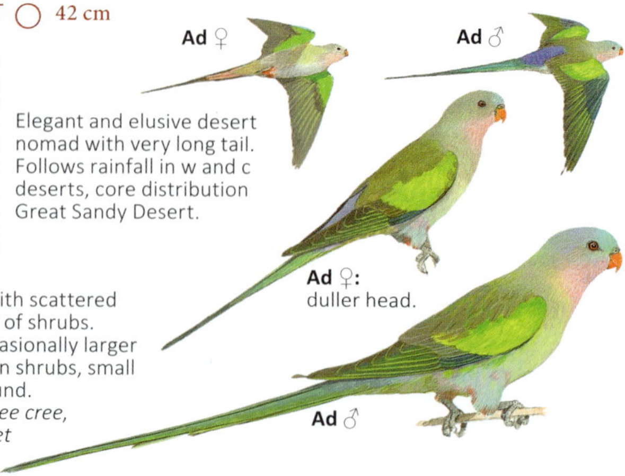

Sand dune country with scattered trees and good cover of shrubs. Small groups and occasionally larger aggregations. Feeds in shrubs, small trees and on the ground.
Voice: far-carrying *cree cree*, also sharp *queet queet* when disturbed.

REGENT PARROT ◑ 41 cm
Polytelis anthopeplus

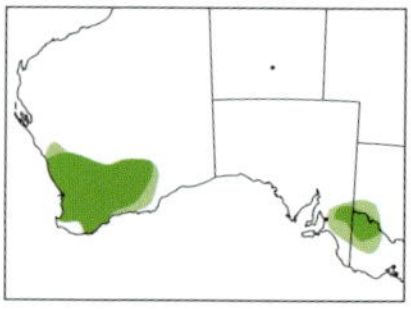

Flight fast and graceful, prefers to fly low over vegetation, black wing contrasting with yellow body.

Long-tailed, black and yellow parrot. Small groups in dry woodland, mallee and farmland with corridors of trees. Feeds in trees, shrubs and on the ground. Roosts and nests in larger trees like River Red Gum.
Voice: rolling harsh *carrack carrack* mostly given in flight.

SUPERB PARROT ◑ 40 cm
Polytelis swainsonii

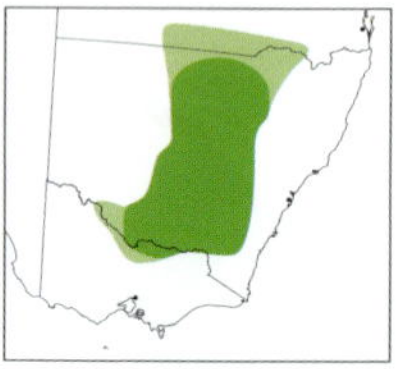

Flight fast and graceful.

Brilliant green parrot. Small flocks in woodland and treed farmland on inland slopes of NSW, also forests on riverine plains of c Murray-Darling Basin. Feeds on ground or in trees and shrubs eating seeds.
Voice: loud, rolling, grating *cureet cureet* mostly given in flight.

AUSTRALIAN KING-PARROT ◕ 42 cm

Alisterus scapularis

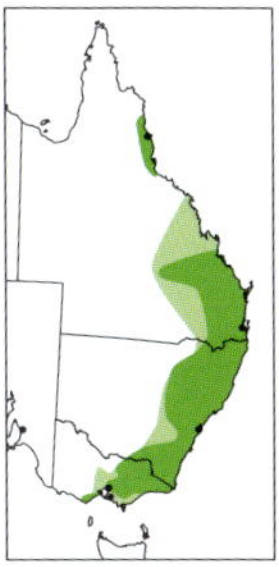

Big red and green parrot of tall wet eucalypt forest, rainforest, adjacent treed farmland and town gardens. Graceful, buoyant flight, languid wing beats with flicking rhythm, doesn't undulate like Crimson Rosella with which it often associates.

Pairs and small flocks feed in trees, shrubs and on ground, can become very tame where food is provided. **Voice:** high-pitched *chack chack*, also single clear whistle.

RED-WINGED PARROT ◕ 32 cm

Aprosmictus erythropterus

Brilliant green with shortish tail. Buoyant flight, deep, languid wing beats, frequently jinks from side to side, weaving through open woodland.

Found in a broad range of tropical and subtropical habitats: rainforest edges, mangroves and dry shrubland with scattered trees in the interior. Pairs, small groups feed in canopy or on large bushes. **Voice:** loud, metallic *crillic crillic*, harsh screeches.

COCKATIEL ◕ 30 cm

Nymphicus hollandicus

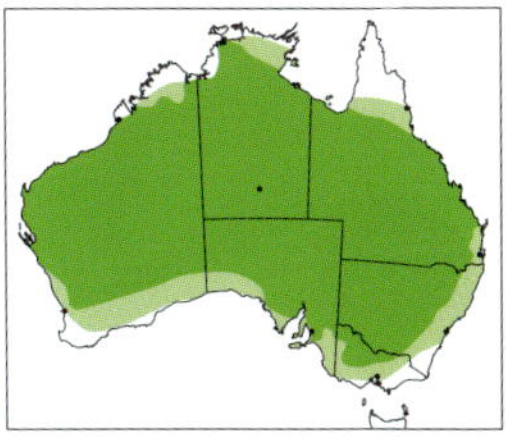

Distinctive grey 'parrot' with oversized crest. Flocks common across much of the inland. Along treed creeklines and in open grassy woodland, avoids treeless deserts. Feeds on ground. **Voice:** loud *queel queel* or *wheero*, alarm call is a low *wee-urp*.

Flight swift, strong and graceful with flicked wing beats. White shoulders, dark underwings and stepped tail obvious.

BUDGERIGAR ◕ 18 cm
Melopsittacus undulatus

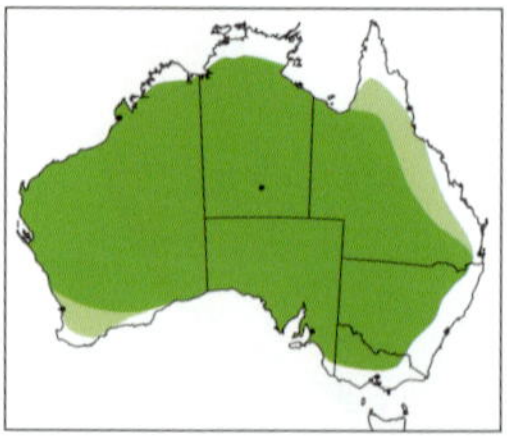

Very familiar, vivid green small parrot. Arid and semi-arid grassy habitats with scattered trees, especially along creeklines of inland. Feeds on ground. **Voice:** musical warbling chatter.

Ad ♂: blue cere.

Ad ♀: brown cere.

Gregarious in mobile, dense flocks often in the thousands, flying with tightly coordinated twists and turns.

EASTERN GROUND PARROT ◔ 30 cm
Pezoporus wallicus

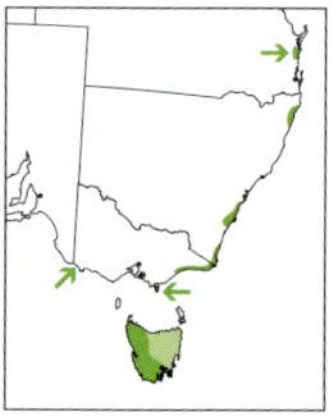

Long-tailed, terrestrial parrot within dense heath and sedgeland. Localised and near coast on mainland, more widespread and secure in Tas. Rarely seen unless flushed, then bursts away with rapid wing beats followed by a curving glide on bowed wings before plunging back to cover.

Voice: at dusk and dawn gives thin, mournful whistles *tee tee te-eee.*

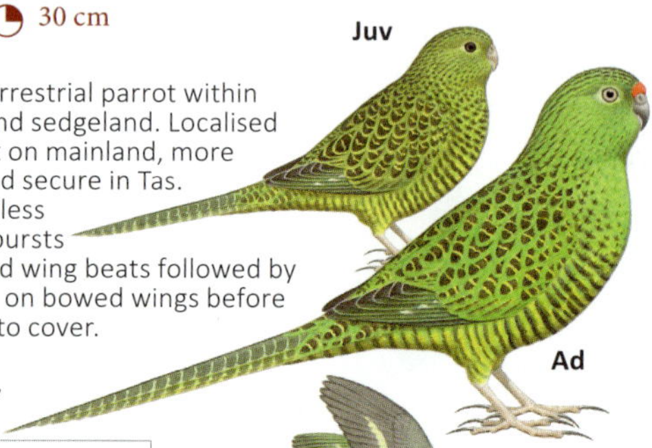

Juv

Ad

WESTERN GROUND PARROT ○ 30 cm
Pezoporus flaviventris

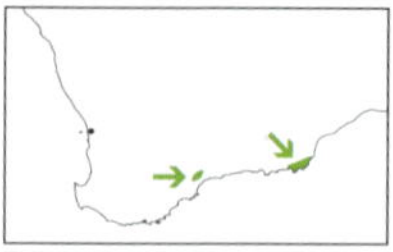

Like Eastern, but critically endangered and restricted to heath in Cape Arid National Park, WA.

In flight note long tail and slightly bowed wings.

NIGHT PARROT ○ 23 cm
Pezoporus occidentalis

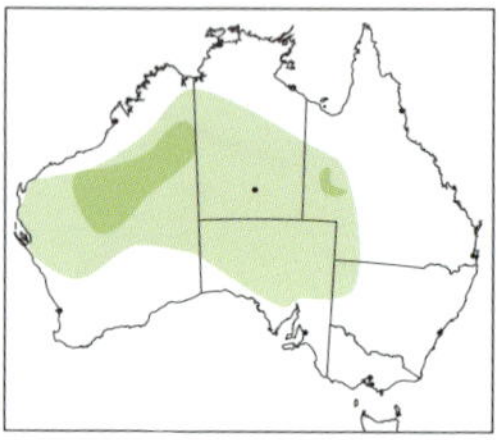

Juv: greyish with bold yellow belly.

Ad: sturdy and short-tailed green parrot with bold yellow belly.

Extremely rare and cryptic, terrestrial and nocturnal. Uses *Triodia* for roosting and nesting, with nearby chenopod habitats for feeding. **Voice:** mournful *deer dit deer dit* and hoarse whistle recalling Pallid Cuckoo with final inflection *pirrr-it.*

AUSTRALIAN RINGNECK ● 36 cm
Barnardius zonarius

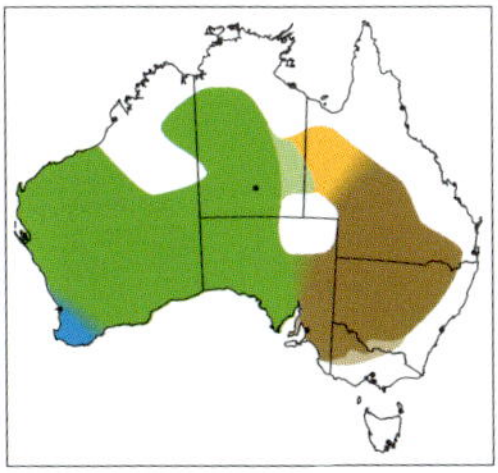

● Cloncurry Parrot

● Mallee Ringneck

Widespread species with four distinct ssp. Mostly open dry woodland with semi-arid scrub on plains or stony hill country, and along inland watercourses. Twenty-eight confined to wetter, tall, dense eucalypt forest in sw WA. Usually in pairs or family groups, feeds on ground. Ssp hybridise along narrow zones of intergradation.
Voice: Cloncurry and Mallee: bell-like piping *tink-tink-tink* and *pit-ink pit-ink*. Port Lincoln: 2-syllable *twen-ty*. Twenty-eight: 3-syllable *twen-ty-eight*.

● x ● **hybrid:**
Flinders Ranges SA.

● Twenty-eight Parrot

● Port Lincoln Parrot

BOURKE'S PARROT ◔ 21 cm
Neopsephotus bourkii

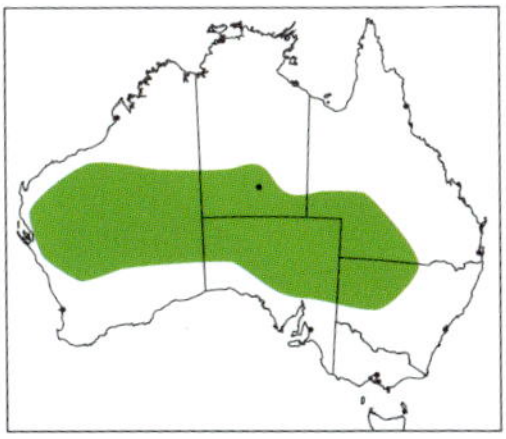

Small, pastel-coloured parrot of inland arid and semi-arid shrublands, especially mulga woodland.

Somewhat crepuscular, feeding on ground at the cooler ends of day and visiting water at dusk or in darkness after sunset. Usually spends most of the day quietly resting within cool, shady tree.
Voice: a pleasant *chu-wee* or *chirrup*, sharp alarm chatter *kik-kik-kik*.

Ad ♂

Juv: brown bill. **Ad** ♀ also shows reduced blue in face and wing but has black bill.

MULGA PARROT ◑ 27 cm
Psephotellus varius

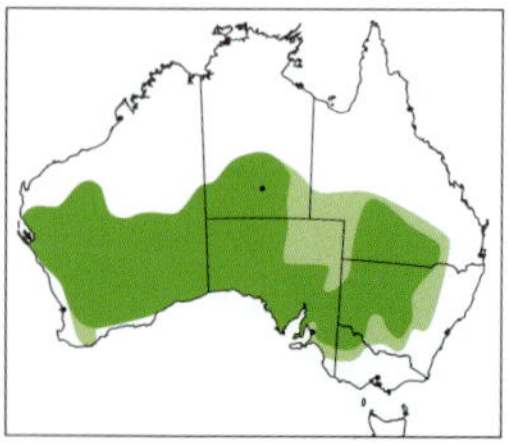

In semi-arid woodland and shrubland, including mallee, *Acacia* and sandplain shrubland. Pairs or family parties feed on ground. Flight swift and low with slight undulations. Can occur with Red-rumped Parrot near inland watercourses.
Voice: soft *sweet-sweet* repeated three or four times.

GOLDEN-SHOULDERED PARROT ○ 25 cm
Psephotellus chrysopterygius

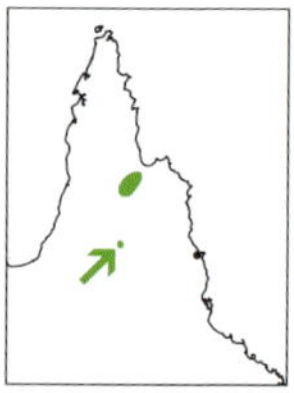

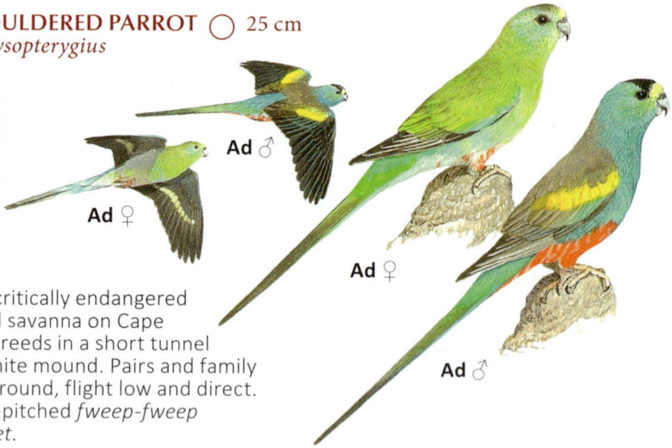

Highly localised critically endangered parrot of tropical savanna on Cape York Peninsula. Breeds in a short tunnel dug into tall termite mound. Pairs and family groups feed on ground, flight low and direct.
Voice: soft, high-pitched *fweep-fweep* and a sharp *wheet*.

HOODED PARROT ◔ 27 cm
Psephotellus dissimilis

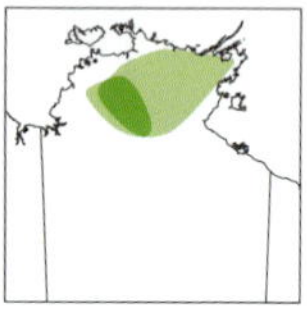

In monsoonal open forest, tropical woodland and savanna of the Top End of NT. Usually in pairs or family groups. Breeds in a short tunnel dug into tall termite mound. Pairs and family groups feed on ground, flight fast and direct, often above the canopy.
Voice: whistled *chu-weet chu-weet*, also shrill chatter.

RED-RUMPED PARROT ● 29 cm
Psephotus haematonotus

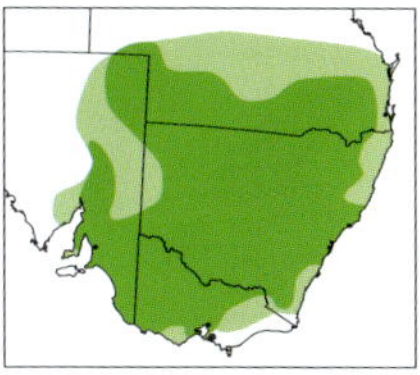

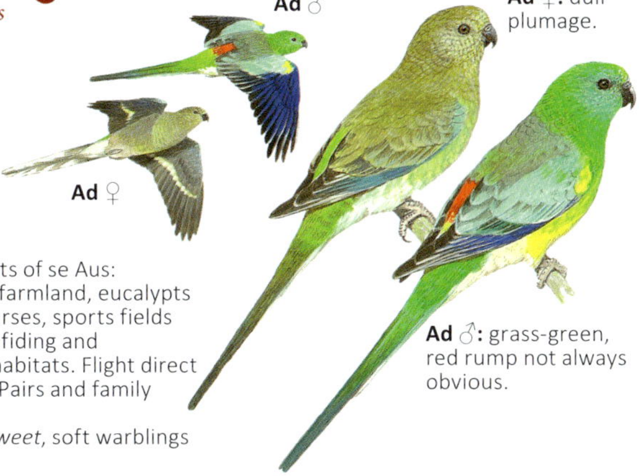

Common in open habitats of se Aus: grassy woodland, treed farmland, eucalypts lining roads or watercourses, sports fields and parkland. Often confiding and approachable in urban habitats. Flight direct with slight undulations. Pairs and family groups feed on ground.
Voice: a repeated *su-suweet*, soft warblings between pair.

EASTERN BLUE BONNET ◑ 30 cm
Northiella haematogaster

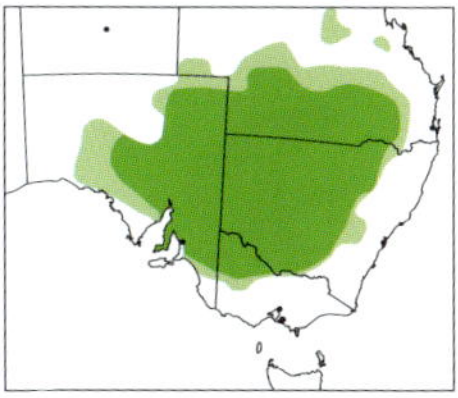

Mid-sized parrot of open dry woodlands, especially with bull-oak. Also sparsely treed arid and semi-arid shrubland often with saltbush, sparsely treed roadsides and farmland. Pairs or family groups feed on ground. Fast, undulating flight.
Voice: harsh *chack chack*, also rosella-like piping whistle.

NARETHA BLUE BONNET ◔ 29 cm
Northiella narethae

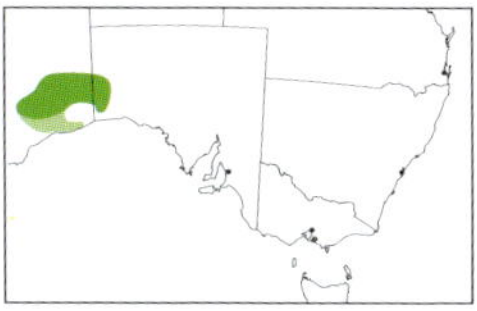

In open, arid shrubland fringing the Nullarbor Plain. Pairs and family groups.
Voice: more melodic and softer than Eastern Blue Bonnet, a flute-like *cloot-cloot*, loud harsh alarm call *yak-yak*.

ORANGE-BELLIED PARROT ◯ 23 cm
Neophema chrysogaster

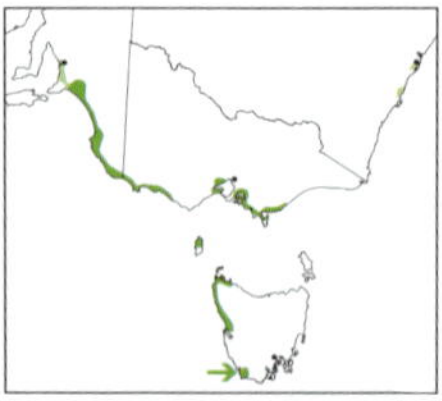

Small parrot close to extinction in wild, breeds only in sw Tas and winters along the Vic and se SA coast in saltmarsh, primary dunes or weedy pasture. Feeds on ground or in low shrubs.
Voice: when flushed gives a rapid buzz, in flight a single *zeet* at 1 sec intervals.

TURQUOISE PARROT ◐ 21 cm
Neophema pulchella

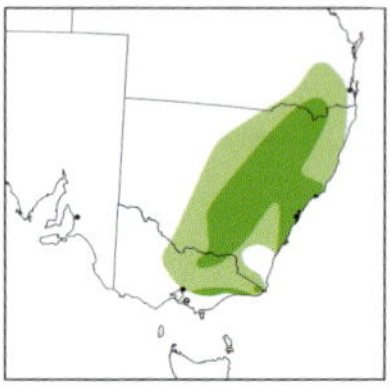

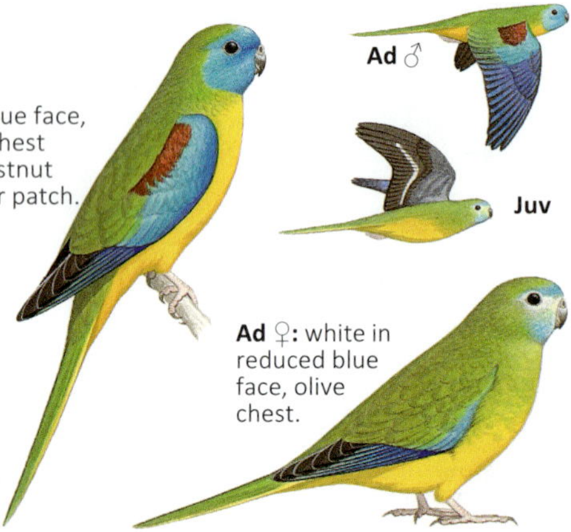

Bright olive-green and yellow small parrot of grassy or heathy open forest and woodland, mostly in foothills. Pairs and small groups feed on ground.
Voice: when flushed a rapid *zit-zit-zit*, in flight a sharp *tzeet tzeet*.

SCARLET-CHESTED PARROT ◯ 20 cm
Neophema splendida

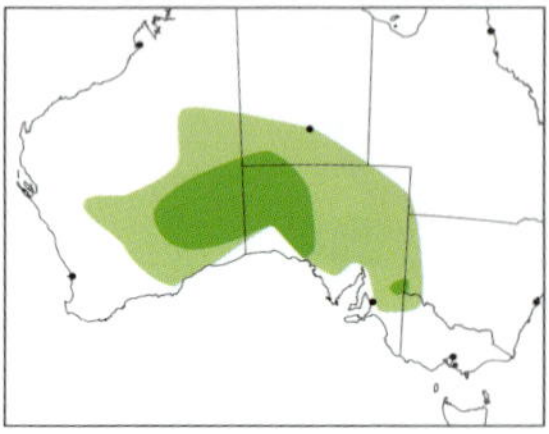

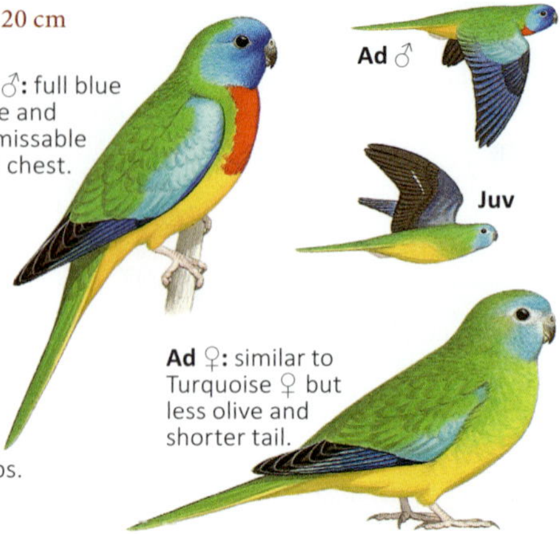

Bright green, shorter-tailed, small parrot of arid scrub, mallee and *Acacia* woodland. Pairs or small groups feed on ground or in low shrubs.
Voice: alarm call a clear whistled *kee-up*, in flight quiet soft chirrups.

BLUE-WINGED PARROT ◑ 22 cm
Neophema chrysostoma

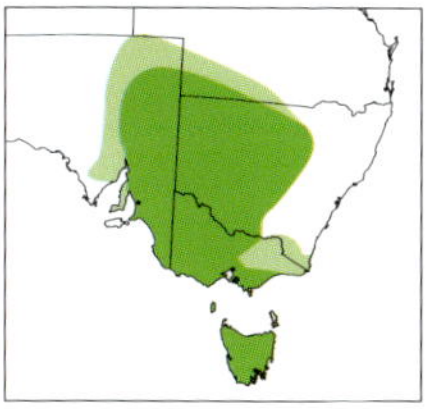

Ad ♂: extensive royal blue in wing, blue band on forehead does not extend behind eye, powdery blue on breast, *cf* Elegant Parrot.

Ad ♀: duller than ♂, less yellow in face.

Small, bluish-olive and yellow parrot. Feeds on ground in open woodland, grassland, saltmarsh, rough pasture. Post-breeding dispersal to more arid inland areas.
Voice: when flushed a staccato burst of *tsit tsit tsit*, in flight a repeated tinkling *tsleet-sleet*.

ELEGANT PARROT ◑ 23 cm
Neophema elegans

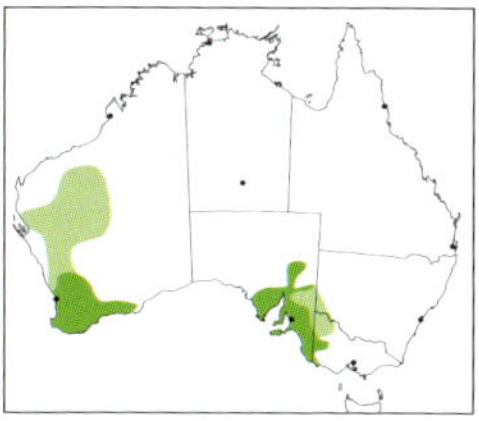

Ad ♂: 2-toned blue in wing less extensive than Blue-winged, blue band on forehead extends slightly beyond eye, body generally a richer golden-olive, longer tail.

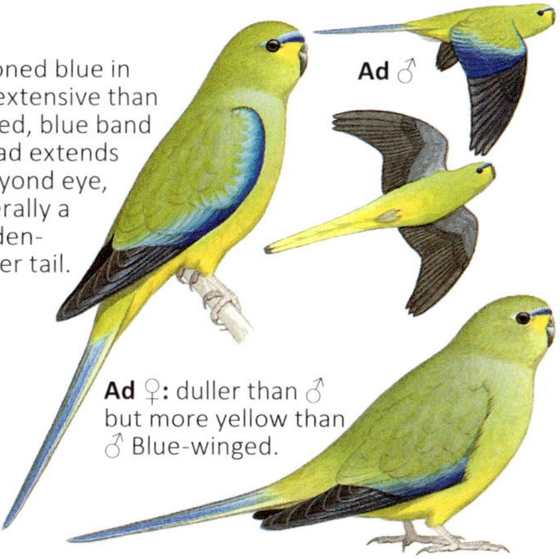

Ad ♀: duller than ♂ but more yellow than ♂ Blue-winged.

Bright yellow-olive small parrot easily confused with Blue-winged Parrot. Mostly in dryer country than Blue-winged, but both species may overlap in SA and w Vic.
Voice: similar to Blue-winged Parrot.

ROCK PARROT ◑ 23 cm
Neophema petrophila

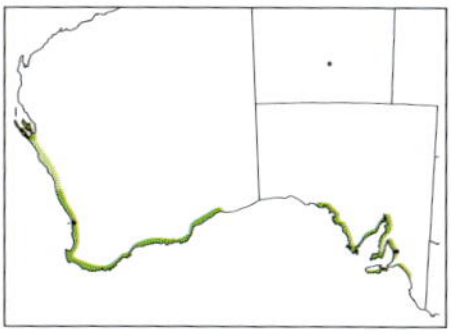

Ad ♂: royal-blue band on forehead joins small blue face mask, very narrow blue on wing.

Ad ♀: duller than ♂.

Small stocky, dull-olive parrot of coastal grassy herbfield and scrub, also rocky headlands and nearby islands. Feeds on ground in pairs or family groups.
Voice: when flushed a rapid, high-pitched *tseet-set tseet-set*, in flight a thin *sleet* at 1 sec intervals.

FERAL PIGEON 32 cm
Columba livia

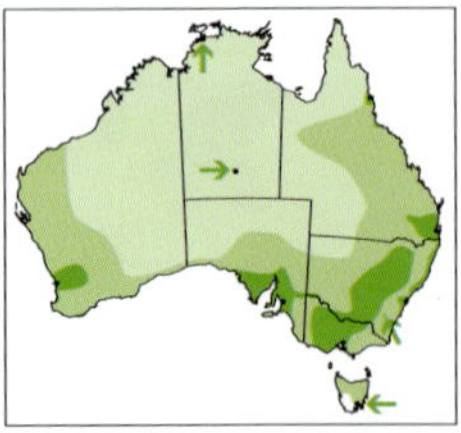

Introduced species. Feral flocks occur widely in cities and rural areas, especially grain-growing regions or where coastal cliffs provide nesting sites.

Many colour patterns but note two broad black wing bars and whitish rump.

Voice: series of deep, drawn-out coos. Courtship call a moaning *drruoo* or *coo-oo-co-cuu*.

LAUGHING DOVE 26 cm
Spilopelia senegalensis

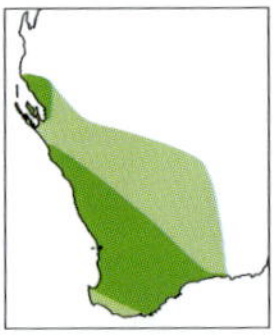

Introduced species. Confined to urban and modified rural areas: streets, parks, gardens, farmyards and grain handling areas.

Voice: pleasant burble of 4–8 continuous coos, *curucoo-cu-cucroo*.

Small, slim, ground-feeding dove, blue-grey rump and innerwing.

SPOTTED DOVE 31 cm
Spilopelia chinensis

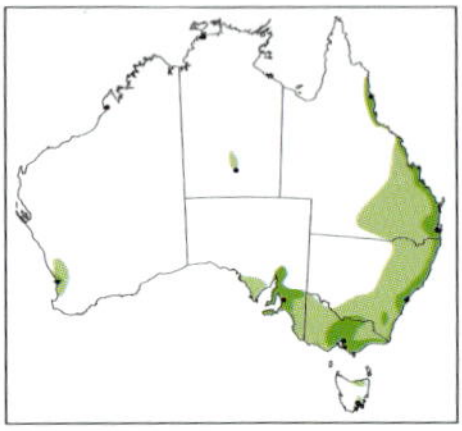

Large, long-tailed, ground-feeding dove with distinctive hindneck. **Voice:** loud repeated *coo-cu-curoo* or *k-coo-curoo*.

Introduced species. Confined to urban areas, parks and gardens, heavily modified rural areas.

BARBARY DOVE 29 cm
Streptopelia roseogrisea

Introduced species. Pale with narrow, black hindcollar. Feral in small parts of Adelaide and perhaps elsewhere. **Voice:** repeated emphatic coos ending in drawn-out *cooroo*.

WHITE-HEADED PIGEON ◐ 39 cm
Columba leucomela

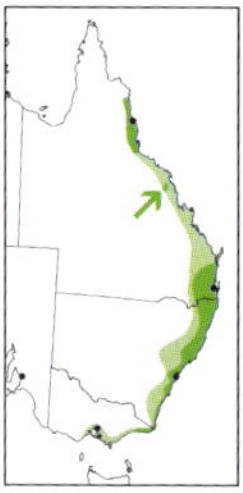

Large slate-grey and white pigeon of rainforest, gallery forest, farmland with remnant rainforest trees, lush parks and gardens. Confiding. Flight strong and low weaving through vegetation.

Feeds on fruits including the introduced Privet and Camphor Laurel. Often seen on ground under isolated Camphor Laurels in farm paddocks. **Voice:** a single low *boo* or *oom*, slow drawn-out *oom … cooo*.

BROWN CUCKOO-DOVE ◐ 42 cm
Macropygia phasianella

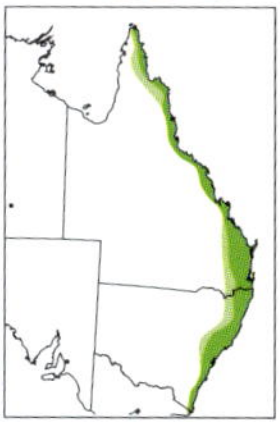

Common, large-tailed pigeon of rainforest and remnant patches in farmland and along roads. Flight strong and low, weaving through vegetation.

Juv: barring on head and neck.

Ad ♂: head and neck with mauve and green iridescence. **Ad ♀:** lacks iridescence.

Feeds on fruits and seeds, often at mid-level of forest, also on ground along tracks. **Voice:** commonly heard, repeated *oo-WUP* or *coo-oo-WUP*.

PACIFIC EMERALD-DOVE ◐ 25 cm
Chalcophaps longirostris

Small, compact, terrestrial dove of rainforest, monsoon scrubs and mangroves.

Pairs or small family groups walk rapidly and erratically across forest floor searching for food. **Voice:** monotonous series of low *oos*, increasing in volume.

DIAMOND DOVE 21 cm
Geopelia cuneata

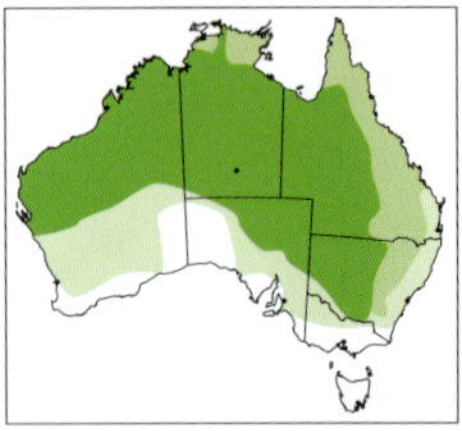

Tiny, terrestrial dove with very long pointed tail. Occurs in a wide variety of arid and semi-arid habitats but mostly dry, grassy woodland and shrubland, never far from a water source.
Voice: a pleasant liquid *coo-coo coo-coooo*, also 2-note *coorrh-coo*.

PEACEFUL DOVE 22 cm
Geopelia placida

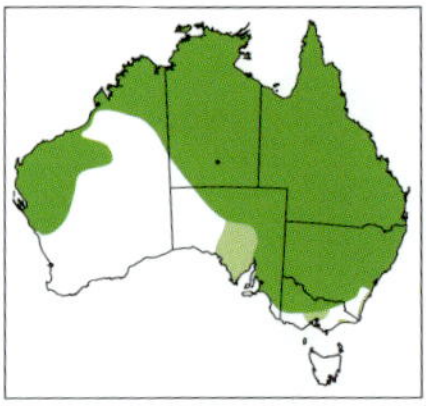

Slightly larger than Diamond Dove. Common in monsoonal forest and scrub, semi-arid areas, dry woodland, agricultural areas, parks, gardens and sports fields. Never far from water. Feeds on ground in pairs and small groups.
Voice: pleasant, repeated *doodle-do* or *doo-le-doo-do*.

BAR-SHOULDERED DOVE 28 cm
Geopelia humeralis

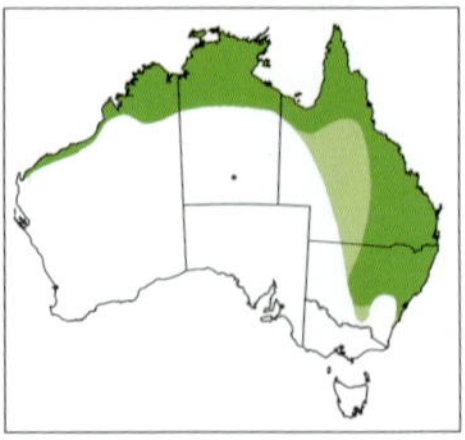

Large, terrestrial dove. In most of coastal and subcoastal, tropical and subtropical Aus, decreasing numbers inland. Open eucalypt forest, coastal scrub, mangroves and *Pandanus*, parks and gardens.
Voice: highly vocal, a loud, repeated *cook-coo-woo*, a musical *coolicop* followed by a single *coo*, also a rapid series of laughing *coos*.

WHITE-QUILLED ROCK-PIGEON 29 cm
Petrophassa albipennis

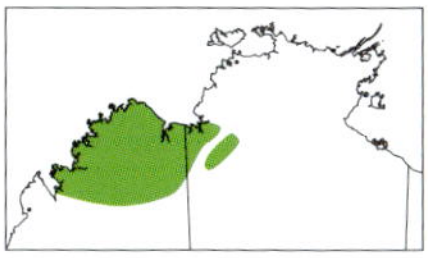

Ad: reddish-brown in w NT.

Small, dark, bulky dove with small head. Terrestrial, confined to jumbled boulder and cliff habitats. **Voice:** loud, deep, laughing *coo-coo-roo-roo-coo-roo.*

CHESTNUT-QUILLED ROCK-PIGEON 30 cm
Petrophassa rufipennis

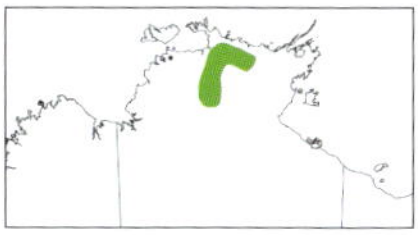

Rocky sandstone escarpments. Noisy flapping and long glides on flat wings.

Voice: loud, repeated, musical *kukarook*, when flushed a sharp high-pitched *coo.*

SPINIFEX PIGEON 22 cm
Geophaps plumifera

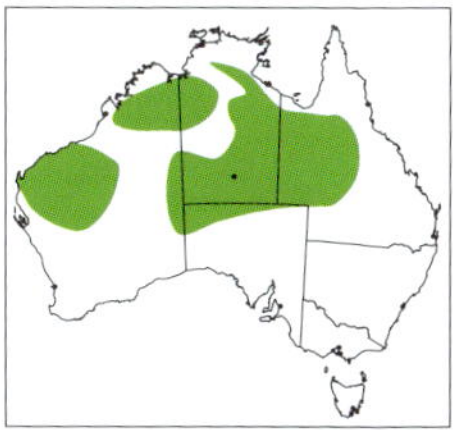

Runs ahead of observer before a quail-like explosion from ground followed by a long, curving glide.

Ad: rufous belly in w.

Small, compact, terrestrial pigeon. Usually small groups in arid rocky country, stony *Triodia* slopes and on nearby plains, never far from water. **Voice:** soft *cu-whoo*, also *coo-oo-oo-oo-whoo.*

CRESTED PIGEON 33 cm
Ocyphaps lophotes

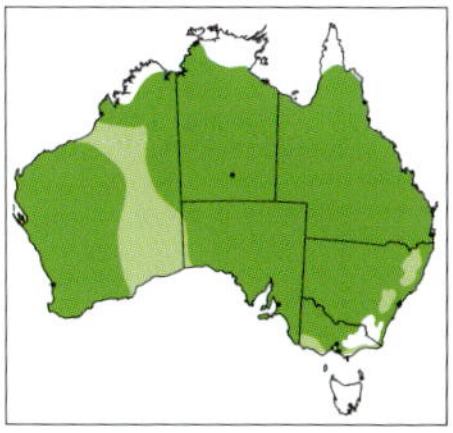

Swift, direct flight, pulse of rapid, whistling wing beats followed by long glide.

Common terrestrial pigeon over most of Aus, in open habitats, parks and gardens, avoiding colder wet areas. **Voice:** loud *coo-whoo*, displaying ♂ gives a short harsh *wook.*

COMMON BRONZEWING ◑ 32 cm
Phaps chalcoptera

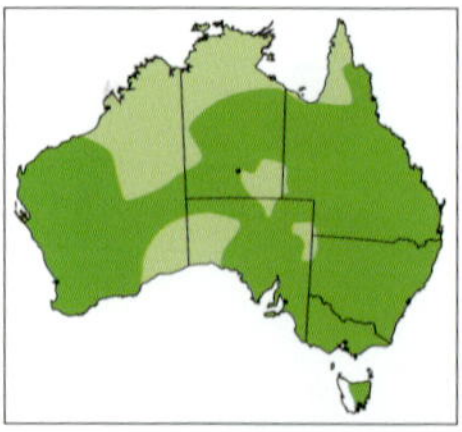

Large, bulky, terrestrial pigeon. Widespread in forest and open woodland with nearby water source. Explodes from ground with loud wing claps. Fast direct flight often low, weaving between trees. Eats seeds, especially *Acacia*.
Voice: a series of deep, downslurred *ooms*, repeated at intervals of 2.5 sec, deeper than Brush Bronzewing.

BRUSH BRONZEWING ◑ 29 cm
Phaps elegans

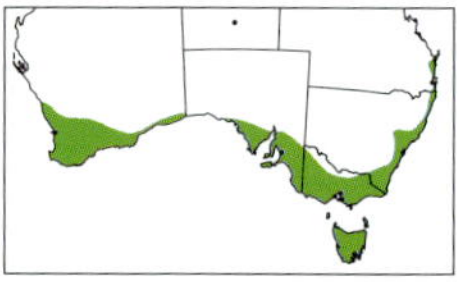

Compact, terrestrial pigeon inhabiting forest and scrub. Prefers a tall, dense, shrub layer including coastal scrub, heathy forest and mallee. Explodes from ground with loud wing claps. Around parks and camp grounds can become tame and will feed out on open grassy areas.
Voice: a series of loud *whoos*, repeated at intervals of 2 sec, not downslurred and higher-pitched than Common Bronzewing.

WONGA PIGEON ◑ 41 cm
Leucosarcia melanoleuca

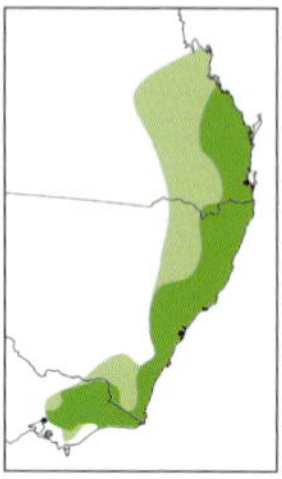

Large, bulky, terrestrial pigeon found in wet forest, forest edges, parks and gardens. Walks purposefully on longish legs.
Voice: a rather high-pitched and monotonously repeated *whoo-whoo-whoo-whoo-whoo*.

FLOCK BRONZEWING 29 cm
Phaps histrionica

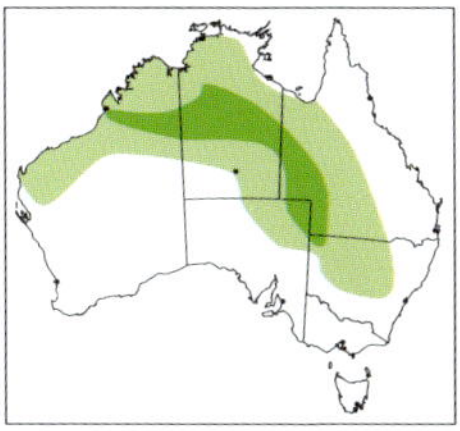

Big-winged pigeon of inland treeless grassland, savanna and the channel country, especially where Mitchell Grass predominates. Strong and direct flight in large flocks, often in the thousands.
Voice: mostly silent, soft contact *coos* when feeding.

PARTRIDGE PIGEON 26 cm
Geophaps smithii

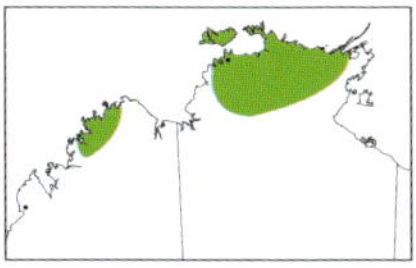

Medium-sized terrestrial pigeon of tropical grassy woodland and open forest. Prefers areas of open ground cover, including recently burnt areas and roadsides. Pairs and family groups. When flushed bursts from ground with fast wing beats followed by glide on bowed wings.
Voice: drawn-out, low *coooo*, soft rather melancholy *oo-poo-poop*.

SQUATTER PIGEON 29 cm
Geophaps scripta

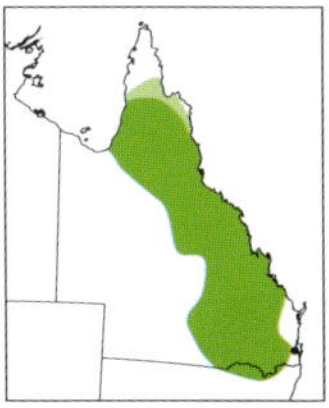

Qld equivalent of Partridge Pigeon. Prefers open tussock-grass woodland with much bare ground, often seen on roadsides. As name suggests, reluctant to fly, preferring to run away well ahead of danger.
Voice: soft *ooop-oop-oop*, also bubbly series of *coo-coos* during display.

TORRESIAN IMPERIAL-PIGEON ◔ 41 cm
Ducula spilorrhoa

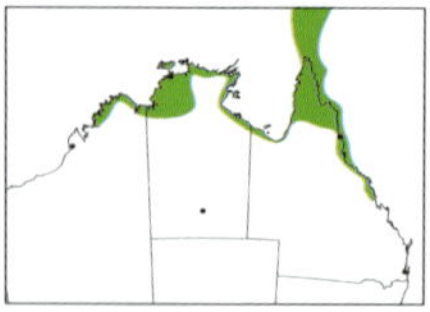

Large, black and white pigeon. Most abundant in near-coastal, lowland rainforest, gallery forest, mangroves, parks and gardens. Usually roosts and breeds on nearby offshore islands, making daily commutes to mainland to feed on fruit. Flies in flocks, fast and direct, often well above canopy. Largely migratory in NT and Qld, absent Apr–Oct. **Voice:** a loud double coo, *who-whoo*.

TOPKNOT PIGEON ◑ 42 cm
Lopholaimus antarcticus

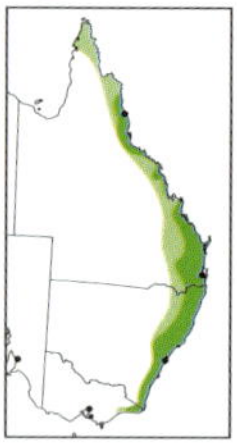

Flocks fly strongly, low over canopy or across farmland to isolated patches of trees.

Large grey pigeon. Nomadic flocks search for fruiting trees in upland rainforest, lowland remnants and isolated trees in farmland. Clambers acrobatically in foliage searching for fruit, flaps wings noisily to balance. **Voice:** mostly silent, short screeches, quiet croaks, *corr-or*.

Ad: unique crest, single pale band in dark tail.

BLACK-BANDED FRUIT-DOVE ◔ 34 cm
Ptilinopus alligator

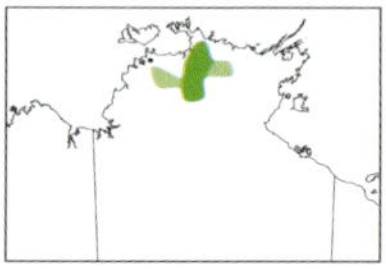

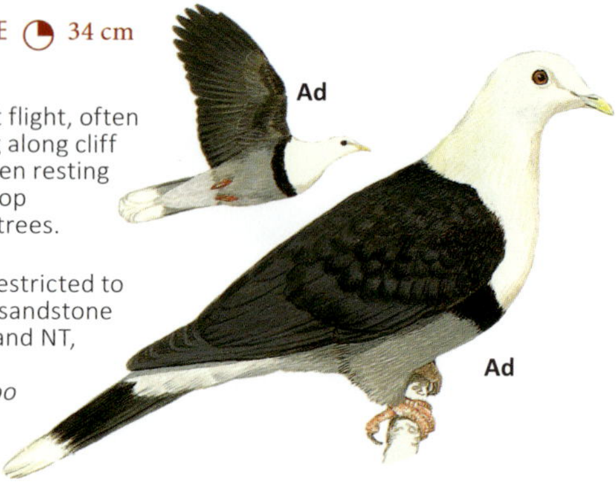

Strong fast flight, often seen flying along cliff edges. When resting perches atop emergent trees.

Largish black and white pigeon. Restricted to monsoonal and riparian forest of sandstone escarpment country in Arnhem Land NT, wherever there are fruiting trees, especially figs. **Voice:** loud, low *coo* of 1 sec duration, repeated at 5 sec intervals.

WOMPOO FRUIT-DOVE ◑ 40 cm
Ptilinopus magnificus

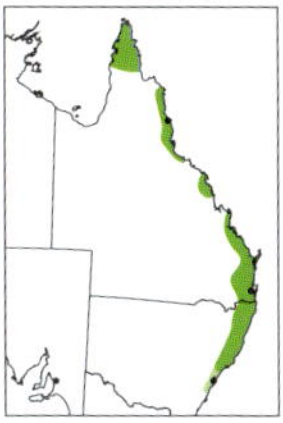

Can be surprisingly difficult to see in canopy. Listen for falling fruit or bird making short flight.

Large, colourful fruit-dove with long tail. Singles or pairs common in tropical and subtropical rainforest, occasionally parks and well vegetated gardens bordering rainforest. **Voice:** familiar, loud *wallock-a woo*, at distance this may sound like *womp-poo*. Other calls *book-a-roo*, loud explosive *hwuck and pak-pak-pak*.

SUPERB FRUIT-DOVE ◑ 23 cm
Ptilinopus superbus

Small, compact fruit-dove of rainforest, vine thickets and nearby secondary growth or mangroves. Common on Cape York and the Wet Tropics, regular but mostly a summer migrant further s. **Voice:** a rapidly repeated *wooh-wooh-wooh*, also a repeated *whoo-oop* or *whoop*.

ROSE-CROWNED FRUIT-DOVE ◑ 23 cm
Ptilinopus regina

Small, compact fruit-dove of rainforest, monsoonal and gallery forest, vine thickets and nearby secondary growth or mangroves. Seasonal movement – more common in summer in s of range. **Voice:** 4–5 slow *wooh*s given at increasingly shorter intervals, followed by 10+ increasingly rapid *wook-wook-wook*s.

CHESTNUT-BREASTED CUCKOO ◔ 22 cm
Cacomantis castaneiventris

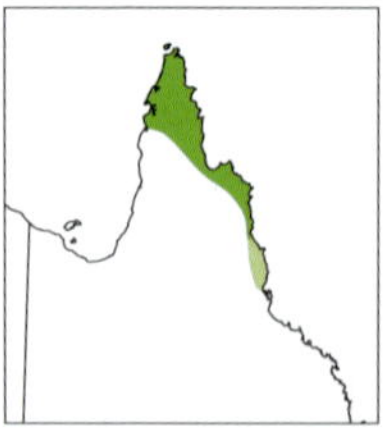

Darker than Fan-tailed Cuckoo; narrow white barring on tail only visible from below.

Juv: unmarked upperparts and underparts.

Ad: uniformly chestnut underparts.

Inconspicuous resident in rainforest canopy. **Voice:** downward trill, very similar to Fan-tailed Cuckoo and Yellow-billed Kingfisher, but slightly shorter.

FAN-TAILED CUCKOO ◕ 26 cm
Cacomantis flabelliformis

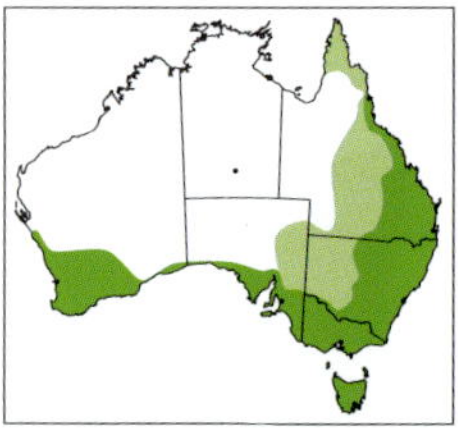

Juv: densely mottled breast.

Ad ♀: duller with faint barring on belly.

Broad white barring of outertail visible from sides and above.

Ad ♂: pale rufous underparts darkest on chest.

Common in forest and woodland with thick understorey. Partial migrant, in s Aus mostly seen spring and summer. **Voice:** ♂ strong downward trill *peer* repeated persistently in spring, also sad whistle *p-wee*. ♀ Shrill *chirree*.

PALLID CUCKOO ◑ 31 cm
Cacomantis pallidus

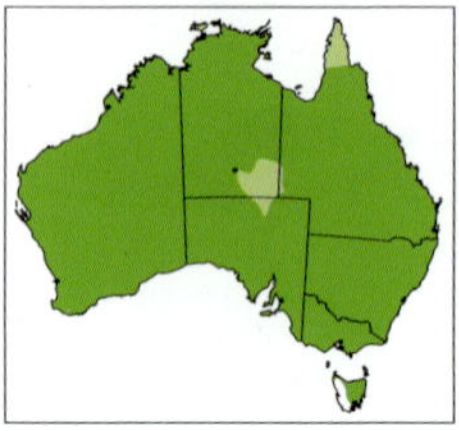

Ad ♀: black stripe behind eye and chequered wing.

Bold white spotting on sides of tail.

Ad ♂

Falcon-like flight often prompts alarm calls.

Juv: with White-plumed Honeyeater foster parent.

In lightly timbered areas. Summer migrant in s Aus, present year-round in n.

Voice: ♂ a series of loud, throaty whistles: 4–5 staccato notes followed by about a dozen loud ascending whistles.

BRUSH CUCKOO ◑ 21 cm
Cacomantis variolosus

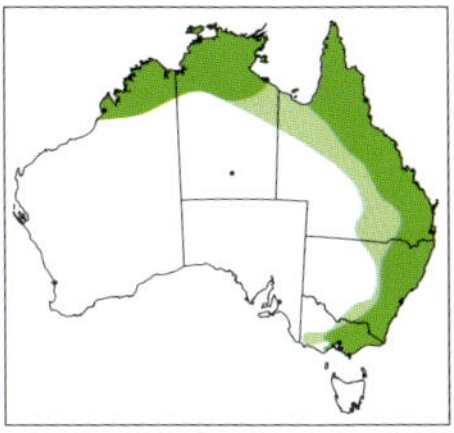

Juv: heavily mottled underparts; rufous and brown barring on upperwing.

Smaller and shorter-tailed than Fan-tailed Cuckoo; narrower white bars on tail not visible from above. In canopy or dense understorey of forest and (in n Aus) woodland.
Voice: ♂ plaintive, penetrating series of 3–16 descending whistles *fear fear fear …*; also repeats 3-note phrase *where's the tea* building to excited frenzy.

Ad ♂: buff belly grades to greyer breast.

Ad ♀: some look like ♂; many have varied barring on underparts.

ORIENTAL CUCKOO ◔ 31 cm
Cuculus optatus

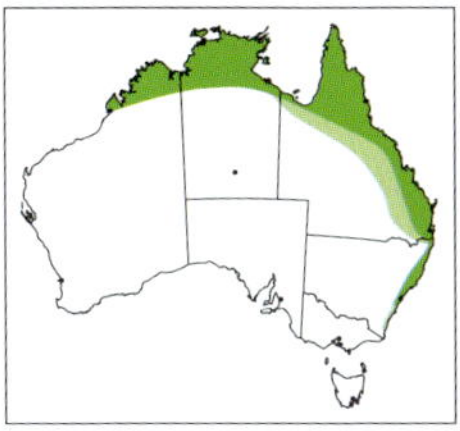

Juv

Always has barred underparts, yellow feet.

Ad ♂

Ad ♀ rufous morph

Migrant from n Asia, present in Aus Sep–May (mainly Nov–Mar). Unobtrusive and arboreal; found singly or occasionally in small groups in wide range of forests and woodlands, edges of riparian forest.
Voice: mainly silent when in Aus.

BLACK-EARED CUCKOO ◔ 19 cm
Chrysococcyx osculans

Much smaller than Pallid Cuckoo. Diagnostic black mask.

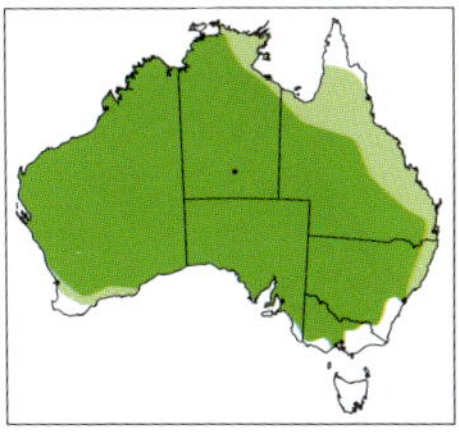

Ad: buff underparts in fresh plumage.

No barring on breast. Beware, Juv Horsfield's Bronze-Cuckoo can look similar.

Juv

Pale rump.

Ad: grey underparts when worn.

Solitary and unobtrusive, in open woodlands and shrublands; in n Aus also in riverine forest.
Voice: descending whistle *peer*, uttered singly or repeated; more mournful and slower than similar call of Horsfield's Bronze-Cuckoo.

HORSFIELD'S BRONZE-CUCKOO ◕ 16 cm
Chrysococcyx basalis

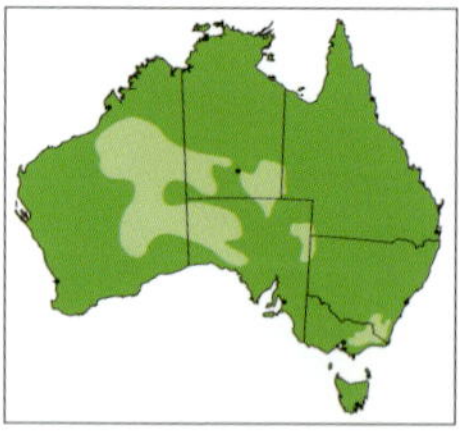

Only bronze-cuckoo with dark mask. However, some ♀ Shining Bronze-Cuckoos can look similar.

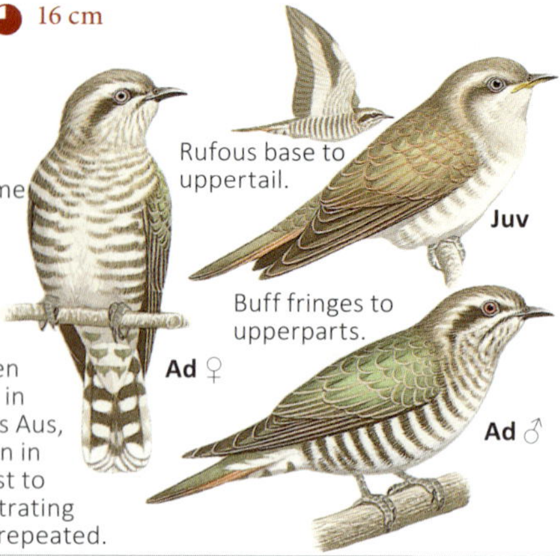

Bronze-cuckoos are small; glittering green upperparts when sunlit, dull and greyish in shade. Horsfield's is a summer visitor to s Aus, most migrate to n Aus in winter. Common in lightly wooded habitats, from open forest to heaths and wetland fringes. **Voice:** penetrating descending whistle *tseeuw*, persistently repeated.

SHINING BRONZE-CUCKOO ◑ 15 cm
Chrysococcyx lucidus

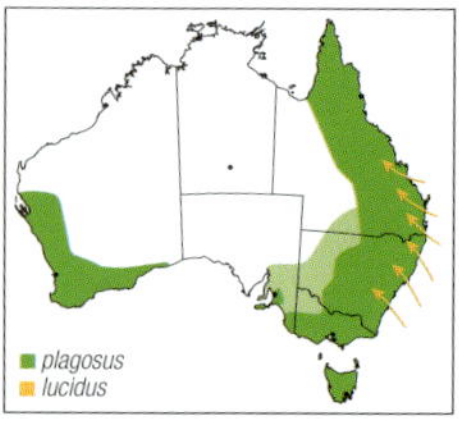

Highly glossy, no eye stripe, no rufous in uppertail.

Mainly in canopy of forest and woodland. Ssp *plagosus* breeds s Aus in spring and summer; migrates to or through n Aus in winter. Ssp *lucidus* breeds NZ, migrates to Solomons, stages en route in e Aus Feb–Apr, Aug–Nov. **Voice:** a series of clear whistles *fwee fwee fwee ...*, each note rising; often ends sequence with downslurred whistle.

LITTLE BRONZE-CUCKOO ◑ 15 cm
Chrysococcyx minutillus

Smaller than Shining Bronze, with broad orbital ring, faint face mask, some rufous in undertail. Mainly in canopy of dense vegetation, including mangroves, vine thickets and gallery forest. **Voice:** brisk series of 4–8 plaintive whistles *tew-tew-tew-tew*; also utters a prolonged, descending trill.

PHEASANT COUCAL 58 cm
Centropus phasianinus

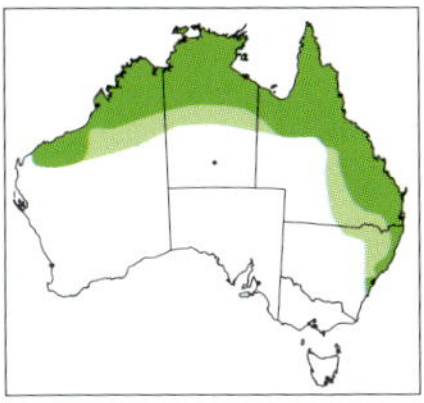

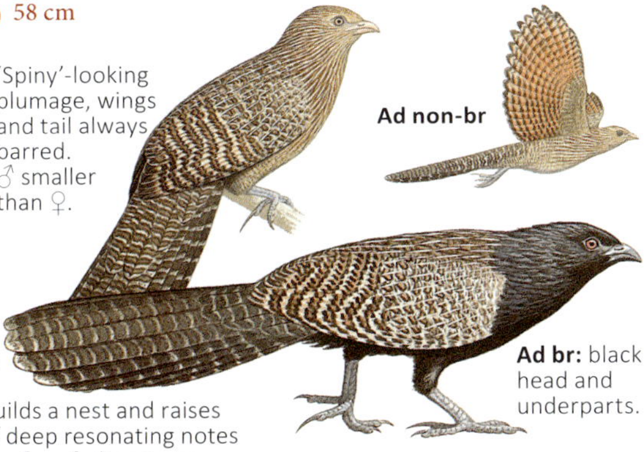

Very large, skulks in dense grassy understorey of open forest and woodland. The only Aus cuckoo that builds a nest and raises own young. **Voice:** series of deep resonating notes *oop-oop-oop*, accelerating before fading away.

CHANNEL-BILLED CUCKOO 63 cm
Scythrops novaehollandiae

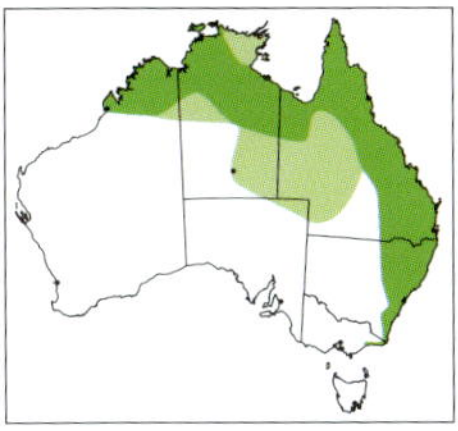

Seen in canopy of forest and woodland, usually with fig trees; as singles or pairs but small flocks can occur in fruiting trees. **Voice:** noisy; loud, harsh calls given day and night. Main call *ee-awk ee-awk ee-awk*, *ca-ca-ca-ca-ca* easily confused with calls of cranes or Blue-winged Kookaburra.

PACIFIC KOEL 41 cm
Eudynamys orientalis

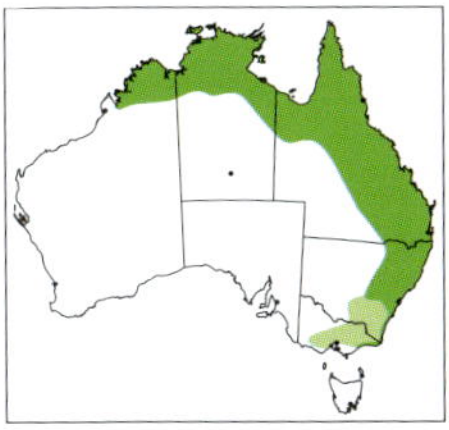

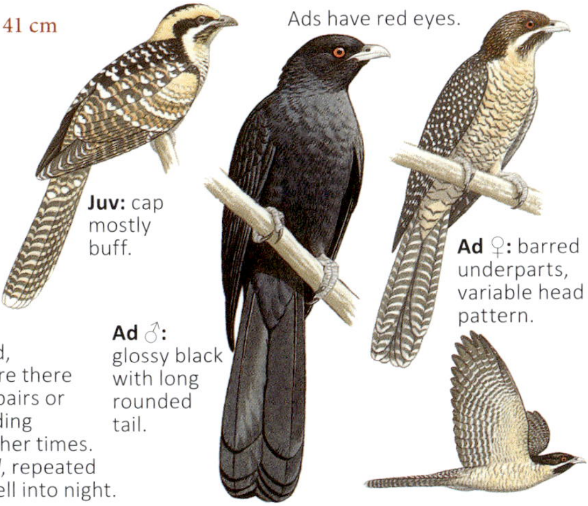

Large, canopy-dwelling cuckoo of forest, woodland, orchards and gardens where there are fruiting trees. Singles, pairs or small flocks. Noisy in breeding season, shy and quiet at other times. **Voice:** loud *coo-ee* or *ko-el*, repeated persistently, sometimes well into night.

AZURE KINGFISHER ◑ 17 cm
Ceyx azureus

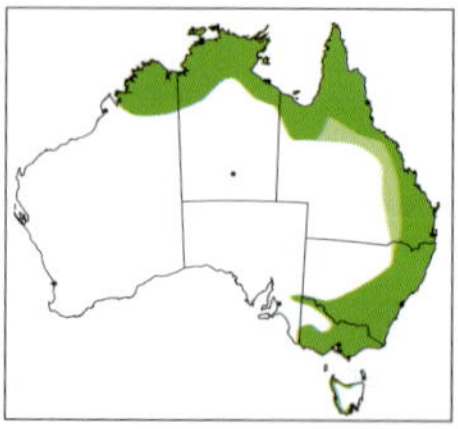

Perches quietly in shady vegetation above creeks, rivers and billabongs; dives head-first into water to catch fish. **Voice:** high-pitched penetrating *pseet* repeated several times.

Juv: slightly duller than Ad; small white bill tip.

Ad: brilliant violet-blue upperparts.

Flies fast and low over water, often calling.

LITTLE KINGFISHER ◔ 12 cm
Ceyx pusillus

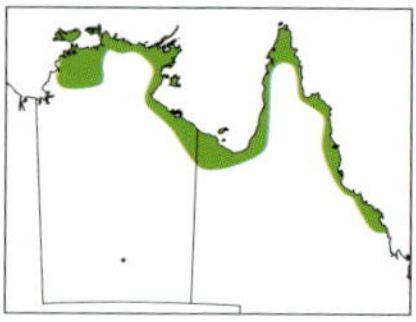

Perches inconspicuously in vegetation overhanging rivers and creeks, including mangroves. Plunges head-first into water to grab prey.
Voice: thin but penetrating *tsee*, higher-pitched than Azure Kingfisher and inaudible to some observers.

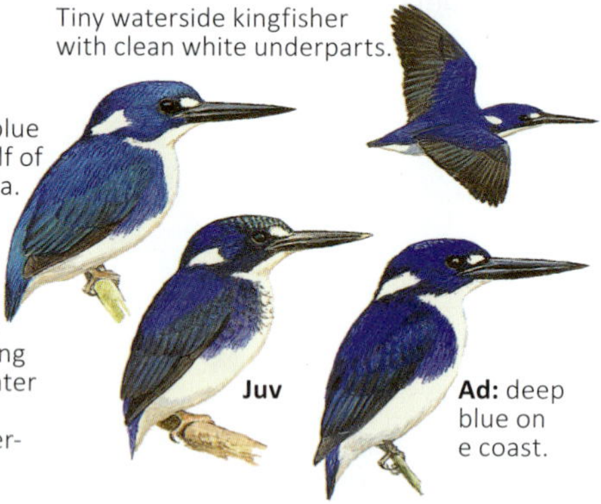

Tiny waterside kingfisher with clean white underparts.

Ad: paler blue NT and Gulf of Carpentaria.

Juv

Ad: deep blue on e coast.

TORRESIAN KINGFISHER ◑ 25 cm
Todiramphus sordidus

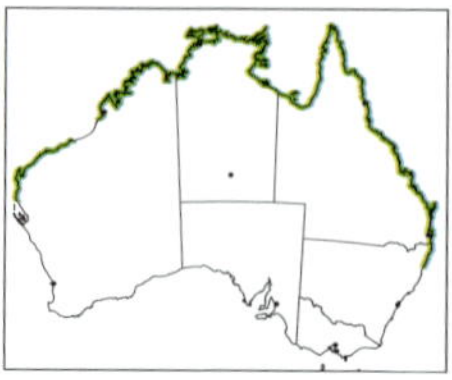

In Aus, restricted to mangroves. Beware confusion with Sacred Kingfisher, which also uses mangroves. Larger and heavier-billed than Sacred Kingfisher. Perches quietly above shallow pools or wet mud, pouncing on crabs or mudskippers.
Voice: explosive *kik-kik*; unlike Sacred, call is usually disyllabic.

Juv: dark scaling on breast and collar.

Ad ♂**:** ♀ similar but with weaker blue tinge on folded wing and crown.

Neat white spot on forehead.

White underwing coverts *cf* buff on Sacred Kingfisher.

FOREST KINGFISHER 19 cm
Todiramphus macleayii

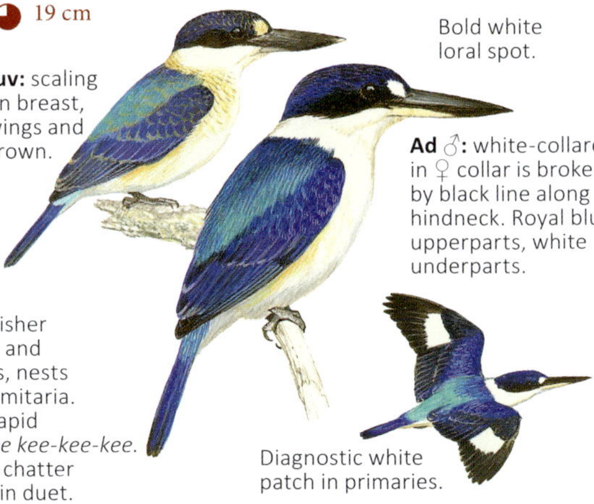

Medium–small tree-kingfisher of open sclerophyll forest and woodland. Usually in pairs, nests in burrows in arboreal termitaria. **Voice:** strident series of rapid high-pitched notes *kee kee kee-kee-kee*. Pairs give scratchy trilling chatter *scissor-weya scissorweya* in duet.

SACRED KINGFISHER 22 cm
Todiramphus sanctus

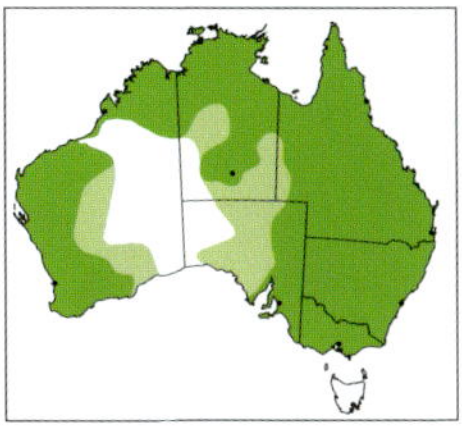

Our commonest tree-kingfisher, widespread in open forest, woodland, town parks and mangroves. Perches quietly, pounces on prey on ground. Summer visitor in s Aus, year-round in n. **Voice:** strident repetition of 3–7 notes: *kek-kek-kek ...*

RED-BACKED KINGFISHER 23 cm
Todiramphus pyrrhopygius

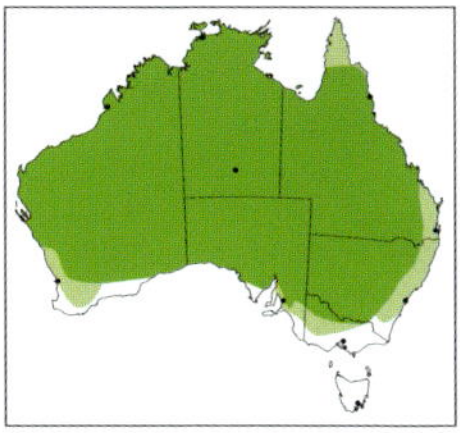

Tree-kingfisher of dry, sparsely treed habitats including savanna and farmland. Nests in burrow. **Voice:** downslurred, sad whistle *chyew* repeated at 3 sec intervals.

YELLOW-BILLED KINGFISHER ◔ 20 cm
Syma torotoro

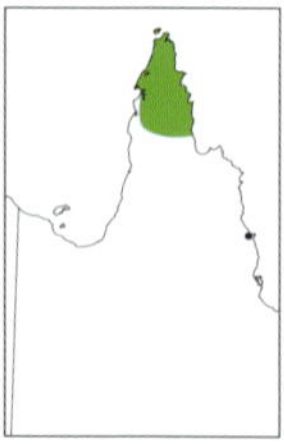

Small tree-kingfisher restricted to rainforest, including small patches abutting woodland. Difficult to see, easy to hear.

Voice: repeated downslurred trill *peer*, very similar to Chestnut-breasted Cuckoo but often builds up to a long trill.

LAUGHING KOOKABURRA ● 44 cm
Dacelo novaeguineae

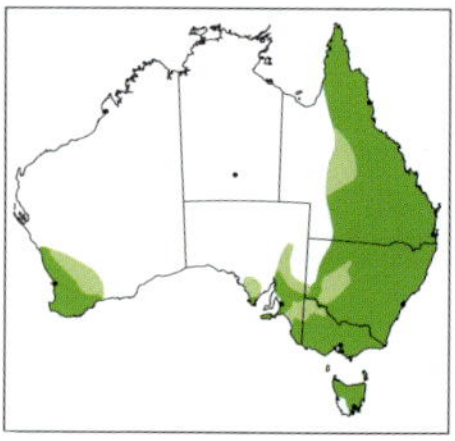

Huge, familiar tree-kingfisher of open eucalypt forest and woodland, including urban areas. In territorial groups, a pair with 1–7 helpers. Forage singly, pouncing on prey on ground; roost and call in groups. **Voice:** unmistakable, raucous, laughing call, given in discordant chorus by all group members.

BLUE-WINGED KOOKABURRA ◕ 39 cm
Dacelo leachii

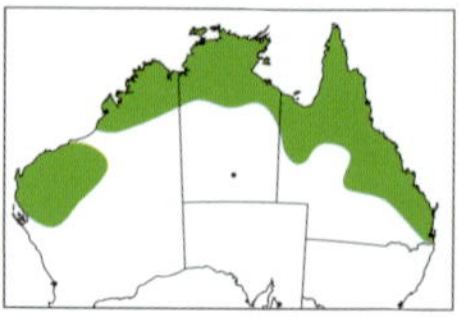

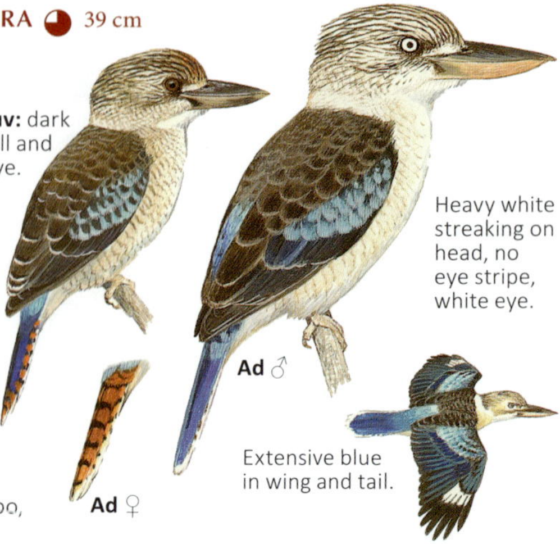

In open eucalypt forest and woodland of tropics and subtropics. Similar behaviour to Laughing Kookaburra. **Voice:** loud and manic; staccato throaty *yok* notes building to excited climax of hoarse screeches, yelps and cackles before ending abruptly. Surprisingly similar to calls of cranes and Channel-billed Cuckoo, but usually given in chorus.

BUFF-BREASTED PARADISE-KINGFISHER ◔ 33 cm
Tanysiptera sylvia

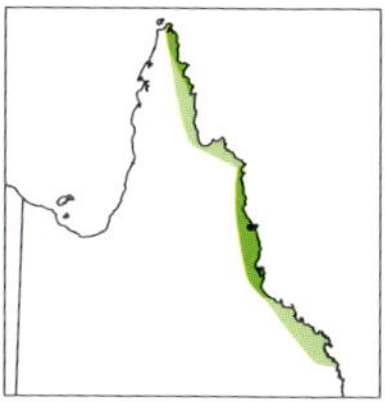

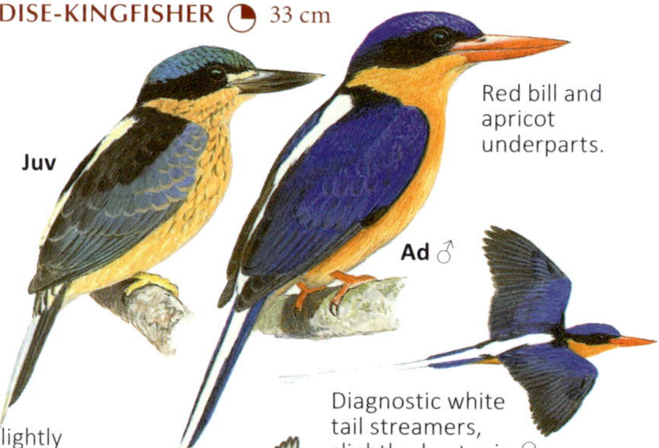

Wet-season migrant to monsoon rainforest. Shy, in shady understorey, most often seen in flight. **Voice:** a pulsing series of slightly hoarse disyllabic pipes: *tcherwill tcherwill tcherwill …*

RAINBOW BEE-EATER ● 25 cm
Merops ornatus

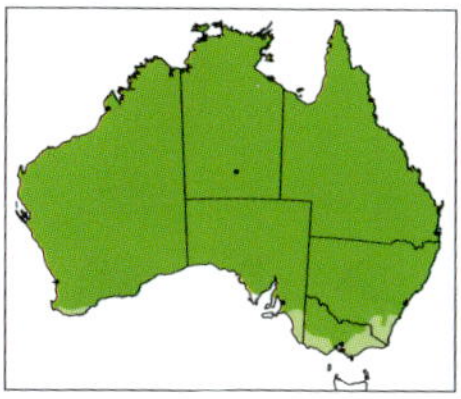

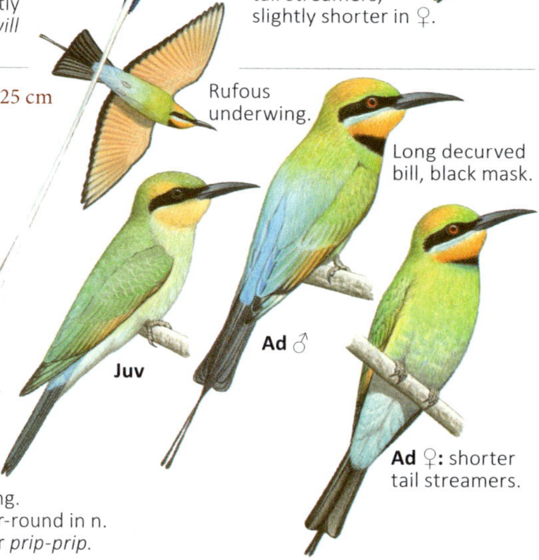

Slim, colourful aerialist. Often seen on high exposed perches in lightly timbered country, sallying to catch flying insects. Pairs nest in burrow, sometimes semi-colonially; forms flocks when not breeding. Summer migrant to s Aus, year-round in n. **Voice:** loud pleasing trill *trrt* or *prip-prip*.

ORIENTAL DOLLARBIRD ◑ 27 cm
Eurystomus orientalis

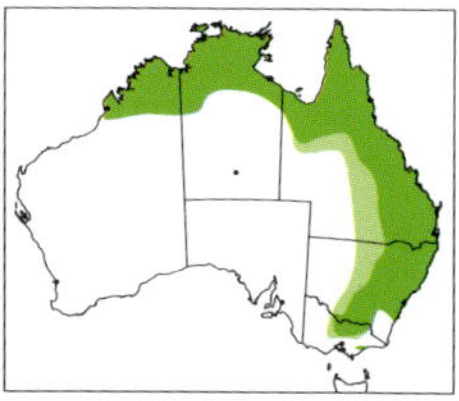

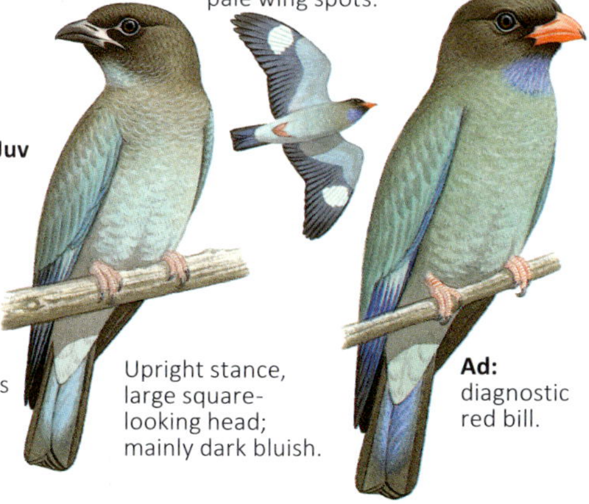

In woodland and open forest, preferring sites with tree hollows and nearby water. Makes acrobatic flights from high perches to catch flying insects. Singles, pairs and small flocks. **Voice:** loud, grating, accelerating chatter *kek kek kek-kek-kek-kek*.

Aerial insectivores: Although not closely related, these three species groups pose similar ID challenges as they are usually seen high overhead, hunting flying insects. They are usually seen in flocks which may include several different species.

Swifts and swiftlets: The most aerial of birds, only landing at nests or perhaps when roosting at night. Note very long, stiff, tapered wings with curved leading edge. They fly fast, with bursts of shallow, flickering wing beats interspersed by glides.

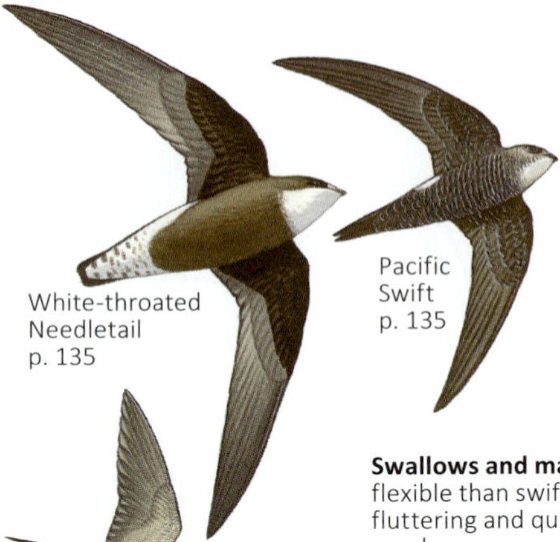

White-throated Needletail p. 135

Pacific Swift p. 135

Australian Swiftlet p. 135

Swallows and martins: Wings are more angular and flexible than swifts; flight is more agile with rapid fluttering and quick turns. Often land on exposed perches.

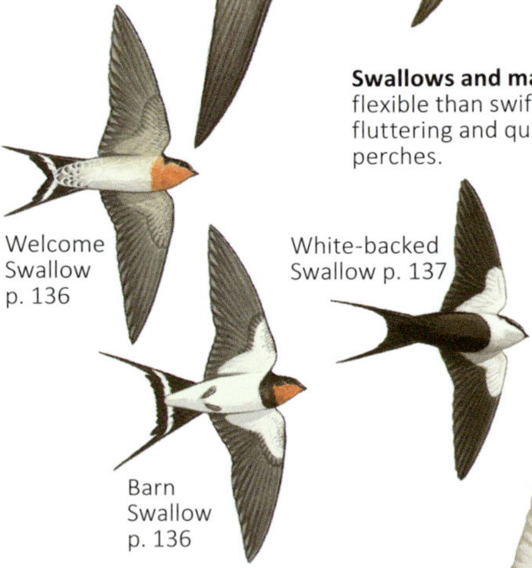

Welcome Swallow p. 136

White-backed Swallow p. 137

Barn Swallow p. 136

Tree Martin p. 137

Fairy Martin p. 137

Woodswallows: Shorter, broader triangular wings. Almost as agile in flight as swallows, but woodswallows soar for long periods, and often perch.

Dusky Woodswallow p. 200

Little Woodswallow p. 200

White-breasted Woodswallow p. 201

Black-faced Woodswallow p. 200

Masked Woodswallow p. 201

White-browed Woodswallow p. 201

WHITE-THROATED NEEDLETAIL 20 cm
Hirundapus caudacutus

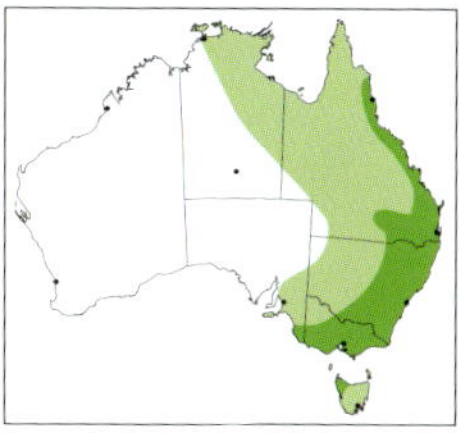

Summer migrant from Asia, seen in flocks high overhead. Most common over forest, hills and cliffs where there are updrafts. Seldom seen landing but roosts at night in outer foliage of tall trees. **Voice:** rapid, high-pitched twittering *chee-chee-chee*. Dramatic loud swoosh of wing beats on uncommon occasions when birds fly low.

PACIFIC SWIFT 19 cm
Apus pacificus

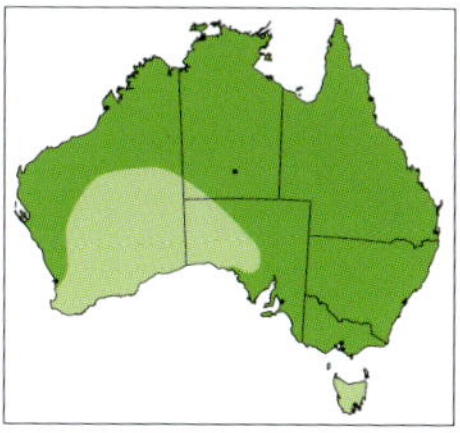

Summer Asian migrant, in flocks high overhead. Over most habitats, but especially inland plains. **Voice:** thin shrill scream *sree* sometimes draws attention to flocks so high they are barely visible with naked eye.

AUSTRALIAN SWIFTLET 11 cm
Aerodramus terraereginae

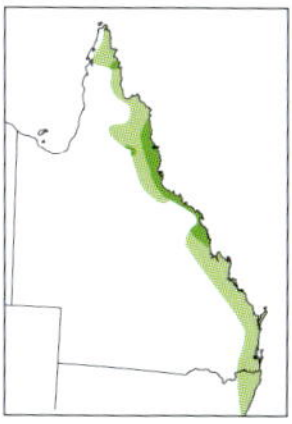

Feeds in flocks, often with swallows and martins. Over forest, woodland and farmland within 30 km of caves where they roost and nest colonially. **Voice:** high-pitched *chee*; in full darkness of nesting caves they echolocate using metallic double click *cli-ik*.

The remaining species in this book belong to one taxonomic group, the Order Passeriformes (also known as passerines, perching birds, or songbirds). It is by far the most diverse order of birds in the world, with many lineages having originated in Australia. Passerines include most of our smaller bush birds and the majority of our best songsters. They are characterised by three forward-pointing toes and a large strong hind-toe.

WELCOME SWALLOW ● 15 cm
Hirundo neoxena

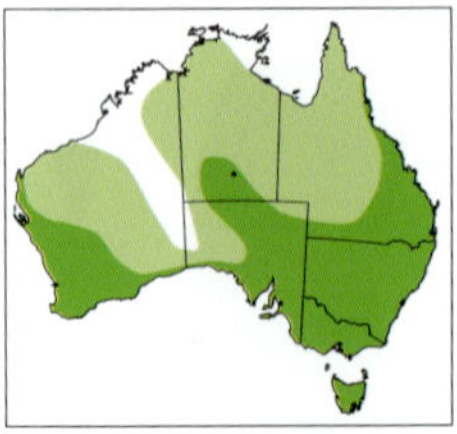

Familiar swallow with glossy black back and rump, deeply forked tail. Forages over open habitats; common in settled areas, most common near water. Partly migratory, in s Aus most common in summer. **Voice:** short *tswit* and sharper *tswee* or *tit-swee* in flight; pleasant twittering song when breeding.

Builds a mud nest under overhangs, especially verandas and eaves of buildings.

BARN SWALLOW ◔ 16 cm
Hirundo rustica

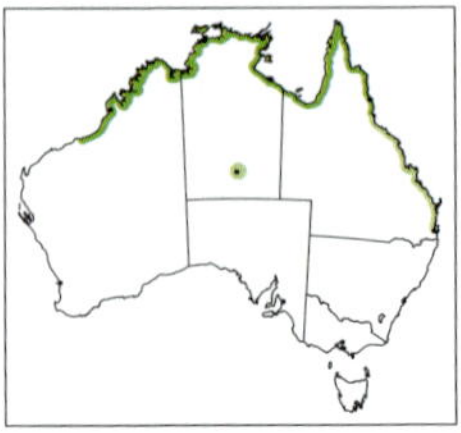

Summer migrant from N Asia, regular in near-coastal lowlands of tropical Aus, especially near fresh water. **Voice:** similar to Welcome Swallow.

Larger than Welcome Swallow with clean white underparts, black breast band, smaller rufous forehead and cheeks.

WHITE-BACKED SWALLOW 14 cm
Cheramoeca leucosterna

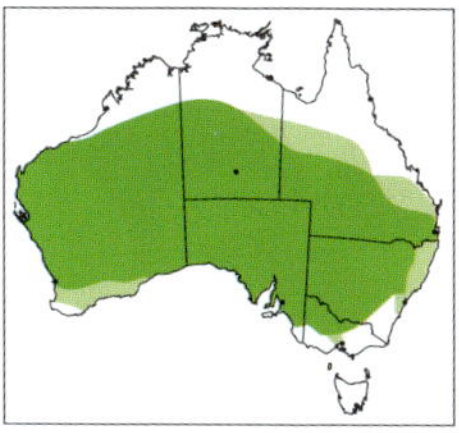

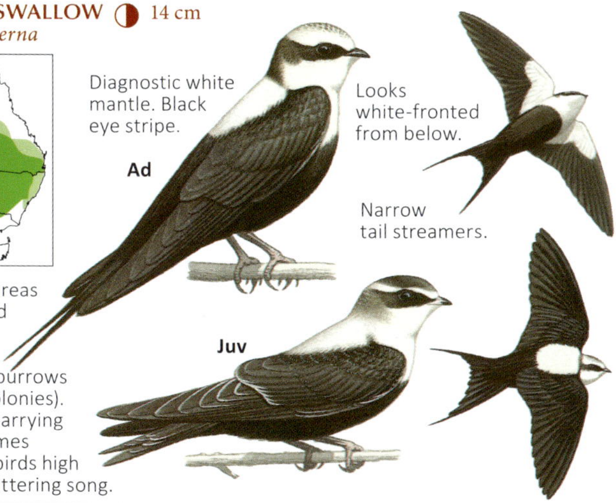

In lightly timbered areas of arid and semi-arid zones, usually near sandy banks where they excavate nest burrows (singly or in small colonies). **Voice:** soft but far-carrying *chek* or *jk jk* sometimes draws attention to birds high overhead; also a twittering song.

FAIRY MARTIN 12 cm
Petrochelidon ariel

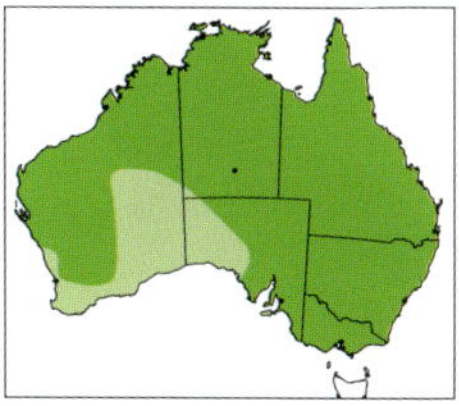

Flocks in open or lightly timbered country, often near water; avoids forest. Partly migratory, in s Aus mainly seen in summer. **Voice:** soft pipit-like *djiit* in flight, slightly deeper and more chirring than Tree Martin. Also a twittering, insect-like song.

TREE MARTIN 13 cm
Petrochelidon nigricans

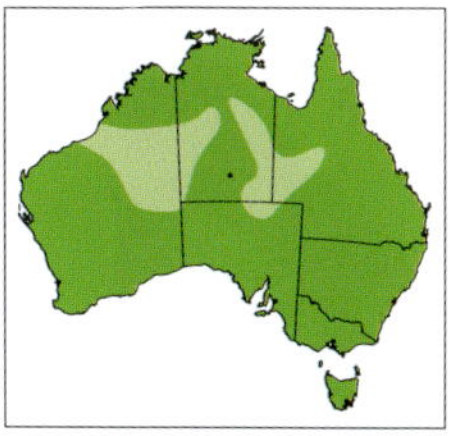

Forages in flocks over most habitats, from grasslands to forests, preferring areas with large hollow-bearing trees for nesting. Partial migrant, in s Aus mainly seen in summer. **Voice:** dry *tzweit* or *chit* in flight, pleasant twittering song.

NOISY PITTA ◑ 21 cm
Pitta versicolor

Pittas are colourful, long-legged and stumpy-tailed denizens of the rainforest floor.

Seen singly or in pairs, foraging on forest floor. Breeds in upland rainforest; in non-br season many migrate to lowland rainforest, wet sclerophyll or gardens.
Voice: loud, brisk, throaty whistle *walk-to-work* given from ground or perch in canopy.

Buff underparts, black face and throat, red vent.

PAPUAN PITTA ◔ 18 cm
Erythropitta macklotii

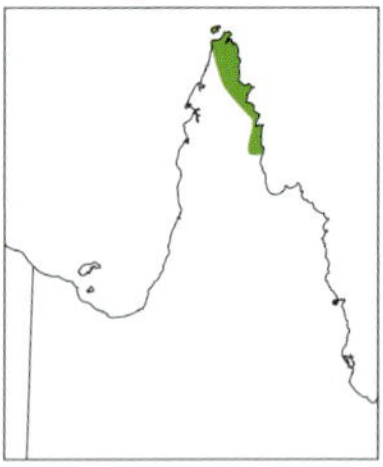

Breeds in closed rainforest of Cape York Peninsula, Dec–Apr; in dry season migrates to NG.

Voice: deep, throaty, drawn-out whistle *kwoor-kwoor*; also a single whistle *kwoor* similar to corresponding call of Noisy Pitta.

Extensively dark blue in flight with rusty hindneck.

Juv: largely brown, unlike our other Juv pittas.

Blue breast band, bright red below.

RAINBOW PITTA ◑ 17 cm
Pitta iris

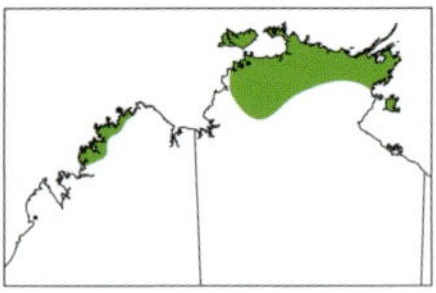

Green upperparts, black head and underparts.

Singles and pairs forage on floor of closed rainforest patches, including parks in Darwin.
Voice: loud, brisk, throaty whistle *tewo-whit tewo-whit* given from ground or trees. Often first detected by distinctive sound of bird hopping on dry leaf-litter (1–6 steps followed by a pause).

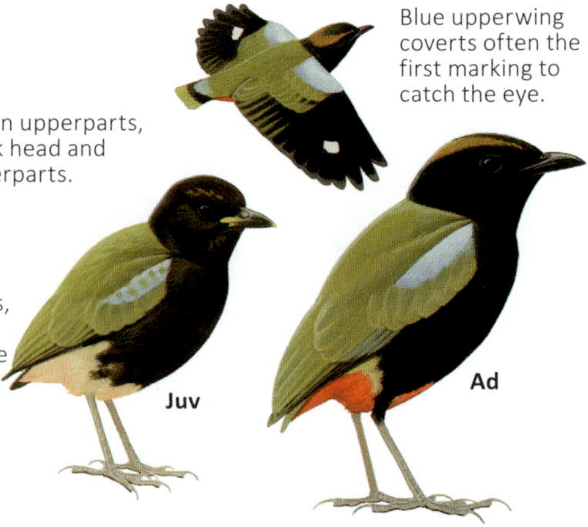

Blue upperwing coverts often the first marking to catch the eye.

SUPERB LYREBIRD ◑ 100 cm
Menura novaehollandiae

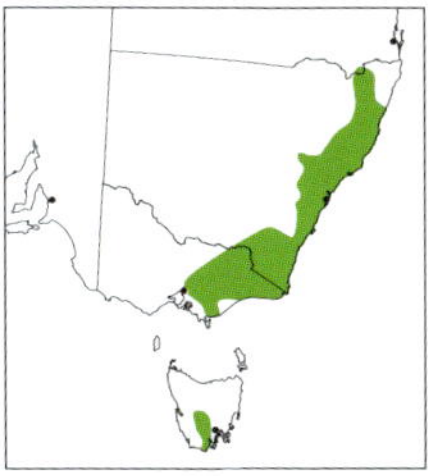

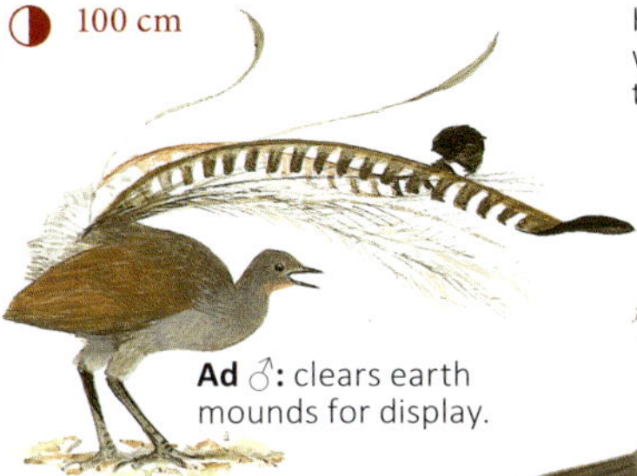

Has short, rounded wings but can fly e.g. to roost in canopy.

Ad ♂: clears earth mounds for display.

Ad ♀: shorter, plainer tail than ♂ without filamentous feathers.

Our largest passerine: long-legged ground-dweller in moist forest. Famous for its ornate tail and display accompanied by amazing song. Singles, pairs or small family groups scratch through leaf-litter.

Ad ♂: spectacular long tail with lyrate and filamentous feathers.

Voice: song most often heard in winter when ♂ displays; very loud medley of mimicry of many bird species plus loud *plik* or *plik plik* and rhythmic thuds. Ear-splitting shriek *quisst* when alarmed.

ALBERT'S LYREBIRD ◔ 89 cm
Menura alberti

Ad ♀: shorter, plainer tail than ♂ without filamentous feathers.

Ad ♂: displays from fallen branches or vines, does not make display mounds.

Smaller, more rufous-tinged than Superb Lyrebird. Restricted to rainforest and wet sclerophyll with moist dense understorey and leaf litter. Wary, hard to see.

Rufous flanks and undertail coverts.

Ad ♂

Voice: powerful song dominated by mimicry; does not utter the loud *plik* of Superb Lyrebird, instead often includes short, loud, gruff notes *gronk*.

AUSTRALIAN LOGRUNNER ◑ 19 cm
Orthonyx temminckii

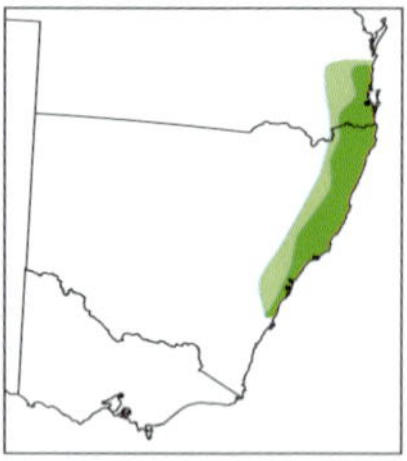

Juv

Ad ♀: orange throat.

Ad ♂: white throat.

Unobtrusive ground dweller in temperate and subtropical rainforests. Strong sexual dimorphism. Rakes leaf litter with large, strong feet, rarely flies. **Voice:** loud, excited *be-kweek-kweek-kweek* by members of family group. Alarm shriek.

CHOWCHILLA ◑ 26 cm
Orthonyx spaldingii

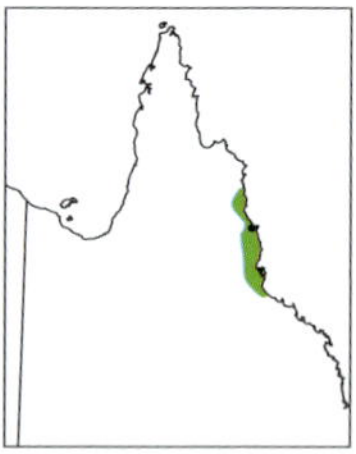

Juv

Ad ♀: orange throat.

Ad ♂: white throat.

Largish, dark ground bird of n Qld rainforest. Strong sexual dimorphism. Bounds on long legs, rakes leaf litter with strong feet. Strongly territorial in family groups. **Voice:** loud, rollicking chorus by family group *chowchilla-chowry-chook-chook*, dominates the dawn chorus.

RUFOUS BRISTLEBIRD ◔ 25 cm
Dasyornis broadbenti

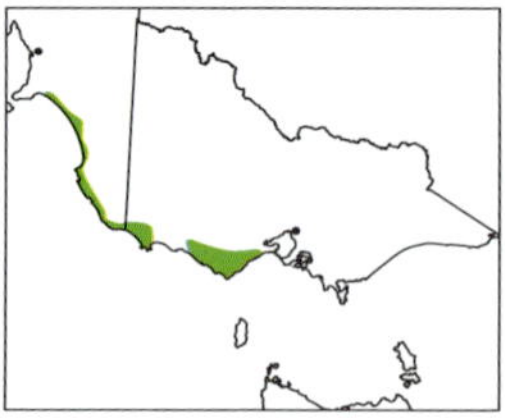

Juv

Ad

Shy ground dweller in coastal heath, dense gullies and shrubby gardens. Runs to cover, rarely flies.

Voice: territorial song with squeaky, silvery notes building to a loud, rollicking *chip-chip-chip-chooee*. Pairs perform duets.

EASTERN BRISTLEBIRD ◯ 19 cm
Dasyornis brachypterus

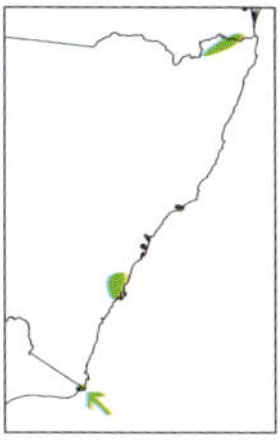

Secretive ground bird, in dense coastal heath or tussocky montane forest. Runs fast, scrambles through dense, low vegetation.

Localised remnant populations in NSW and extreme e Vic.

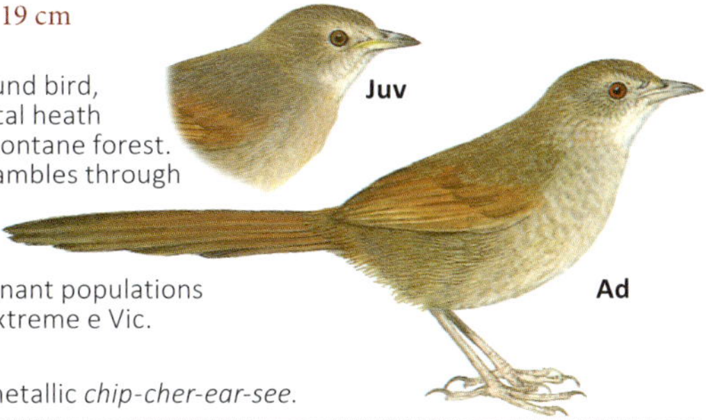

Voice: territorial song a loud, metallic *chip-cher-ear-see*.

WESTERN BRISTLEBIRD ◯ 17 cm
Dasyornis longirostris

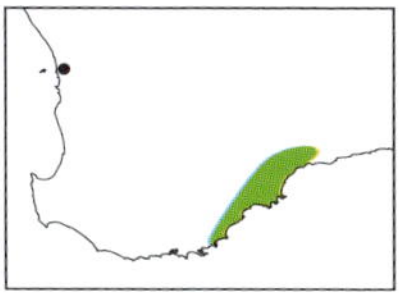

Secretive ground bird, restricted to dense, low coastal heath in sw WA. Emerges to feed along quiet tracks, ♂ may sing from atop a shrub.

Voice: territorial song a series of loud, clear, melodious notes *chip-per-tee-peedle-peet*, mate often responds with *quick-more-beer*.

NOISY SCRUB-BIRD ◯ 21 cm
Atrichornis clamosus

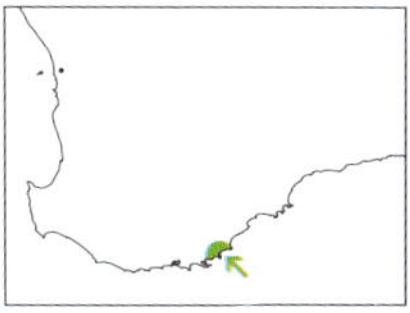

Scurries across paths.

Ad ♂: white throat with black centre.

Extremely secretive ground bird, often heard, rarely seen. Inhabits long-unburnt, low, closed forest and heath in sw WA.
Voice: territorial song a series of 10–20 very loud, clear notes building to a crescendo. Sings all year but particularly May–Oct *chee chee chee chip-ip-ip-ip chewit*.

RUFOUS SCRUB-BIRD ◯ 17 cm
Atrichornis rufescens

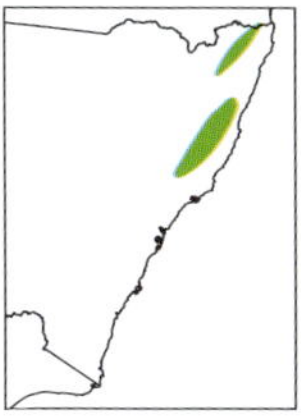

Extremely secretive ground bird, allowing only briefest of views. In dense wet undergrowth, especially with ferns, of upland rainforest in n NSW, just reaching Qld.

Ad ♂: black barring on throat.

Voice: amazingly loud song of ♂ given year-round, especially Aug–Dec, a variable series of phrases, sometimes lasting for 20 min, based on a ringing chip note.

TROPICAL SCRUBWREN ◔ 11 cm
Sericornis beccarii

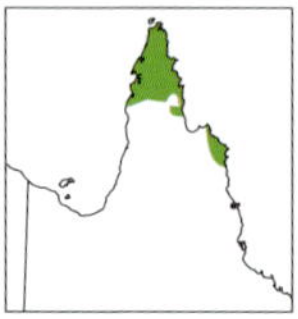

Only scrubwren in range on Cape York. Intergrades with Large-billed s of Cooktown.

White markings on face and wing, pink legs.

Ad ♂: plainer face on birds in s of range.

Rainforest and vine thickets with dense understorey. Bark-gleans from tall shrubs and small trees. Often forages on ground. **Voice:** like Large-billed Scrubwren.

LARGE-BILLED SCRUBWREN ◑ 12 cm
Sericornis magnirostra

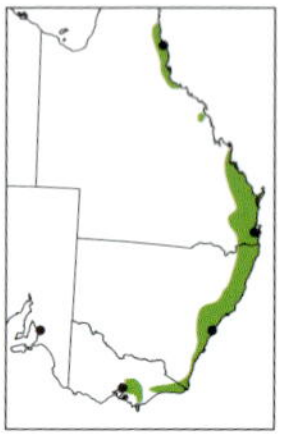

Small nimble scrubwren of wet forest; bark-gleans in mid-storey. **Voice:** not loud, but talkative: sharp *sip-sip* when foraging, chirring alarm call, sweet twittered song includes phrase *sa-leep sa-leep sa-leep*.

Bill long, slightly upturned. Cute contrast of dark eye with plain face.

Pink legs rule out thornbills.

ATHERTON SCRUBWREN ◔ 12 cm
Sericornis keri

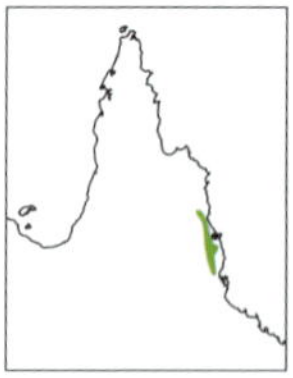

Very similar to Large-billed but slightly sturdier with shorter bill; subtly darker than Large-billed, usually with trace of supercilium.

Ad: Mt Lewis, yellower belly-tinge.

Ad: Atherton Tablelands.

Usually forages on ground or in low foliage like White-browed.

Restricted to upland rainforest. **Voice:** soft *tip* or *chup* when foraging, song a repeated *che-wee* or *tzee-you*, alarm calls similar to Large-billed Scrubwren.

YELLOW-THROATED SCRUBWREN ◕ 14 cm
Neosericornis citreogularis

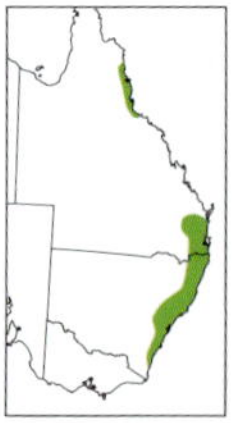

Singles or pairs on ground or in shady understorey of rainforest and wet sclerophyll, especially in gullies. In n Qld restricted to uplands.

Bold supercilium, yellow throat.

Yellow panel in folded wing.

Voice: melodious warbling song interspersed by short trills and mimicry. Also scolding alarm calls and a hard *tac*.

WHITE-BROWED SCRUBWREN ● 12 cm
Sericornis frontalis

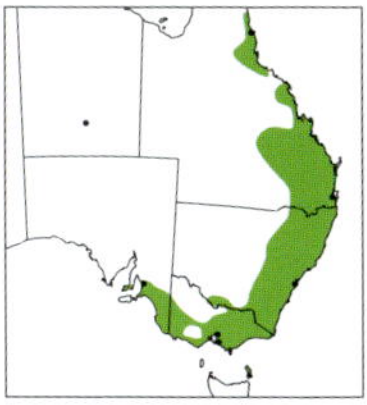

Varies geographically. All ssp have dark facial mask and bend of wing, pale iris, white submoustachial stripe. In dense undergrowth of rainforest, sclerophyll forest and woodland, shrubland and coastal heath. Alert but not timid, often seen on open ground near cover. **Voice:** harsh staccato chirring *tzzz* in alarm like Brown Thornbill. Loud musical song of repeated notes *tseer* or short phrases *seat-you* or *whee-a-chee*.

SPOTTED SCRUBWREN ● 12 cm
Sericornis maculatus

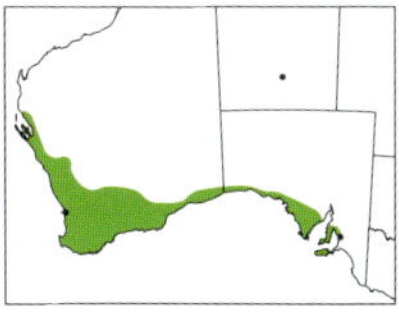

Formerly lumped with White-browed Scrubwren, has similar behaviour, sex differences and calls. Differs in strongly streaked underparts, black subterminal tail band, occupies more arid habitats. **Voice:** similar to White-browed.

TASMANIAN SCRUBWREN ● 13 cm
Sericornis humilis

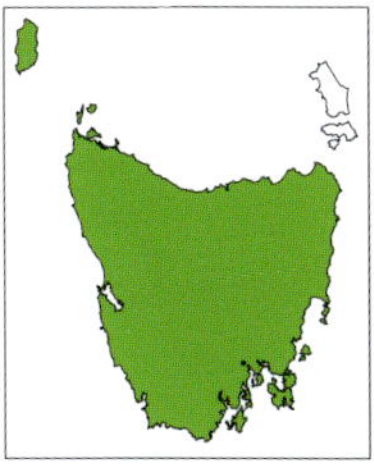

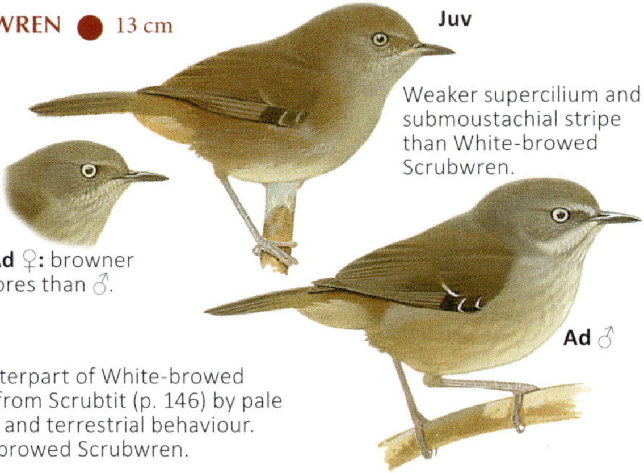

Faintly marked Tas counterpart of White-browed Scrubwren. Distinguish from Scrubtit (p. 146) by pale brow, shape of wing bar and terrestrial behaviour. **Voice:** similar to White-browed Scrubwren.

CHESTNUT-RUMPED HEATHWREN ◔ 13 cm
Hylacola pyrrhopygia

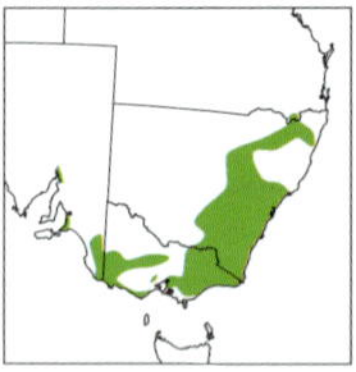

Secretive, in low heath or heathy understorey of sclerophyll forest. Forages on ground, hides in thick cover. **Voice:** ♂ sometimes sings atop bush or low branch just above shrub layer: melodious, sustained string of trills, warbles and mimicry. Sharp *tzeet* or *zweet zweet* in alarm.

SHY HEATHWREN ◑ 13 cm
Hylacola cauta

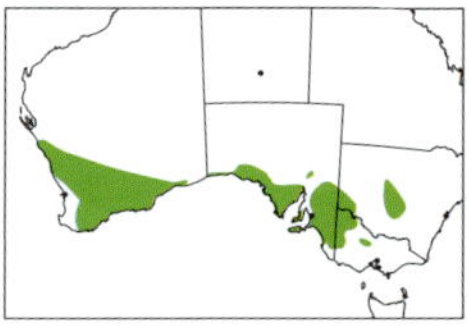

Shy, but less so than Chestnut-rumped. Singles or pairs in low shrubby or heathy understorey of mallee woodland. Forages on ground, hides in thick cover. **Voice:** clear sustained canary-like trilling, e.g. *chee-chee chick-a-dee*; quieter than Chestnut-rumped with less mimicry. Sharp *tchak* in alarm.

REDTHROAT ◑ 12 cm
Pyrrholaemus brunneus

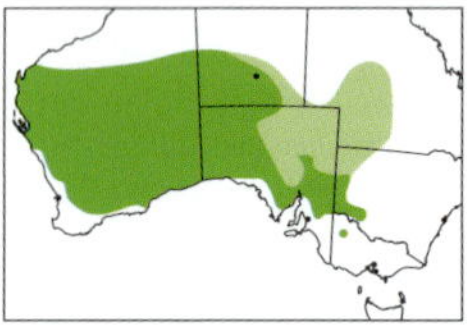

In arid shrublands, especially *Acacia* and chenopods. Forages on ground or thornbill-like in low shrubs. Unobtrusive but not shy, ♂ often sings atop shrub or small tree. **Voice:** beautiful sustained canary-like trilling and warbling often interspersed by mimicry. Scolding chatter in alarm.

STRIATED FIELDWREN ◑ 13 cm
Calamanthus fuliginosus

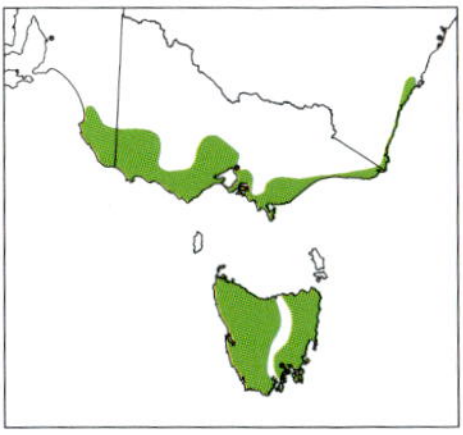

Singles or pairs in low, dense heath, saltmarsh, sedges and tussock grasses. ♂ often sings atop a shrub, otherwise inconspicuous, feeding on ground and skulking in vegetation. **Voice:** melodious and prolonged song a series of warbles and trills, often with two sharp notes followed by pause and trill.

RUFOUS FIELDWREN ◑ 12 cm
Calamanthus campestris

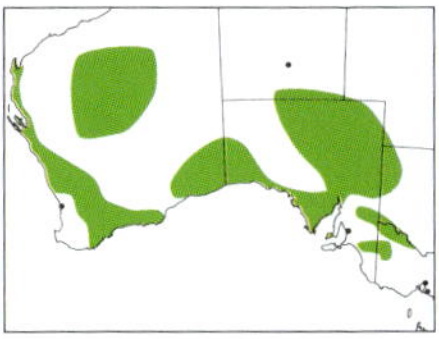

Variable; differs from Striated by unstreaked rufous uppertail coverts, rufous on cheek, greyer upperparts, longer bill, short hindclaw. Inland fieldwren of low, sparse to dense shrublands, especially chenopods including samphire. ♂ sings from exposed perch. Otherwise shy, singles or pairs feeding on ground, taking cover in dense bushes. **Voice:** loud melodious song of repeated warbles and trills, similar to Striated Fieldwren.

SPECKLED WARBLER ◑ 13 cm
Pyrrholaemus sagittatus

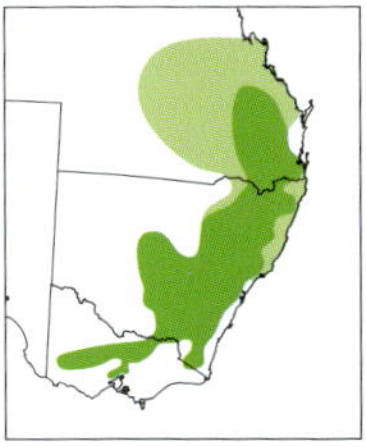

Dry sclerophyll forest and open woodland, often with scattered shrubs and tussock grasses. Rather shy; mostly forages on ground, takes cover in shrubs or trees. Singly or in pairs, often joins mixed feeding flocks in winter. **Voice:** sweet undulating musical whistle of 4–8 sec, sometimes includes mimicry. Rattling scrubwren-like chatter when agitated.

FERNWREN
Oreoscopus gutturalis 13 cm

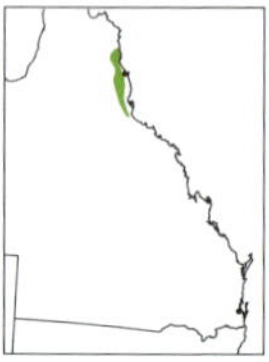

Small, dark scrubwren of upland rainforest in n Qld. In pairs on forest floor, feeding birds toss leaf litter aside with long bill. **Voice:** song a series of long pure whistles *pee-pee-pee-pee-peeee*.

SCRUBTIT
Acanthornis magna 12 cm

In mid-storey of wet forest in Tas. **Voice:** trilled jumble of fast notes *chi chi* and prolonged whistles *cheweet*.

ROCKWARBLER
Origma solitaria 14 cm

Sturdy, active ground bird restricted to rock outcrops in NSW.

Voice: shrill, melancholy *good-bye* or *tid-ee-dah* repeated 3–4 times; also a penetrating *pink* and mimicry.

PILOTBIRD
Pycnoptilus floccosus 18 cm

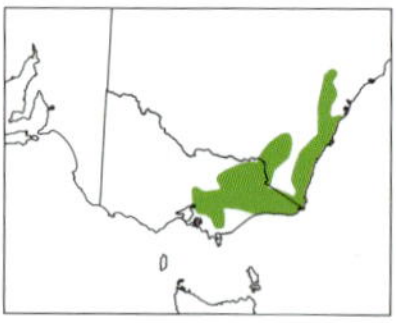

Plump, terrestrial resident of wet forest and coastal scrub. Scratches through leaf-litter, often raises and fans tail, flicks it up and down. In pairs or small family groups.
Voice: loud ringing territorial call *guinea-a-week*.

SOUTHERN WHITEFACE ◔ 12 cm
Aphelocephala leucopsis

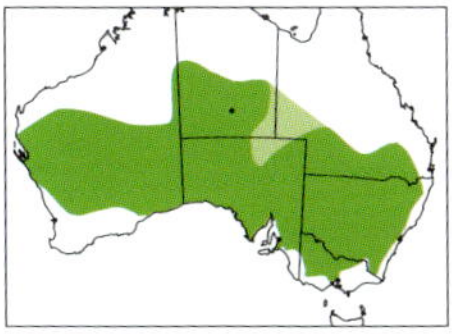

Ad: rufous flanks in WA.

Greyish upperparts, no breast band.

Singles, pairs and small groups in arid and semi-arid shrublands; forages on ground or low shrubs, often joins mixed feeding flocks.
Voice: fast, loud, high-pitched twittering; varied when feeding, given in bursts of 4 notes in flight.

CHESTNUT-BREASTED WHITEFACE ○ 11 cm
Aphelocephala pectoralis

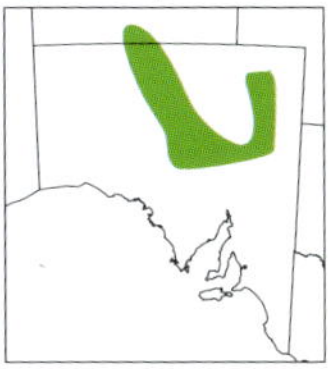

Juv: broad but faint breast band.

Rufous upperparts and pale-edged tertials.

Ad: broad rufous breast band.

Elusive whiteface of arid stony shrubland on plains, slopes and ridges. Avoids dense cover or sites where stock have depleted low herbs.

Voice: fast twittering; also a plaintive, whistling song.

BANDED WHITEFACE ◑ 11 cm
Aphelocephala nigricincta

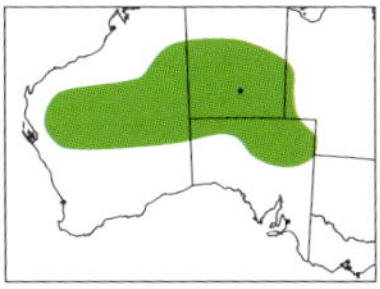

Juv: faint breast band.

Rufous upperparts and pale-edged tertials.

Narrow black breast band.

Arid, open shrubland, especially with mulga and saltbush, also grassland with a few scattered shrubs or trees. Pairs or small parties, often with other species. **Voice:** rich, fluty, fast twittering; also sweet whistles, a piping *pee-pee-pee* and harsh buzzing.

WEEBILL ◕ 9 cm
Smicrornis brevirostris

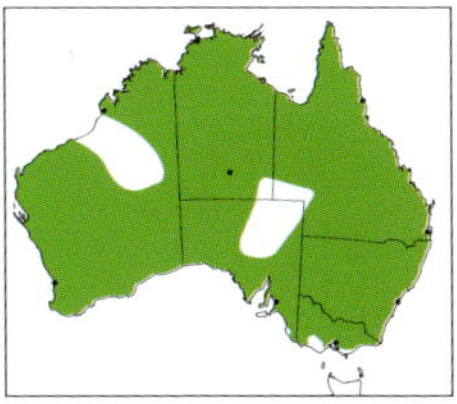

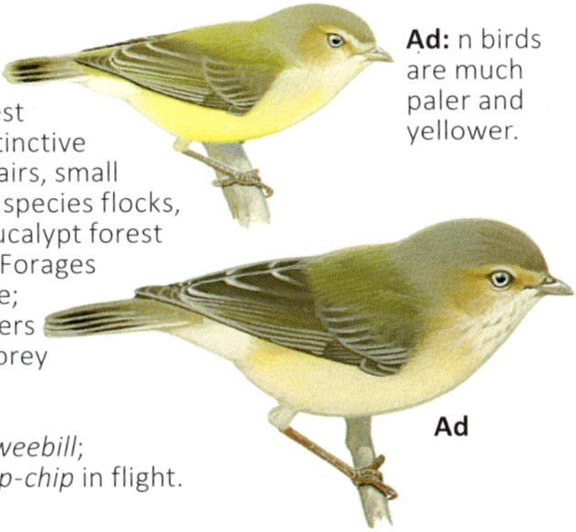

Ad: n birds are much paler and yellower.

One of our tiniest birds with a distinctive stubby bill. In pairs, small flocks or mixed species flocks, mostly in dry eucalypt forest and woodland. Forages nimbly in foliage; sometimes hovers while gleaning prey from leaves.

Voice: vocal; diagnostic whistled call *I'm a weebill*; also loud trill, high-pitched *trip* and soft *chip-chip* in flight.

YELLOW THORNBILL ◑ 10 cm
Acanthiza nana

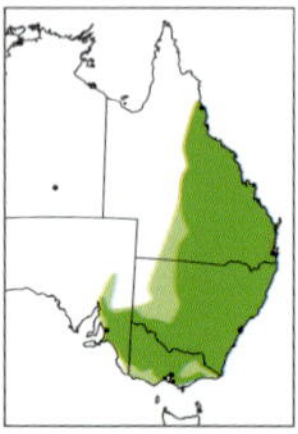

Plain forehead, dark eye, streaked ear coverts and orange wash on throat.

Ad: bright yellow in n Qld.

Tiny foliage gleaner in pairs or small flocks. Tall understorey of woodland, open forest and shrubland, often dominated by trees other than eucalypts. **Voice:** call *tzid-it* or *tis tis*, sometimes run together in longer sequence.

STRIATED THORNBILL ◕ 10 cm
Acanthiza lineata

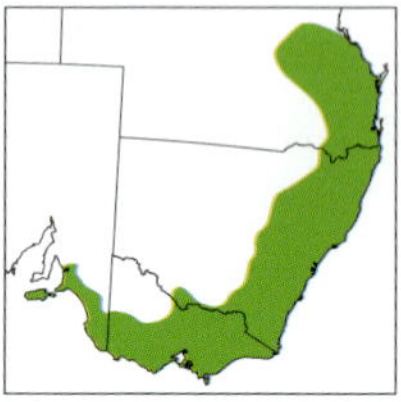

White streaking on rufous crown; olive upperparts.

Coarse white streaking on ear coverts; streaky breast.

Foliage gleaner found in canopy of eucalypt forest and woodland. Gregarious: in small parties, flocks of 10–20 birds or mixed species flocks.
Voice: thin insect-like *tsip*, singly or in a brisk string *tizis-tizis*. Also snatches of pleasant trilled song in spring.

MOUNTAIN THORNBILL ◑ 11 cm
Acanthiza katherina

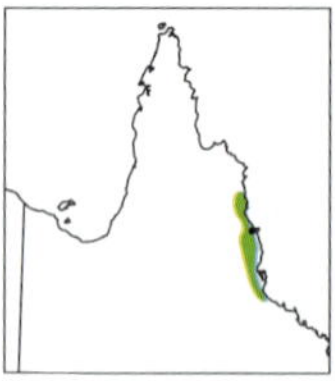

Pale iris, cream scalloping on forehead.

In montane rainforest of Wet Tropics where the only thornbill present. Confusion only likely with Brown Gerygone. Singles, pairs and small flocks in foliage.

Voice: recalls related Brown Thornbill: twittering contact calls and complex song of melodious notes and trills.

SLATY-BACKED THORNBILL ◔ 11 cm
Acanthiza robustirostris

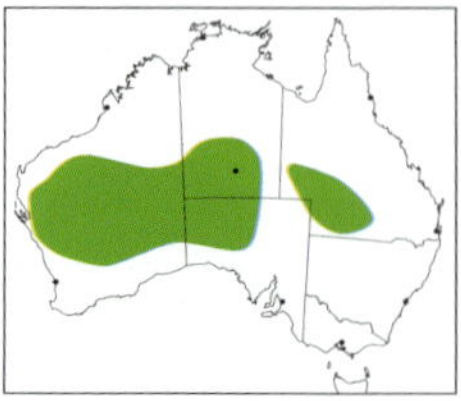

Easily confused with other thornbill species when in mixed species flocks.

Cold brownish grey upperparts.

Juv: plain forehead.

Black streaks on forehead, short white supercilium.

Uncommon and unobtrusive foliage gleaner in arid mulga woodland.
Voice: *tseeu* contact call similar to Chestnut-backed; harsh chirring trills and short snatches of warbling song.

TASMANIAN THORNBILL ◕ 11 cm
Acanthiza ewingii

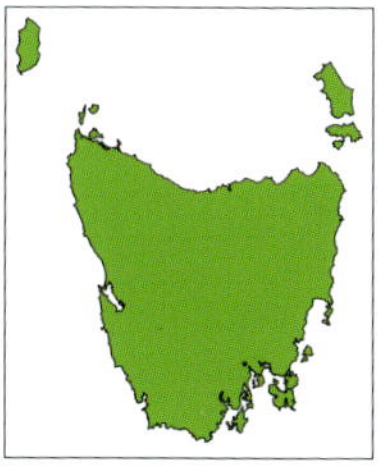

In shrub layer of wet sclerophyll forest.

Voice: song more liquid than Brown *tit-tit-too-woo*.

BROWN THORNBILL ● 11 cm
Acanthiza pusilla

Common in forest, woodland and heath with dense shrub layer. In pairs or family parties, joins mixed species flocks.

Voice: loud, deep calls for a tiny bird. Harsh *tzzt* or *tchirt* like White-browed Scrubwren; pleasant trilled song *to-weet-et-wrrtt*.

INLAND THORNBILL ◕ 11 cm
Acanthiza apicalis

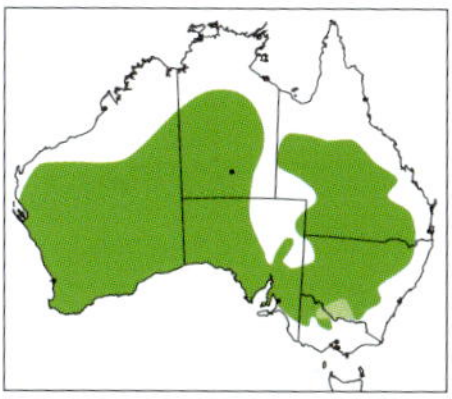

Tall shrubland and dense understorey of woodland; in s WA also in shrub layer of forest. **Voice:** similar to Brown Thornbill; also thin short *tsee* contact call.

CHESTNUT-RUMPED THORNBILL ◕ 10 cm
Acanthiza uropygialis

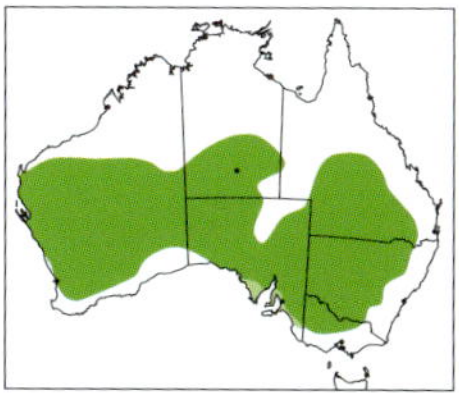

Small groups in dry open woodland and shrubland; forages in trees and shrubs, occasionally on ground. **Voice:** high-pitched single note *tseeu*, also a short melodious song *pit-pee-teu*.

YELLOW-RUMPED THORNBILL 11 cm
Acanthiza chrysorrhoa

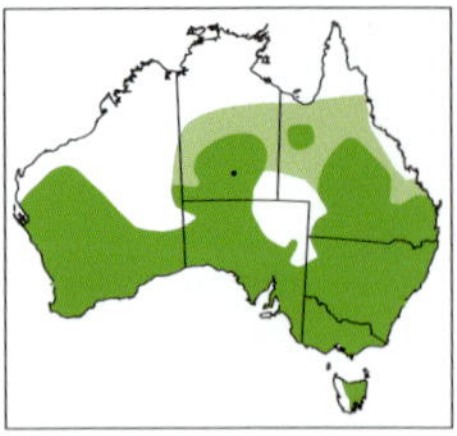

Flocks of up to 30 in woodland and lightly wooded grassland, including farms, roadside verges. Forages on ground.

Black forehead with white spots.

Bright yellow uppertail coverts.

Voice: lively, tinkling, descending song, soft *chek* contact calls when feeding.

Yellow rump easily seen as flock flies from ground to cover.

BUFF-RUMPED THORNBILL 11 cm
Acanthiza reguloides

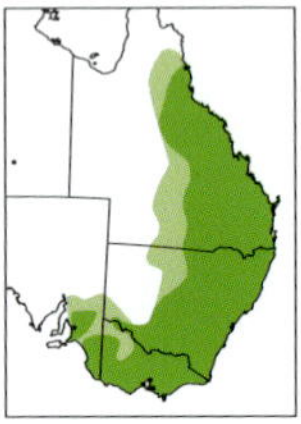

In eucalypt woodland and open forest with sparse understorey.

Pairs or small flocks forage in leaf-litter or glean prey from tree branches and foliage.

Buff-scalloped forehead, pale eye.

Buff uppertail coverts.

Voice: pleasing reel *pit-pit-pititta-pit*, less varied in pitch than similar song of Yellow-rumped Thornbill.

SLENDER-BILLED THORNBILL 10 cm
Acanthiza iredalei

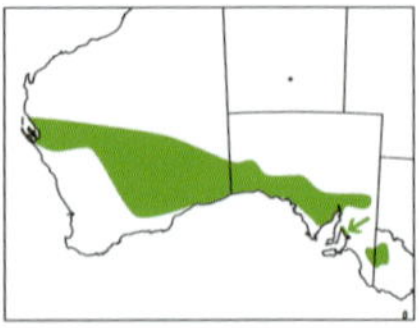

In pairs or small flocks, rather shy, doesn't join mixed species flocks.

Black and white scalloping on forehead, pale eye.

Narrow, pale rump patch.

In low shrublands with few or no trees: chenopods in inland, coastal samphire near Adelaide, dry heath around SA–Vic border.
Voice: rapid high-pitched call of repeated single notes *tsit-tsit-tsit-tsit*; also wavering trilled song in spring *preeur*.

WESTERN THORNBILL 10 cm
Acanthiza inornata

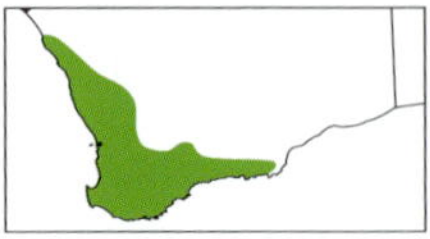

Plain WA counterpart of Buff-rumped Thornbill.

Buff-scalloped forehead, pale eye.

Plain uppertail and rump.

In pairs or small groups, in forest and woodland with some low shrubs; feeds on ground or by bark-gleaning.
Voice: pleasant reel *pitta-pitta-pitta*, sometimes ending in fast trill, interspersed by metallic *dzink*.

SPOTTED PARDALOTE ● 9 cm
Pardalotus punctatus

All pardalotes are foliage gleaners of eucalypts. Can be difficult to see when high in canopy. Singly or pairs in forest and woodland. **Voice:** chiming call a constant backdrop in many forests: *s-wit PIWIP*, loud, final phrase recalling rosella.

Nests in hole in ground.

STRIATED PARDALOTE ● 10 cm
Pardalotus striatus

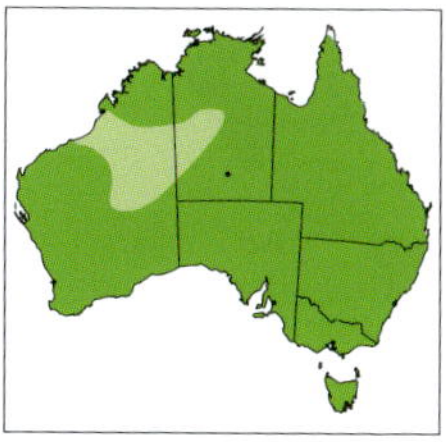

Largest pardalote. Mostly in eucalypt forest and woodland, especially smooth-barked gums.

Voice: repetitive song 2–4 clear notes, *wit-wit*, *witta-witta* or *witchi-chew*.

RED-BROWED PARDALOTE ◑ 10 cm
Pardalotus rubricatus

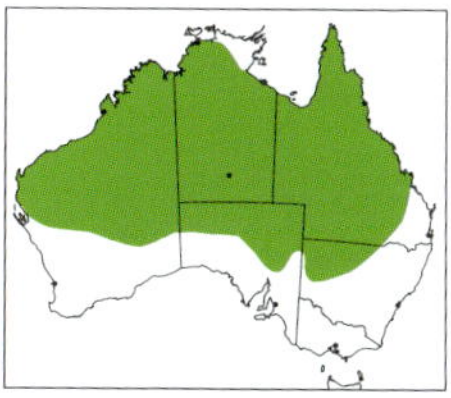

Inland and tropical pardalote of open eucalypt woodland, especially along watercourses.

Voice: rosella-like chiming whistle *few-wh-wh-wh-wh-whit*.

FORTY-SPOTTED PARDALOTE ○ 9 cm
Pardalotus quadragintus

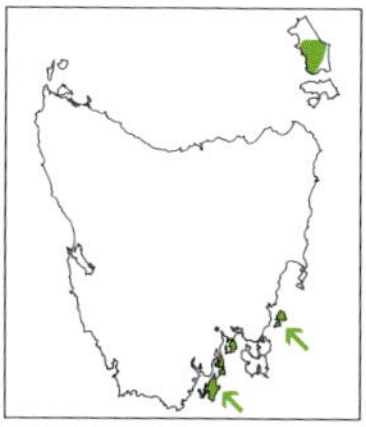

Small, rare pardalote restricted to foliage of dry woodland and forest dominated by White Gum *Eucalyptus viminalis*. Singles and pairs, joins feeding flocks in non-breeding season. **Voice:** soft piping *whi-whi*; loud, sharp *kchoo* when breeding.

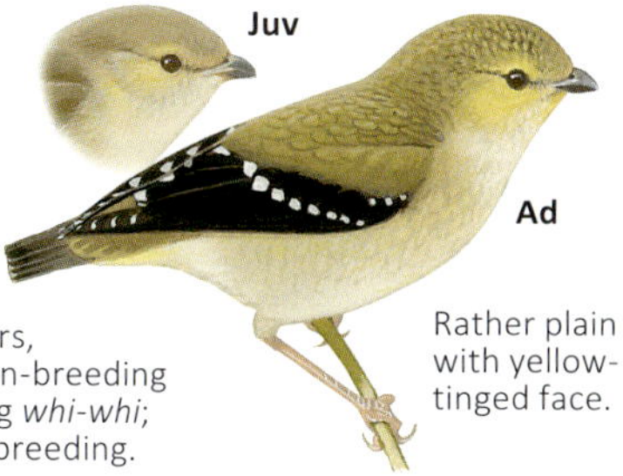

WHITE-THROATED GERYGONE ◔ 10 cm
Gerygone olivacea

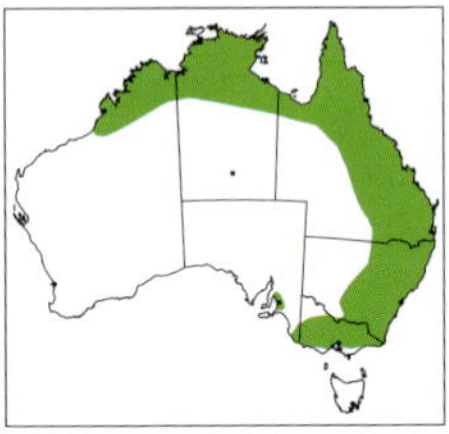

Singles and pairs in open eucalypt forest and woodland. Resident in n Aus, breeding visitor to foothill forests of se Aus. Inconspicuous in foliage, usually first detected by song. **Voice:** a sweet, musical, far-carrying song, initial whistles blend into liquid cascading warble.

FAIRY GERYGONE ◑ 10 cm
Gerygone palpebrosa

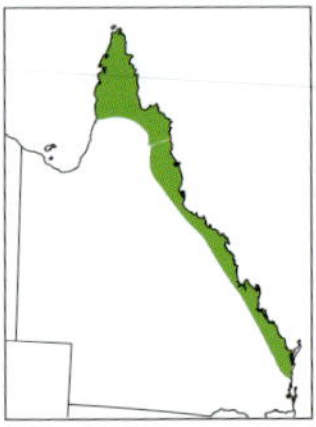

In rainforest fringes. Lacks white spot on undertail *cf* White-throated Gerygone.

Paler yellow underparts than White-throated Gerygone.

Voice: lively, frequently repeated warble, often ends in louder descending note *witchee cheeweet tew*.

GREEN-BACKED GERYGONE ◑ 10 cm
Gerygone chloronota

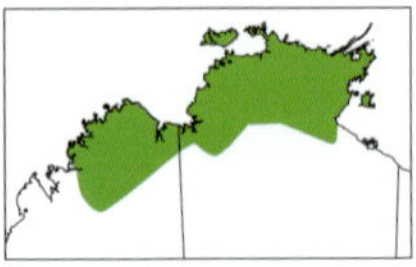

Small heavy-billed gerygone.

In closed forest, including rainforest, mangroves and gardens e.g. in Darwin. **Voice:** oft-repeated song, a chattering reel of ~10 notes.

DUSKY GERYGONE ◑ 11 cm
Gerygone tenebrosa

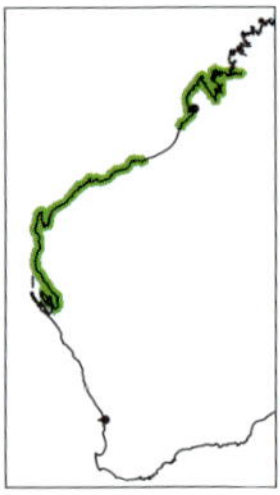

Plain, slender gerygone restricted to mangroves of n WA. Mainly forages in outer canopy of mangroves but also perches on pneumatophores, takes prey from ground. No white in tail. **Voice:** repeated series of hesitant, plaintive whistles *chee chee chew-wee witwee*, slower than most gerygone calls, recalls a subdued whistler.

WESTERN GERYGONE ◕ 10 cm
Gerygone fusca

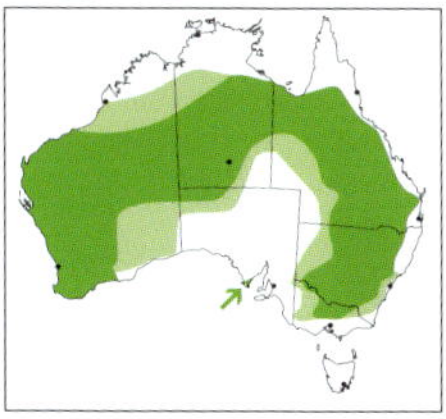

Pied tail pattern.

Juv: brown eye.

Small plain gerygone with charming song.

Ad: red eye.

In dryish forest and woodland, mulga and along watercourses.

No white line behind eye *cf* Mangrove Gerygone.

Voice: often sings; sweet musical series of rising and falling whistles, often ending abruptly as if bird ran out of breath.

BROWN GERYGONE ◕ 10 cm
Gerygone mouki

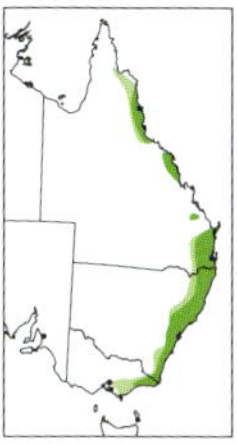

Grey face contrasts with brown crown and underparts.

Juv: brown eye.

Small rainforest gerygone, mostly seen in canopy. Most readily distinguished from thornbills by voice, white eyebrow and white spot under tail.

Ad: red eye.

Voice: vocal; repeats brisk twittering song *which-is-it* or *diddle-it-did-dit*.

MANGROVE GERYGONE ◑ 11 cm
Gerygone levigaster

Plain grey gerygone with long white eyebrow extending behind eye.

Juv: browner upperparts, yellower underparts than Ad; brown eye.

Ad: red eye.

In mangroves, but in n WA mainly in *Melaleuca* thickets (most gerygones in n WA mangroves are Dusky).

White tail band.

Voice: sustained melodious song, moving sweetly up and down scale without the hesitancy of Western Gerygone or cascading trill of White-throated Gerygone.

LARGE-BILLED GERYGONE ◑ 11 cm
Gerygone magnirostris

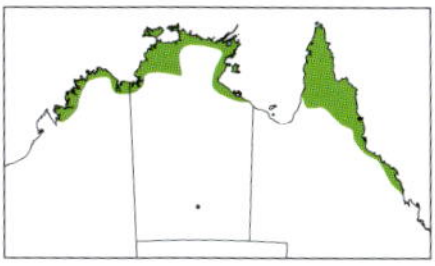

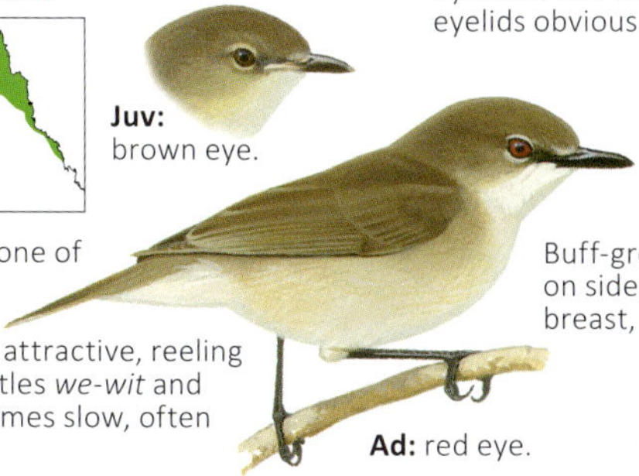

Lacks clear white eyebrow but white eyelids obvious.

Juv: brown eye.

Hefty-billed gerygone of mangroves and dense riverine vegetation. **Voice**: attractive, reeling song of clean whistles *we-wit* and *will-we-wit* sometimes slow, often loud and cheery.

Buff-grey wash on sides of breast, plain tail.

Ad: red eye.

Large pendant nest over water.

MALURIDAE. Australasian family, found mostly on the ground or in low cover; long tails usually held cocked. **Fairy-wren** males are brilliantly coloured, females have plain, unstreaked upperparts; they are social, usually in small groups. **Emu-wrens** are inconspicuous residents of dense, low cover with dark-streaked upperparts and distinctive tail structure. **Grasswrens** have white-streaked upperparts; they are very secretive, usually running into cover rather than flying when disturbed; in pairs or small family groups; most species have very restricted ranges and habitat requirements.

SUPERB FAIRY-WREN ● 12 cm
Malurus cyaneus

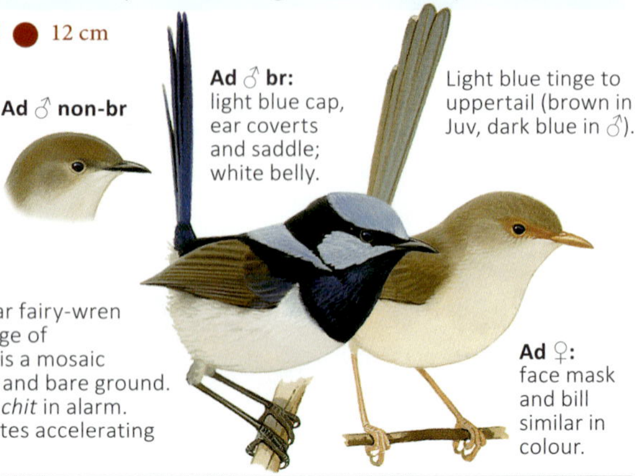

Boldest and most familiar fairy-wren of se Aus. Uses wide range of habitats provided there is a mosaic of dense low vegetation and bare ground. **Voice:** sharp *tsit*, louder *chit* in alarm. Reeling song of short notes accelerating to rippling trill.

SPLENDID FAIRY-WREN ◕ 12 cm
Malurus splendens

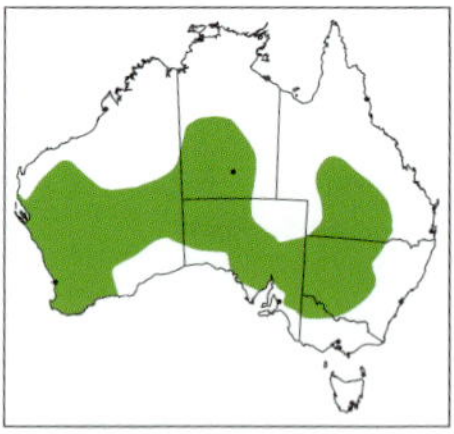

Shrubland and woodland of arid and semi-arid regions, with combination of shrubby to heathy understorey, bare ground and emergent trees or tall shrubs. **Voice:** similar to Superb Fairy-wren.

PURPLE-CROWNED FAIRY-WREN ◔ 14 cm
Malurus coronatus

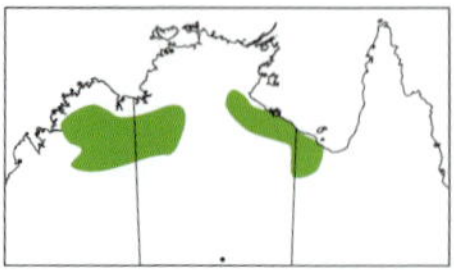

In 'brown' plumages, the only fairy-wren with darker ear coverts. Juv has brown cap.

Largest fairy-wren. In thickets of *Pandanus* or canegrass beside rivers of wet-dry tropics. **Voice:** strong *chet* contact call, sharp *zit* in alarm. Loud reeling song, *cheepa-cheepa-cheepa*.

WHITE-WINGED FAIRY-WREN ◕ 12 cm
Malurus leucopterus

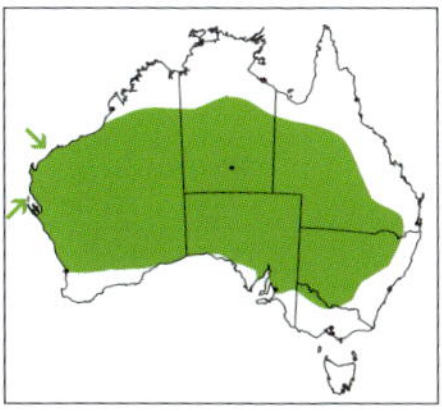

Arid and semi-arid zones: occurs in low open shrubland with much bare ground, few or no trees. Usually in groups of 2–11 birds that mostly include only one blue ♂.
Voice: soft *tsit*. Song of 3–5 chirps followed by prolonged trill wavering around the same pitch.

RED-BACKED FAIRY-WREN ◕ 11 cm
Malurus melanocephalus

Tropical and subtropical habitats with grassy understorey, including grassland, wetland fringes, savanna woodland and remnants in urban areas.
Voice: soft and unobtrusive contact call *ssst*, sharper *zit* in alarm, song a twittering reel.

LOVELY FAIRY-WREN ◑ 12 cm
Malurus amabilis

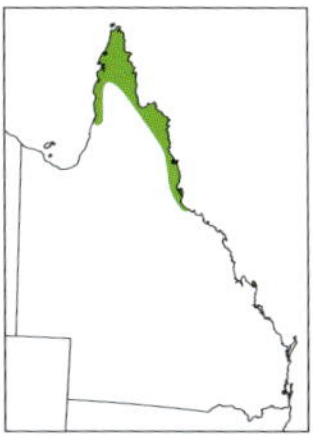

Shrubby margins of rainforest; the most arboreal fairy-wren, gleaning prey from leaves and branches of shrubs and small trees.
Voice: similar to Purple-backed Fairy-wren.

PURPLE-BACKED FAIRY-WREN ◕ 13 cm
Malurus assimilis

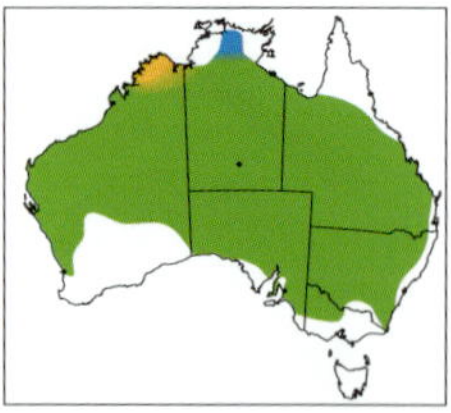

Ad ♂ br: purple mantle; ear tufts slightly paler than deeper blue crown. ♂ of all ssp similar.

Ad ♂ non-br: whitish eye ring.

Small lilac patch.

● **Ad ♀:** rufous lores darker than pale bill.

● **Ad ♀**

● **Ad ♀**

In Kimberley and Top End, NT, confined to rocky country; ♀ have smoky blue head and upperparts.

Understorey of mallee scrub, *Acacia* or chenopod shrubland, lignum thickets. **Voice:** soft sibilant *see*; sharper *tsit* or *trrt-trrt* in alarm; trilling song.

VARIEGATED FAIRY-WREN ◕ 13 cm
Malurus lamberti

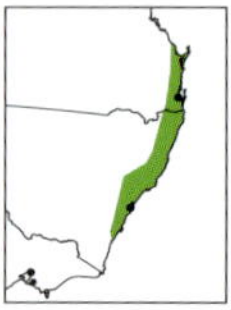

Ad ♂ br: cobalt cap and ear coverts paler than Purple-backed.

Brown ♀ similar to Purple-backed. Coastal heath, and shrubby understory of dry sclerophyll forest and woodland. **Voice:** similar to Purple-backed.

BLUE-BREASTED FAIRY-WREN ◕ 13 cm
Malurus pulcherrimus

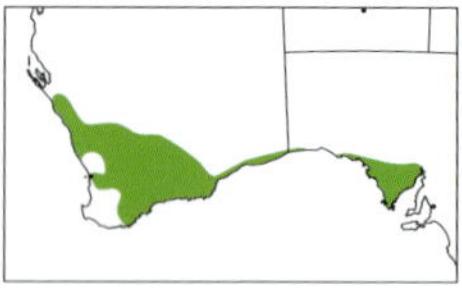

Ad ♂ br: dark indigo breast, looks black in shade. Violet-blue cap, ear coverts and back.

Ad ♀: rufous lores coloured like bill, eye ring paler.

Ad ♂ non-br: black lores, pale blue eye ring.

Tall sandy heath and woodland with shrubby understorey. Shy and seldom far from cover. **Voice:** *tsse* contact calls, sharper *tsit* in alarm; chirped song runs into a trill.

RED-WINGED FAIRY-WREN ◕ 14 cm
Malurus elegans

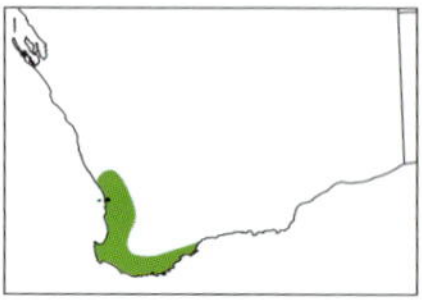

Ad ♂ br: pale blue ear-tufts, forehead and back, dusky blue crown. Dark slate-blue throat.

Ad ♀: black bill, rusty lores, no eye ring. Grey head contrasts with brown back.

Ad ♂ non-br: black lores.

Humid forests of sw WA. **Voice:** soft sibilant *see-see* contact calls. Song has introductory notes *cher-cher-cher* followed by a rippling trill.

SOUTHERN EMU-WREN ◔ 16 cm
Stipiturus malachurus

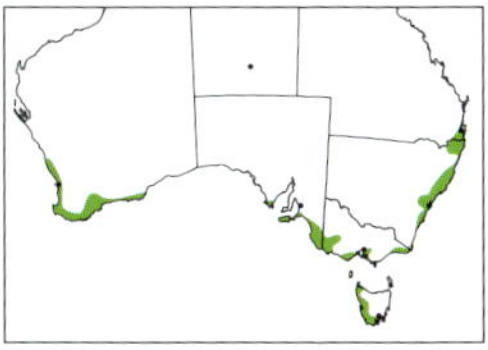

Longest-tailed emu-wren. In heath, with or without tree cover. Sometimes in sedge or tussocks. **Voice:** contact call similar to fairy-wrens but softer, higher-pitched, more insect-like. Song a high-pitched, twittering reel lasting 1–2 sec.

MALLEE EMU-WREN ○ 13 cm
Stipiturus mallee

Tiny emu-wren restricted to Murray Mallee of Vic. Mainly in large *Triodia* hummocks within long-unburnt mallee; some in mallee heath. Shy; listen for soft calls and scan for birds singing from emergent stems. **Voice:** soft contact call *tseep* easily confused with insects, inaudible to some. Song a short, fast, high-pitched reel.

RUFOUS-CROWNED EMU-WREN ◔ 13 cm
Stipiturus ruficeps

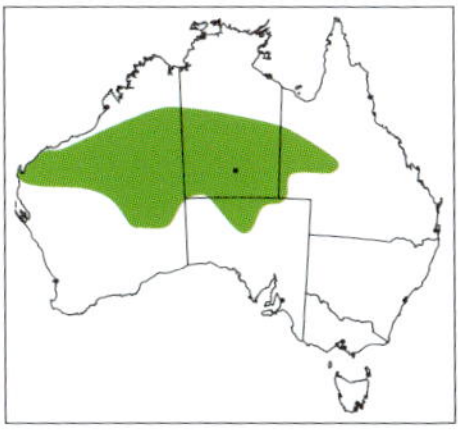

Tiny emu-wren, arguably the smallest Aus bird. Occurs patchily in tall, long-unburnt *Triodia* on plains and rocky hills of c Aus, sometimes with overstorey of shrubs or low woodland. **Voice:** similar to Mallee Emu-wren; incessant insect-like contact call *tseep*, song a fast twittering reel.

GREY GRASSWREN ○ 19 cm
Amytornis barbatus

Restricted to lignum swamps (whether wet or dry) in Bulloo and Cooper-Diamantina basins.
Voice: persistent metallic chirps *tsit-tsit-tsit*. Song similar but ends with downslurred *trrt tirrew*.

DUSKY GRASSWREN ◑ 16 cm
Amytornis purnelli

Rather plain, dark plumage with white streaking on head, upperparts and breast.

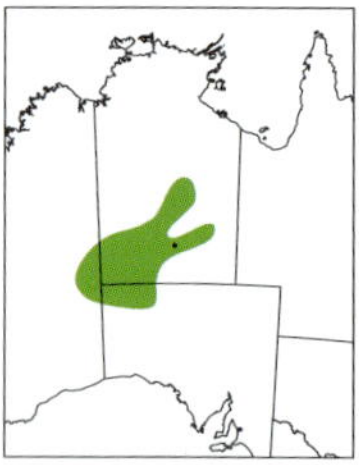

Thickset grasswren of rocky *Triodia* clad slopes in c Aus ranges.
Voice: drawn-out, high-pitched *seep* and twittering trills. Sharp, staccato *tchk-tchk* in alarm; song a loud reeling trill.

KALKADOON GRASSWREN ◔ 16 cm
Amytornis ballarae

Greyer underparts and coarser white streaking than Dusky Grasswren.

Nw Qld counterpart of Dusky Grasswren. Rocky slopes, ridges and gullies with long-unburnt *Triodia*.
Voice: high-pitched peeps and squeaks. Song a short series of varied high pitched trills.

EYREAN GRASSWREN ◯ 16 cm
Amytornis goyderi

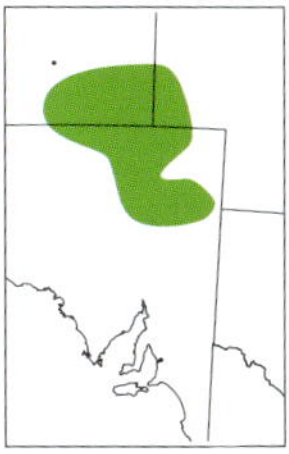

Small, long-tailed with sandy-rufous upperparts, mostly plain white underparts.

Deep finch-like bill, moustachial stripe indistinct.

Restricted to canegrass tussocks on slopes and ridges of dunes in Simpson and Strzelecki deserts. Furtive, runs from observers when they are 10s of m away. Slightly offset paired footprints often a good clue to presence.
Voice: soft, high-pitched, cricket-like trill. Song a jumble of whistled trills and buzzes.

THICK-BILLED GRASSWREN ◔ 16 cm
Amytornis modestus

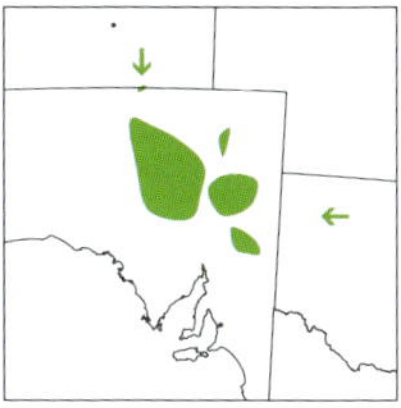

Small, rather plain and pale, light brown above, creamy-white below with stout bill.

Restricted to arid chenopod shrubland on plains and low rocky ridges. Often along drainage lines where shrubs are larger and thicker.
Voice: quietest grasswren; soft, high-pitched contact calls *see-see* difficult to hear. Also short, quiet song *sip-sip-tsip-twee*.

WESTERN GRASSWREN ◔ 16 cm
Amytornis textilis

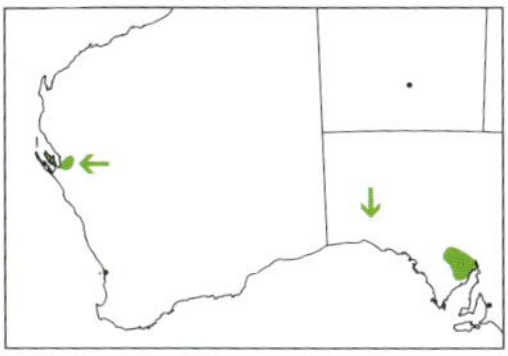

Longer-tailed than Thick-billed Grasswren. Darker brown upperparts, pale brown underparts, more boldly streaked on head, back and throat.

Acacia shrubland with low cover near Shark Bay. Low chenopod shrubland on Eyre Peninsula, sometimes with open woodland cover and especially with shrubs of Australian Boxthorn.
Voice: soft twittering contact calls, harder *chet*, sharp *tik* in alarm. Short song ends in complex trills, louder and more musical than Thick-billed Grasswren.

STRIATED GRASSWREN ◔ 16 cm

Amytornis striatus

Slender bill. Black moustachial stripe contrasts with rufous lores and white throat.

Ad ♀: rufous flank spot.

Secretive and hard to see; restricted to *Triodia* in long-unburnt mallee, preferring tall, dense tussocks. **Voice:** high-pitched *seep*, inaudible to some. Louder, sharper *tchritt* in alarm. Sweet varied song starts *tew tew tew*, merges into ripple of buzzes and trills.

RUFOUS GRASSWREN ◔ 16 cm

Amytornis whitei

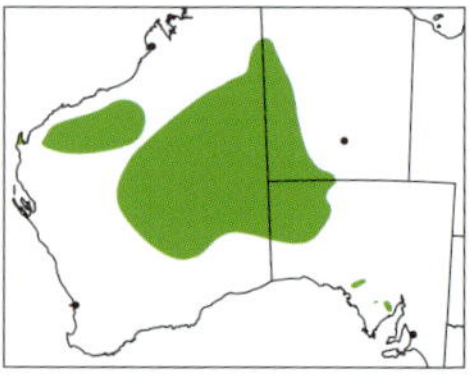

Brighter rufous upperparts with less black streaking than Striated Grasswren. Less rufous in c Aus and s of range.

Small ssp with broad but patchy distribution in mature *Triodia* and heath on arid sandy soils. Large ssp found on *Triodia*-clad rocky hills of Pilbara and North West Cape.

OPALTON GRASSWREN ◔ 16 cm

Amytornis rowleyi

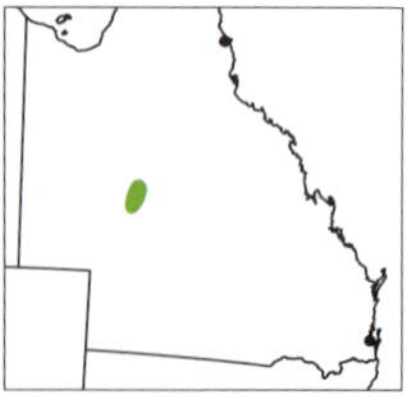

Restricted to *Triodia* within Normanton Box mallee on gravel substrates, c Qld. Like Rufous, but with darker head streaking and cleaner white underparts.

SHORT-TAILED GRASSWREN ◔ 15 cm

Amytornis merrotsyi

Shorter tail and stouter bill than Striated Grasswren.

Ad ♀: rufous flank spot.

Tail often cocked well forward.

Smudgy black on face, lacks clear moustachial stripe, has only faint rufous in lores.

Restricted to *Triodia*-clad stony hills of Flinders and Gawler Ranges, SA. **Voice:** similar to Striated Grasswren.

BLACK GRASSWREN ◔ 19 cm
Amytornis housei

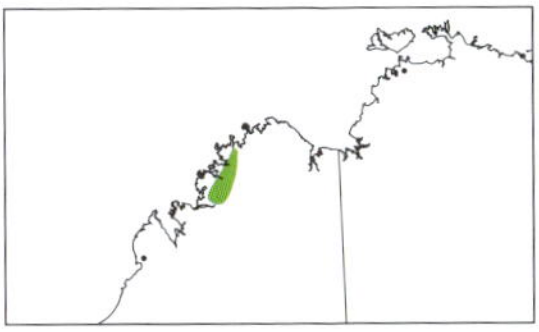

Large grasswren restricted to sandstone escarpment of n Kimberley, usually with large *Triodia* tussocks. Hops and runs, bounds between boulders, seldom flies or cocks tail.
Voice: presence often revealed by metallic chatter or chirped contact calls. Also a brief complex song.

WHITE-THROATED GRASSWREN ◯ 21 cm
Amytornis woodwardi

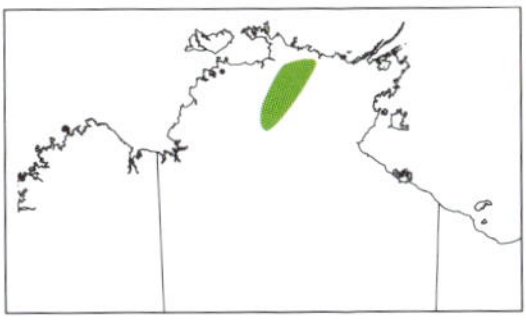

Largest grasswren, restricted to Arnhem Land escarpment with bare rock and large *Triodia* tussocks.
Voice: sharp contact calls *tzzt* louder and deeper than fairy-wrens. Rich song from exposed perch: starts with sharp trills, ends in sweet warbles.

CARPENTARIAN GRASSWREN ◯ 16 cm
Amytornis dorotheae

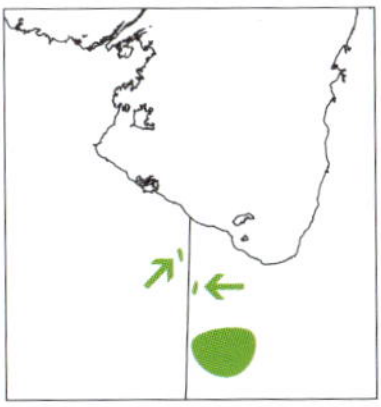

Restricted to rocky hills, plains, slopes and creeklines with long-unburnt *Triodia* along Qld and NT border. Intermediate between White-throated and Rufous Grasswrens. Cryptic, even by grasswren standards.
Voice: high-pitched, cricket-like *szzip*; also a sweet song of jumbled trills, buzzes and downslurred whistles.

ORANGE CHAT ◑ 11 cm
Epthianura aurifrons

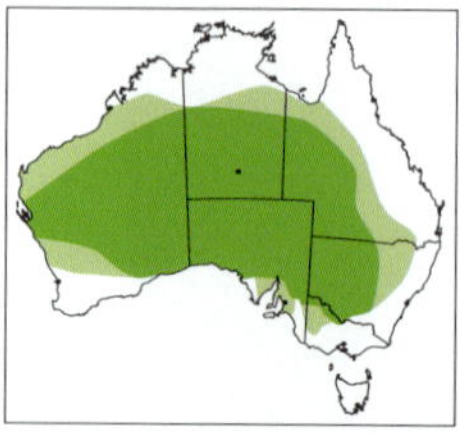

Yellowish to vibrant orange-yellow chat with dark eye. Forages on ground and in low shrubs. Desert-dwelling, especially saltbush plains, often around fringes of salt lakes. **Voice:** a metallic *tang*.

YELLOW CHAT ○ 11 cm
Epthianura crocea

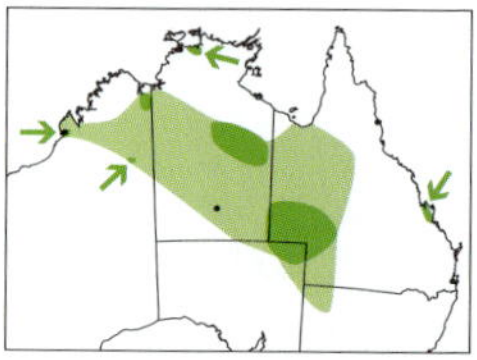

Pale yellow to vibrant yellow chat with pale eye. Scarce to rare and localised on coastal plains, floodplains and inland ephemeral wetlands, bore drains. **Voice:** 3-note, high-pitched call *te tsu te* with middle note higher or lower.

GIBBERBIRD ◔ 12 cm
Ashbyia lovensis

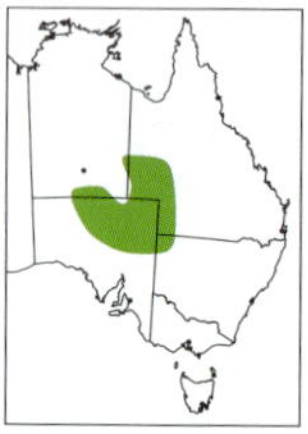

Yellowish chat with pale eye, restricted to treeless gibber desert. When flushed lands on elevated stone (*cf* small shrub for Orange Chat). **Voice:** *whit-whit-whit* during display flights and musical chatter.

CRIMSON CHAT ◑ 12 cm
Epthianura tricolor

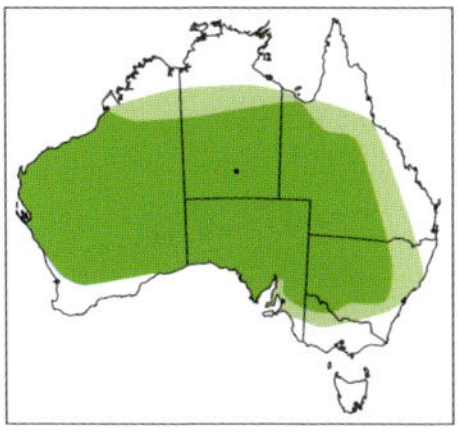

Widespread, red-rumped chat of dry shrubby habitats. Sometimes in large flocks, irruptive at edges of range. **Voice:** a metallic *tang*.

WHITE-FRONTED CHAT ◕ 12 cm
Epthianura albifrons

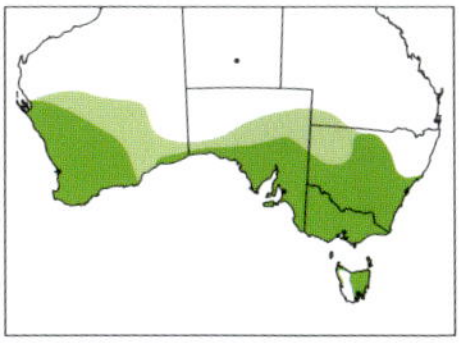

Pied chat of s Aus, bold grey or black breast band. In coastal and damp open areas, inland areas including samphire flats and saltbush plains. Often in mixed flocks with other chat species.
Voice: a short metallic *buzz* recalls Zebra Finch.

GREY HONEYEATER ○ 11 cm
Conopophila whitei

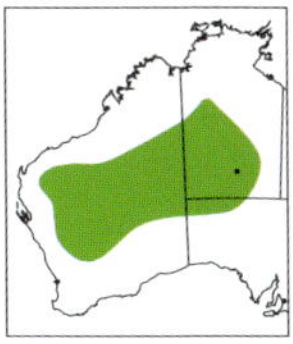

Beware Western Gerygone which has straight bill, distinct black and white tail pattern.

Small, greyish honeyeater with pale-tipped undertail, otherwise devoid of field characters. Mostly associated with mulga woodland, but also flowering shrubs and eucalypts.
Voice: a 2-note *cre-seek*.

PIED HONEYEATER ◔ 17 cm
Certhionyx variegatus

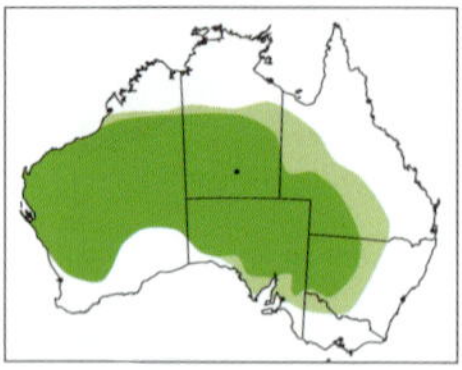

Arid zone honeyeater with striking sexual dimorphism, long decurved bill. Arid and semi-arid shrubland and woodland. Nomadic and irruptive. **Voice:** drawn-out, mournful *pe-pipee-pee-pee* often given in diving display flight.

BLACK HONEYEATER ◑ 11 cm
Sugomel niger

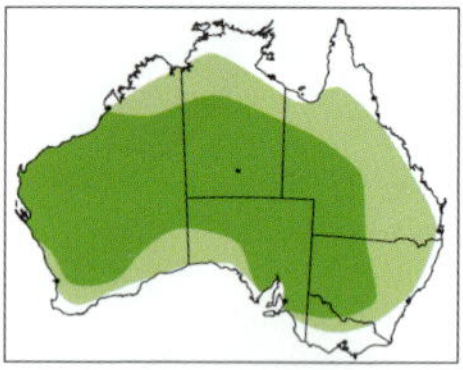

Small, short-tailed arid zone honeyeater with long, slender, decurved bill. Arid and semi-arid woodland, especially where nectar abundant. *Eremophila* (Emu-bush) is a favoured food plant. **Voice:** a high-pitched drawn out *se-seeee* given repeatedly.

BANDED HONEYEATER ◑ 12 cm
Cissomela pectoralis

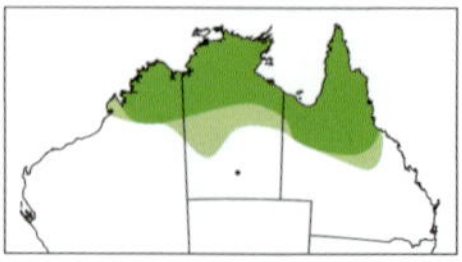

Small black and white (Ad) or brown and white (Juv and Imm) honeyeater with neat, narrow breast band. Tropical grassy woodland and forest, highly mobile in response to flowering. **Voice:** loud, buzzing *tzeep tzeep*. Also high-pitched double whistle.

RED-HEADED HONEYEATER ◑ 11 cm
Myzomela erythrocephala

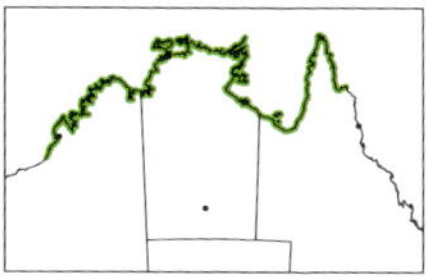

Small, red-headed or red-faced honeyeater with slender, decurved bill. Largely restricted to mangroves and adjacent dense scrub and forest.
Voice: repetitive metallic buzzing *caseep*.

Much darker below than Scarlet Honeyeater, with sharply cut-off red hood.

SCARLET HONEYEATER ◕ 10 cm
Myzomela sanguinolenta

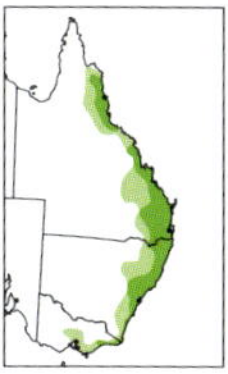

Does not normally co-occur with Red-headed Honeyeater.

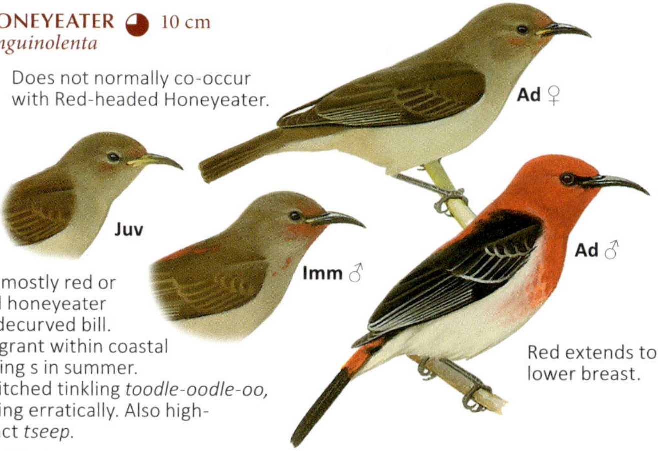

Small, bright, mostly red or reddish-faced honeyeater with slender decurved bill. An e coast migrant within coastal forest extending s in summer.
Voice: high-pitched tinkling *toodle-oodle-oo,* rising and falling erratically. Also high-pitched contact *tseep*.

Red extends to lower breast.

DUSKY HONEYEATER ◕ 14 cm
Myzomela obscura

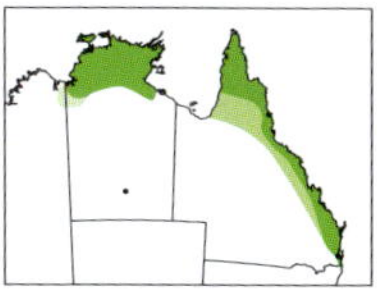

Lacks the warm brown or olive tones of Brown Honeyeater. Rather dark, often appearing sooty grey.

Small, slender, unmarked honeyeater with slender decurved bill. Dense coastal vegetation, rainforest, wetland fringes and gardens.
Voice: loud repeated melodious chattering including the phrase *pe-pee*.

GREY-HEADED HONEYEATER ◐ 14 cm
Ptilotula keartlandi

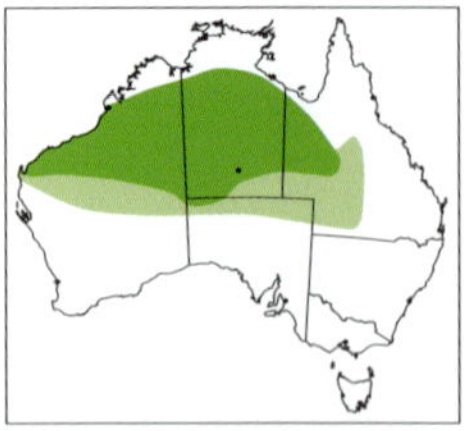

Juv: paler with puffy, yellow gape.

Ad br

Ad non-br, base of lower mandible and gape yellowish.

Olive-yellow honeyeater of arid n Aus with steel-grey head and yellow plume. Low eucalypt woodland and scrub in stony hill country, also rocky gorges; occasionally on sandy plains. **Voice:** cheery whistles *wee-wee-wee* or loud *kwoyt*. Contact call frequent scratchy *chip*.

GREY-FRONTED HONEYEATER ◐ 15 cm
Ptilotula plumula

Common name refers to inconspicuous grey patch on forehead.

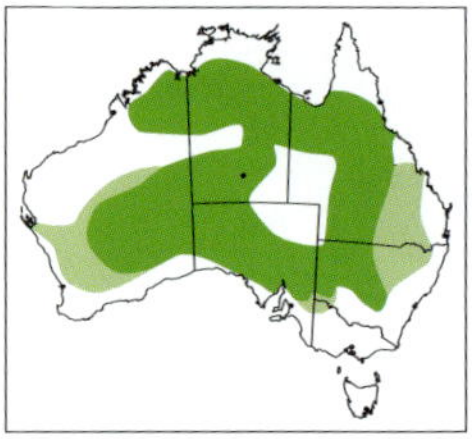

Juv: duller, much reduced plume, pale base to bill.

Ad br

Underparts lightly streaked.

Fan-shaped, yellow plume bordered above by black. Semi-arid shrubland and eucalypt associations. Often in regrowth after fire. **Voice:** loud *it-wirt wirt wirt wirt*. Sharp *twip* as contact call.

YELLOW-PLUMED HONEYEATER ◕ 16 cm
Ptilotula ornata

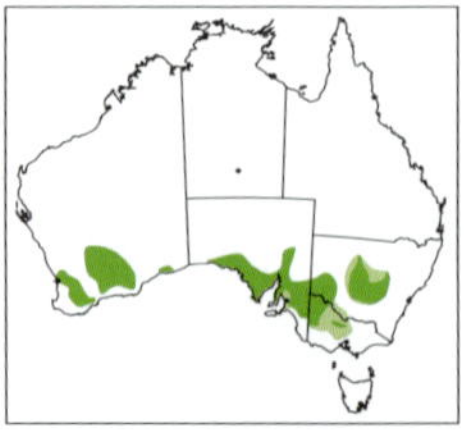

Juv: resembles Ad non-br but duller with reduced plume.

Ad br

Underparts with obvious streaking.

Ad br bill and gape black. Ad non-br base of lower mandible and gape yellow.

Narrow, yellow plume with fine, black upper edge. Abundant in mallee woodland, small numbers extend to box-ironbark woodland. **Voice:** loud, clear *chier wit chier* from perch or in flight. Contact call *chip*; rattling *chap chap*; trilling alarm call.

YELLOW-TINTED HONEYEATER 14 cm
Ptilotula flavescens

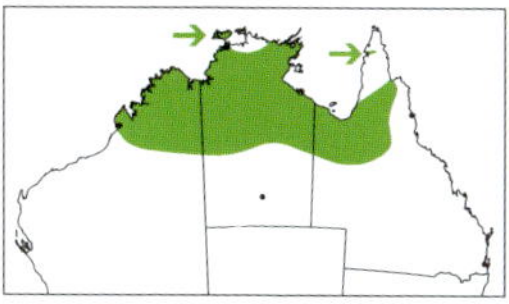

Narrow, black upper edge to yellow plume.

Northern counterpart of Fuscous Honeyeater, restricted to humid tropics; paler with brighter yellow face, more distinct plume. Eucalypt and *Acacia* woodland, riparian thicket. **Voice:** *porra-cheu porra-cheu porra cheu cheu*. Alarm call repeated *wi-wi-wi-wi*.

FUSCOUS HONEYEATER 15 cm
Ptilotula fusca

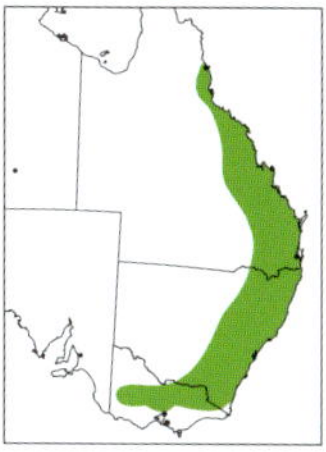

Uniformly grey-olive head, faint yellowish plume.

Plainest of the plumed honeyeaters with indistinct neck plume. Mostly drier eucalypt forest and woodland, inland of Dividing Range, extending to coast in n. **Voice:** clear, fluty *cheer tor cheer*, rollicking *arig arig a taw taw* and incessant chips.

WHITE-PLUMED HONEYEATER 15 cm
Ptilotula penicillata

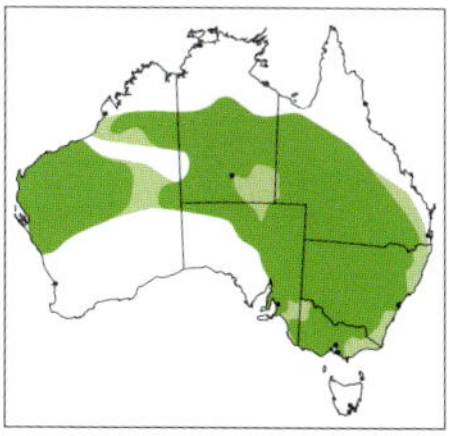

Juv: browner backed with puffy yellow gape, indistinct plume.

Noisily active with chases and bill-clapping. Chases off other small birds.

Ad: yellower in n and w.

Widespread yellow-olive honeyeater with clean-white neck plume. Mostly a bird of eucalypt-lined rivers and creeks, especially those with smooth barked gums, but also urban environments with eucalypts. **Voice:** *chick-chick-o-wee* and *chick-a-brick*.

PURPLE-GAPED HONEYEATER ◑ 17 cm
Lichenostomus cratitius

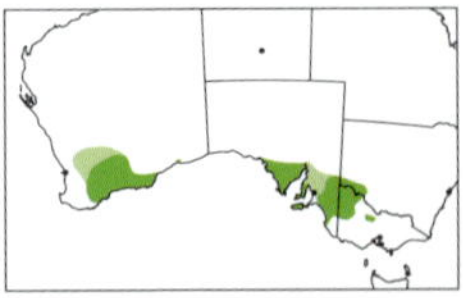

Juv: browner, gape and gape extension yellow.

Grey cap, small yellow ear tuft.

Purple gape.

Olive honeyeater with grey head. Purple gape extension diagnostic but indistinct. Mostly mallee with dense understorey, also tall heath. Extends to woodland on Kangaroo I.
Voice: clear *toweet toweet toweet* followed by high-pitched *yeep-yeep-yeep*. Also metallic chatter.

YELLOW-TUFTED HONEYEATER ◕ 18 cm
Lichenostomus melanops

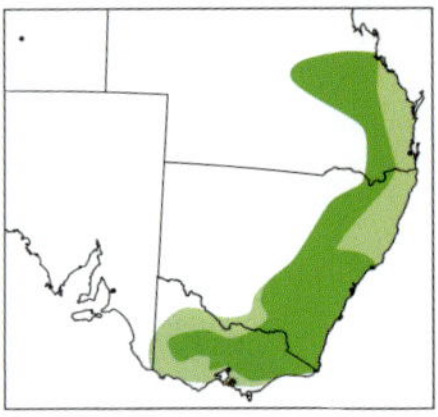

Smallest and dullest form, widespread in drier inland forests.

Boldly marked yellow, black and olive honeyeater. Occurs in loose colonies throughout drier inland eucalypt woodland, also more dense eucalypt forest of the se mostly within riparian zones.
Voice: loud, metallic *cheet* contact call; whistled *tooey-t tooey-t*; harsh *churl*.

Critically Endangered 'Helmeted Honeyeater' restricted to single location near Melbourne. Birds in other moist forests of se Aus appear very similar.

WHITE-EARED HONEYEATER ◕ 18 cm
Nesoptilotis leucotis

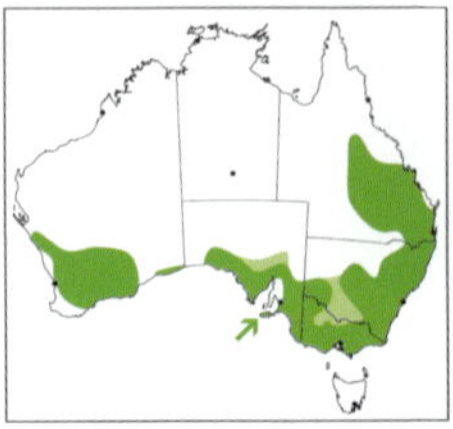

Juv: browner with olive crown, lacks black bib.

Large black bib, white ear patch, grey crown.

Olive honeyeater with blackish head and white 'ear' patch. Widespread in almost all treed habitats, especially eucalypts with peeling bark.

Voice: loud, ringing *chwok* repeated in bursts; similar note repeated rapidly, but slower and more guttural than Lewin's Honeyeater call.

YELLOW-THROATED HONEYEATER ◕ 20 cm
Nesoptilotis flavicollis

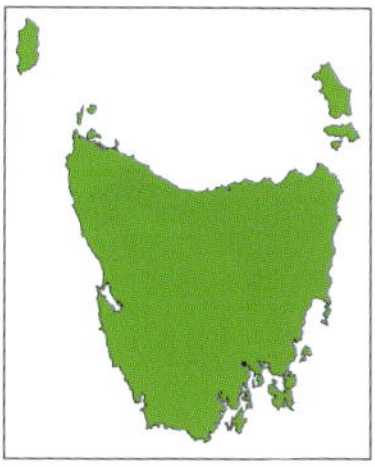

Grey and green honeyeater with bright yellow chin and throat. Tas endemic. Forest and woodland especially with tall, dense shrub layer.

Voice: loud, repeated *chwok chwok* ... or *choka-wok*.

BLACK-HEADED HONEYEATER ◕ 14 cm
Melithreptus affinis

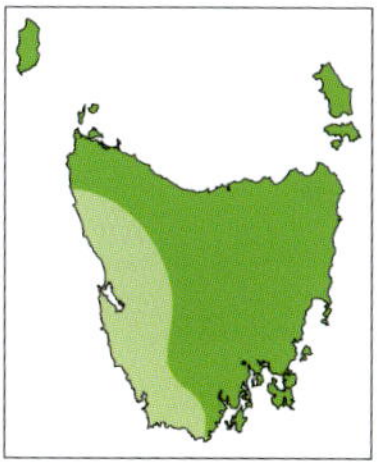

Only honeyeater in Tas with all-black head. Widespread in eucalypt forest but most common in dry forest of c and e Tas.

Voice: loud *sherp sherp* contact call. Sharp, repeated, piping whistle often given in flight.

STRONG-BILLED HONEYEATER ◑ 15 cm
Melithreptus validirostris

Largest *Melithreptus* with mostly black head except broad white nape band and malar stripe. Favours taller eucalypt forest, especially with hanging bark upon which it forages.

Voice: loud *cheep* frequently repeated. Flight song a rapid series of *twips*.

WHITE-THROATED HONEYEATER 13 cm

Melithreptus albogularis

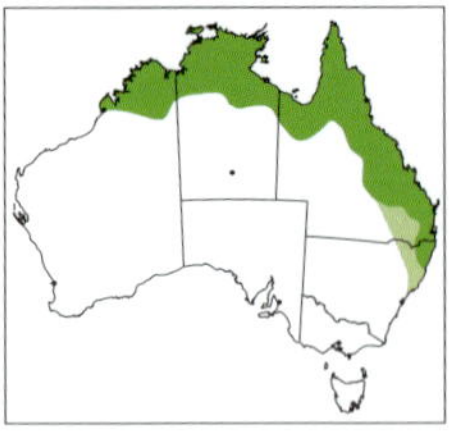

Black-capped honeyeater with clean white underparts. Tropical and subtropical woodland and forest. Often high in canopy.
Voice: rapid shrill piping *peep-peep-peep* ... Also sharp *tip*.

GILBERT'S HONEYEATER 13 cm

Melithreptus chloropsis

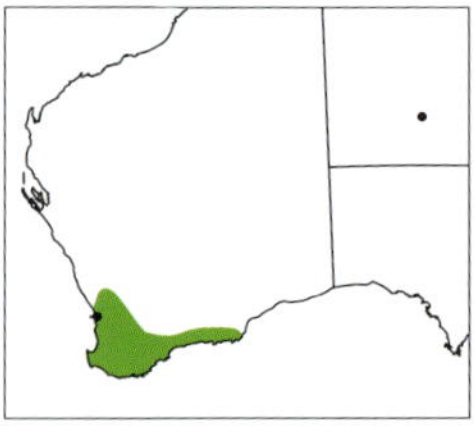

Only black-headed honeyeater in sw WA. Bare skin above eye white. Eucalypt forest and woodland.
Voice: lisping *slerp slerp* given while foraging and in flight. Incessant *tssip* contact calls.

WHITE-NAPED HONEYEATER 13 cm

Melithreptus lunatus

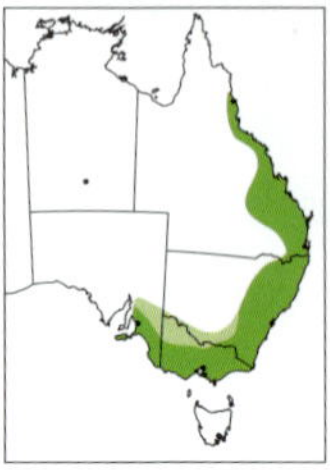

Very similar to White-throated Honeyeater. Eucalypt forests of se Aus where common and familiar.
Voice: lisping *slerp slerp* from foraging flocks. Incessant *tssip* contact calls.

BLACK-CHINNED HONEYEATER ◑ 15 cm
Melithreptus gularis

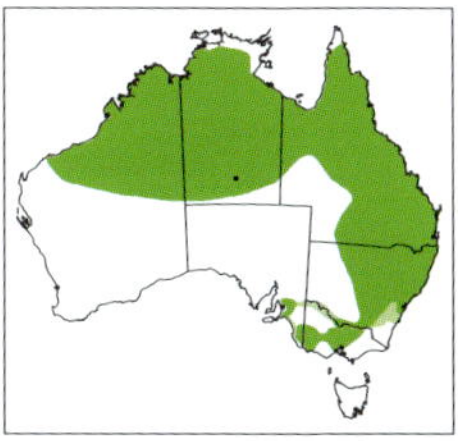

Ad: yellow-green back and yellow fleshy brow in n.

Ad: blue fleshy brow in se.

Juv

Stocky mainland honeyeater with obvious dusky chin. Southern form in drier woodland and red gum forest. Northern form in tropical eucalypt woodland extending into arid zone along watercourses. **Voice:** far-carrying, somewhat scratchy song *chee chee creep creep creep* or *chur chur chur*.

BROWN-HEADED HONEYEATER ◕ 13 cm
Melithreptus brevirostris

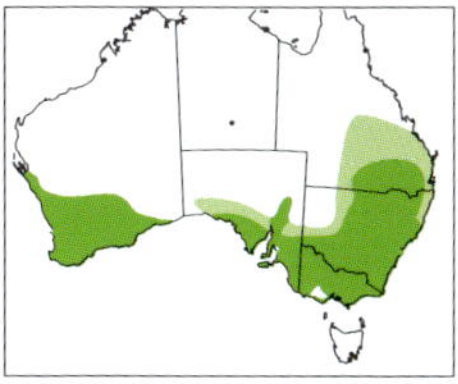

Indistinct buff nape band.

Juv: pale blue eye ring.

Ad

Black bill rules out Juv of other *Melithreptus*.

Small brown-headed honeyeater invariably in noisy groups. Common in most eucalypt forest and woodland from coast to alpine regions. **Voice:** a rattling of sharp *chip* notes delivered in quick succession, often whilst in flight.

BROWN HONEYEATER ● 13 cm
Lichmera indistincta

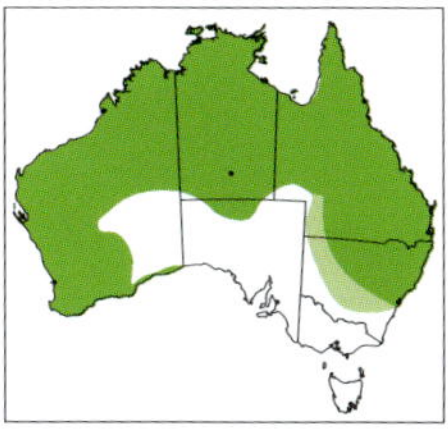

Juv: lacks yellow eye patch.

Ad: small yellow eye patch contrasting with darker surrounds to eye.

Voice: loud, pure, rhythmic *sweet-sweet-querty-querty* and many variants often incorporating *twips* and scratchy notes. Also repeated scratchy *ke-ke-ke*.

Widespread, small and nondescript. Broad range of wooded and shrubby habitats but avoids tall, dense forest.

BAR-BREASTED HONEYEATER ◑ 13 cm

Ramsayornis fasciatus

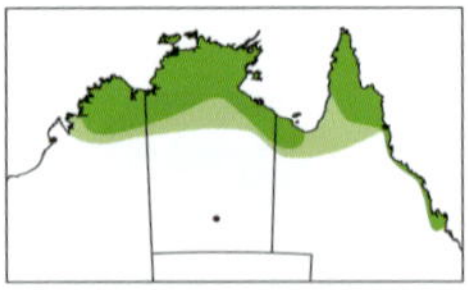

Short-tailed, brown and white honeyeater with black, scaly breast. Associated with rivers and wetlands especially *Melaleuca* forests. Also eucalypt woodland, vine forest, mangroves, gardens. Follows flowering events. **Voice:** sharp piping *chwee-chwee-chwee*. Sharp repeated *plip plip*.

BROWN-BACKED HONEYEATER ◑ 12 cm

Ramsayornis modestus

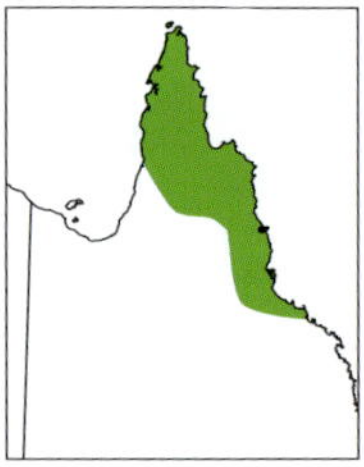

Plain, short-tailed, brown and white honeyeater. Coastal lowlands, islands, woodland, rainforest edges, gardens. Routinely associated with freshwater habitats, especially *Melaleuca* swamps. **Voice:** loud, clipped whistles *seee-chwee seee-chwee* and *weeek-weeek-weeek*. Also staccato chatter.

GREEN-BACKED HONEYEATER ○ 12 cm

Glycichaera fallax

Small, plain, olive and lemon-yellow honeyeater. Recalls a long-billed gerygone but bill longer and more slender. Restricted to e Cape York rainforest where unobtrusive, often high in canopy. **Voice:** pleasant whistled *twee twee-twee-twit-twi-twee*. Also repeated *chit* as contact call.

RUFOUS-BANDED HONEYEATER ◑ 13 cm
Conopophila albogularis

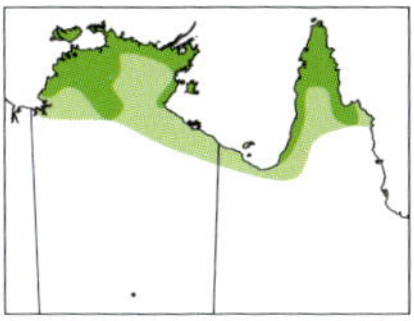

Juv: traces of rufous breast band. Not easily distinguished from Juv Rufous-throated Honeyeater.

Small honeyeater with clean white throat and bold rufous breast band and yellow wing panel. Lowland tropical woodland, monsoon forest, mangroves and gardens. Preference for riparian zones.
Voice: high-pitched melodious twittering *swee-whit-chi-ti*, oft repeated; also squeaky *svee*.

RUFOUS-THROATED HONEYEATER ◕ 12 cm
Conopophila rufogularis

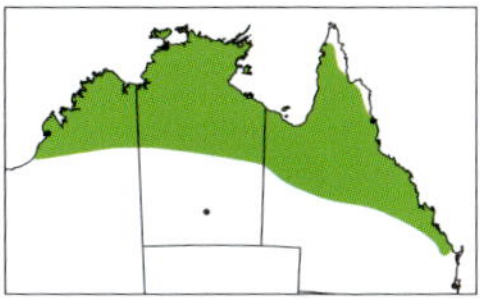

Juv: uniformly pale throat and breast.

Ad: dark rufous throat.

Small honeyeater with distinct rust-coloured throat patch and yellow wing panel. Widespread in woodland, tropical savanna, rainforest edges and gardens. Often associated with drainage lines.
Voice: rapid, melodious *pretty-pete-pretty-pete*, oft repeated. Incessant scratchy chatter *chuur-chuur-churr.*

YELLOW HONEYEATER ◕ 17 cm
Stomiopera flava

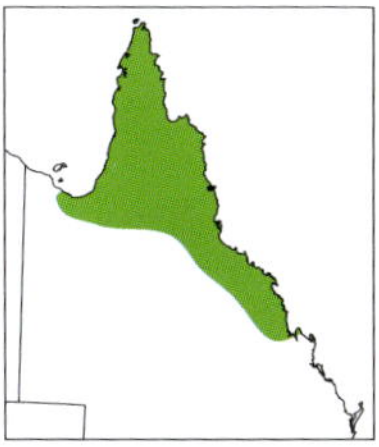

Juv: slightly darker head, puffy yellow gape, yellow base to bill.

Ad: relatively plain olive-yellow plumage.

Plump honeyeater with remarkably uniform olive-yellow plumage. Noisy and conspicuous in variety of wetter wooded habitats.
Voice: loud rollicking song, metallic whistles *wheeet* or *wheet-wruu*. Scolding chatter.

WHITE-GAPED HONEYEATER ◑ 19 cm
Stomiopera unicolor

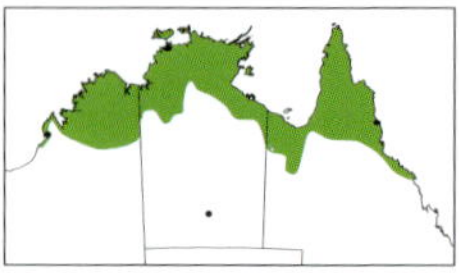

Juv: lacks white gape flange.

Ad: expanded fleshy, white gape flange.

Mid-sized, plain grey honeyeater of tropical n with fleshy white gape flange. Riparian vegetation, rainforest patches, mangroves, gardens. **Voice:** loud, sharp, rollicking *chiep-whiep tipa-tipa* or *tchicka-tichicka-whiep*.

WHITE-LINED HONEYEATER ◔ 18 cm
Meliphaga albilineata

Ad: flared white line curves behind eye, narrow white crescent at end of ear coverts. Gape puffy in all ages.

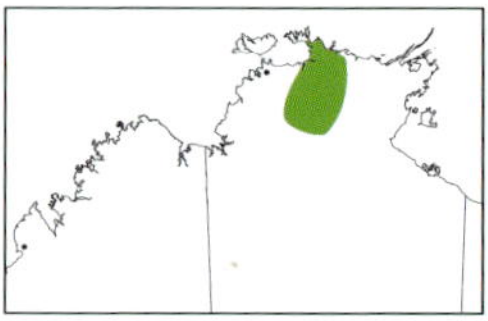

Ad: indistinct streaking on breast.

Mid-sized honeyeater with silvery-white line below eye. Rainforest pockets and riverine forest of sandstone gorges and escarpment. Restricted to the W Arnhem Land Plateau. **Voice:** powerful fluting song of tremulous notes, thrush-like, echoes off surrounding rock faces.

KIMBERLEY HONEYEATER ◔ 18 cm
Meliphagas fordiana

Ad: very similar to White-lined Honeyeater. White line below eye flares slightly but is otherwise straight.

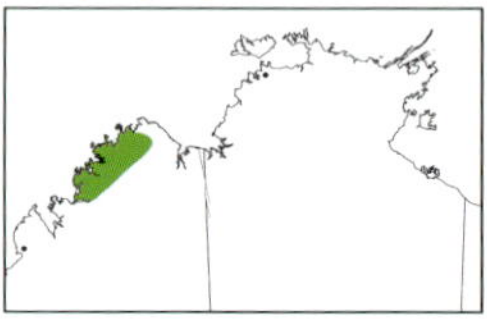

Ad: indistinct streaking on breast.

Kimberley equivalent of White-lined Honeyeater, the two species never co-occur. Subtle differences in facial pattern. Restricted to deep sandstone gorges where associated with vine thickets and rock figs. **Voice:** powerful fluting song of tremulous notes, thrush-like.

LEWIN'S HONEYEATER 20 cm

Meliphaga lewinii

Mid-sized, olive-grey honeyeater with large, pale-yellow crescent on side of head. Rainforest and wet eucalypt forest, mostly above 600 m in n but to sea level in s. **Voice:** loud abrupt chatter *cho-to-ti-ti-ti-ti-ti* ... ~11 notes per sec. Occasional single *toc*, harsh *schwep*.

Softly streaked underparts.

Ad: larger with thicker bill in s of range.

Grey area on face between blue-grey eye and crescent-shaped ear patch. Yellow line under eye joins with straight white gape.

Ad: n Qld.

YELLOW-SPOTTED HONEYEATER 18 cm

Meliphaga notata

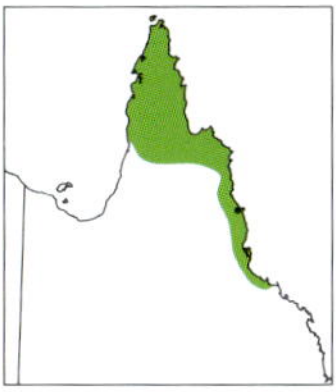

Resembles Lewin's Honeyeater but slightly smaller. Wet tropical habitats mostly below 400 m altitude.

Ear patch ~circular or diamond-shaped.

Voice: loud, high-pitched *ee-yeu ee-yeu ear ear ear* ... with metallic or wheezy quality ~3 notes per sec.

Dark eye, pale yellow line under eye and fleshy gape bulges slightly.

CRYPTIC HONEYEATER 16 cm

Meliphaga imitatrix

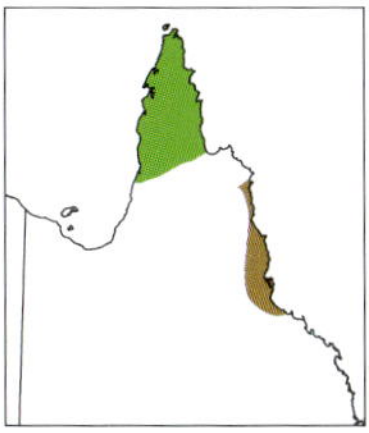

Smallest and slimmest of this difficult *Meliphaga* group in Wet Tropics of ne Qld. Rainforest, *Melaleuca* thickets, mangroves and gardens, to 500 m altitude.

Bill more slender and decurved than Yellow-spotted Honeyeater.

Weak line of pale yellow feathers under eye joins with brighter yellow, fleshy gape. Ear patch similar to Yellow-spotted Honeyeater, more rounded than in Lewin's Honeyeater. Faint pale-yellow midline in unstreaked belly. **Voice:** simple yet loud and resonating *chip* or *plik* repeated at well-spaced intervals.

GRACEFUL HONEYEATER

Meliphaga gracilis

Recently described species. Very similar to but slightly yellower and paler than Cryptic Honeyeater. Lowland rainforest and adjacent riverine habitats to 500 m altitude.

BRIDLED HONEYEATER ◑ 21 cm
Bolemoreus frenatus

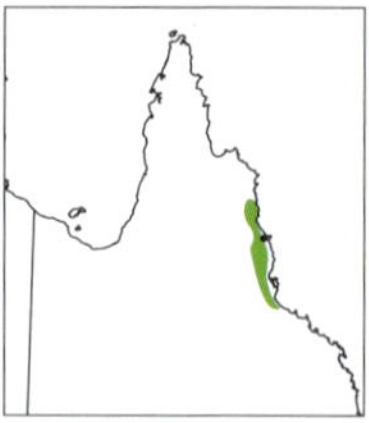

Juv: dull bare spot below eye, plainer brown back and wings.

Ad: pale bare spot below eye.

Mid-sized dusky honeyeater of Wet Tropics with distinct bicoloured bill. Rainforest and wetter eucalypt forest mostly above 300 m altitude, some movement to lower areas in winter.

Voice: loud, scratchy, descending notes *wichit-chit-chit-chit-chit-suwheet*. Harsh scolding.

EUNGELLA HONEYEATER ◔ 18 cm
Bolemoreus hindwoodi

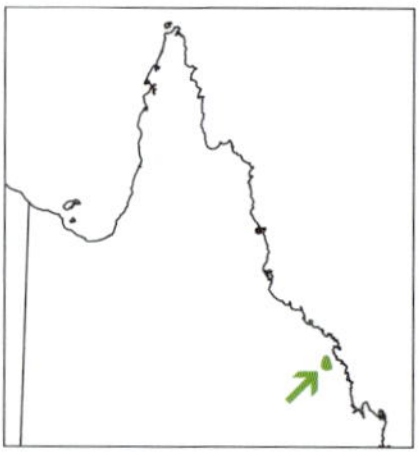

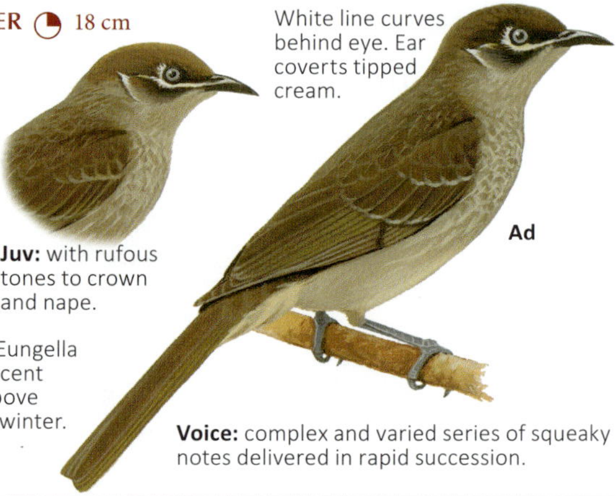

White line curves behind eye. Ear coverts tipped cream.

Juv: with rufous tones to crown and nape.

Ad

Sooty-grey honeyeater of Eungella Range. Rainforest and adjacent Rose Gum forest mostly above 900 m but moves lower in winter. Localised movements in response to flowering.

Voice: complex and varied series of squeaky notes delivered in rapid succession.

YELLOW-FACED HONEYEATER ◕ 16 cm
Caligavis chrysops

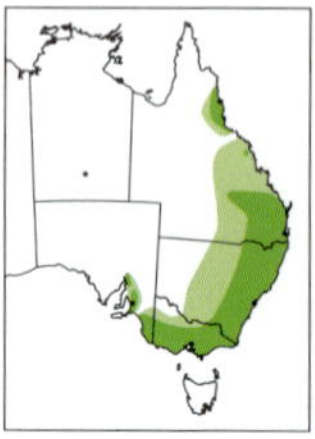

Juv: reduced facial markings, browner head and upperparts.

Ad: bold black facial stripes.

Small, olive-brown honeyeater with bold yellow and black facial stripes. Woodland and forest throughout range but avoids semi-arid environments. In s, most individuals migratory so scarce in winter.

Voice: loud, bright series of cheery *chichup* or *quitchup*; a familiar sound in range.

WHITE-STREAKED HONEYEATER ◔ 15 cm
Trichodere cockerelli

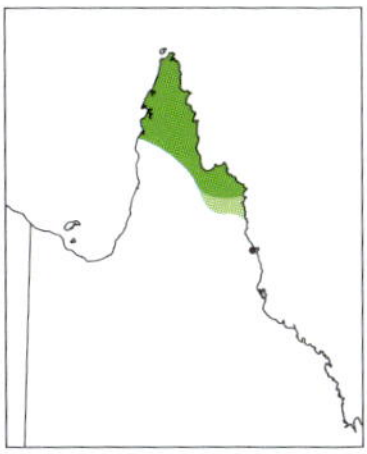

Juv: browner above, minimal streaking on throat, flesh-coloured base to bill.

Pale blue base to long robust bill.

Cape York endemic with distinct silvery-streaked gorget and yellow wing panel. Active, noisy and conspicuous. Generally dry open forest, tropical heath, coastal dunes and *Melaleuca* swamps. **Voice:** sweet, 4-note whistle interspersed with chattering, warbling. Also rapid staccato rattle and harsh metallic *chirr*.

Ad: mostly blackish above and white below.

MACLEAY'S HONEYEATER ◑ 19 cm
Xanthotis macleayanus

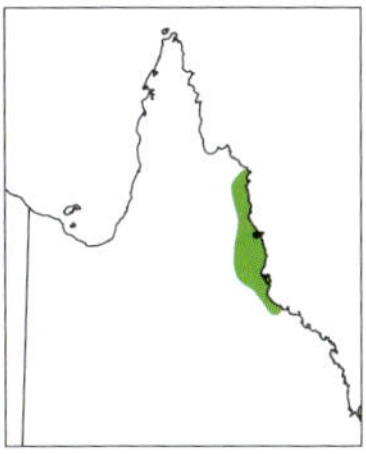

Juv: streaks much reduced, lacks white gape stripe.

Ad

Plump rainforest honeyeater with dark plumage boldly streaked and mottled white. Orange-brown face. Mostly rainforest, extending to adjacent eucalypt forest and gardens.

Voice: a whistled *t-whi-t-weee* ... given in rolling series. Loud ringing *chip*.

TAWNY-BREASTED HONEYEATER ◑ 19 cm
Xanthotis flaviventer

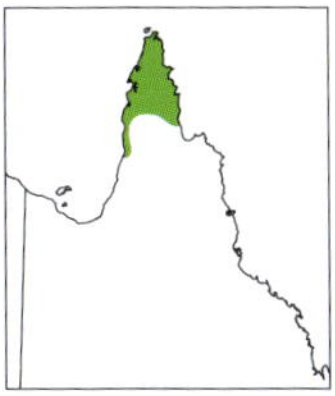

Dark cap, narrow white line through face, streaks on nape.

Juv: lacks streaks on nape.

Ad

Plump, rather plain, warm-brown honeyeater of Cape York. Rainforest, monsoon forest and mangroves, extending to adjacent habitats. **Voice:** loud and distinctive whistled *which-witch-is-which* ... given in steady measured series.

Body feathers, especially flanks, long and fluffy.

SINGING HONEYEATER ● 20 cm
Gavicalis virescens

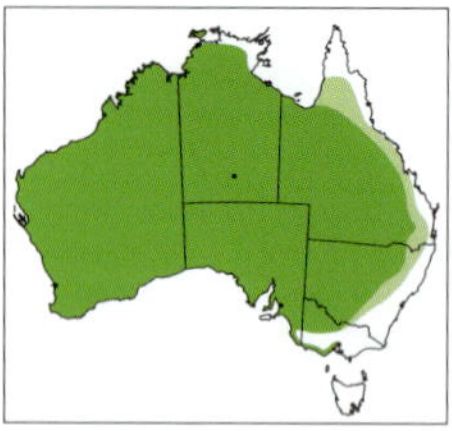

Juv: plainer, paler and warmer toned.

Dark se form and paler inland form.

Ad

Faintly streaked breast.

Widespread and common mid-sized honeyeater with broad, black eye stripe from bill to ear coverts. Wide range of shrubby habitats from coast to the arid interior. Often in homestead gardens. Usually in singles or pairs.

Voice: a distinctive *pirrt* sometimes given as extended trill. Song varies across range, commonly a melodious *wheer we what*.

VARIED HONEYEATER ◕ 21 cm
Gavicalis versicolor

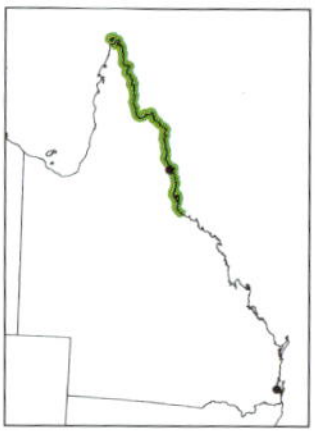

Juv: plainer, paler and warmer toned.

Ad

Clear yellow throat. Pale yellow, streaked grey-brown below.

Noisy, mid-sized honeyeater of coastal n Qld. Pale-yellow underparts with diffuse streaking. Mangroves, coastal scrub, vine thickets, gardens in coastal towns.

Voice: loud, rich bubbling calls, fluted duets, much scolding.

MANGROVE HONEYEATER ◕ 19 cm
Gavicalis fasciogularis

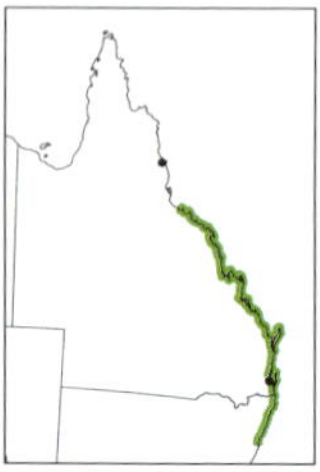

Pale lower face and throat with dusky barring.

Juv: with less barred throat.

Ad

Coastal specialist with black mask and dusky breast. Associated with mangroves, ranges into adjacent wooded habitats, gardens. Noisy, active parties.
Voice: loud melodious fluting calls *whit u wee u*, harsh scolding.

WHITE-FRONTED HONEYEATER ◑ 16 cm
Purnella albifrons

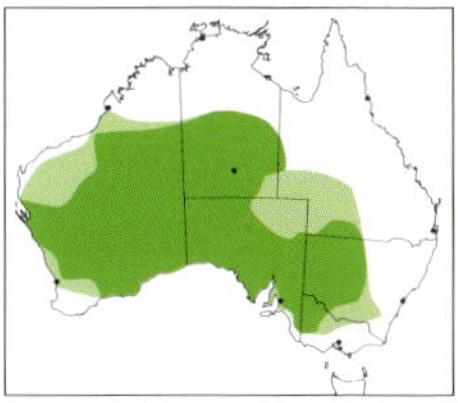

Small, slender honeyeater with white face. Highly nomadic nectarivore, mostly in semi-arid shrubland or shrubby woodland.

Voice: broad repertoire of loud metallic notes; musical *kzeep chrok-chrok-chrok*, trilling *peter-pete-pete*, rapid ringing *kziep kziep*.

NEW HOLLAND HONEYEATER ● 18 cm
Phylidonyris novaehollandiae

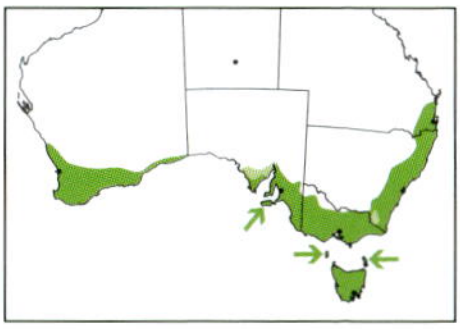

Common and familiar.
Small, black and white striped honeyeater with yellow wing panel. Active and conspicuous in heath, shrubby forest and gardens.
Voice: loud single *tchik*, oft-repeated. Whistled *tseee* in flight. Rapid *chwiep chwiep* scolding notes.

WHITE-CHEEKED HONEYEATER ◑ 18 cm
Phylidonyris niger

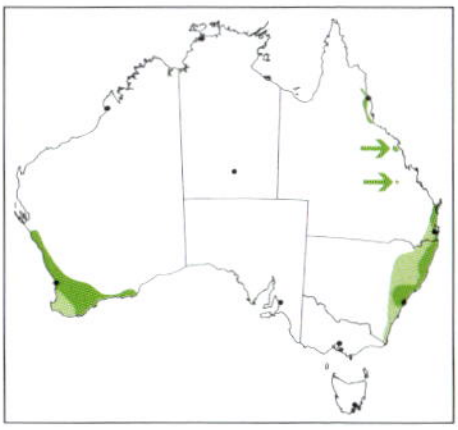

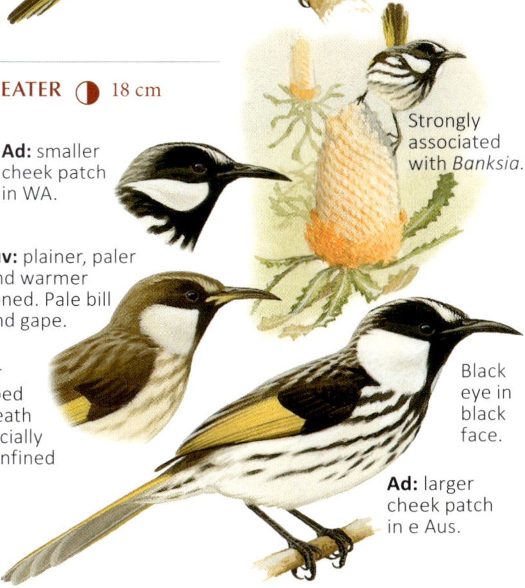

Like New Holland Honeyeater but has large, white, fan-shaped cheek patch. Mostly dense heath and eucalypt woodland, especially with banksias, but in n Qld confined to high-altitude tall forest.
Voice: loud *echip* or *chakup*. Pure, melodious *chwippy-choo chwippy-choo*. Double whistle in display flight.

PAINTED HONEYEATER ◔ 14 cm

Grantiella picta

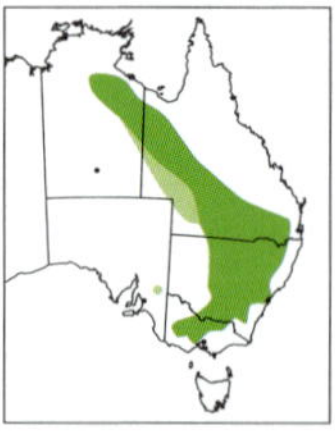

Juv: browner, dull bill and minimal streaks on breast.

Ad ♂

Small black and white honeyeater with yellow wing panel and pink bill. Associates with mistletoe in open forest and woodland. A summer migrant in s of range. **Voice:** far-carrying, high-pitched whistle *georg-ee georg-ee georg-ee* with second syllable inflected.

Distinctive black and white patterning when seen from below.

TAWNY-CROWNED HONEYEATER ◑ 16 cm

Gliciphila melanops

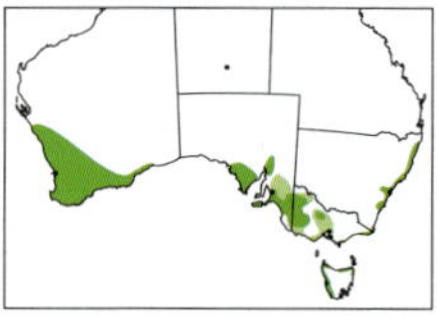

Juv: brown mask, yellow throat and pale shaft streaks on back.

Ad

Small honeyeater with tawny crown and black face mask that extends down sides of breast. Mobile in response to flowering. **Voice:** a long, clear whistle, followed by drawn-out, mournful note, fluty but metallic. Often given in climbing song flight or perched on exposed emergent branch; a characteristic sound of coastal and semi-arid heathlands.

Salmon underwing.

CRESCENT HONEYEATER ◑ 15 cm

Phylidonyris pyrrhopterus

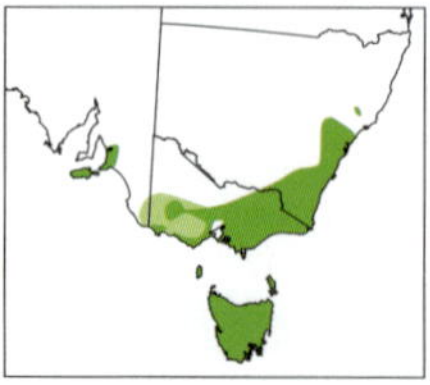

Ad ♀: with indistinct markings, shadow of crescent.

Juv: dull brown, lacks crescents. Yellow gape.

Ad ♂

Small honeyeater with black or brown crescents on breast sides. Frequents both montane woodland and forest, and cooler coastal forest, scrub and heath. Common in Tas, more localised on mainland. **Voice:** loud emphatic *ee-gypt* and extended chatters with similar qualities. Sharp *jik*.

Broad yellow wing patch; duller in Ad ♀ and Juvs.

EASTERN SPINEBILL
Acanthorhynchus tenuirostris

14 cm

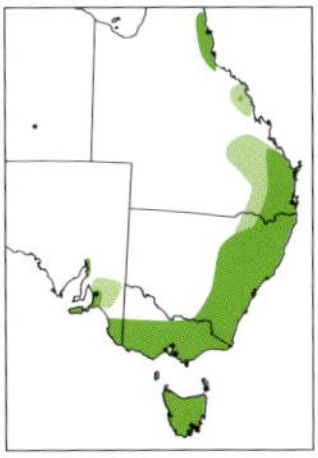

Ad ♀: grey crown.

Juv: olive crown, plain buff throat and chest.

Ad ♂: black crown.

Small, well-marked honeyeater with long, slender, decurved bill. Heathland and a wide variety of wooded habitats including gardens. Birds at higher altitude and in wet forest move lower in winter.
Voice: loud, rapid piping *pip-pip-pip* … often 10–30 notes with rate of delivery increasing towards end.

In flight wings create a *frrrp frrrp* sound as it flits through the understorey.

WESTERN SPINEBILL
Acanthorhynchus superciliosus

14 cm

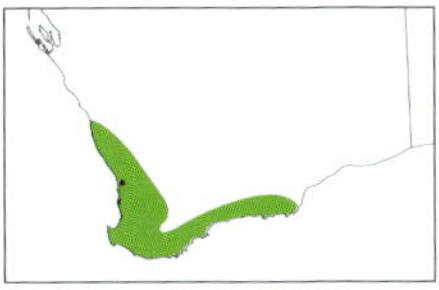

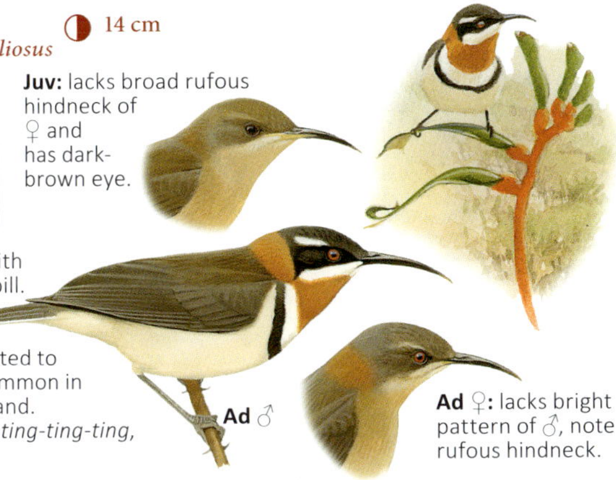

Juv: lacks broad rufous hindneck of ♀ and has dark-brown eye.

Very small honeyeater with long, slender, decurved bill. Restricted to sw WA.
A nectar specialist attracted to tubular flowers. Most common in heath and heathy woodland.
Voice: loud, rapid piping *ting-ting-ting*, clear *ca-chip ca-chip*.

Ad ♂

Ad ♀: lacks bright pattern of ♂, note rufous hindneck.

BELL MINER
Manorina melanophrys

18 cm

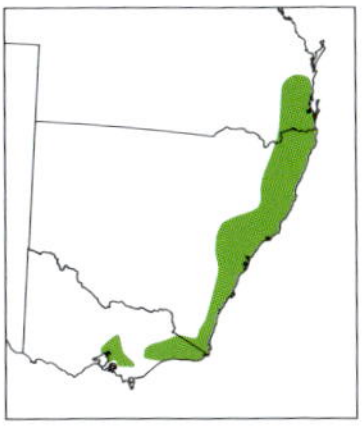

Juv: duller and paler than Ad.
Lacks red-orange triangle of bare skin behind eye.

Ad

Robust, uniform olive-green honeyeater with stout yellow bill and red-orange triangle of bare skin behind eye. Large colonies occupy eucalypt forest and woodland with dense understorey, typically along waterways.

Voice: diagnostic, bell-like *ping* resonates incessantly throughout forest inhabited by colony. Almost always heard first.

NOISY MINER ● 26 cm
Manorina melanocephala

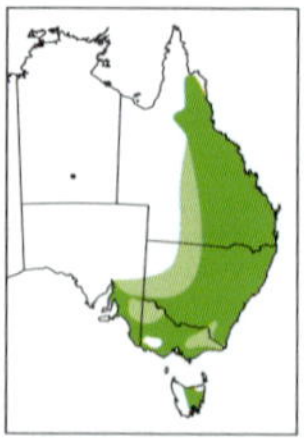

Juv: less boldly marked, browner back.

Ad: bandit-like black mask extends over crown. White forehead, grey rump.

Common, robust, grey honeyeater of forest edge, woodland and modified environments. Colonial with complex social structure.

Voice: *meee, meee, meee* oft repeated, *chur-chur-chur* as general alarm call higher-pitched to indicate aerial predators.

YELLOW-THROATED MINER ● 25 cm
Manorina flavigula

Juv: less boldly marked, browner back.

Yellow on neck sides.

Pale-grey crown.

Lower jaw pale, like throat.

Darker ssp *obscura* recalls Black-eared Miner but restricted to sw WA.

Pale rump.

Widespread, colonial miner with pale rump. Frequents open wooded areas, especially along watercourses, also gardens and towns.
Voice: similar to Noisy Miner.

BLACK-EARED MINER ○ 24 cm
Manorina melanotis

Dark rump.

Juv: less boldly marked, browner back.

Dark-grey crown.

All-black ear coverts.

Lower jaw darker than throat.

Ad

Little or no pale tip to tail.

Voice: similar to Noisy Miner.

Very rare, dark-rumped miner restricted to a few sites in Murray Mallee of se Aus. Occupies intact, long-unburnt mallee habitat. Presence of hybrids with Yellow-throated Miner makes ID difficult.

STRIPED HONEYEATER ◑ 22 cm

Plectorhyncha lanceolata

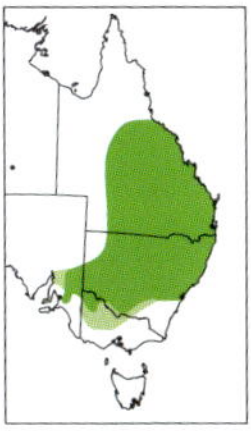

Juv: stripes much reduced, buff on back and wing.

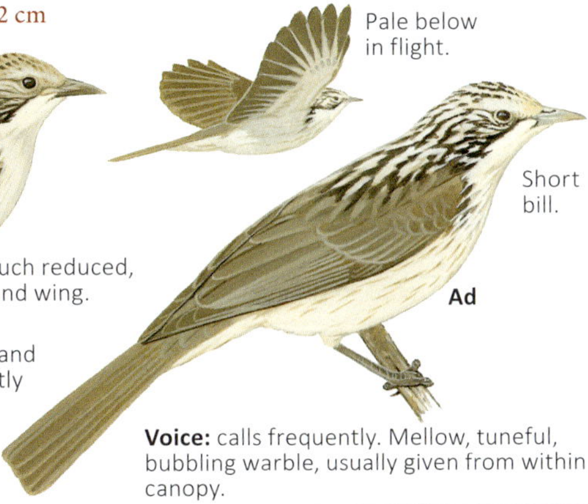

Pale below in flight.

Short bill.

Ad

Pale honeyeater with bold black and white streaked head. Inland mostly in woodland, especially *Acacia*, she-oaks and native pine. Extends to swamp forest on coast in n of range.

Voice: calls frequently. Mellow, tuneful, bubbling warble, usually given from within canopy.

SPINY-CHEEKED HONEYEATER ● 24 cm

Acanthagenys rufogularis

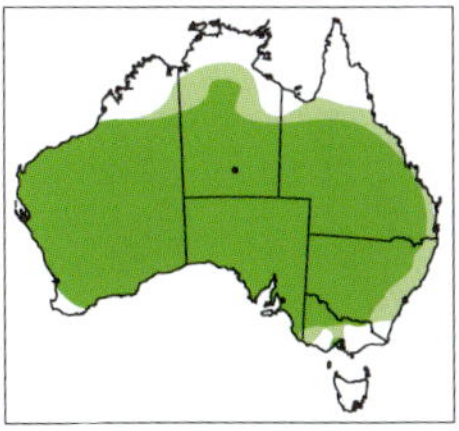

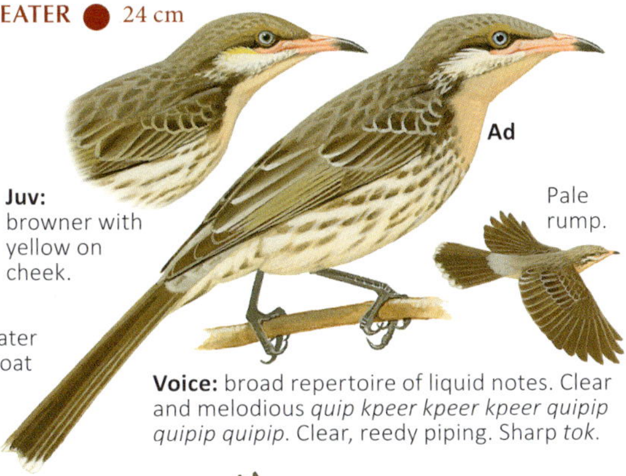

Juv: browner with yellow on cheek.

Ad

Pale rump.

Common, mid-sized honeyeater with pink bill and apricot throat and breast. In shrubland, woodland with shrubby cover and gardens from arid interior to coast. Active and conspicuous.

Voice: broad repertoire of liquid notes. Clear and melodious *quip kpeer kpeer kpeer quipip quipip quipip*. Clear, reedy piping. Sharp *tok*.

REGENT HONEYEATER ○ 22 cm

Anthochaera phrygia

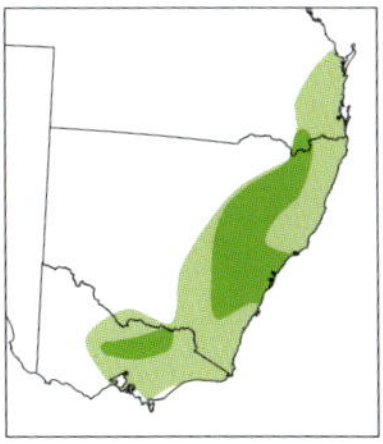

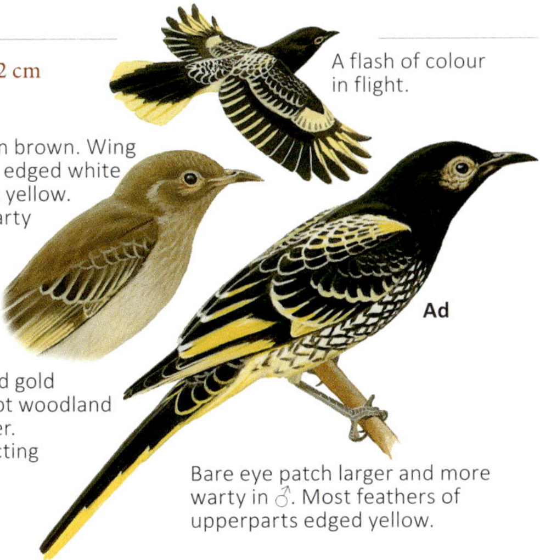

A flash of colour in flight.

Juv: plain brown. Wing feathers edged white and pale yellow. Lacks warty face.

Ad

Extremely rare, brilliant black and gold honeyeater. A bird of dry eucalypt woodland with coastal movements in winter. Population declining and contracting to a few key refugia.

Voice: highly vocal. Song a liquid series of notes *plink-ple-plink*, bell-like metallic *tinks*.

Bare eye patch larger and more warty in ♂. Most feathers of upperparts edged yellow.

RED WATTLEBIRD ● 35 cm
Anthochaera carunculata

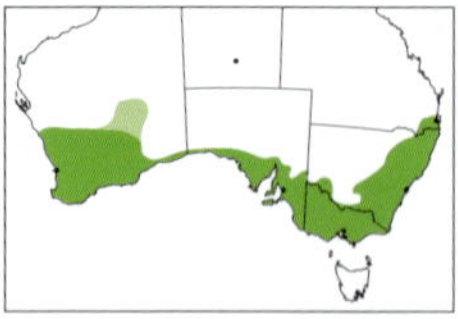

Common and conspicuous, large grey-buff honeyeater with long, pale-tipped tail. In forest, woodland, mallee, parks and gardens. Mobile in response to nectar availability, travelling in loose flocks when not breeding.

Voice: loud *Kwok,* a familiar sound in s Aus wherever there are eucalypts, including cities and towns. Also a loud, hoarse, coughing crow *yak-ah-yak*.

WESTERN WATTLEBIRD ◑ 30 cm
Anthochaera lunulata

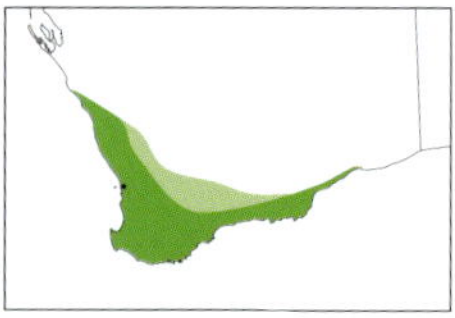

Medium–large, grey-brown honeyeater with extensive fine pale streaking; especially on face, neck sides. Energetic and aggressive. A nectar nomad, frequents heath, and woodland with a tall shrub layer, especially with *Banksia*.

Voice: very vocal. Loud *choks* and bill clapping builds to ringing, cackling *I've got the hiccups*. Also repeated *cook-cackle cook-cackle* and harsh warning *graaak*.

LITTLE WATTLEBIRD ◕ 31 cm
Anthochaera chrysoptera

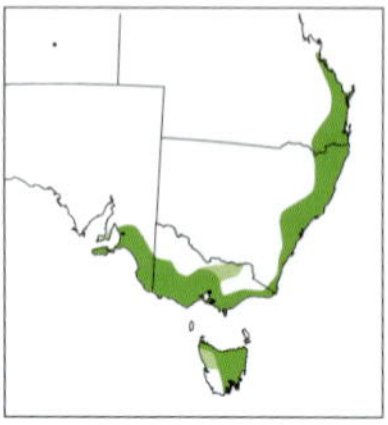

Eastern counterpart of Western Wattlebird. Common in heath and woodland with a tall shrub layer, especially with *Banksia*. Has expanded range into city gardens in recent decades. Pugnacious, active and noisy, usually seen in pairs.

Voice: very vocal. Loud raucous *kook-kwa-krock* or a mechanical *kok kok kwa kwok kra-kwok kra-kwok,* also a harsh warning *graauk*.

YELLOW WATTLEBIRD 43 cm
Anthochaera paradoxa

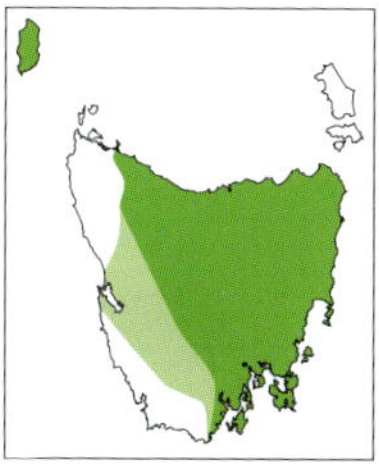

Restricted to Tas

Very long, graduated, white-tipped tail.

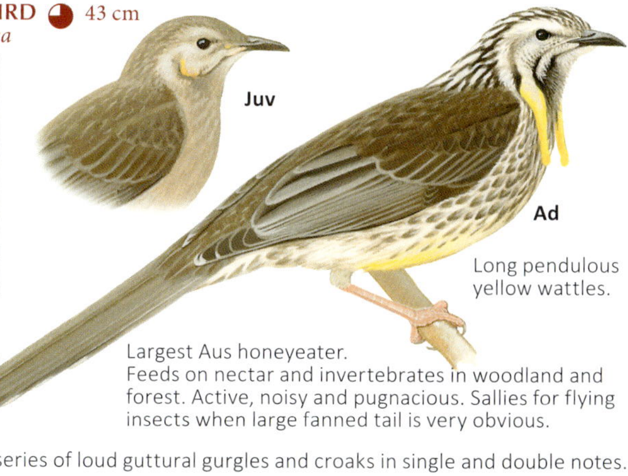

Long pendulous yellow wattles.

Largest Aus honeyeater.
Feeds on nectar and invertebrates in woodland and forest. Active, noisy and pugnacious. Sallies for flying insects when large fanned tail is very obvious.

Voice: series of loud guttural gurgles and croaks in single and double notes.

BLUE-FACED HONEYEATER 29 cm
Entomyzon cyanotis

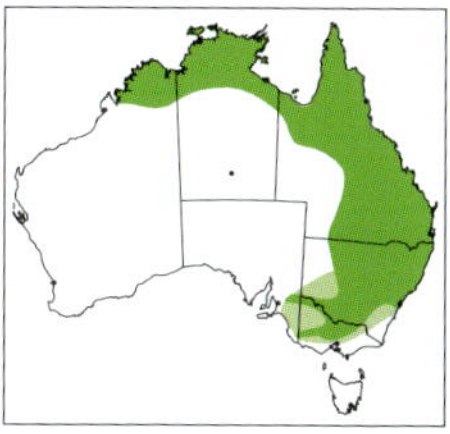

Large, green-backed honeyeater with extensive, bright-blue, bare facial patch. In woodland and open grassy eucalypt forest, especially along rivers. Also parks and gardens.

Juv: green skin around eye.

Voice: noisy; repeated *queet*, harsh mewing and chatter, *quorrick quorrick*.

E Aus, orange in wing.

NT and Kimberley, white in wing.

LITTLE FRIARBIRD 27 cm
Philemon citreogularis

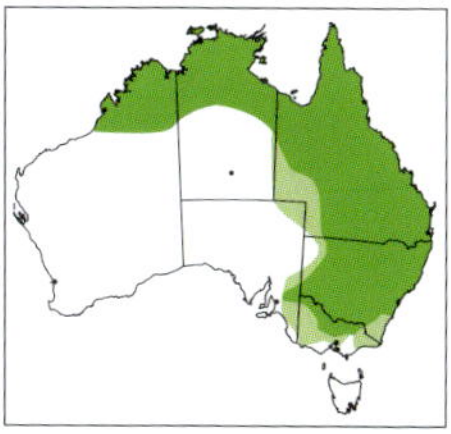

Small, nondescript friarbird with blue-grey facial skin. Wide range of forest and wooded habitats especially riverine forest. Partial summer migrant in s, elsewhere nomadic.

Lacks casque on bill of other friarbirds.

Juv: dark face, yellow throat.

Imm: pale scalloping on back.

Voice: repeated *chee-whip* or *chee-whip-will*, also raucous chatter *chowik* and *rackety crookshank*.

HORNBILL FRIARBIRD ◑ 32 cm
Philemon yorki

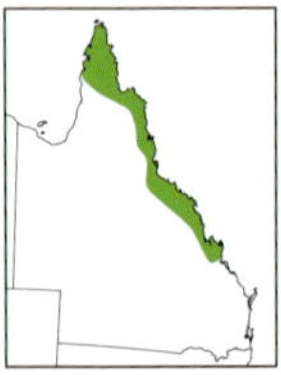

The common friarbird in Cairns. In rainforest edges, eucalypt forest and gardens.

Voice: monotonous, loud, nasal, downslurred *wheert* also *kurr-rk*, *poor devil* and repeated *watch-out*.

HELMETED FRIARBIRD ◑ 32 cm
Philemon buceroides

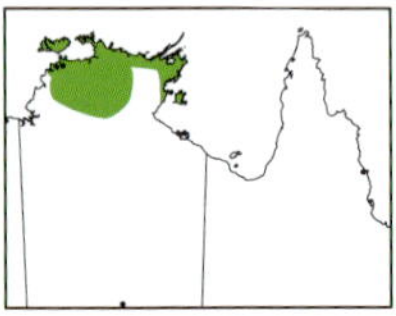

The common friarbird in Darwin.

In riparian woodland, monsoon forest, parks and sandstone escarpment.
Voice: harsh cackling and rollicking *kurr-rk* slowly repeated, more lyrical than Silver-crowned Friarbird.

SILVER-CROWNED FRIARBIRD ◑ 28 cm
Philemon argenticeps

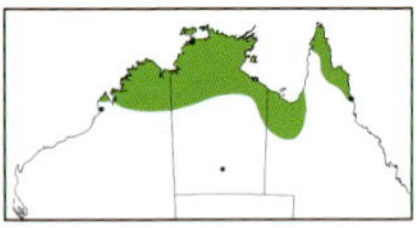

Northern friarbird with silvery crown. Humid woodland, also monsoon forest, mangroves, parks.
Voice: harsh guttural croaking and squawking repeated *more-tobacco-huh* and *aark-coo-arrk-coo* or *what-jack*.

NOISY FRIARBIRD ◕ 32 cm
Philemon corniculatus

All friarbirds have square-ended tail.

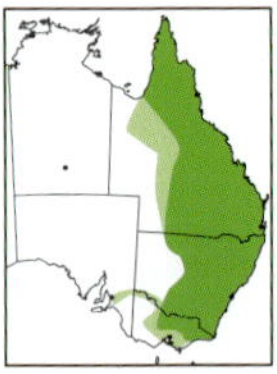

Large honeyeater of open eucalypt woodland and forest, extending to coastal *Melaleuca* and heath in n of range.

Voice: cackling and rollicking *four-o'clock*, *chock chock* and *ya-cob ya-cob*.

EASTERN WHIPBIRD ◑ 26 cm
Psophodes olivaceus

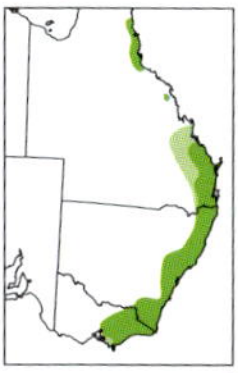

Mostly terrestrial, long-tailed skulker of undergrowth. Wet forest and scrub, especially riparian zones.

Bold white throat patches. Black triangular crest.

Voice: very loud whipcrack, often given as duet. ♂ *chuk-chuk* followed by prolonged rising whistle, terminating in loud abrupt whipcrack. ♀ follows with *chew-chew*.

WHITE-BELLIED WHIPBIRD ○ 22 cm
Psophodes leucogaster

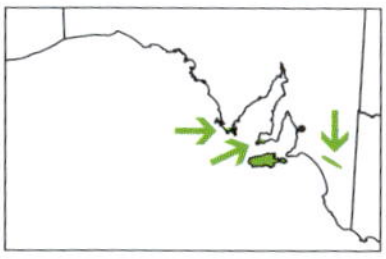

Restricted to SA. Highly cryptic, pairs keep close to ground in heath, coastal scrub and mallee. **Voice:** a mechanical reel, sometimes only briefly at sunrise and sunset. Regional calls differ slightly.

Black throat patch.

Pale belly.

Graduated tail with pale tips.

BLACK-THROATED WHIPBIRD ○ 22 cm
Psophodes nigrogularis

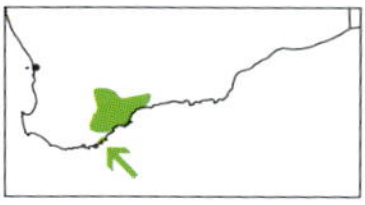

Extensive dark throat. Dark belly.

Very similar to White-bellied Whipbird in habits, habitat and call.

CHIRRUPING WEDGEBILL ◑ 20 cm
Psophodes cristatus

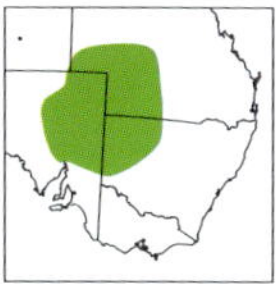

Restricted to Lake Eyre Basin. In arid shrubland of *Acacia*, chenopod, lignam or canegrass, often near claypan or drainage line.

Sings from exposed perch.

Graduated tail with white tips.

Voice: squeaky, mechanical 3-note song, first 2 notes subdued, last loud and shrill *tutsi-CHEER*. In duet, female follows with loud *chir-ru*.

CHIMING WEDGEBILL ◑ 20 cm
Psophodes occidentalis

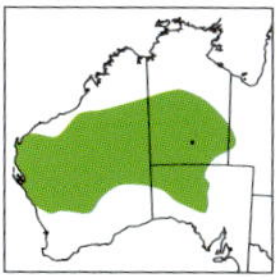

C and w arid interior. Very similar to Chirruping Wedgebill in habits and habitat.

Plain breast.

Juv: pale bill.

Plain greyish crested songbird with faint shaft streaks on breast.

Voice: sweet, bell-like, descending chime of 4–6 notes *did-you-get-drunk*, repeated incessantly.

CHESTNUT QUAIL-THRUSH ◑ 24 cm
Cinclosoma castanotum

All species of quail-thrush have a weak, high-pitched contact call, a piping or twittering *tsit-tsit-tsit* ... Inaudible to some.

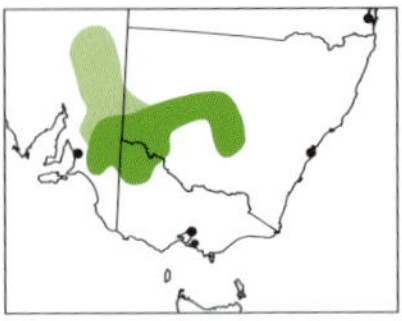

Black throat and breast.

Band of deep chestnut across back of Ad ♂. Occupies mallee habitats and adjacent semi-arid shrubland. Unobtrusive and shy, runs ahead of observer. **Voice:** song a high-pitched, repeated, pulsating treecreeper-like *see see see see* ... or a faster, higher-pitched *whit whit whit whit* ...

COPPER-BACKED QUAIL-THRUSH ◑ 24 cm
Cinclosoma clarum

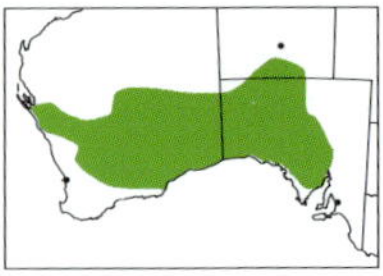

Ad ♀: extensive copper back.

Western counterpart of Chestnut Quail-thrush with similar calls; differs by more extensive copper saddle and rump. Occupies semi-arid woodland and shrubland, especially mallee.

SPOTTED QUAIL-THRUSH ◑ 27 cm
Cinclosoma punctatum

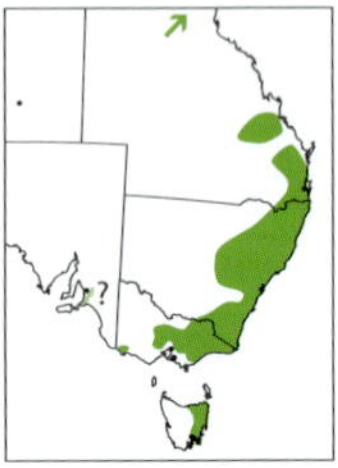

Flushes from vehicle tracks. Quail-like flight but long tail.

Ad ♀: buff spot on face.

Both sexes have blue-grey breast.

The only quail-thrush in eastern forests. On gravelly ridges with tussock grass. Wary, walking stealthily into cover when disturbed. **Voice:** song a high-pitched, repeated, whistler-like, 2-note whistle *weee-it weee-it weee-it* ... can be given at different speed and tone; often first means of detection. Also a faster, higher-pitched series of repeated single notes.

CHESTNUT-BREASTED QUAIL-THRUSH ◔ 23 cm
Cinclosoma castaneothorax

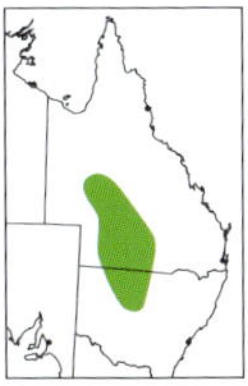

Ad ♀: olive-grey breast.

Ad ♂: rich rufous-brown breast.

Shy in pairs and small family groups in stony hills and breakaway country with *Acacia* shrubland, especially mulga.
Voice: song a haunting, high-pitched, plaintive or tremulous whistle, *whit-what-whittiteeee*.

WESTERN QUAIL-THRUSH ◔ 23 cm
Cinclosoma marginatum

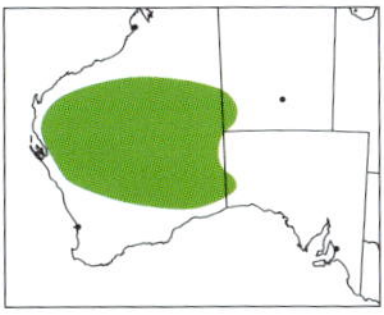

♀ like ♀ Chestnut-breasted Q-t. Stony plains, and breakaways with sparse cover of *Acacia* shrubland, often associated with quartz outcrops.

Ad ♂

White border to black breast band.

Shy, in pairs and small family groups.
Voice: similar to Chestnut-breasted Q-t.

CINNAMON QUAIL-THRUSH ◔ 21 cm
Cinclosoma cinnamomeum

Ad ♀: pale-grey breast *cf* ♀ Chestnut-breasted.

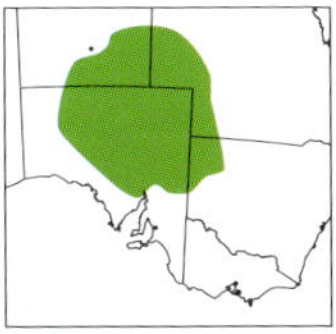

Smaller and shorter tailed than other quail-thrush. Saltbush and bluebush on stony gibber plains and tablelands, also rocky rises and low ridges.

Ad ♂: white centre of chest.

In pairs and family groups. Shy when disturbed, often freezes at base of bush, or runs swiftly or flies suddenly in a low dash to cover.
Voice: song a high-pitched, 3-note *see-see--see*, or *see-see--seeit*, or lower and slower in 4 notes. Also a higher-pitched, fast, repeated series of the same note *si-si-si-si-si* ...

NULLARBOR QUAIL-THRUSH ◔ 21 cm
Cinclosoma alisteri

Only bird species restricted to Nullarbor Plain. Notoriously shy, generally staying well ahead of observer. In arid shrubland, especially bluebush.
Voice: similar to Cinnamon Q-t.

Ad ♂: chin stripe joins broad breast band.

GREY-CROWNED BABBLER ◕ 25 cm
Pomatostomus temporalis

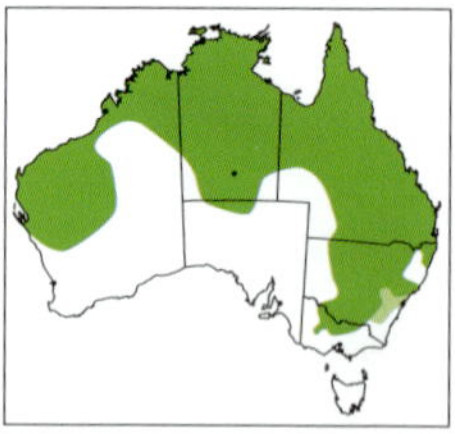

Largest babbler, with dark mask in otherwise pale head. Open forest and woodland, especially with some bare ground and fallen timber.
Voice: noisy with constant chatter dominated by *chuck*. Loud duet *ya-hoo*, first note by ♀, second by ♂.

WHITE-BROWED BABBLER ◕ 20 cm
Pomatostomus superciliosus

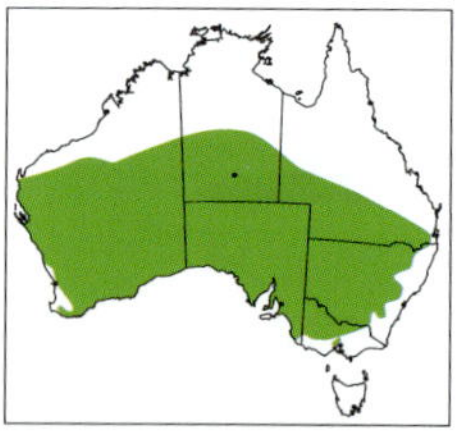

Small, widespread babbler with long, narrow, white brow stripe. Woodland, open forest and shrubland with tall or dense cover of shrubs.
Voice: noisy active parties, oft-repeated *chuck*, whistled contact call *wee-wee-weet*.

CHESTNUT-CROWNED BABBLER ◑ 21 cm
Pomatostomus ruficeps

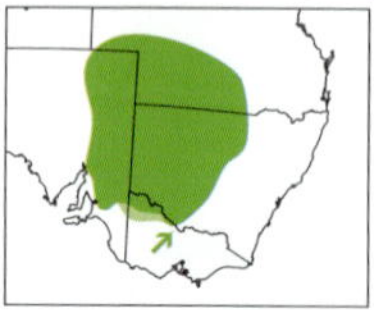

Only babbler with white wing markings and chestnut crown.
Long, narrow eyebrow, extensive white front. Plains country with large domed shrubs interspersed with bare ground.
Voice: constant chatter, higher-pitched more grating than White-browed Babbler.

HALL'S BABBLER
Pomatostomus halli

20 cm

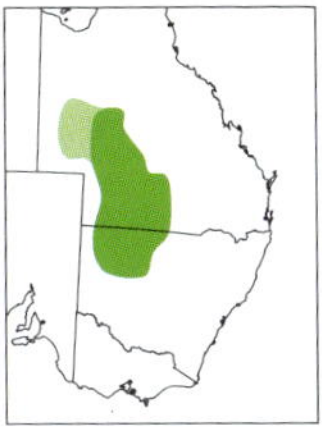

Nest smaller and neater than White-browed Babbler.

Very broad white brows and sharply defined white bib.

Dark sooty-brown babbler of *Acacia* shrubland, especially mulga. Along watercourses, plains and stony ridges.
Voice: noisy, constant chatter with variably repeated *chirp*, staccato *chit-chit* …

VARIED SITTELLA
Daphoenositta chrysoptera

12 cm

Variable plumage across five ssp.

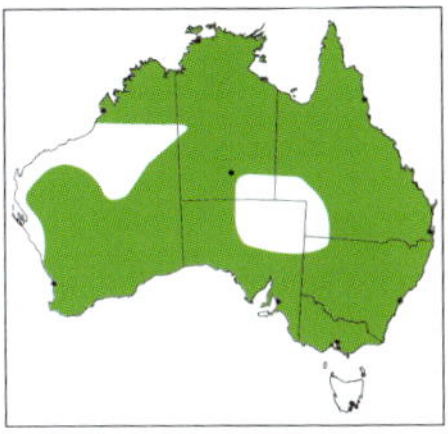

Ad ♂: se Aus.

Juv

Ad ♂: sw and s Aus.

Ad: se Qld.

Orange wing panel on s and e coast ssp. Short undulating flight between trees.

Ad ♀: sw and s Aus.

Small bark foraging specialist with narrow up-tilted bill and stubby tail. Small flocks, noisy, constantly active in eucalypt woodland and forest. Often lands in uppermost branches and forages downwards.

Voice: repeated high-pitched *chip chip* contact call, also *sweit swee* as group moves off.

Ad ♂: nw Aus.

Ad ♀: nw Aus.

White wing panels on both n ssp.

Ad ♀: Cape York.

Ad ♂: Cape York.

RED-BROWED TREECREEPER ◑ 15 cm
Climacteris erythrops

Arboreal forest dweller with diagnostic rusty eye patch. Eucalypt specialist, especially wetter forests with either peppermints or smooth-barked gums. **Voice:** softer call than White-throated Treecreeper. A rapid series of sibilant notes *tzup sip-sip-sip-sip ...*

WHITE-THROATED TREECREEPER ◕ 15 cm
Cormobates leucophaea

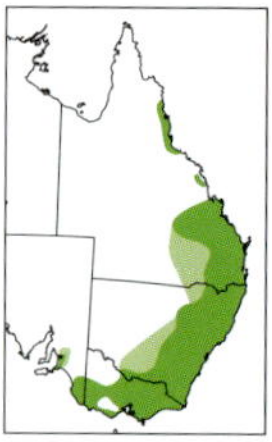

Common arboreal treecreeper with clean white throat. Crown, nape and saddle uniform grey-brown. Wide variety of forested habitats, invariably with eucalypts. **Voice:** loud resonating piping call *pee - pee-pee-pee* ... a characteristic sound in eastern forests.

RUFOUS TREECREEPER ◕ 17 cm
Climacteris rufus

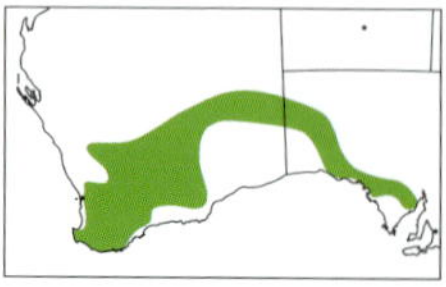

Only treecreeper with rufous face and underparts. Arboreal and terrestrial in family parties. Forest, woodland and tall mallee with open ground. Dead standing and fallen timber important habitat elements. **Voice:** noisy, often first detected by alarm and contact calls; shrill *peep*, given with varying intervals. Also shrill whistled chirr *tsoo-tsoo-tsoo* or *tsit-tsit-tsit*.

WHITE-BROWED TREECREEPER ◔ 15 cm
Climacteris affinis

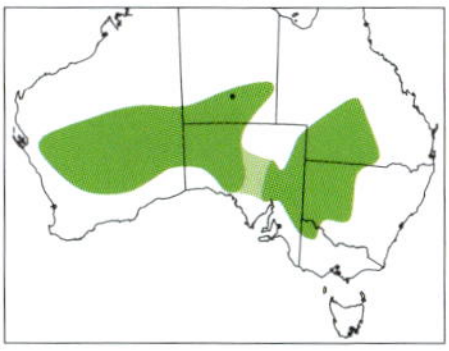

Mostly arboreal grey-brown treecreeper of arid interior with streaked belly. Largely restricted to *Acacia*, she-oak and native pine woodland.
Voice: softer call than Brown Treecreeper. Insect like ringing *prrpit-prrpit* ... or *prrit-prrit* ... sometimes in long series, also faster trill.

BROWN TREECREEPER ◕ 16 cm
Climacteris picumnus

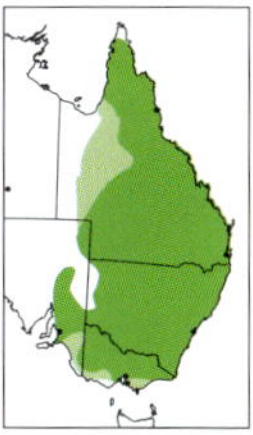

Arboreal and terrestrial treecreeper with plain brown upperparts. Eucalyptus dominated woodland especially with grassy understorey, much dead or fallen timber, and many hollows.
Voice: noisy, a staccato *pink* singly or repeated 5–10 times.

BLACK-TAILED TREECREEPER ◑ 17 cm
Climacteris melanurus

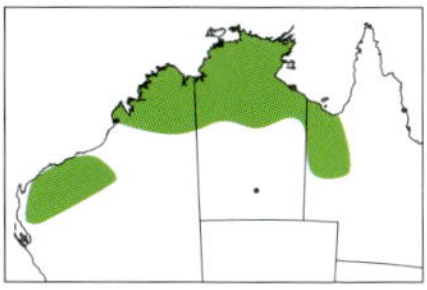

Largest and darkest treecreeper. Range does not overlap with other treecreepers. Eucalypt woodland and savanna of humid and semi-arid zones, prefers grassy understorey.
Voice: a loud metallic *ching* or *chee-ting*, singly or repeated at ~1 sec intervals.

COMMON CICADABIRD ◑ 24 cm
Edolisoma tenuirostre

Dimorphic cuckoo-shrike of tall eucalypt forest canopy. Summer migrant to e and s Aus.
Voice: varies with range, in e Aus a cicada-like fast pulsing buzz *kee-kee-kee* ..., 4–5 notes per sec, in n Aus similar but slower paced with 1–2 notes per sec.

VARIED TRILLER ◕ 19 cm
Lalage leucomela

Bold double wing bar, orange-buff undertail coverts and finely barred underparts (can be faint). Narrow pale brow in all plumages. Rainforest, vine thicket, riparian forest and mangroves.
Voice: loud chirring trill *drr-eea - drr-eea* ...

WHITE-WINGED TRILLER ◕ 18 cm
Lalage tricolor

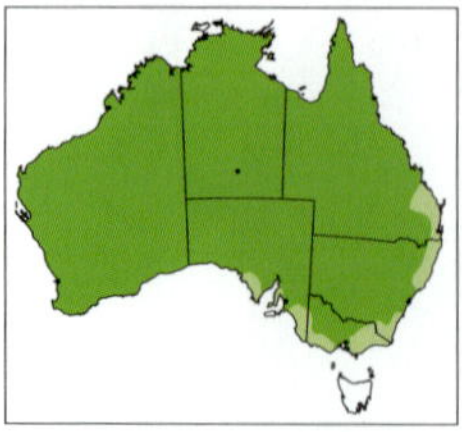

Widespread in open woodland and shrubland. Spring–summer migrant to s Aus.
Voice: extended series of crisp notes, descending slightly, then ending with canary-like trill *chiff-chiff-chiff joey joey joey.*

BLACK-FACED CUCKOO-SHRIKE ◕ 32 cm
Coracina novaehollandiae

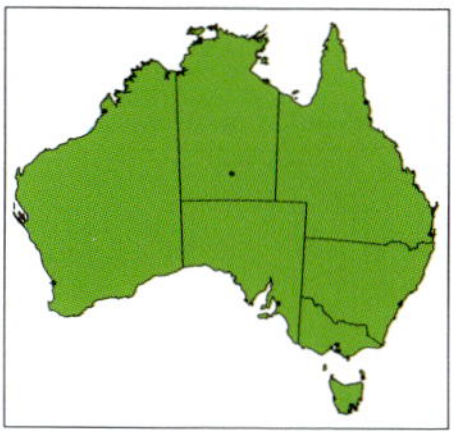

Large, familiar cuckoo-shrike widespread in wooded habitats. Many but not all from s Aus migrate n in winter.
Voice: common call a pleasant rattling trill *cher reer,* uttered singly or 3–5 times when perched and in flight.

WHITE-BELLIED CUCKOO-SHRIKE ◕ 27 cm
Coracina papuensis

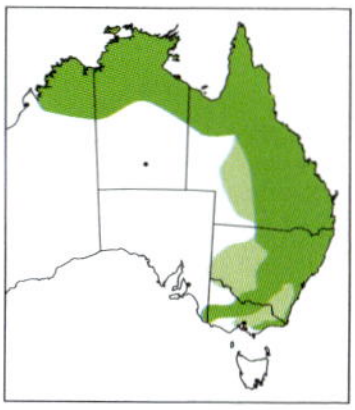

Medium-sized cuckoo-shrike, most with neat black mask restricted to lores; some with extensive black head and throat. Widespread in eucalypt dominated forest and woodland including tropical savanna.
Voice: shrill call *kiseek-kiseek.*

BARRED CUCKOO-SHRIKE ◑ 26 cm
Coracina lineata

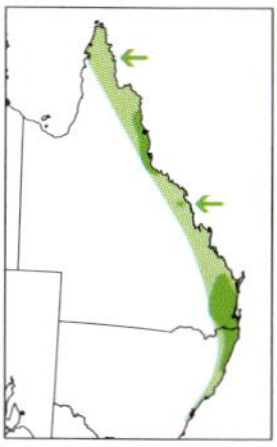

Medium-sized, finely barred cuckoo-shrike of rainforest and rainforest edges. Visits isolated fruiting trees to forage.
Voice: calls in flight or from high perch, pleasant ringing reminiscent of toy mouth organ *we-we-loo, aw-loo-ack.*

GROUND CUCKOO-SHRIKE ◔ 34 cm
Coracina maxima

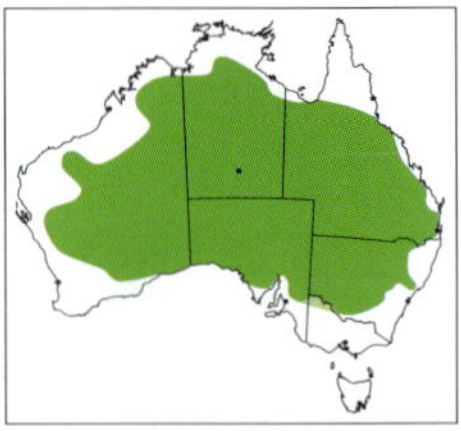

Long-tailed, terrestrial cuckoo-shrike of semi-arid and arid interior. Open woodland and shrubland with little to no ground cover. Struts purposefully whilst foraging.
Voice: a shrill *queel* or *chew chew*, often from elevated perch or in flight.

WHITE-WINGED CHOUGH ◕ 45 cm
Corcorax melanorhamphos

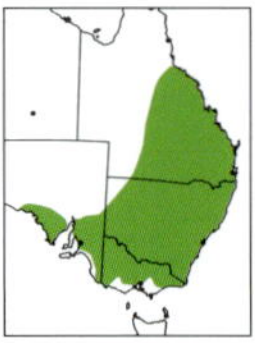

Crow-sized, gregarious ground forager with large white wing panels. Families of 5–20 in open forest, woodland, mallee; wherever ground cover is sparse and leaf litter plentiful.
Voice: noisy; contact call a mournful descending whistle given by the flock *pieew-pieew* ..., alarm call harsh shrieks *ccchhrr* and sinister grating trill.

APOSTLEBIRD ◕ 31 cm
Struthidea cinerea

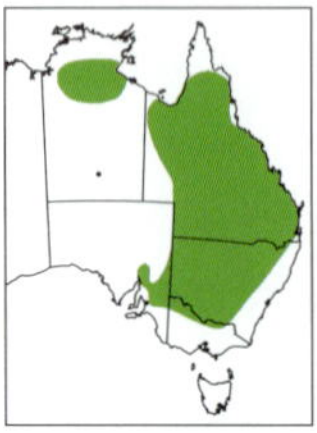

Gregarious ground forager with short, robust bill. Families of 5–20 in arid and semi-arid woodland, often along watercourses and around homesteads.
Voice: noisy; constant chatter of flock with many harsh, scratchy, squeaky and scolding notes.

PIED CURRAWONG ● 47 cm
Strepera graculina

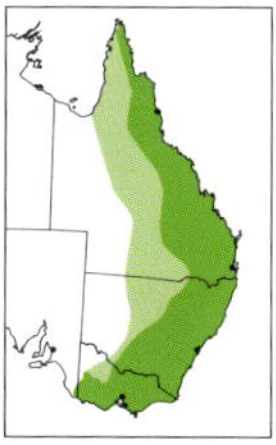

Crow-sized bird of wooded habitats usually with white base to tail. Size of white wing patch varies across range.

Ad: sw Vic, reduced white in tail base and wing.

Widespread in most wetter wooded habitats. Flocks move to more open habitats in winter.
Voice: vocal; named after far carrying, rollicking call *curra-wong curra-wong*. Calls are otherwise highly variable.

GREY CURRAWONG ◕ 49 cm
Strepera versicolor

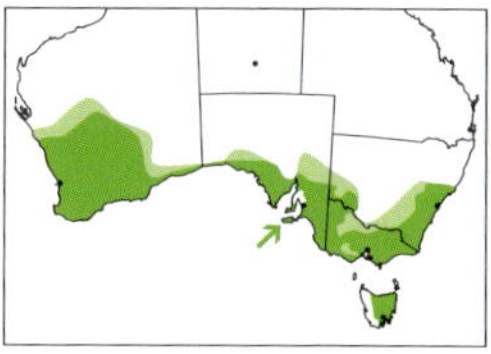

Ad: Vic and SA mallee, mostly black, white vent and tail tips.

Ad: se and sw Aus, grey with white wing patch.

Ad: Tas, black with white wing patch.

Ad: grey with darker face.

Southern currawong with much geographic variation. Grey plumage with darker face in most of range. Blackish forms in mallee and Tas. Can be confused with Black and Pied Currawongs; note straight bill profile.
Voice: clinking calls; 2–3 abrupt notes *clink-clink* (se Aus), *tew-tew* (s WA), *ker-link* (Tas).

BLACK CURRAWONG ◔ 48 cm
Strepera fuliginosa

Tas endemic. Widespread but most abundant in uplands.

Voice: loud, somewhat musical goose-like cackling *kar-week-week-ka*.

Mostly black except for white-tipped wings and tail.

AUSTRALIAN MAGPIE ● 40 cm
Gymnorhina tibicen

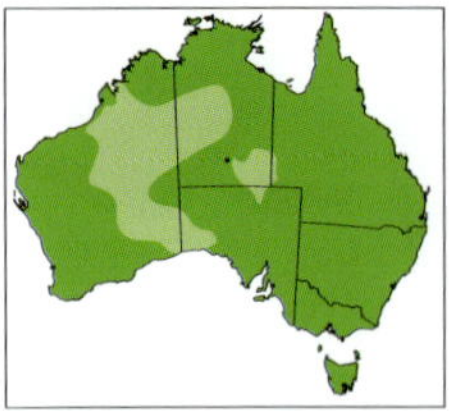

Ad ♂: Pilbara to Broome WA, white 'trousers'.

Ad ♂: 'black-backed'.

Ad ♂: 'white-backed'.

Common, familiar and conspicuous ground forager in open country in rural and urban areas; white-backed forms in s quarter of Aus, black-backed forms further n. **Voice:** a characteristic Aus sound, loud and melodious *quardle oodle ardle wadle doodle*, also conversational warbling.

Ad ♀: 'white-backed' pale-grey back with white scaling.

Juv

GREY BUTCHERBIRD ◕ 28 cm
Cracticus torquatus

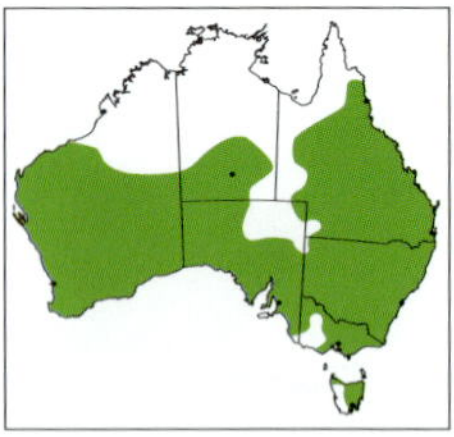

Perches watchfully, takes prey from vegetation or ground.

Small grey-backed butcherbird with black 'helmet' and white throat. Open forest, woodland, farmland, and urban areas.

Juv

Ad ♂

Ad ♀

Voice: loud, rollicking, fluty song finishing with tumbling series of notes.

SILVER-BACKED BUTCHERBIRD ◑
Cracticus argenteus
28 cm

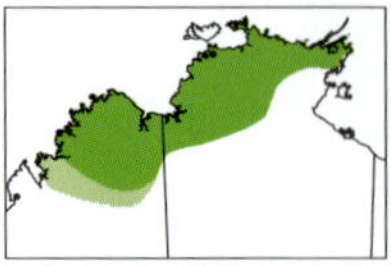

Pale-grey back, no white in lores.

Ad

Large white wing panels.

Northern counterpart of Grey Butcherbird. Tall woodland and riparian forest. **Voice:** like Grey Butcherbird but less vocal.

BLACK BUTCHERBIRD ◕ 37 cm
Melloria quoyi

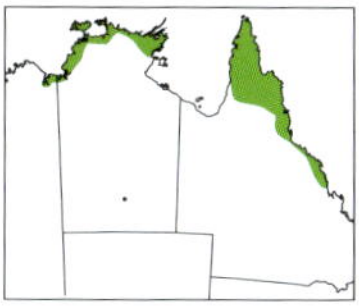

Juv black morph

Ad

Very large, all-black butcherbird (except Juvs in s part of range, which are rufous-brown). Occurs in dense tropical vegetation, mangroves, also rainforest and gallery forest. Wary, but can become tame in urban areas.

Juv: Wet Tropics.

Separate from crows by upright stance and straight, mostly pale bill.

Voice: loud varied calls, including rich, mellow yodelling and a ringing *kurr-ra-tung* reminiscent of currawongs. Often in duet from deep within forest.

PIED BUTCHERBIRD ◕ 30 cm
Cracticus nigrogularis

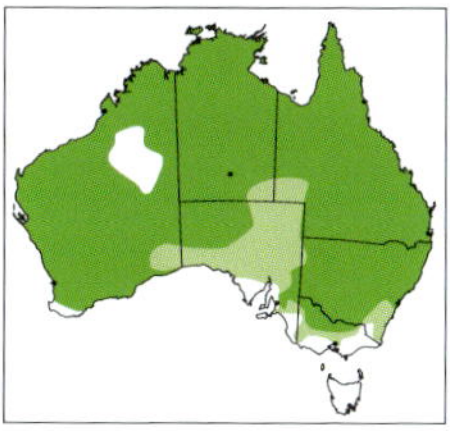

Juv

Imm

Large butcherbird with complete black hood. Widespread in open country, drier woodland and forest.
Voice: song is one of the finest in Aus. Melodious call consisting of a varied sequence of pure, fluty whistles, interspersed with throaty warbles.

Ad: complete black hood.

BLACK-BACKED BUTCHERBIRD ◑ 26 cm
Cracticus mentalis

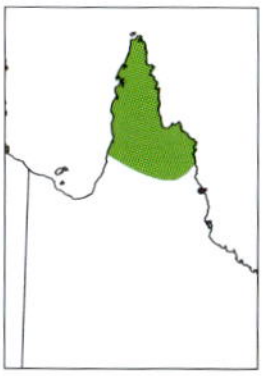

White throat, smaller size and narrower white collar help rule out Pied Butcherbird.

Juv

Ad

Small butcherbird restricted to Cape York. Open eucalypt forest and woodland.
Voice: song shares characteristics with that of Grey Butcherbird.

BLACK-FACED WOODSWALLOW ◕ 17 cm
Artamus cinereus

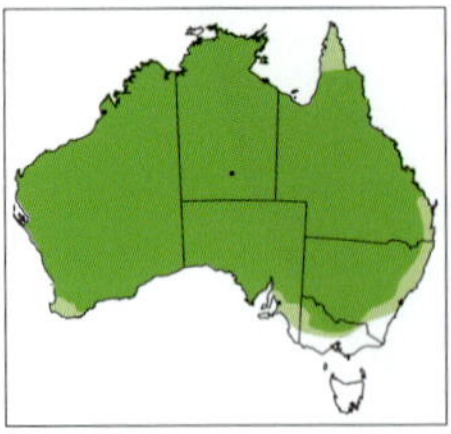

Pairs or small flocks in arid and semi-arid regions. Uses dry open woodland, shrubland and farmland with exposed perches, e.g. dead trees, fences, termite mounds.
Voice: vocal; varied chattering contact calls including scratchy *chiff chiff;* loud throaty *tchat-tchat-tchat-tchat* in alarm.

DUSKY WOODSWALLOW ◕ 18 cm
Artamus cyanopterus

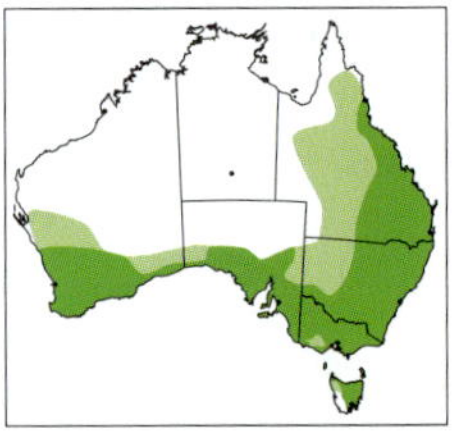

Pairs or small flocks in open forest and woodland, including remnant patches in farmland.
Voice: loud, coarse *zweet* in flight, chattering and chirping in contact and in song.

LITTLE WOODSWALLOW ◑ 14 cm
Artamus minor

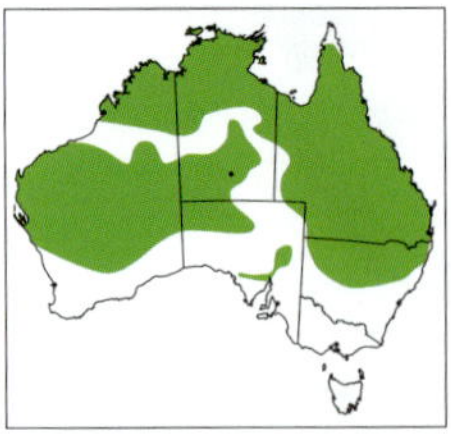

Pairs or small flocks usually near rocky outcrops in open woodland and shrubland. Perches on emergent bare branches.
Voice: brisk repeated *peet* in contact. Less vocal than other woodswallows.

WHITE-BREASTED WOODSWALLOW ◕ 20 cm
Artamus leucorynchus

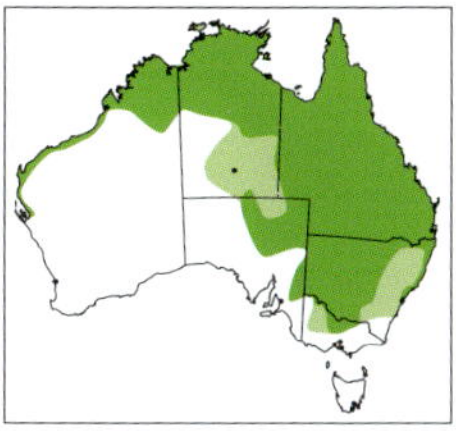

Largest woodswallow. Wooded habitats near water; in tropics often seen in urban areas. Typically seen on high exposed perches, or foraging on the wing.
Voice: nasal *pirt* in contact, harsher calls in alarm.

MASKED WOODSWALLOW ◑ 19 cm
Artamus personatus

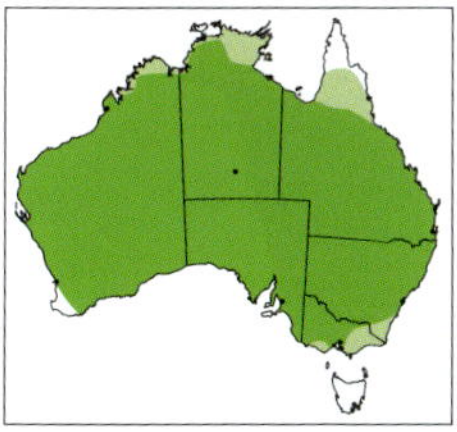

Found in small to very large flocks, usually with White-browed; Masked predominates in WA, White-browed in e Aus. In open forest, woodland and shrubland, often high overhead.
Voice: incessant chirped contact calls *chyep* draws attention to overhead flocks.

WHITE-BROWED WOODSWALLOW ◑ 19 cm
Artamus superciliosus

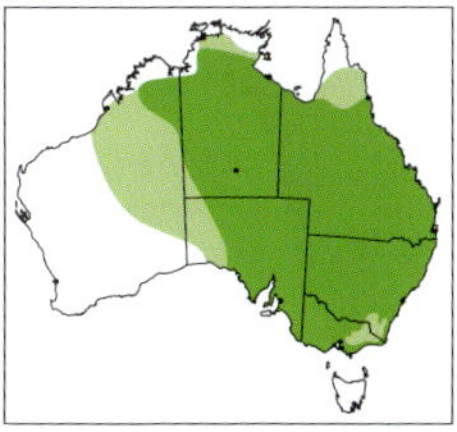

Found in small to very large flocks, usually with Masked. White-browed predominates in e Aus. In open forest, woodland and shrubland, often high overhead. Habitat, behaviour and calls like Masked.
Voice: incessant chirped contact calls *chyep* draw attention to overhead flocks.

AUSTRALIAN RAVEN ● 51 cm

Corvus coronoides

The usual corvid in Sydney and only corvid in Perth.

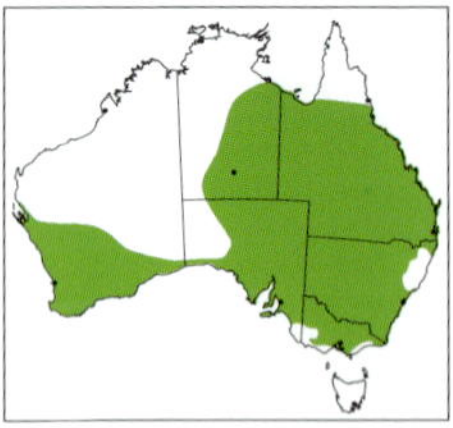

Widespread raven with long throat hackles forming distinct 'beard'.
Voice: high-pitched territorial call a slow, drawn out wail, *aiah-aaah-aaah-aaaaahhh*, the last wail protracted and dropping in pitch and intensity. Also gravelly rattle.

FOREST RAVEN ● 51 cm

Corvus tasmanicus

The only corvid in Tas, extends to coastal se and e mainland.
Voice: the harshest and lowest-pitched of Aus corvid calls. Slow, clipped, nasal *korr-korr-korr-korr,* the last note sometimes drawn out and descending.

LITTLE RAVEN ● 49 cm

Corvus mellori

Call often accompanied by wing flicking.

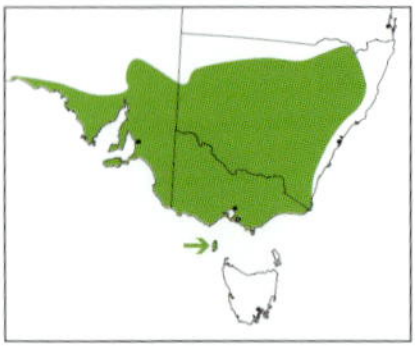

SE Aus, only corvid in urban Melbourne. Routinely forms flocks. In farmland, open woodland and alpine areas.
Voice: calls are short, rapid, medium-toned, guttural *ark-ark-ark* or longer *ark-arrk-arrrk* usually ending abruptly. If end of call is drawn out it is shorter and lower-pitched than Australian Raven.

TORRESIAN CROW ● 50 cm
Corvus orru

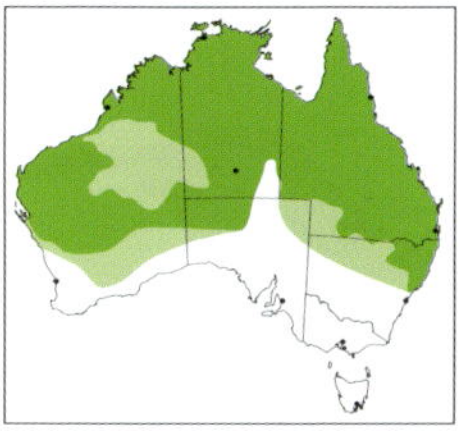

White bases to hackles sometimes seen when calling, throat hackles not as obvious as in ravens.

Thick bill shorter than ravens.

Large crow, less bulky than ravens, occurring across much of c and n Aus. Throat hackles short, no obvious beard. The common corvid in major Qld cities and towns. **Voice:** usual call a high-pitched short, sharp, nasal *ok-ok-ok* with a barking quality, the last 1–2 notes sometimes extended.

LITTLE CROW ◕ 46 cm
Corvus bennetti

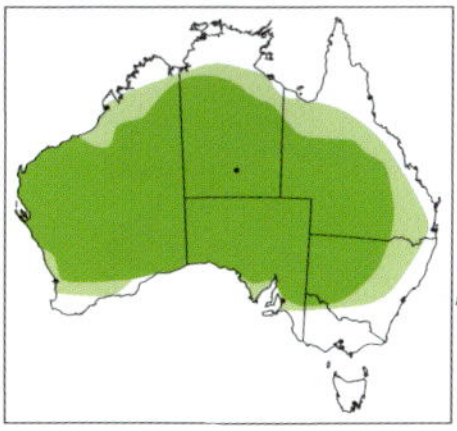

White bases to throat hackles sometimes seen when calling.

Flocks readily soar in thermals.

Shorter bill than Torresian Crow, trim head can often appear rather squarish.

Small, gregarious crow of arid and semi-arid zone, the common corvid in Alice Springs. Throat hackles short, no obvious beard. **Voice:** a short, sharp, nasal *nark-nark* slightly longer and lower-pitched than Torresian Crow.

TRUMPET MANUCODE ◑ 33 cm
Phonygammus keraudrenii

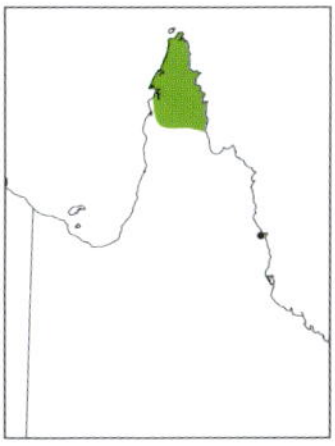

Juv: less glossy and neater head.

Ad: shaggy nape.

Broad wings.

Large, glossy, blue-black bird of paradise restricted to n Cape York. Slightly larger than Spangled Drongo. A rainforest inhabitant, mostly remains in forest canopy. Occasionally appearing in adjacent woodland and mangroves.

Voice: usually first detected by contact call, a loud, hollow rasp *oonng*. Also higher-pitched *keow* and abrupt *skowp*.

PARADISE RIFLEBIRD ◑ 28 cm
Ptiloris paradiseus

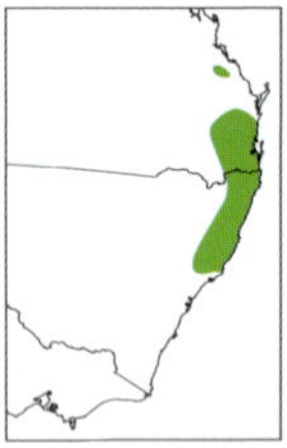

Riflebird wings are short, broad and rounded. In flight, ♂ wings make a distinctive rustle.

Riflebirds have a distinctive, downcurved bill and a short tail.

Inhabits subtropical rainforest above 500 m altitude in s Qld and n NSW. Mostly in canopy.
Voice: ♂ advertising song loud, rasping, repeated *yaas yaas*.

VICTORIA'S RIFLEBIRD ◑ 25 cm
Ptiloris victoriae

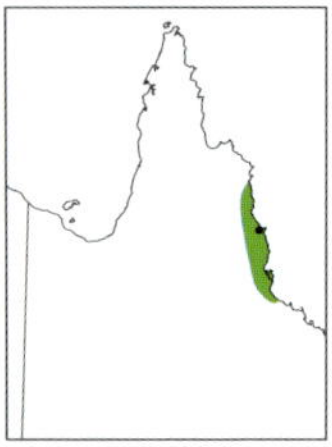

Restricted to Wet Tropics, n Qld.

♂ riflebirds perform an extravagant courtship display on exposed perch.

Smallest riflebird. In tropical rainforest and adjacent wet eucalypt forest and gardens at all elevations.
Voice: ♂ advertising song loud, rasping *ya-a-as*.

MAGNIFICENT RIFLEBIRD ◑ 30 cm
Ptiloris magnificus

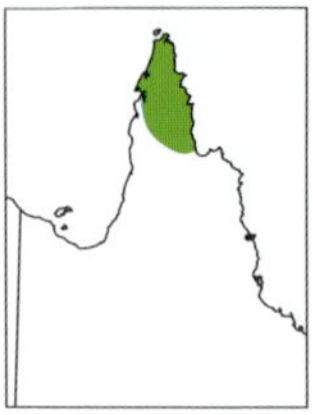

Largest, loudest riflebird.

Lowland and foothill rainforest and adjacent habitats of n Cape York Peninsula.
Voice: unlike other riflebirds; loud, clear whistles *we ee-oop*, the final note upslurred.

GOLDEN BOWERBIRD 24 cm
Prionodura newtoniana

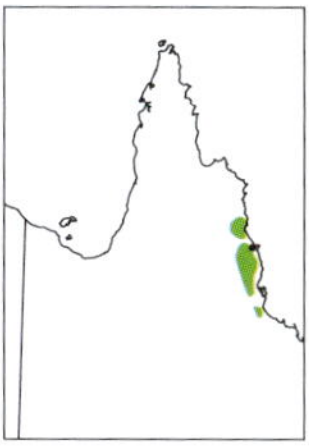

Small bowerbird of upland rainforest in n Qld, mostly above 900 m altitude. ♂ sits quietly near bower or works at maintaining the huge bower.

Voice: ♂ advertising song a pulsating rattle of 1–2 sec duration. Good mimic.

♂ at bower.

REGENT BOWERBIRD 27 cm
Sericulus chrysocephalus

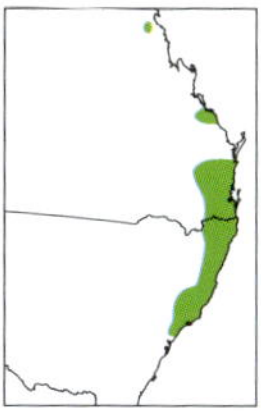

Small bowerbird of subtropical rainforest, adjacent parks and gardens. **Voice:** mostly quiet, courtship song includes mimicry of other species.

♂ at bower.

SATIN BOWERBIRD 31 cm
Ptilonorhynchus violaceus

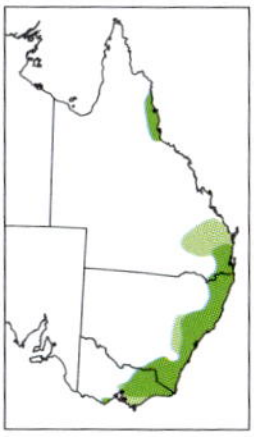

Large, stocky bowerbird. In wet forest and adjacent modified habitats including gardens.

Voice: a variety of grating chirrs and buzzes with mimicry of other birds.

♂ at bower which it decorates with blue objects.

SPOTTED BOWERBIRD ◑ 29 cm
Chlamydera maculata

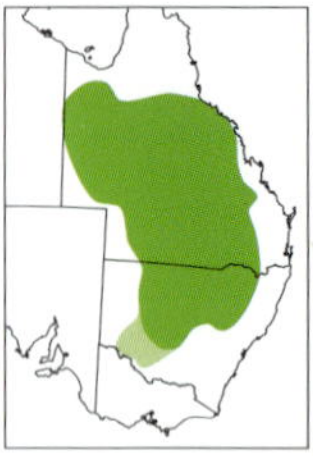

Medium-sized bowerbird of semi-arid woodlands and pastoral country, often in homestead and town gardens.

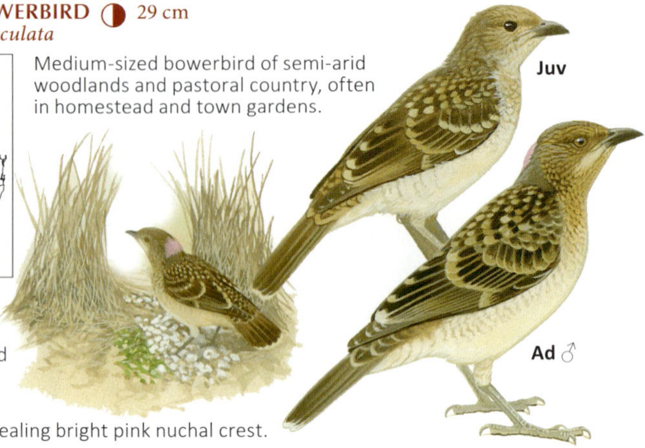

Voice: loud harsh chirring, an accomplished mimic.

♂ at bower revealing bright pink nuchal crest.

WESTERN BOWERBIRD ◑ 27 cm
Chlamydera guttata

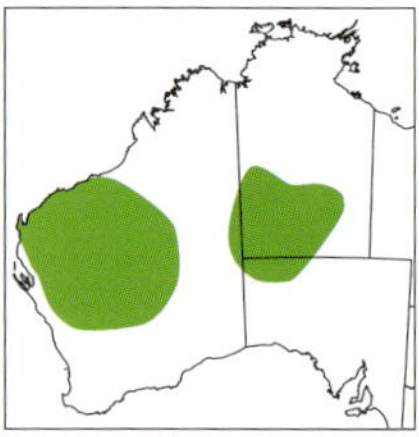

Equivalent of Spotted Bowerbird in c and w Aus but darker and warmer coloured. Often in rocky gorges with fig trees, also homestead gardens.
Voice: as for Spotted Bowerbird.

GREAT BOWERBIRD ◕ 36 cm
Chlamydera nuchalis

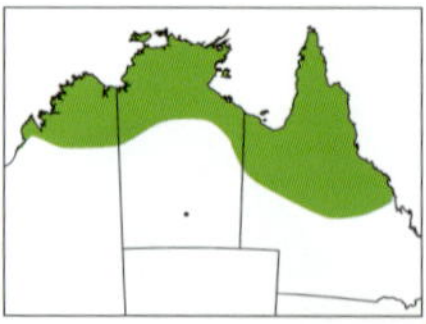

Largest bowerbird, mostly plain grey plumage. Bold and inquisitive, common in towns, homestead gardens and riverine habitats.

Voice: variety of loud, harsh chattering, hissing and cat-like sounds.

♂ at bower revealing bright pink nuchal crest.

FAWN-BREASTED BOWERBIRD ○ 29 cm
Chlamydera cerviniventris

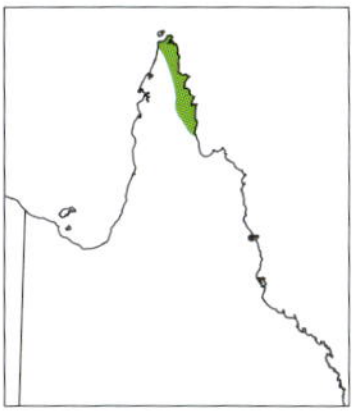

Uncommon and shy in lowland eucalypt and paperbark woodlands, especially adjacent to riparian forest.

Voice: range of harsh chirring, rattling and sputtering, hoarse *chee chee*. Skilled mimic.

GREEN CATBIRD ◐ 30 cm
Ailuroedus crassirostris

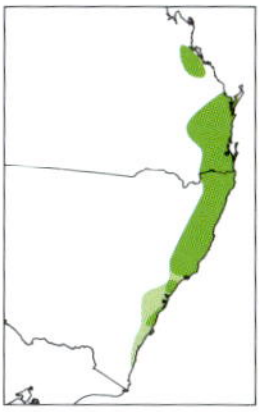

In middle and upper canopy of temperate and subtropical rainforest. Can be hard to see, usually first detected by call. Chunky with heavy pale bill.

Voice: like a yowling cat, a long undulating *yow-owl-owl*. Contact call a sharp, high-pitched *tic*.

SPOTTED CATBIRD ◐ 27 cm
Ailuroedus maculosus

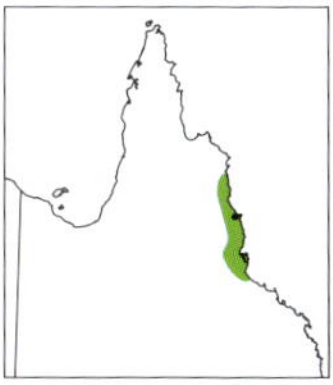

In Wet Tropics rainforest, forages at all levels of forest, usually first detected by call.

Chunky build, conspicuous black ear coverts, green flanks with cream streaks.
Voice: as for Green Catbird.

BLACK-EARED CATBIRD ◐ 27 cm
Ailuroedus melanotis

In rainforests of n Cape York Peninsula. Chunky build, conspicuous black ear coverts, cream flanks, cleaner white spotting on head.
Voice: as for Green Catbird.

TOOTH-BILLED BOWERBIRD ◔ 29 cm
Scenopoeetes dentirostris

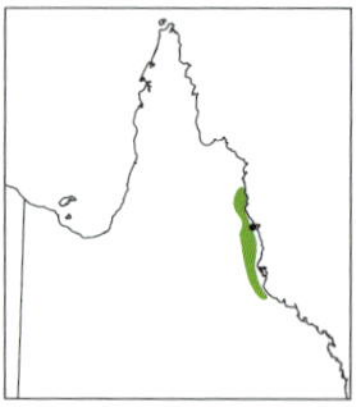

Singing ♂ beside display court of scattered, pale-green leaves.

In upland rainforest of Wet Tropics in ne Qld above 500 m altitude. Heavily streaked underparts, heavy black bill.
Voice: mostly quiet. Displaying ♂ gives powerful, varied and sustained song of loud, harsh screeches, chuks and mimicry.

GREEN ORIOLE ◕ 28 cm
Oriolus flavocinctus

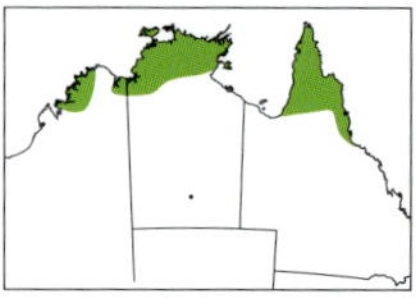

Canopy of rainforest, riparian forest, mangroves, parks and gardens. Yellow-green with blackish wing feathers edged white. Often difficult to see but distinctive call reveals presence.
Voice: rich, deep, variable bubbling *yok-yok-yoddle*, a characteristic sound in tropical Aus.

OLIVE-BACKED ORIOLE ◑ 27 cm
Oriolus sagittatus

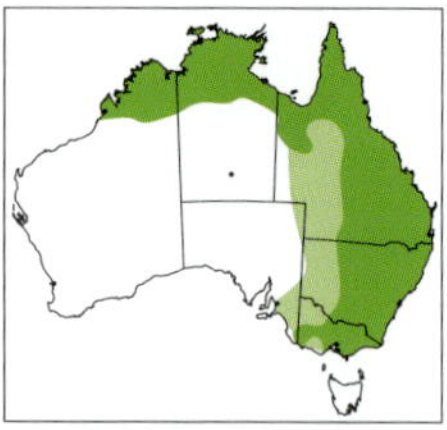

In canopy of more open and drier forests than Green Oriole. Pale and streaked underparts, mostly grey wing feathers. Present year round in n Aus, spring–summer migrant to s Aus. Usually heard before being seen.
Voice: distinctive, pleasant and far-carrying, melodious *orri-olly-oriole*.

AUSTRALASIAN FIGBIRD ● 27 cm
Sphecotheres vieilloti

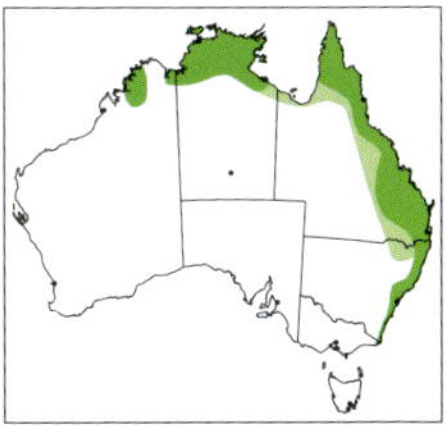

Stocky, variable species, with large bare facial patch. Eats mostly fruit, especially figs, found in most habitats with fruiting trees. Conspicuous in noisy flocks, common in cities and towns.
Voice: loud, fluted whistles.

SPANGLED DRONGO ◕ 29 cm
Dicrurus bracteatus

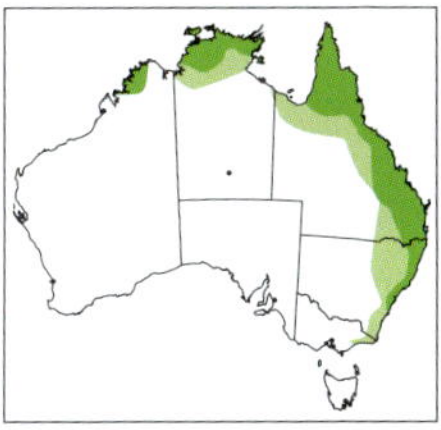

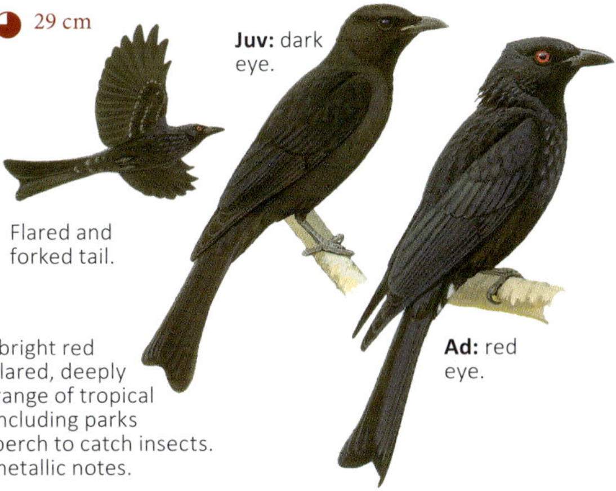

Glossy, all-black plumage, bright red eye, only bird in Aus with flared, deeply forked 'fish' tail. In broad range of tropical and subtropical habitats, including parks and gardens. Sallies from perch to catch insects.
Voice: harsh rattling and metallic notes.

MAGPIE-LARK ● 27 cm
Grallina cyanoleuca

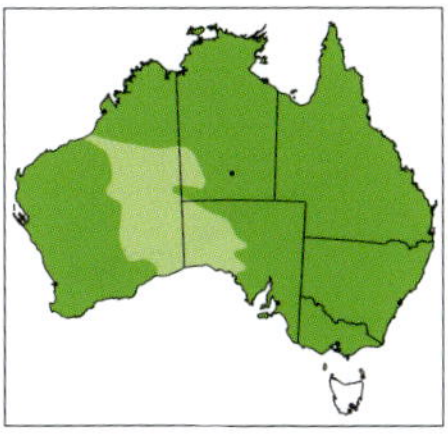

Common and familiar across most of continent. Forages on ground in short grass or on muddy shores, including urban areas. Distinctive pair bonding display involving loud duet with rhythmic opening of wings and fanning of tail.
Voice: loud, ringing *peewee*, often a duet between a pair.

YELLOW-BREASTED BOATBILL ◑ 11 cm

Machaerirhynchus flaviventer

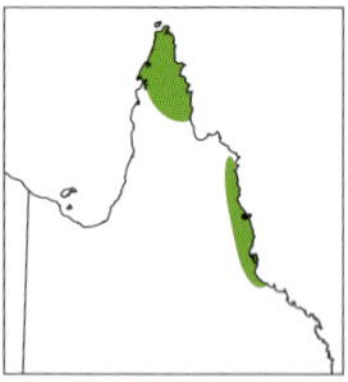

Small, unobtrusive flycatcher with broad flat bill, tail cocked or vibrated. Pairs in rainforest canopy and subcanopy at all altitudes. Sallies and gleans for insects in outer foliage.
Voice: insect-like trill *wit-zee-ee-eewit*.

RESTLESS FLYCATCHER ◑ 20 cm

Myiagra inquieta

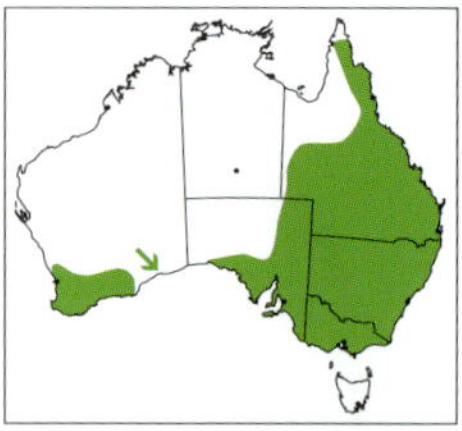

Confiding, glossy-black flycatcher. White underparts extend to throat *cf* Willie Wagtail (p. 215). In dry open forest and scrub, catches insects from low perch, or hovers above ground while searching.
Voice: best known call a distinctive, continuous grinding *bsrrt* often given while hovering, also a pleasant, clear whistle *tuii-tuii-tuii*.

PAPERBARK FLYCATCHER ◕ 19 cm

Myiagra nana

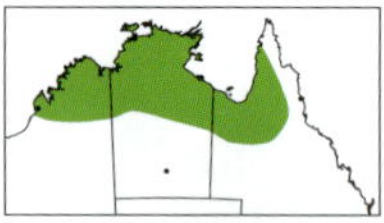

Smaller, glossier tropical equivalent of Restless Flycatcher. In waterside habitats including paperbark swamps, *Pandanus*, mangroves and vine thickets. More widespread during dry season.

Voice: like Restless Flycatcher.

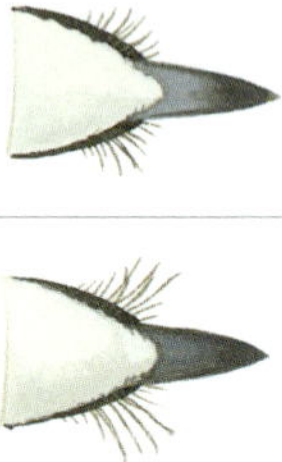

BROAD-BILLED FLYCATCHER ◑ 15 cm
Myiagra ruficollis

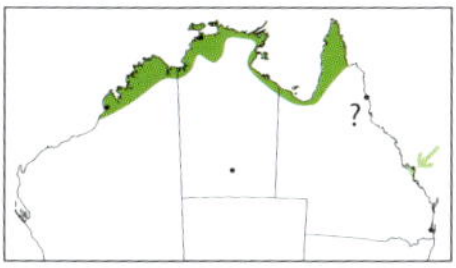

In mangroves and adjacent vegetation.

Voice: a loud repeated *chinny chinny* or *chew chew*, grinding *tzeep*.

LEADEN FLYCATCHER ◕ 16 cm
Myiagra rubecula

Active and noisy, shivers tail. Summer migrant in s where mostly in canopy in dry forest. Also coastal and riverine habitats in n Aus.
Voice: a loud, pleasant *towhee towhee*, repeated buzzing *tzeep*.

SATIN FLYCATCHER ◑ 17 cm
Myiagra cyanoleuca

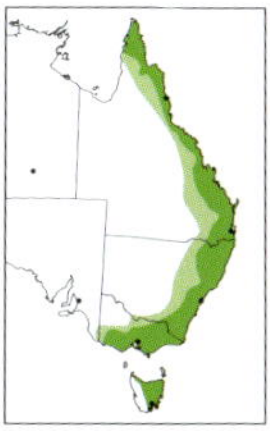

Active and noisy, shivers tail. Mostly in canopy of moist forest, at most altitudes.

Voice: similar to Leaden.

SHINING FLYCATCHER ◑ 18 cm
Myiagra alecto

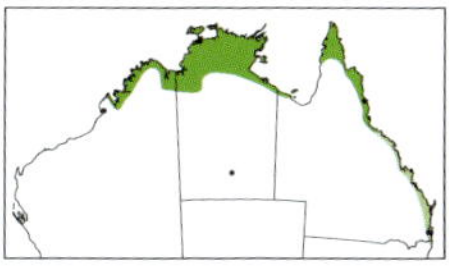

Mangrove and streamside habitats in tropics and subtropics.
Voice: loud, clear, piping whistle *towwhit-too-towhit*, also grating and rasping sounds.

SPECTACLED MONARCH ◕ 15 cm

Symposiachrus trivirgatus

Southern populations migrate to n Qld for the cooler months.

Small, active monarch, gleans insects from leaves in mid to lower levels of rainforest, riverside forest and mangroves. **Voice:** territorial song a clear, ascending *sweet-sweet* or *pree-pree-pree*, also scratchy buzzing and scolding.

BLACK-FACED MONARCH ◑ 18 cm

Monarcha melanopsis

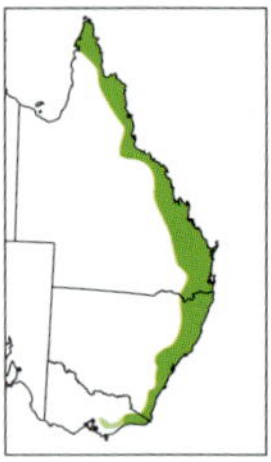

Migrates to NG Apr–Sep.

Uniformly grey upperparts.

Large, sedate monarch. In lower to mid-levels of rainforest, gallery forest, waterside and wet sclerophyll forest. Methodical and deliberate, gleans insects from leaves and branches. **Voice:** a pleasant clear whistle, rising then falling *whee-you* or *why you witch yueew*.

BLACK-WINGED MONARCH ◔ 18 cm

Monarcha frater

Black tail and wings.

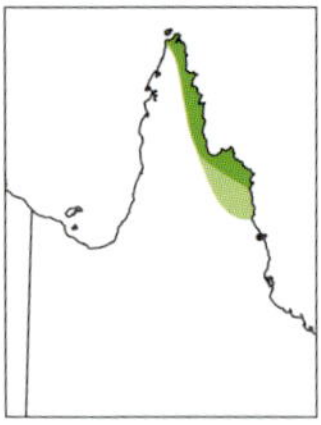

Breeds in ne Cape York, n of Cooktown, migrates to NG Mar–Sep.

Large, sedate monarch with pearl-grey and black upperparts. In lower to mid-levels of lowland rainforest, gallery forest and vine forest. Methodical and deliberate, gleans insects from leaves and branches. **Voice:** cheery 4-note whistle *wherii-chiioo*, recalls Black-faced Monarch.

WHITE-EARED MONARCH ◑ 15 cm
Carterornis leucotis

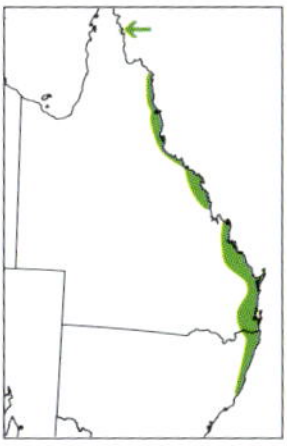

Small, active monarch, although often very difficult to see. In rainforest, regrowth thickets, streamside remnants and mangroves. Altitudinal migrant in s, moving lower in winter.

Forages high up, often in outer canopy searching for insects. When at lower levels of forest can be confiding. Also perch sallies. **Voice:** 4-note song *you get away*. Also downslurred *phew-phew* recalling Horsfield's Bronze-Cuckoo.

FRILL-NECKED MONARCH ◑ 15 cm
Arses lorealis

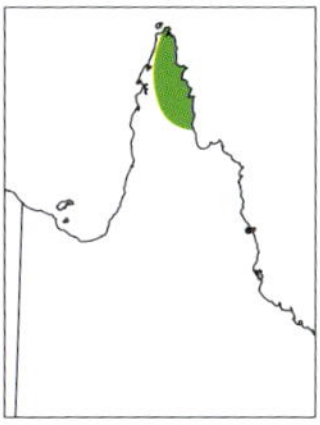

In rainforest, deciduous vine forest and gallery forest on n Cape York Peninsula.

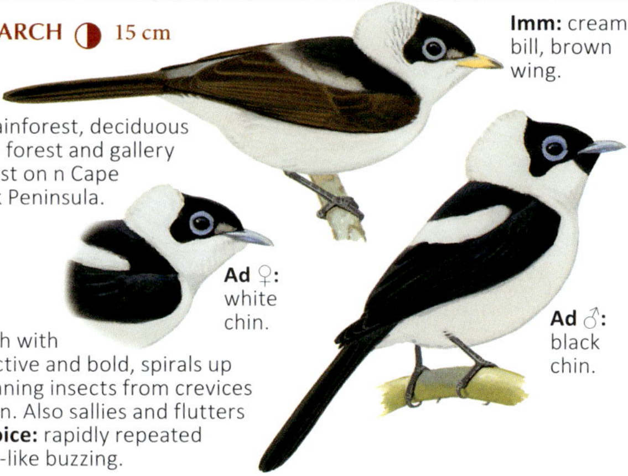

Imm: cream bill, brown wing.

Ad ♀: white chin.

Ad ♂: black chin.

Black and white monarch with distinctive white ruff. Active and bold, spirals up and down branches gleaning insects from crevices and clumps of vegetation. Also sallies and flutters after flushed insects. **Voice:** rapidly repeated nasal *tyu-tyu-tyu*, insect-like buzzing.

PIED MONARCH ◑ 15 cm
Arses kaupi

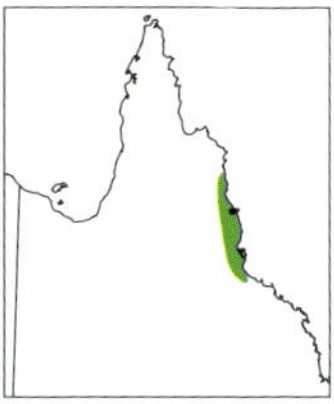

Ad ♀: black helmet and breast band joined.

Imm: cream bill, dark bars in frill and throat.

Foraging on branches.

Ad ♂: all white collar.

Black and white monarch with distinctive white ruff and black breast band. Active, but unobtrusive, in tropical rainforest and adjacent wet eucalypt forest. Similar foraging behaviour to Frill-necked Monarch. **Voice:** whistled *quee-quee-quee*, harsh scolding *zzree zzree*.

GREY FANTAIL ● 15 cm
Rhipidura albiscapa

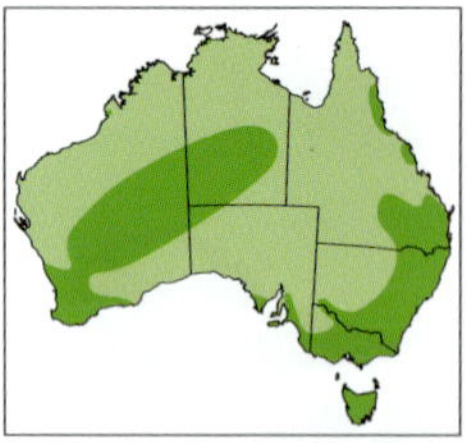

Small grey and white fantail. Widespread, occupies most terrestrial habitats, most abundant in drier woodlands. Constantly active with flitting and fanning of tail. Se and sw populations migratory, many moving n and inland in winter.
Voice: high-pitched song of pleasant ascending squeaks and chatters ending in trill.

MANGROVE FANTAIL ◕ 14 cm
Rhipidura phasiana

Like Grey Fantail but paler and smaller. Mostly restricted to mangrove habitats of n Aus coastline, sometimes in adjacent habitats.
Voice: softer than Grey Fantail, more feeble.

NORTHERN FANTAIL ◑ 17 cm
Rhipidura rufiventris

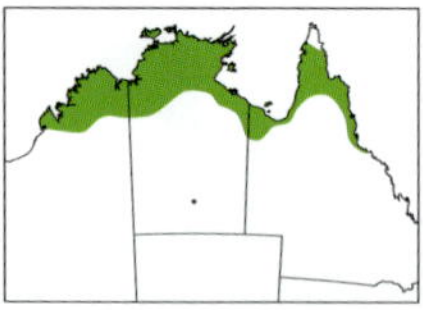

Dark-grey fantail with proportionally large head and square-tipped tail.

Inhabits dense, moist habitats e.g. paperbark swamps, monsoon forest, mangrove edges.
Voice: melodious series of descending notes.

RUFOUS FANTAIL ◑ 16 cm
Rhipidura rufifrons

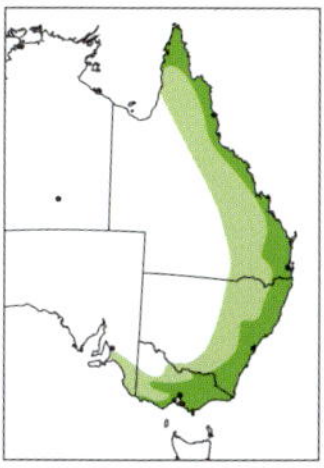

Thicket-loving fantail. Constantly moving, flitting to snatch insects in moist gullies, dense understorey. Migratory, absent from s Aus in winter. **Voice:** thin tinkling notes, higher-pitched than Grey Fantail.

ARAFURA FANTAIL ◔ 16 cm
Rhipidura dryas

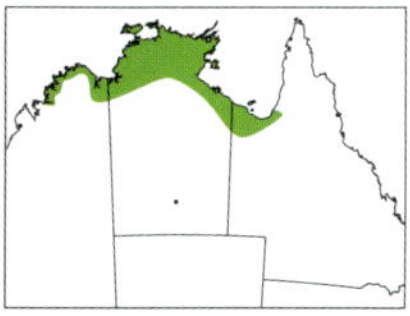

Nw Aus equivalent of Rufous Fantail. Frequents monsoon forest, gallery forest and mangroves. **Voice:** call like Rufous Fantail.

WILLIE WAGTAIL ● 20 cm
Rhipidura leucophrys

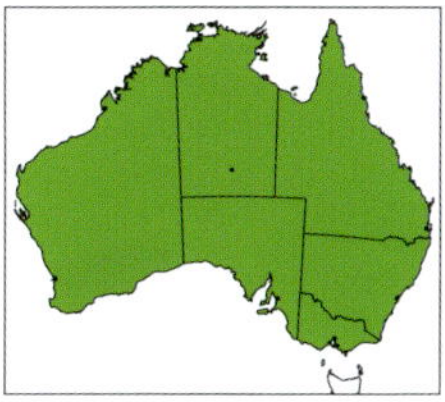

Ground frequenting, black and white fantail. Common in wide range of open habitats. Habitually wags tail side to side.

Voice: *chitit-chitit-chitit*. Song *sweet-pretty-creature* given at all times of day or night.

JACKY WINTER ◔ 13 cm
Microeca fascinans

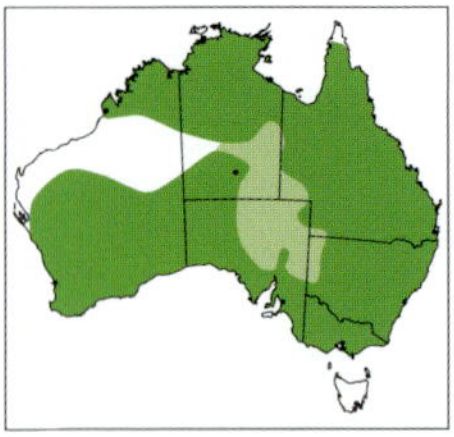

Plain plumage except for black tail with white sides. Tail swung from side to side when perched.

Open forest and woodland with bare ground and sparse shrub layer. Perches low, sallies to catch flying insects or prey from ground. **Voice:** loud melodious song dominated by a fast phrase *witta-witta-witt* ...

LEMON-BELLIED FLYCATCHER ◑ 13 cm
Microeca flavigaster

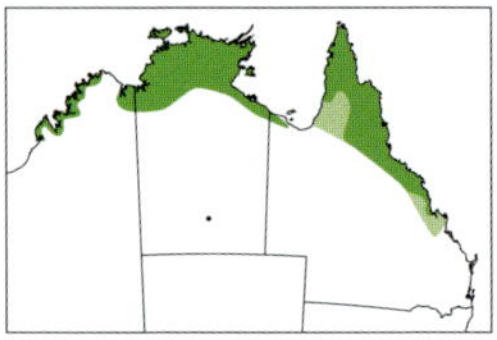

Ad: 'Kimberley Flycatcher' in mangroves of nw WA. No yellow, can be confused with Jacky Winter.

Plain uppertail without white sides, shorter wings than Jacky Winter.

Small flycatcher with upright stance. Two ssp groups, posing different ID problems. Makes short sallies to snatch insects from air, outer foliage or ground. Open forest and woodland, monsoon forest, mangroves and closed vegetation near wetlands. **Voice:** loud, melodious, cheery song of 5–9 brisk warbling whistles over 2–3 sec *pa-treeter-treeter-treeter* and *wi-choo wi-choo we-choo* or *do be sweet to Cynthia*. Sharp contact call *k-chip*.

Ad: yellower on Cape York.

Slimmer bill than Grey Whistler (p. 225) with yellower underparts and black legs, more active behaviour.

YELLOW-LEGGED FLYCATCHER ◔ 13 cm
Kempiella griseoceps

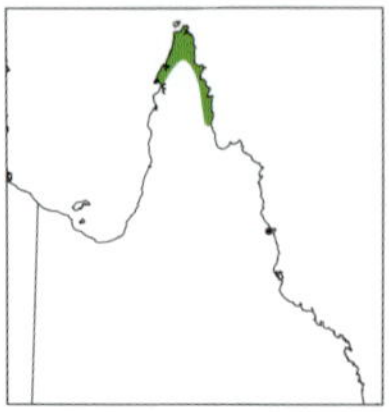

High outer canopy of rainforest and monsoon forest on Cape York Peninsula. Very active: often cocks tail, flits wings, makes short flycatching sallies before returning to perch.

Broad bill with yellow underside.

Bright yellow legs.

Voice: cheery, variable song of chirrups and trills e.g. *chewit chewit chreee chewit* ... Also a rapid trill.

WHITE-BROWED ROBIN ◑ 15 cm
Poecilodryas superciliosa

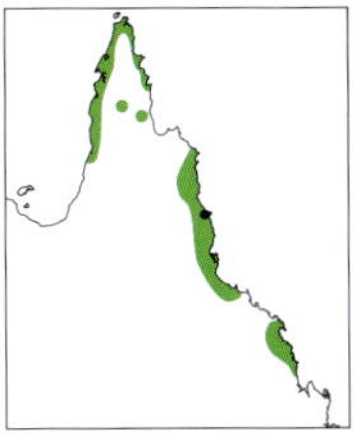

Singly or in pairs in thickets of lowland rainforest, riparian forest or *Pandanus*. Sallies from low perches to take prey from ground or low foliage.

Tail long, often slightly cocked. Wings often flicked when perched.

Ad

Voice: 3–5 clear piping whistles, sometimes ending in sharper note *peet ee ee chak*.

BUFF-SIDED ROBIN ◑ 15 cm
Poecilodryas cerviniventris

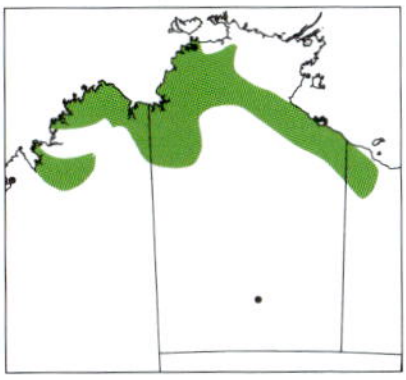

Juv: Buff-sided and White-browed Robin similar.

Ad

Handsome robin of dense riverside vegetation, including rainforest, paperbark, bamboo and *Pandanus*. Singly or in pairs. Usually forages on the ground.
Voice: sings from a low perch: 3–5 loud, piping, rosella-like whistles often ending in louder descending note *peet ee ee chak*.

Similar behaviour to White-browed: cocks tail, flicks wings.

GREY-HEADED ROBIN ◕ 19 cm
Heteromyias cinereifrons

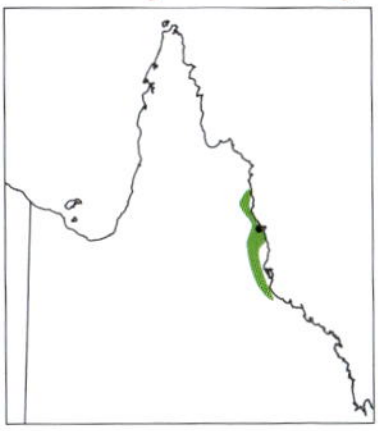

Juv

Ad

Largest robin, almost whistler-size. Tortoiseshell plumage pattern and upright stance. Only in montane rainforest. Takes prey from ground, often scanning for it from low branch or trunk before pouncing.
Voice: song a monotonous series of loud, plaintive whistles *weet* sometimes in groups of 2–3 notes, occasional quiet chattering.

Pink legs.

RED-CAPPED ROBIN 11 cm
Petroica goodenovii

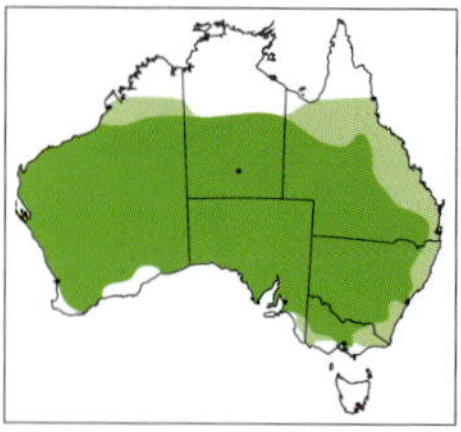

Small robin of dryish woodland and scrub. Singles or pairs perch low and pounce on ground prey.
Voice: insect-like song: a dry trill *dit dit durrrur-it*. Sharp contact call *tick* or *ptek*.

SCARLET ROBIN 12 cm
Petroica boodang

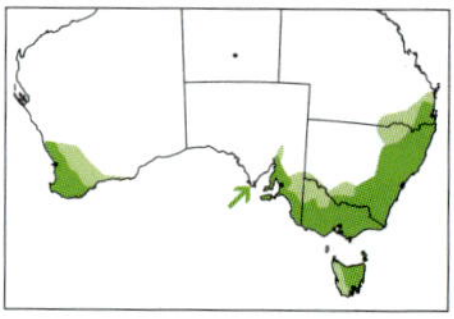

Medium-sized robin of dry sclerophyll woodland and open forest. Singly or in pairs. Perches low, pounces on prey on ground, bark or low foliage.
Voice: sweet song *we chee-dallee-dallee*. Sharp contact call *chup* or *ptek*.

FLAME ROBIN 13 cm
Petroica phoenicea

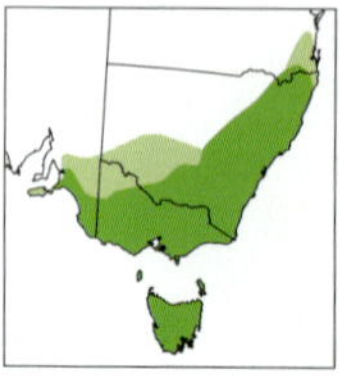

Breeds in upland eucalypt forest and woodland with open understorey or small clearings, often in recently burnt areas. In autumn and winter, flocks migrate to more open lowland areas including grassy woodland and forest.
Voice: warbling song *you may come, if you wish, to the sea*. Contact call a single note *tlip*, seldom given away from breeding grounds.

ROSE ROBIN ◐ 12 cm
Petroica rosea

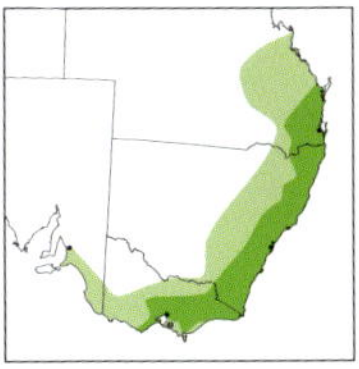

Slimmest, longest-tailed robin. Active; makes fantail-like sallies to catch insects.

In canopy or tall mid-storey of wet eucalypt forest and rainforest. In winter some move to dryer lowland forest and woodland. **Voice:** trilled song *dick didditt deer deer deer*, the last 2–3 notes rising in pitch. Quiet but distinctive contact call; a nasal *neep*.

PINK ROBIN ◐ 12 cm
Petroica rodinogaster

Perches low, feeds on ground or gleans prey from base of trees.

Shy, in denser cover than other robins. Shady shrub layer of wet sclerophyll and rainforest, especially in wet gullies with *Nothofagus* and *Atherosperma*. Many, mainly ♀ and Imm, spend winter in drier, more open lowland forest or coastal scrub. **Voice:** song a rapid flat trill *cht-tr-tr-tr-r-r*. Contact call a hard *tic,* like tapping two stones together.

WHITE-FACED ROBIN ◐ 13 cm
Tregellasia leucops

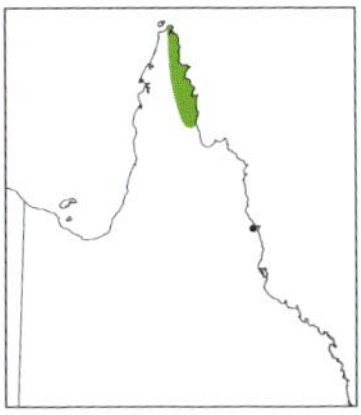

Perches quietly low down, often on side of vertical trunk or vine. Mostly takes prey from ground.

Small robin with unique clown-like facial pattern. Lower and mid-storey of tropical rainforest. **Voice:** similar to Pale-yellow Robin but quieter.

PALE-YELLOW ROBIN ◕ 13 cm
Tregellasia capito

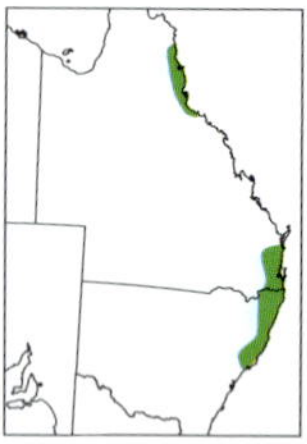

Small, large-headed robin of moist eucalypt forest and rainforest, sometimes in adjacent clearings and gardens. Perches low and still, pounces on prey on ground. **Voice:** soft thin contact call of 2–4 notes; harsh *scriatch* in alarm; dawn song an accelerating series of squeaks *kwee-kwee-kwee-kwee.*

EASTERN YELLOW ROBIN ◕ 15 cm
Eopsaltria australis

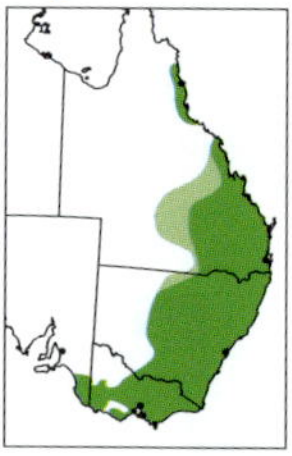

Forest with a tall shrub layer, sparse ground cover, and vertical stems used as perches to scan for terrestrial prey. **Voice:** clear piping whistle throughout day; loud double-noted territorial call at dawn and dusk *chop chop*; grating scold or chattering when agitated.

WESTERN YELLOW ROBIN ◑ 15 cm
Eopsaltria griseogularis

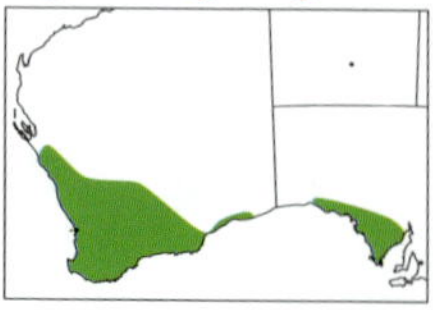

In sclerophyll forest and woodland with thickets, or a moderately dense shrub layer. Avoids densest and wettest thickets where, in s WA, they are replaced by White-breasted Robin. **Voice:** similar to Eastern Yellow Robin but territorial call is more drawn out, a whistled *tchair tchair.*

WHITE-BREASTED ROBIN ◕ 15 cm
Quoyornis georgiana

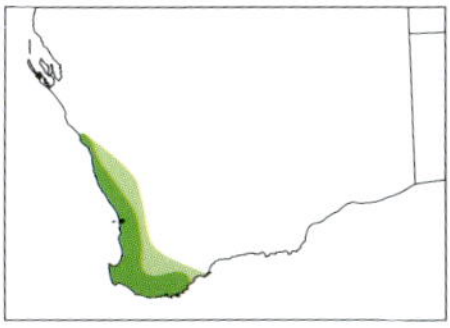

Similar size and behaviour to Western Yellow Robin.

Ad: clean white underparts.

In wetter forests of s WA: thickly vegetated creeklines and understorey of eucalypt forests s of Perth, dense coastal scrubs n of Perth.
Voice: loud *zhip*. Also a whistler-like song: a loud penetrating *see-ow*, sometimes repeated several times, sometimes ends in a whipcrack. Harsh chatter in alarm.

DUSKY ROBIN ◕ 15 cm
Melanodryas vittata

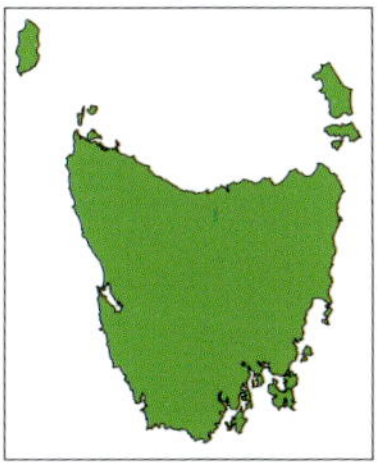

Open forest, woodland and adjacent clearings, including gardens and farmland; avoids dense forest. Perches low, takes prey from ground.
Voice: rather quiet; clear plaintive song *choo-wee* or *choo wee-er*, mainly at dawn.

Plain, sombre brown, larger than Flame Robin.

MANGROVE ROBIN ◑ 14 cm
Peneothello pulverulenta

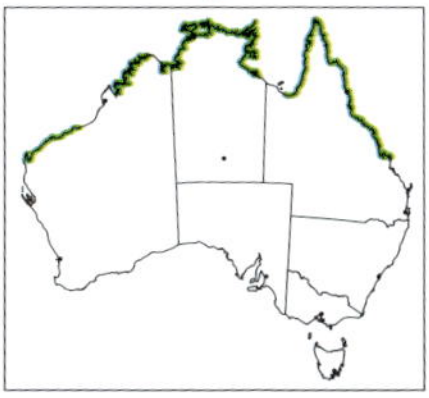

White bases to outer tail feathers.

Rather long bill for a robin.
Grey upperparts contrast with black wings, clean white underparts. Restricted to tropical mangroves, especially stilt-rooted *Rhizophora*. Perches low, forages on ground.
Voice: clear plaintive whistle *pyu* or *pu-pyu*. Also a whistling song, and harsh repeated *chak*.

HOODED ROBIN ◑ 16 cm
Melanodryas cucullata

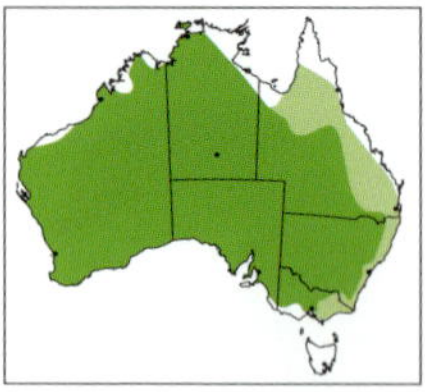

Medium–large, unobtrusive robin of drier, lightly timbered habitats, especially woodland and shrubland of eucalypt and *Acacia*. Often perches on fallen timber before taking prey from ground.
Voice: soft, monotonous piping. Song only given by ♂ at dawn *kwee kwoo kwoo kwoo*.

SOUTHERN SCRUB-ROBIN ◑ 20 cm
Drymodes brunneopygia

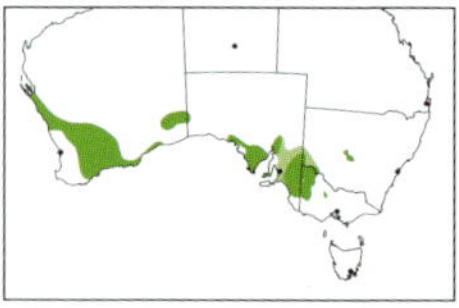

Large, ground-dwelling robin, runs on long legs. In mallee and other semi-arid scrub with dense tall shrubs over sparse ground layer. Easily overlooked, but often inquisitive.
Voice: long, thin, high-pitched whistle. Song given from perch a loud, clear, 3-note *did you eat*, the last note drawn out and ascending.

NORTHERN SCRUB-ROBIN ◔ 22 cm
Drymodes superciliaris

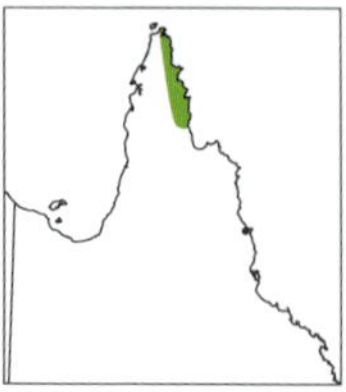

Large, ground-dwelling robin preferring areas of dense leaf litter and low to mid-level cover. In rainforest, monsoonal scrub and vine thicket of n Cape York Peninsula. Initially shy, but also inquisitive, giving patient observers close views.
Voice: a series of slow, high-pitched whistles *sweee-ee*.

RUFOUS WHISTLER ● 16 cm
Pachycephala rufiventris

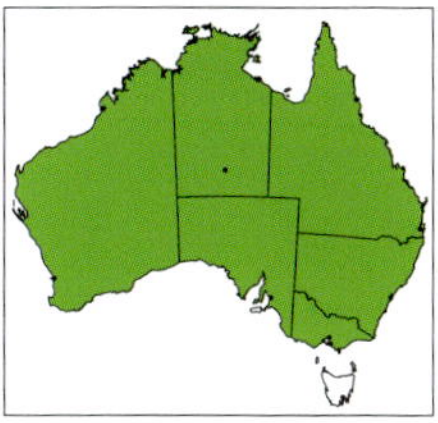

Widespread and common in eucalypt forest, woodland and mallee, avoiding wettest areas. **Voice:** territorial ♂ sing almost constantly in daylight; a loud ringing *EE-chong*, also repeated *joey joey joey* and ringing phrases resembling *with ring and with ripple*.

GILBERT'S WHISTLER ◐ 19 cm
Pachycephala inornata

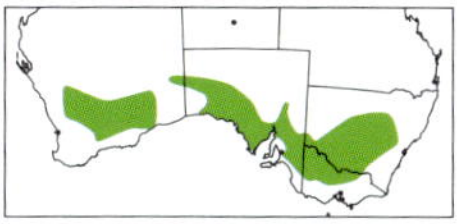

Secretive whistler of dry scrub, woodland and mallee. Requires dense cover of large bushes. Usually heard before seen. **Voice:** territorial call a powerful, swelling, repeated series of *chop chop chop*, also a musical *err-whit err-whit err-whit,* the second note shorter and higher-pitched.

RED-LORED WHISTLER ○ 19 cm
Pachycephala rufogularis

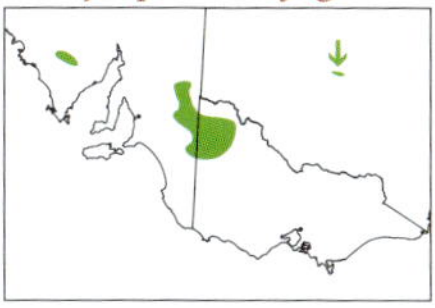

Rare, shy and rather elusive. Restricted to mallee in se Aus with abundant dense cover, also adjacent areas of broombush or cypress pine scrub. **Voice:** a series of loud, slow, swelling *see-saw see-saw see-saw*. Repeated *chong chong chong* like Gilbert's but not as sharp.

GOLDEN WHISTLER ◕ 17 cm
Pachycephala pectoralis

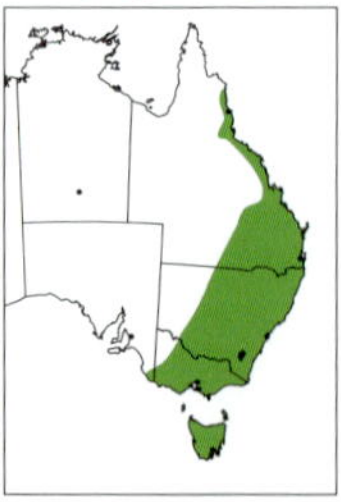

Common whistler of se Aus and e Qld. In forest, woodland and rainforest, from coast to subalpine regions. ♀ plumage and black in ♂ tail vary geographically. **Voice:** song a pleasant *tchee tchee tchee tchuwit*, also a rising whistle ending in whipcrack, a drawn out *seep*.

WESTERN WHISTLER ◕ 17 cm
Pachycephala fuliginosa

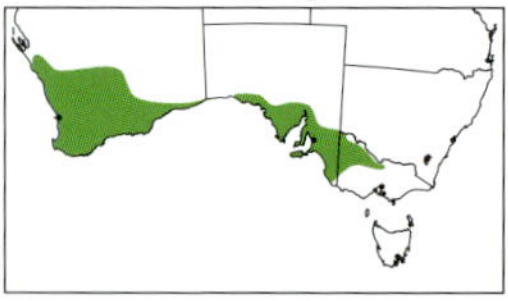

Recently described cryptic sp. Ad ♂ like Golden Whistler, ♀ differs by russet belly and vent. **Voice:** similar to Golden Whistler.

MANGROVE GOLDEN WHISTLER ◑ 16 cm
Pachycephala melanura

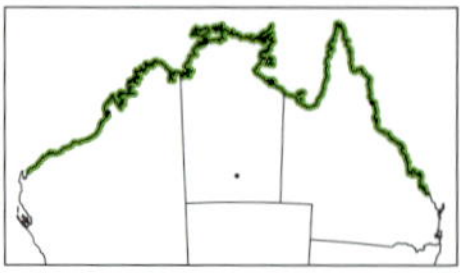

Mangrove specialist, occasionally wanders into other waterside thickets. On islands utilises wider variety of habitats. Very patchily distributed on e coast of Qld. Slimmer than Golden Whistler with longer bill. **Voice:** sweet *wit wit whitchel* recalls Golden Whistler.

GREY WHISTLER ◑ 15 cm
Pachycephala simplex

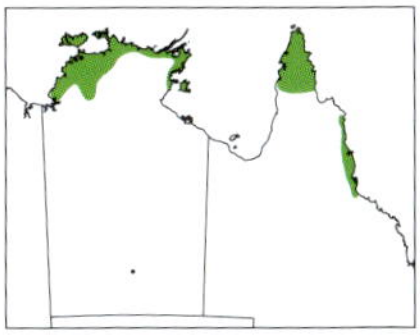

Smallest whistler. In NT inhabits coastal swamp forest, monsoon forest and mangroves. In Qld in lowland rainforest and adjacent eucalypt forest and mangroves. Easily overlooked when silent.
Voice: ringing 3-note *ee-ee-you*, the second note lower than first.

OLIVE WHISTLER ◑ 20 cm
Pachycephala olivacea

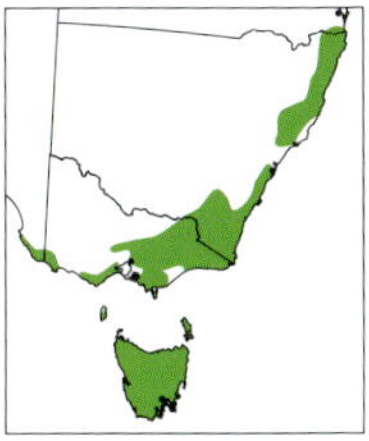

Juv: extensively rufous.

Drab, thickset whistler. In cool, wet, dense undergrowth from coastal scrub and tall heath to wet forest and subalpine woodland. Secretive, more often heard than seen.

Voice: powerful, rich *cho-cho-choo*, sometimes repeated. Also single pure high-pitched whistle.

WHITE-BREASTED WHISTLER ◑ 19 cm
Pachycephala lanioides

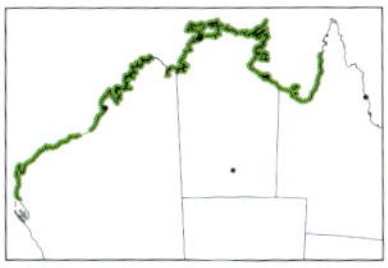

Large, heavy-billed whistler. In dense mangrove forest, usually on the seaward margins, rarely in adjacent riverine vegetation. Takes crustaceans off mud at low tide and gleans insects from foliage.
Voice: rich, loud and musical; ♂ often sings from emergent branch, *cho cho cho cheweet* or *ferweet ferweet ferweet*.

GREY SHRIKE-THRUSH ● 25 cm
Colluricincla harmonica

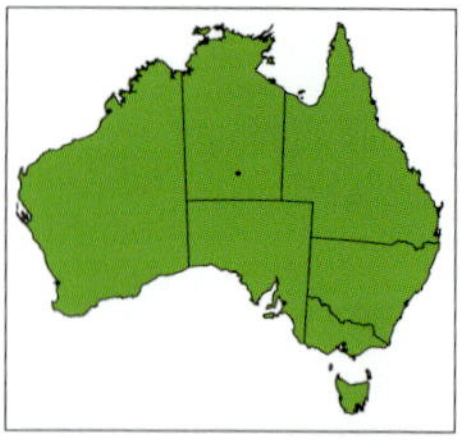

Common in most treed habitats from tall, wet forest to mallee and arid scrub.
Voice: pure, rhythmic song is a characteristic sound of the Aus bush – a ringing *pur pur QUEE YULE*. Also a whistling, repeated *wit-wit-wit* but with many regional dialects, and a loud single note *chong* or *yorrick*.

SANDSTONE SHRIKE-THRUSH ◑ 25 cm
Colluricincla woodwardi

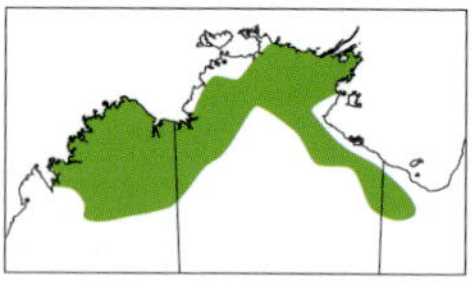

Longish tail, bill and legs. Mostly terrestrial in sandstone escarpments.
Voice: sings from rocky prominence, 2 rapidly repeated whistles.

BOWER'S SHRIKE-THRUSH ◔ 20 cm
Colluricincla boweri

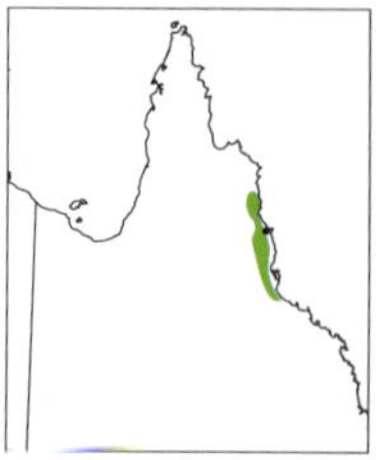

Thickset with short tail. In rainforest above 400 m altitude, mostly in middle and lower strata of forest.
Voice: 4 quiet notes *da-dee da-dee* followed by loud *PON-PON-PON*.

ARAFURA SHRIKE-THRUSH 19 cm
Colluricincla megarhyncha

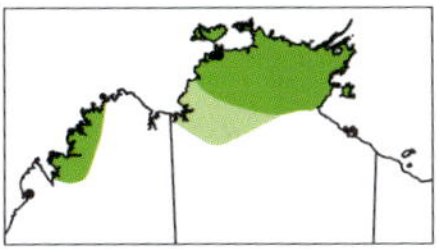

Paler than Rufous Shrike-thrush with whiter face and eyebrow, but similar habits and habitat.

Ad

Voice: rich, melodious *ee butch butch butcher.*

RUFOUS SHRIKE-THRUSH 19 cm
Colluricincla rufogaster

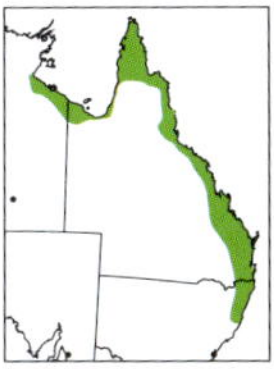

Small shrike-thrush. In Lowland rainforest, vine thicket, coastal woodland, paperbark swamp and mangroves. **Voice:** melodious, rich *cup of tea what-what* or *tea wat-wat* and *tu-whee-wat-wat*. Also harsh wheezing notes.

Pale bill.

Ad

CRESTED SHRIKE-TIT 17 cm
Falcunculus frontatus

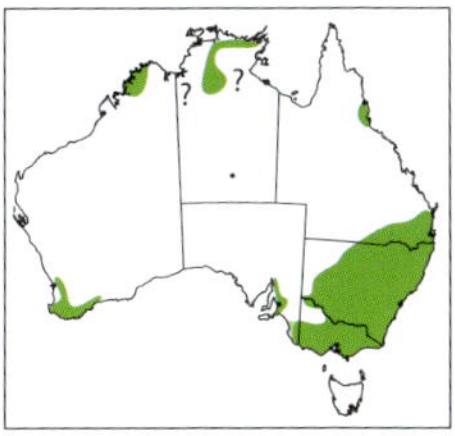

In eucalypt forest and woodland.

Boldly patterned, but often difficult to see, usually heard first. Noisily strips bark searching for insects. **Voice:** mournful, descending piping *keep-keep-keep*, also chatter.

Ad ♂: NT and Kimberley n WA.

Ad ♀: e Aus.

Juv

Ad ♂: sw WA.

WA call *hur hee.*

Ad ♂: e Aus.

CRESTED BELLBIRD 21 cm
Oreoica gutturalis

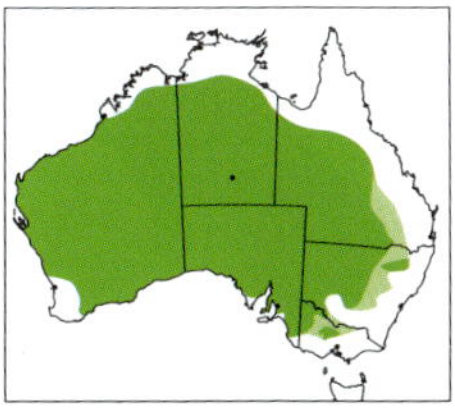

Ad ♀

Juv

Ad ♂

In arid and semi-arid forest and scrub, feeds on ground. Usually heard first. **Voice:** distinctive, far-carrying, mid-toned whistle repeated monotonously *pan pan palella*, often followed by *plonk*.

OLIVE-BACKED SUNBIRD ● 11 cm
Cinnyris jugularis

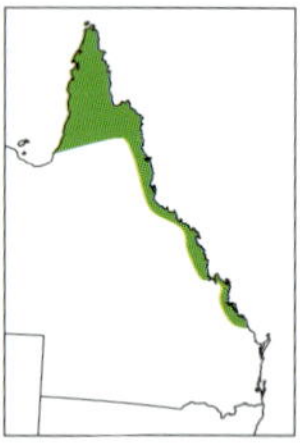

Only Aus sunbird. Tiny and active in forest edges, secondary growth, mangroves, parks and gardens. Feeds on nectar, and invertebrates, especially spiders, gleaned from nooks and crannies, hovers briefly.

Voice: short, ascending, high-pitched buzz, squeaky chatter and short squeaking *chip*.

SILVEREYE ● 12 cm
Zosterops lateralis

Common and widespread.
Ssp vary in colour of throat, back, undertail and amount of buff-brown on flanks. In a wide range of habitats with leafy understorey. Small, active and noisy flocks forage in foliage of shrubbery for flowers and fruit, then move to the next patch.
Voice: a loud, high-pitched, tinkling trill.
Contact call in flight a slurred peevish *psee-psee*.

YELLOW WHITE-EYE ◕ 11 cm
Zosterops luteus

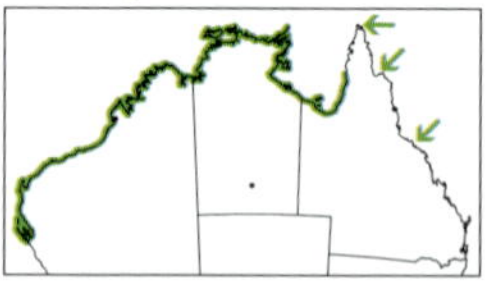

Bright yellow white-eye. In mangroves and adjacent coastal habitats across n Aus.

Voice: constant melodious warbling trills; contact call a plaintive *zeep* or *mew*.

ASHY-BELLIED WHITE-EYE ◔ 11 cm
Zosterops citrinella

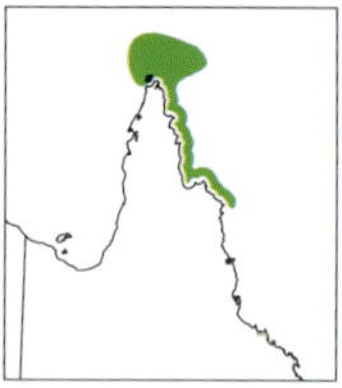

Grey underparts contrast with yellow throat, yellow lores and vent *cf* Silvereye. Only on smaller islands of Torres Strait and off e coast of Cape York Peninsula.
Voice: loud *chew* contact call. Clear, sweet warbling song.

MISTLETOEBIRD 9 cm

Dicaeum hirundinaceum

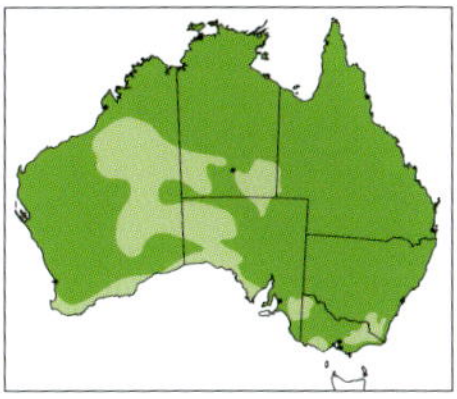

Only flowerpecker on mainland Aus. Tiny and short-tailed, always has red undertail coverts.

Ad ♀

Ad ♂: bright red and glossy.

Feeds mostly on mistletoe fruits. In wide range of woodland and forest habitats wherever mistletoe occurs. **Voice:** often detected by flight call, sharp *dzee*. Song a high-pitched, tinkling twitter *swizzt-a-swit* or *sweet-swit-zeer* and *mistle-toot*.

GOLDEN-HEADED CISTICOLA 10 cm

Cisticola exilis

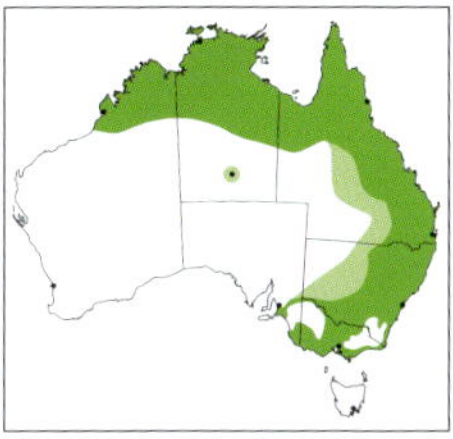

Ad ♀ br

Ad ♂ non-br: streaked cap, tail longer in non-br plumage.

Buff underwing.

Ad br: buff tips to grey undertail.

Ad ♂ br: unmarked golden head.

Tiny warbler. In tall grassland, especially near wetlands. Inconspicuous during winter, but during breeding season ♂ calls continuously from perch within grasses or during fluttery display flight high above grassland. **Voice:** ♂ br song a long, loud buzz *zwee* followed by *wit plink*.

ZITTING CISTICOLA 10 cm

Cisticola juncidis

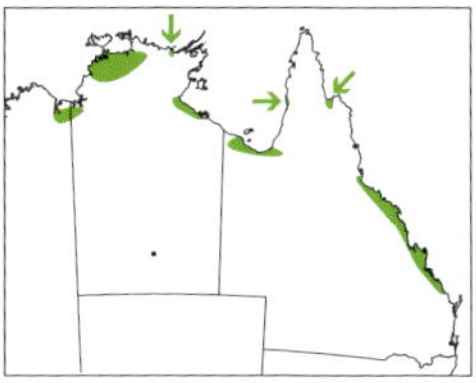

Ad ♂ br: white tips and cinnamon patches to undertail, cream underwing.

Ad ♂ br: dark-brown lores and cap, pale supercilium.

Ad ♂ non-br: tail is longer. Has white tips all year.

Ad ♀ non-br

Tiny, localised warbler, in coastal tropical grassland on freshwater floodplains and margins of saline swamps. Ad ♀ and non-br plumages very similar to Golden-headed, note white tail tips. **Voice:** ♂ br song mainly given during bouncy display flights high above the ground; a loud metallic clinking *lik-lik lik-lik*, also bursts of 2–4 repeated *tzit tzit tzit*.

AUSTRALIAN REED-WARBLER 16 cm
Acrocephalus australis

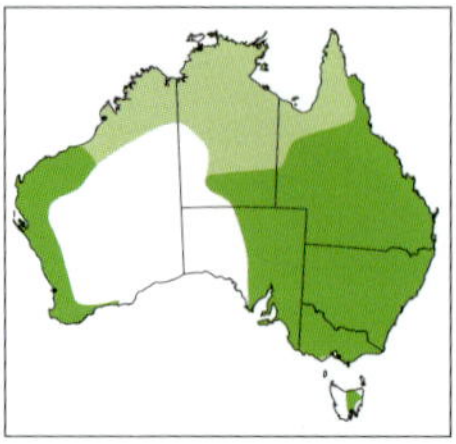

Mainly in reedbeds or rushes in fresh to saline wetlands; when non-br occasionally uses dry shrublands and woodlands.
Voice: constant loud song when breeding; a stream of scratchy and ringing phrases interspersed or ending with melodious snatches, e.g. *chup-chup dzee-dzee-dzee quarty-quarty-quarty* ... Also a sharp *chak* in alarm.

LITTLE GRASSBIRD 13 cm
Poodytes gramineus

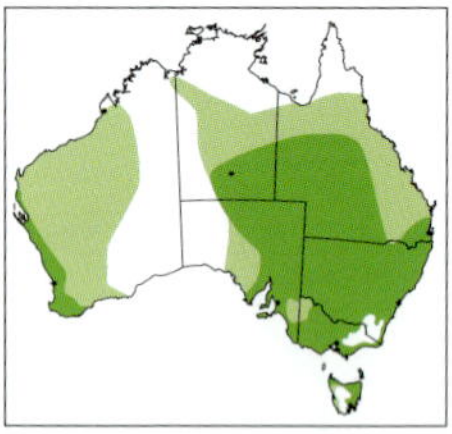

Furtive, in dense wetland vegetation.
Voice: usually detected by repeated plaintive whistles *p-pee-pee*. Also sharp *chuk* and harsh rattling chatter in alarm.

More olive-tinged and shorter-tailed than Tawny Grassbird.

SPINIFEXBIRD 15 cm
Poodytess carteri

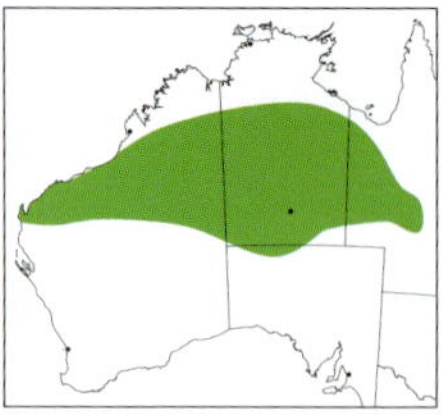

Secretive warbler of arid country where there are no similar species.

In tall, dense *Triodia* tussocks, on plains, dunes or rocky hills, with or without adjacent shrubs. **Voice:** usually detected by call. Short warbling ♂ song *cheer-it* or *cheery-wit*, sometimes answered *jip jip-jip* by ♀. Also a single note *chup* in contact or alarm.

TAWNY GRASSBIRD
Cincloramphus timoriensis 17 cm

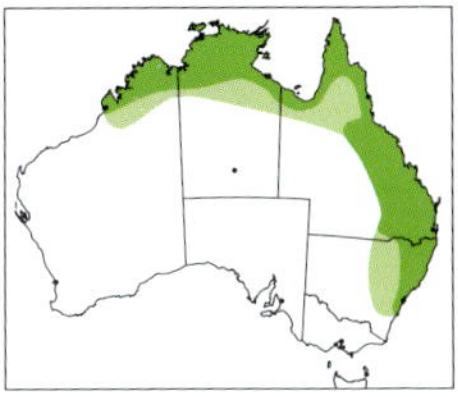

Furtive and inconspicuous. In rank grassland and reeds, usually around wetlands; also crops and shrubland. Larger, stouter-billed and longer-tailed than Little Grassbird. Rufous fringes to tail and wing feathers. Displaying ♂ sings from exposed perch or in display flight.
Voice: song starts with high-pitched squeaks, then melodious trill, ends with harsh chuckling. Also *tjik* or *jk jk* in alarm.

Lacks eye stripe.

Juv

Ad

Imm: duller, with faint crown streaking.

RUFOUS SONGLARK
Cincloramphus mathewsi 18 cm

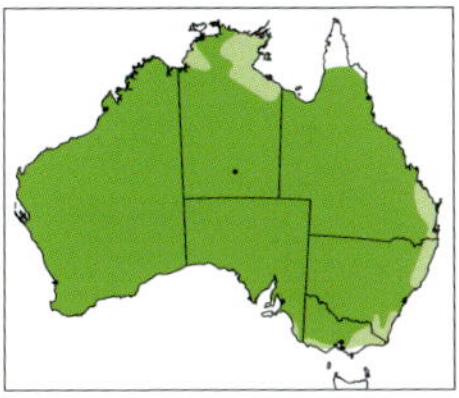

Ad ♂ br: larger than ♀, black bill.

Rufous rump.

Ad ♀

Juv

♂ sings in display flights or from exposed perch.

A spring–summer migrant in s Aus. In woodland with grassy understorey. Forages inconspicuously on ground.
Voice: ♂ song very loud, incessantly repeated series of melodious phrases, e.g. *witcher-weedle* interspersed by long descending trills.

BROWN SONGLARK
Cincloramphus cruralis ♂ 23 cm ♀ 18 cm

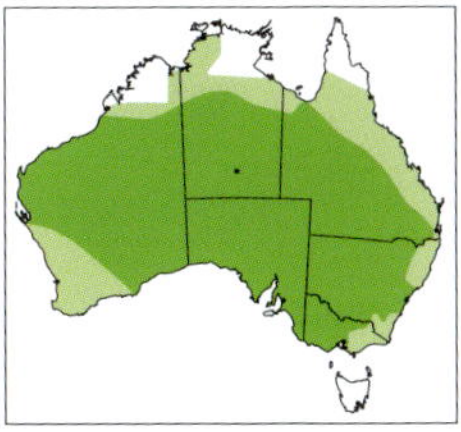

Lanky songlark of treeless grassland, farmland and chenopod plains. Inconspicuous when foraging on ground, but ♂ often sings from exposed perch.

Song flight, upswept fluttery wings and dangling feet.

Juv ♀

Ad ♂ br: sooty plumage with black bill and lores. Bill and underparts paler in non-br.

Ad ♀: much smaller than ♂. Black patch on belly.

Voice: ♂ song very loud and incessantly repeated phrase *skit-scot-a-wheeler*, sounds more scratchy and metallic than Rufous Songlark.

HORSFIELD'S BUSHLARK ◑ 13 cm
Mirafra javanica

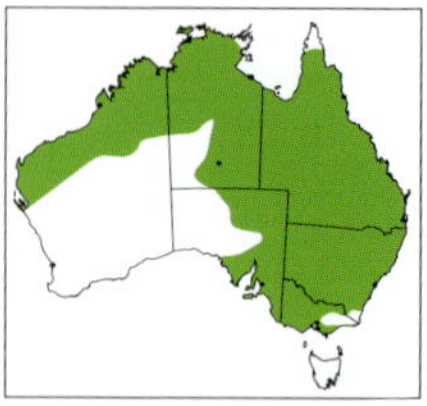

Small, sparrow-like lark, with short tail and thick bill. In flight, jerky wing beats, head lifted slightly and tail depressed, hovers briefly before dropping to cover. In grassland and rank farmland especially with perennial tussocks. **Voice:** sustained, melodious song recalls Skylark but less fluid due to inclusion of much mimicry.

EURASIAN SKYLARK ◕ 17 cm
Alauda arvensis

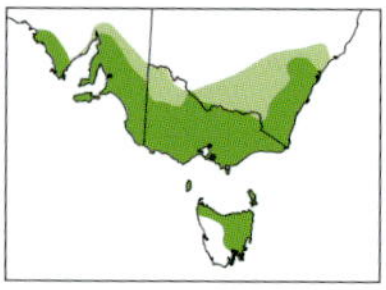

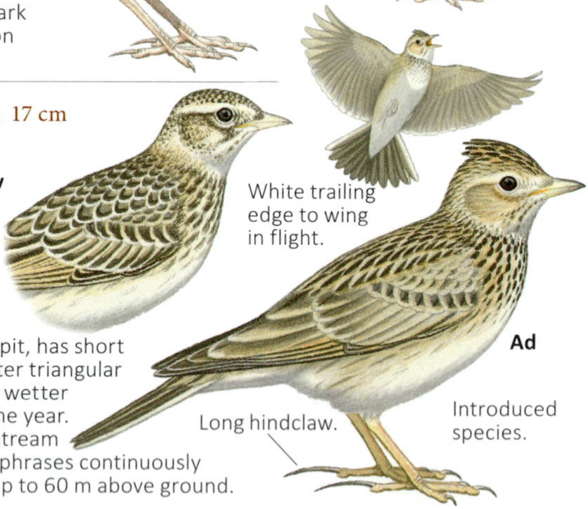

Typical lark. Compared to Pipit, has short crest, shorter legs and shorter triangular bill. Common in farmland in wetter regions. Sings for much of the year. **Voice:** ♂ flight song a loud stream of trills, runs and throbbing phrases continuously performed while hovering up to 60 m above ground.

AUSTRALIAN PIPIT ◕ 16 cm
Anthus australis

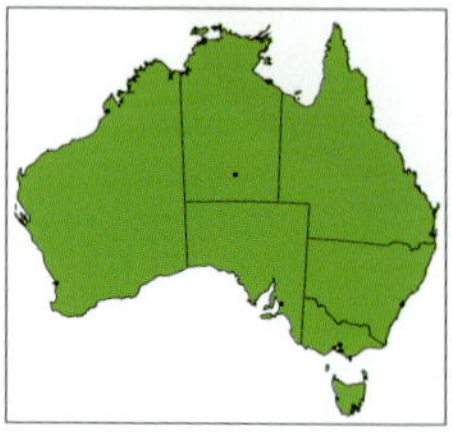

Compared to Skylark, slimmer with more upright stance on longer legs, more slender bill. Runs ahead of observer, often hops up on stone. Habitually bobs tail.

Common over most of Aus in open habitats including; arid and semi-arid plains, native grassland, farmland, alpine meadow, heathland and coastal dunes. **Voice:** when flushed a single *tjsweep*. Song a high-pitched trill given in flight.

EASTERN YELLOW WAGTAIL ◔ 17 cm
Motacilla tschutschensis

Slim build, long legs, slender bill, persistent bobbing of tail. Most birds show at least some yellow in underparts, but Imms in spring plain grey. Annual non-br migrant in n Aus, rare in s. Usually close to muddy edges or mown grass.

Voice: when flushed a slurred *tslie tslie*.

COMMON MYNA ● 24 cm
Acridotheres tristis

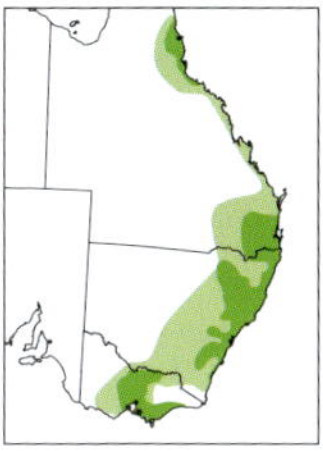

Bold, strutting, raucous urban dweller introduced in 1860s, progressively occupying disturbed rural environments.

Introduced species.

Voice: broad repertoire of grating and melodious calls *chic-uu-chir* and *chee chee chee*.

RED-WHISKERED BULBUL ◑ 21 cm
Pycnonotus jocosus

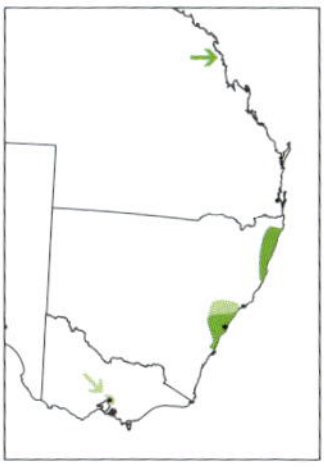

Distinctive tall crest. Introduced in early 1900s. An urban bird in greater Sydney area and locally on n coast NSW. Rare in Mackay, Qld and in Melbourne, Vic where no established population.
Voice: persistent cheerful chatter and scolds. Common call is *kink-a-jou*.

Introduced species.

METALLIC STARLING 24 cm
Aplonis metallica

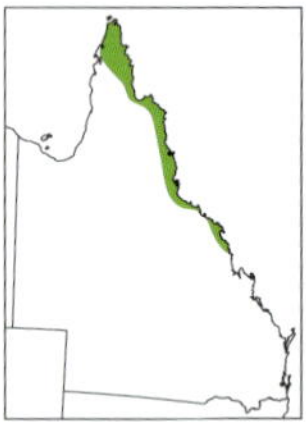

Glossy green-black starling with long-tapered tail. Occupies rainforest, forest and gardens. Breeding migrant Aug–Apr; some overwinter. Flies swiftly in tight flocks just above the forest or skilfully through the canopy.
Voice: oft-repeated, high-pitched *cheeeup*, much chattering.

COMMON STARLING 20 cm
Sturnus vulgaris

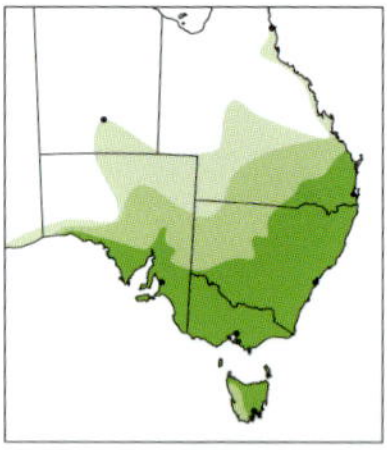

Abundant, short-tailed starling. Frequents grassland, agricultural and urban areas. Nests in cavities including in buildings.
Voice: remarkably complex, melodious song.

COMMON BLACKBIRD 25 cm
Turdus merula

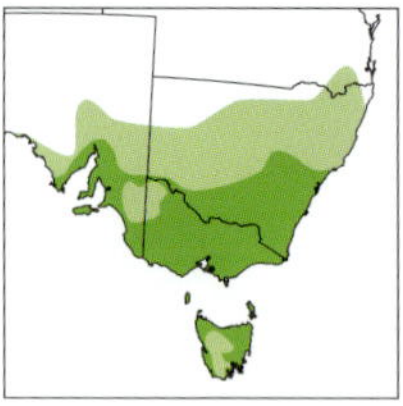

Familiar all-black or brown thrush of se Aus. Common in gardens, creeklines and damp forest.
Voice: melodious dawn songster in winter and spring. Rattling alarm call when flushed.

BASSIAN THRUSH ◑ 27 cm
Zoothera lunulata

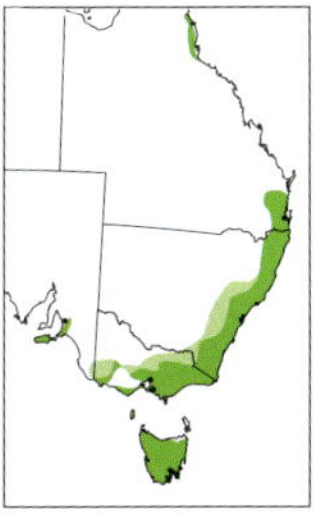

Scaly thrush with olive rump. Mostly in thick cover in wetter forests, occasionally in clearings, especially at half-light. In n, e.g. se Qld and Wet Tropics, only at higher altitudes. **Voice:** song a typically thrush-like melodious warble of complex modulated phrases. Contact call very high-pitched *seep*.

RUSSET-TAILED THRUSH ◑ 26 cm
Zoothera heinei

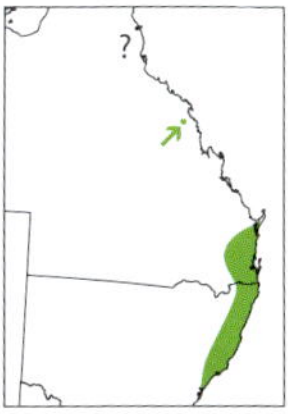

Very like Bassian Thrush but with russet rump. Ad has bold pale-tipped coverts forming two wing bars similar to Juv of both spp and contra Ad Bassian. Mostly in rainforest where both spp can occur, but Russet-tailed generally at lower altitudes in winter. Best separated by simple song. **Voice:** 2-note *whee-dooo*.

SONG THRUSH ◔ 22 cm
Turdus philomelos

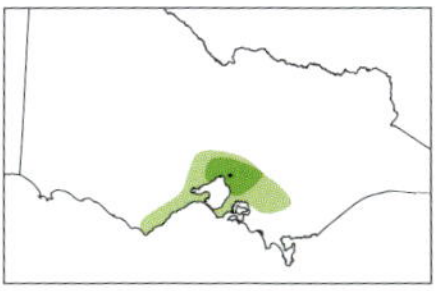

Introduced species.

Dainty, spotted thrush. Scarce and localised in urban areas and damp forested gullies. Often detected by song in winter–spring, otherwise remarkably cryptic. **Voice:** simple but melodious phrases for long periods in early morning.

GOULDIAN FINCH ◔ 13 cm

Chloebia gouldiae

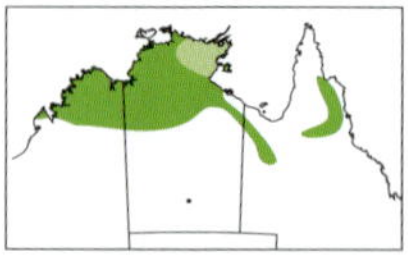

Vibrant, multicoloured finch of humid grassy woodland. Scarce with patchy distribution. Forages in tall grass and recently burnt areas, encountered at waterholes.

Voice: a high-pitched *sitt*.

BLUE-FACED PARROT-FINCH ○ 12 cm

Erythrura trichroa

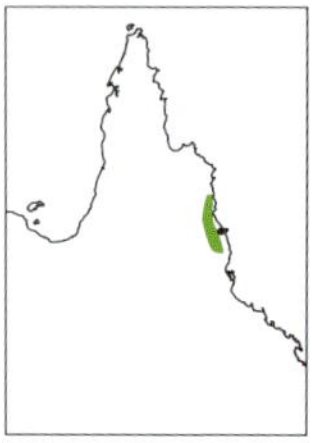

Dark sea-green grassfinch. Small parties, very localised in rainforest and scrub of Wet Tropics. Forages in clearings on seeding grasses.

Voice: a thin, high-pitched and distinctive *tseet tseet*.

CRIMSON FINCH ◕ 13 cm

Neochmia phaeton

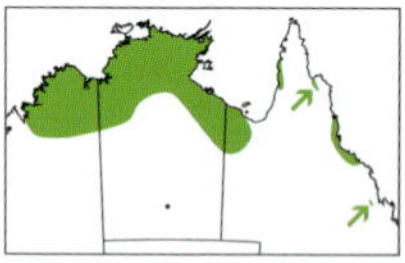

Mostly red grassfinch with long tail. Generally common. Small parties frequent tall grass near *Pandanus*-lined watercourses and wetlands.

Voice: a metallic *che* repeated rapidly.

STAR FINCH ◑ 11 cm

Bathilda ruficauda

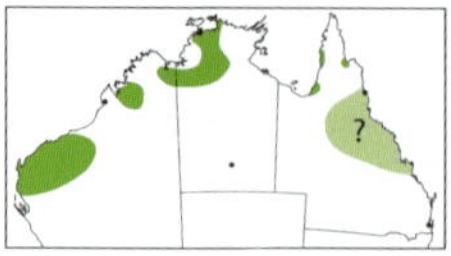

Dull olive-green with striking red face. Can be common but localised in grassland, reedbed and woodland, typically near wetlands and watercourses.

Voice: a soft, distinct *tsit* given repeatedly.

MASKED FINCH ◔ 13 cm
Poephila personata

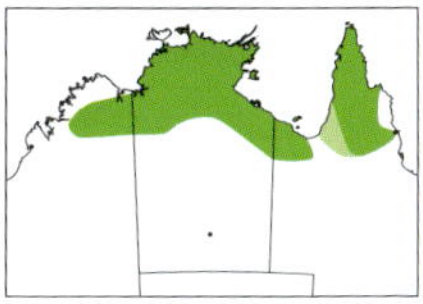

Ad: pale cheeks on Cape York.

White rump.

Long-tailed, pale-brown grassfinch with triangular black mask, large yellow bill and broad black flank patch. Open grassy woodland and grassland of tropics. Often with other finches. **Voice:** a flat nasal whistle *tiat*.

LONG-TAILED FINCH ◔ 15 cm
Poephila acuticauda

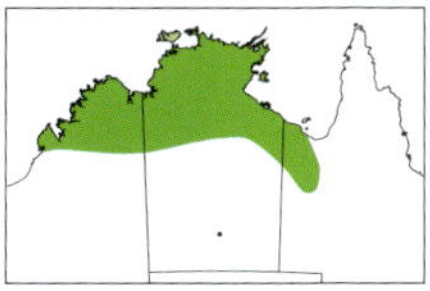

Ad: yellow bill in Kimberley, WA.

Grey-headed grassfinch with prominent black throat, narrow black lores, narrow black flank patch and long wire-like tail. Frequents grassy woodlands of tropics, usually near water. **Voice:** a mournful descending whistle *teeweet*.

BLACK-THROATED FINCH ◑ 12 cm
Poephila cincta

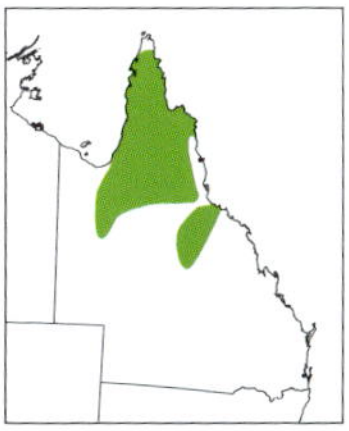

White rump.

Short blunt tail.

Ad: black rump in s.

Stocky, grey-headed grassfinch with prominent black bib and short, square-tipped tail. Open grassy woodlands of e tropics and subtropics. **Voice:** a metallic whistle *pewwww*.

PAINTED FINCH ◑ 11 cm
Emblema pictum

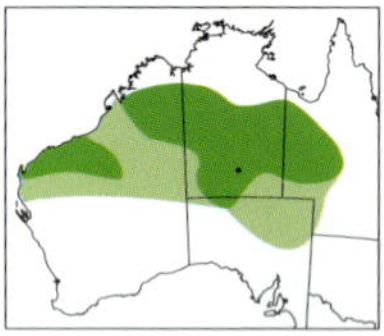

Striking red, black and brown finch. Widespread in arid interior, especially gorges and creek beds. Favours rocky substrates with *Triodia*.
Voice: a loud *tilk*, often given in flight.

BEAUTIFUL FIRETAIL ◑ 11 cm
Stagonopleura bella

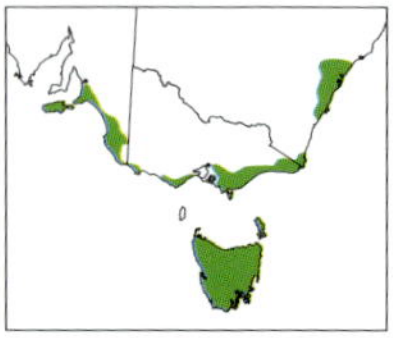

Plump, finely-barred finch with scarlet rump. Occupies heath, shrubby woodland, gullies near running water. Feeds especially amongst *Allocasuarina*.
Voice: a drawn-out, mournful *sweee ... sweee*.

RED-EARED FIRETAIL ◑ 11 cm
Stagonopleura oculata

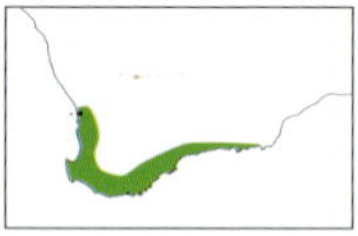

Sw Aus counterpart to Beautiful Firetail with red ear, heavily spotted below. In dense, shrubby, riparian vegetation and heath.
Voice: a mournful *whee-whee*.

DIAMOND FIRETAIL ◑ 12 cm
Stagonopleura guttata

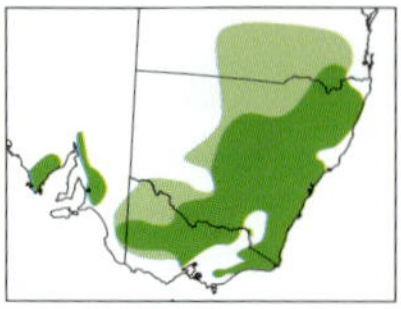

Stocky, scarlet-rumped finch with white spots on black flanks. Occurs in grassy dry forest and woodland, forages on ground in small parties.
Voice: a drawn-out mournful whistle.

RED-BROWED FINCH ◕ 11 cm
Neochmia temporalis

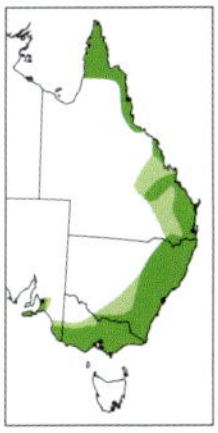

Red-rumped finch with neat red brow. Common in wide variety of wooded and shrubby habitats, often in small flocks. Readily feeds on lawns.

Voice: high-pitched contact call a drawn-out *seet* repeated 2–3 times.

PLUM-HEADED FINCH ◑ 11 cm
Aidemosyne modesta

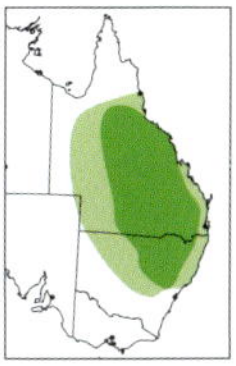

Barred brown and cream finch of e rangelands. Patchy distribution. Frequents grassland, and grassy woodland, usually near a swamp or creekline.

Voice: rather quiet, soft double *tyitt tyitt* given in flight.

ZEBRA FINCH ● 11 cm
Taeniopygia guttata

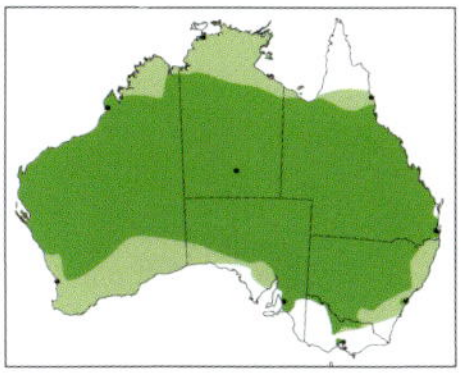

Small finch with orange-red bill, distinctive tear-drop on face and white-spotted rufous flanks. Abundant across much of Aus especially inland grasslands and woodlands. Irruptive breeder when conditions suitable.
Voice: a nasal buzz *tiaah* ♀ or *tia* ♂.

DOUBLE-BARRED FINCH ◕ 11 cm
Stizoptera bichenovii

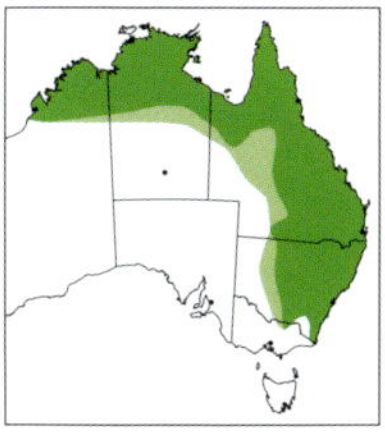

Grey and white finch with two narrow, black breast bands. Occupies wide variety of wooded habitats, parks, gardens.

Voice: single or double *tiaat-tiaat* softer, lower-pitched than Zebra Finch.

PICTORELLA MANNIKIN ◔ 11 cm
Heteromunia pectoralis

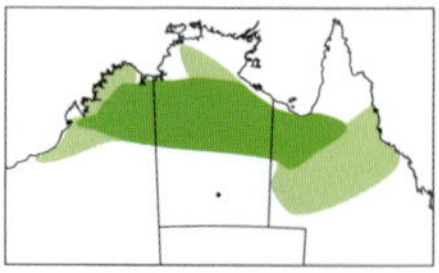

Black face, white scaly breast and uniformly dark rump. Tropical and semi-arid grasslands and woodland, especially with *Triodia*.
Voice: a drawn-out *teet*, also sparrow-like *chip*.

CHESTNUT-BREASTED MANNIKIN ◕ 11 cm
Lonchura castaneothorax

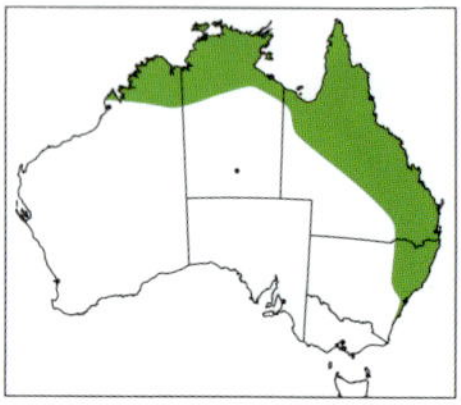

Boldly marked, black facial disc and chestnut breast. In many wooded, grassland and wetland habitats with tall seeding grasses.
Voice: a short bell-like *tilt*.

YELLOW-RUMPED MANNIKIN ◔ 11 cm
Lonchura flaviprymna

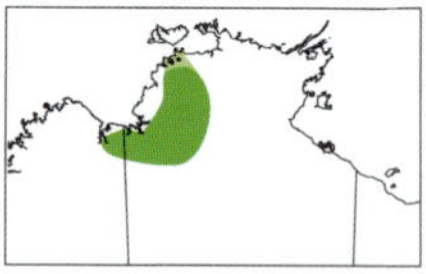

Pale-headed finch of tropical grassland and adjacent grassy woodland. Often in mixed flocks.
Voice: very like Chestnut-breasted Mannikin.

SCALY-BREASTED MUNIA ◕ 11 cm
Lonchura punctulata

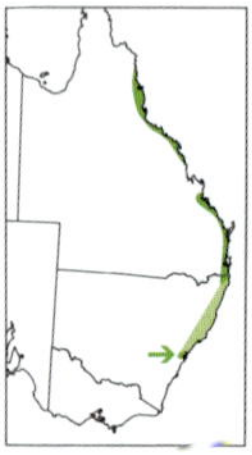

Introduced species.

Mostly dark-brown finch of e seaboard, intricately scaled below. Typically in grassy areas in and around settlements and towns.
Voice: a rather soft *tit-ti*.

HOUSE SPARROW ● 15 cm
Passer domesticus

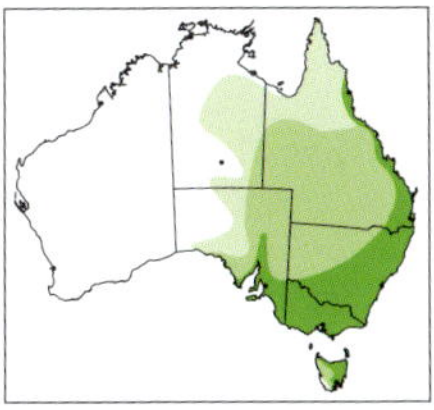

Familiar small plump brown bird of farms, towns and cities. Common, sometimes abundant, routinely underfoot at outdoor cafes etc. **Voice:** an incessant *chirup*.

EURASIAN TREE SPARROW ◑ 14 cm
Passer montanus

Introduced species.

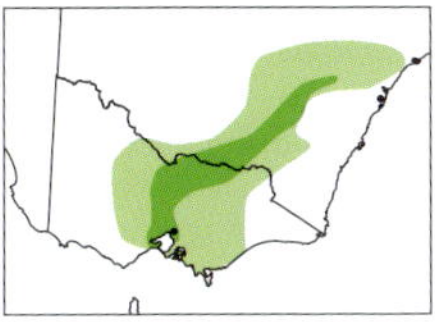

Localised russet-brown sparrow, smaller than House Sparrow. Largely commensal with man, occasionally grasslands and wetlands. **Voice:** like that of House Sparrow but higher-pitched.

EUROPEAN GOLDFINCH ◕ 12 cm
Carduelis carduelis

Introduced species.

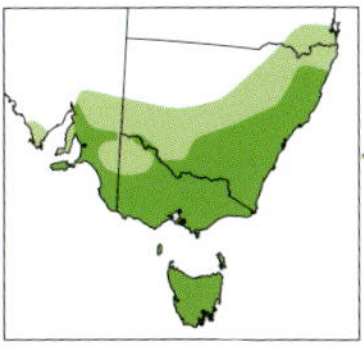

Common in open, modified habitats especially weedy areas with thistles. **Voice:** a series of liquid tinkles and short buzzes. Pleasant contact call *tickelitt* given in flight.

COMMON GREENFINCH ◑ 14 cm
Chloris chloris

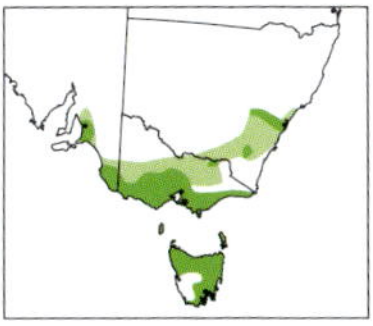

Robust, mostly olive-green, grey and yellow finch. Occupies farmland, plantations, coastal areas especially with pine, elm or oak. **Voice:** drawn out buzzing *birrrzzz*, canary-like twittering contact calls.

Index

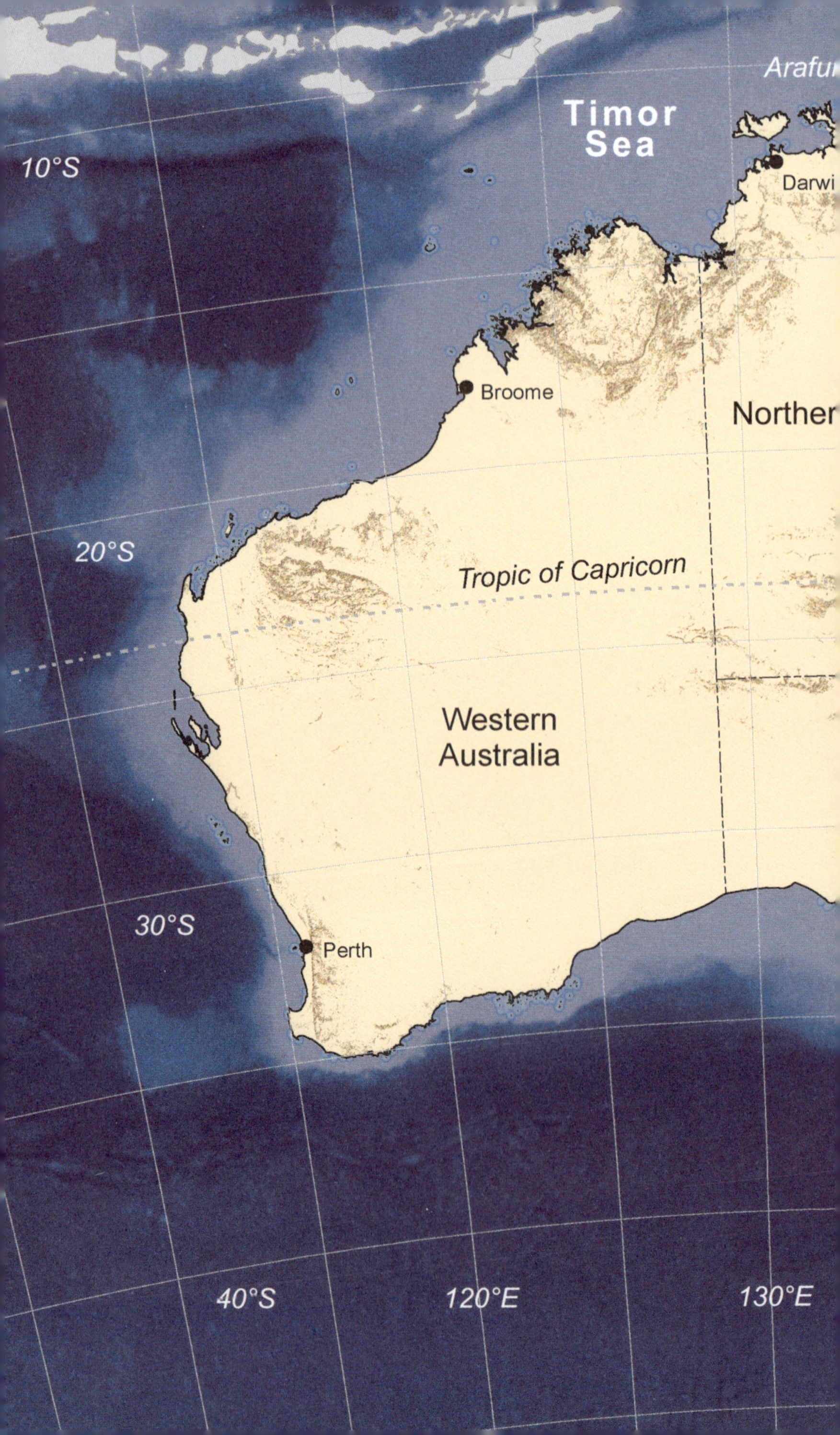
Arafu
Timor Sea
Darwi
10°S
Broome
Norther
20°S
Tropic of Capricorn
Western Australia
30°S
Perth
40°S
120°E
130°E